Myrna Loy

Myrna Loy

The Only Good Girl in Hollywood

Emily W. Leider

UNIVERSITY OF CALIFORNIA PRESS

Berkeley · Los Angeles · London

University of California Press, one of the most distinguished university presses in the United States,
enriches lives around the world by advancing scholar-
ship in the humanities, social sciences, and natural
sciences. Its activities are supported by the UC Press
Foundation and by philanthropic contributions from
individuals and institutions. For more information, visit
www.ucpress.edu.

University of California Press
Berkeley and Los Angeles, California

University of California Press, Ltd.
London, England

Library of Congress Cataloging-in-Publication Data

Leider, Emily W.
    Myrna Loy : the only good girl in Hollywood /
Emily W. Leider.
        p.   cm.
    Includes bibliographical references and index.
    ISBN 978-0-520-25320-9 (cloth : alk. paper)
    1. Loy, Myrna, 1905–1993.   2. Motion picture actors
and actresses—United States—Biography.   I. Title.
    PN2287.L67L46   2011
    791.43'028092—dc22
    [B]   2011011571

Manufactured in the United States of America

20   19   18   17   16   15   14   13   12   11
10   9   8   7   6   5   4   3   2   1

In keeping with a commitment to support environ-
mentally responsible and sustainable printing practices,
UC Press has printed this book on Natures Book, a fiber
that contains 30 percent postconsumer waste and meets
the minimum requirements of ANSI/NISO z39.48-1992
(R 1997) (Permanence of Paper).

For Rosa and Linus,
a new generation of movie lovers

Contents

Plates follow page 180

Plates

Introduction

Myrna Loy's grace and slender elegance, her ease before the camera, and her arresting face had a lot to do with her success on film, but she claimed that stardom entailed more sweat than glamour. In her early days at Warner Bros. she worked nonstop, sometimes moving from set to set in multiple films being shot at the same time. In 1927 alone she played in eleven movies, and she took no vacation until she had been a screen actress nearly ten years. During her six-decade career she appeared in a staggering 124 films, beginning with her debut at age twenty as a dancing chorine in *Pretty Ladies*. Fifty-five years later, in 1980, she made her last appearance on the big screen, as a sassy executive secretary in Sidney Lumet's *Just Tell Me What You Want*.

Loy took her first full-time job, as a prologue dancer at Grauman's Egyptian Theatre, while still in her teens. She needed to support her widowed mother, younger brother, and aunt. As a contract player for Warner Bros. in the 1920s she took part in the sound revolution, playing small roles in *Don Juan,* the first silent with a synchronized score, and *The Jazz Singer,* the groundbreaking Al Jolson musical with some sound dialogue. Hitting her stride in drawing room comedy in the early sound era, she signed with MGM in 1931, striking gold three years later as Nora Charles in *The Thin Man* and making the list of the top ten box-office stars in 1937 and 1938. After taking time off to move to New York and volunteer full time for the Red Cross during World War II, she returned to Hollywood for a memorable performance opposite Fredric

March in *The Best Years of Our Lives,* winner of the Best Picture Academy Award for 1946.

Along the way, in her eighty-eight years, she found the time to marry and divorce four times, fight the House Un-American Activities Committee, become a UNESCO delegate, campaign for various Democratic Party candidates, serve John F. Kennedy on the National Committee against Discrimination in Housing, help found the American Place Theatre, and rack up credits in radio, television, and stage. She lived in four very different cities—Helena, Montana; Los Angeles; Washington, D.C.; and New York—and traveled widely. She could always see the larger world beyond Hollywood.

As a screen actress Loy was best known for her collaborative skills. She was an attuned, responsive screen partner, most famously to William Powell, with whom she made fourteen films, but also to Clark Gable (her second most frequent leading man), Cary Grant, Melvyn Douglas, and a long list of others. Never a stand-alone pillar of female power onscreen, she excelled at sharing the frame and reacting, what Cary Grant called tossing back the ball. Here she differed from her dynamo friend Joan Crawford and from such dominating female screen icons of her generation as Bette Davis, Katharine Hepburn, and Mae West. Being a top-tier movie star didn't define Myrna Loy as it did them, and her career eventually lost momentum as a result.

Most at home in comedy, she achieved her best effects by underplaying, by suggesting meaning rather than hammering it home. No pies in the face for her. The subtle, nuanced action or reaction—a raised eyebrow, wry inflection, or crinkled nose—could say it all. Even in drama she avoided scenery chewing or broad strokes. For Loy, as an actress, less was more. Extremely modern in her minimalist technique, she remains our contemporary in her ability to grow, to stay in the game and continue evolving.

Her greatest acclaim followed the unexpected runaway success of her partnership with Powell in *The Thin Man,* which engendered five sequels. Released just months before strict enforcement of the Production Code began, *The Thin Man* pleased censors by making marriage, the only kind of sexual relationship endorsed by the Code, look like fun. Because Nick and Nora Charles lived a carefree, luxurious life on buckets of money, they made married life look like one big party, with plenty of excitement generated by a murder mystery and enough mink coats, art deco surroundings, martinis, and smart repartee to divert any Depression-weary audience. The screen's Nick and Nora turned wedded bliss into a true partnership of near equals. Although Nick dominates and sometimes condescends, Nora holds up her end. She has wealth, wit, style, and a mind of her own. This kind of balance between complementary spouses had never been shown onscreen and became a model for subsequent couplings in cinema and television.

Comedy itself changed over the decades of Loy's career. The cynical, urban edge of the first *Thin Man* became less cutting in the sequels, and the mingling of wealthy characters with endearing ex-cons no longer worked. Nick and Nora acquired a son and stopped being footloose. During World War II, family values took hold, and murder could no longer be treated lightly. The postwar comedy *Mr. Blandings Builds His Dream House* played to the consumer's dream of achieving happiness by buying a house in the suburbs and fixing it up with multiple bathrooms.

Nora was consistently a good sport, and usually upbeat, as was Myrna Loy offscreen. Although she once took on MGM, going absent without leave and demanding higher pay and more time off, and although from the 1940s on she sounded off periodically against isolationists and right-wingers, in private she usually shunned confrontation, as did the characters she played. In *After the Thin Man* William Powell's Nick tells Nora: "You don't scold, you don't nag, and you look too pretty in the morning." Nora wryly promises to start scolding, but she never does.

Myrna Loy had a well-spoken, relaxed but classy manner that eventually steered her into genteel roles, usually as someone's wife. Darryl Zanuck tried to put her in a few tough-girl parts at Warner Bros. in the late 1920s, but they didn't fit. As one writer put it, caviar suited her, not corned beef and cabbage. At the peak of her stardom in the late 1930s she once asked her boss at MGM, Louis B. Mayer, for permission to play a scrubwoman character. Mayer forbade it, telling her, "You always gotta be a lady."[1]

Loy became known as "the Perfect Wife," a tag she came to despise, in part because it clashed with her record of failed marriages. Even before her first divorce, from producer Arthur Hornblow Jr., Myrna came to feel that the epithet set up impossible expectations. No wife should expect to be perfect. One female fan complained to a reporter that any real husband would look at the movies' all-forgiving, never cranky, and never overworked Nora and inevitably find his own wife wanting.

Ultimately, the repeated Perfect Wife roles began to grate on Loy, all the more so because type casting was boxing her in for the second time. Her first typing occurred at Warner Bros., where she was asked to play dangerous, bizarre, and outré characters. Her widely spaced almond-shaped eyes could easily be made up to appear exotic. In real life she had Celtic ancestry, freckles, and red hair, but makeup, costumes, and black-and-white photography made it possible for this Montana native to be transformed into a seductively sinister other woman, usually an Asian but sometimes Hispanic, mulatto, Gypsy, or Polynesian. Dressed in a sarong, grass skirt, or high-collared sheath, and bearing a name like Azuri or Nubi, she tossed her hips and perfected sloe-eyed come-hither glances. Loy longed to play a more authentic character, someone more like her real self—wholesome, with a sense of humor. MGM's Woody Van Dyke, the director who fought to cast her as Nora, helped her to realize her wish, but she shed the vixen mantle only to be subjected to the casting straitjacket once more. Until she aged into mother roles and then soused old ladies, she continued to play upscale married women. Even her triumph as Milly Stephenson in *The Best Years of Our Lives,* made for Goldwyn after she'd left MGM, affirmed her status as a privileged, steadfast wife.

In her lifetime Loy was underappreciated. She never was nominated for an Academy Award. Other honors came late, as partial compensation. In the 1980s she received a Kennedy Center tribute, a special Academy of Motion Picture Arts and Sciences celebration at Carnegie Hall of her screen career, and at last an honorary Oscar. Although many of her films are available on DVD and are shown regularly on cable television's Turner Classic Movies, she remains relatively unsung, which helps explain why she has never before been the subject of a biography. Another reason is that, by Hollywood standards, Myrna Loy led a relatively quiet life. Though she made headlines when she sued the *Hollywood Reporter* for calling her a fellow traveler, she steered clear of scandal. She never ran off with her leading man (although Leslie Howard and Tyrone Power were temptations), nor did she chatter about the indiscretions and failings of others. When John Ford, who had a yen for her, teased her by calling her "the only good girl in Hollywood," he meant that compared to other alluring young actresses, she stayed on the straight and narrow and avoided bed-hopping. Because she showed abiding concern for the world's problems and for other people, the good girl label resonates beyond Ford's original meaning.

She and her coauthor, James Kotsilibas-Davis, did such a good job with her autobiography, *Myrna Loy: Being and Becoming,* that other biographers may have feared they couldn't match it. Based on extensive interviews with Loy herself, as well as with friends and colleagues, it reveals an intelligent, sensitive, woman with a fierce sense of commitment to her favorite people and beliefs, a woman who after four failed marriages had learned to trust herself. *Being and Becoming* does venture into private territory, illuminating otherwise hidden corners. But it goes only so far. Full disclosure is never attempted, and some events and people get short shrift. She discusses her abortion but leaves out the crushing news that an infection rendered her sterile at age thirty, before her first marriage. The persistent problems she had with her only sibling, her younger brother, David, are never touched upon, even though he died several years before the book was published.

By temperament, Myrna was shy, reserved, and reticent. A good listener who always had just a few close friends, she remained a decidedly private person. Among reporters who covered the film beat, she had a reputation for being a tough interview, a public figure unwilling to disclose much about her personal life. The record she left is full of gaps. She never kept a diary, and very few letters of hers that could be called intimate have survived. She left a large archive at Boston University, but she carefully removed from it every letter from her first husband, Arthur Hornblow Jr., whom she described in her autobiography as the love of her life. The only letters from her mother in the archive were addressed to an agent, not Myrna. Letters from her closest friends are also absent. Myrna Loy wanted to die with many of her secrets intact, and to some extent she achieved that goal.

From day one Myrna Loy's screen image has conjured mystery, a sense of something withheld, something intriguing because it seems unknowable. "Who is she?" was a question posed in the very first published fan magazine article about her, in 1925. This book attempts to fill in some of the gaps and to counter the relative neglect that has befallen her abundant legacy. I want to remind people of Myrna Loy's prodigious achievements onscreen and of the remarkable person she was.

CHAPTER I

The Climb

In the spring of 1905 Della Mae Williams, pregnant with the baby girl she and her husband, David, would name Myrna Adele, decided to take a hike. While David journeyed by rail to Chicago to sell cattle, she set out with friends from her home on the Williams family's ranch in southwestern Montana's Crow Creek Valley, traveling south, probably in a wagon pulled by a team of ranch horses. She packed a knapsack, donned sturdy boots and a sunbonnet, tied a rope around her thickening waist, and joined a group of climbers determined to scale the highest peak in the southern Rocky Mountains. Della climbed all the way to the top, a triumph that someone in the party not only recorded with a Kodak but also made public. A photograph of Mrs. Della Williams, the first white woman known to have packed through to the mountain's summit, would soon adorn the cover of *Field and Stream* (*BB*, 10).

When he saw his wife's picture smiling from the front of a popular magazine, David exploded. Although a genial man, and a free thinker when it came to religion—after being elected to the Montana state legislature in his early twenties, he wrote "none" when asked to name his church— "Honest Dave" 's ideas about womenfolk had always been more conservative than those of his strong-minded, high-spirited wife. He never did come to terms with Della's habit of taking off without him every now and then, a tendency she would indulge periodically during their fourteen years as man and wife. Her love affair with California would one day threaten the stability of their marriage. This spring he soon got over his pique. An openhearted man, he rarely held a grudge.

On August 2, 1905, several months after Della's audacious hike, she and David welcomed their first-born, a child who would share Della's spunk and David's concern for others. The robust infant came into the world in the city of Helena, not at the ranch, and the facts that she was born in a hospital and "attended by a physician" hint of her family's relative prosperity. Doctors were scarce in sparsely populated Montana.[1]

The baby's Celtic good looks immediately commanded attention. She had a well-knit, long-limbed body, gray-green almond-shaped eyes, wide cheeks, a rosebud mouth, fair skin that would freckle easily, and abundant carrot-colored hair. Her pert nose tilted up, like the nose of her Welch-born paternal grandmother, Ann Williams, who also had red hair. Della's Scottish mother, Isabella Johnson, who lived four miles from the ranch in the tiny town of Radersburg, used to press down on that up-tilting nose every time she rocked the baby to sleep, trying in vain to flatten it and make it more like the noses in *her* side of the family. The nose would one day become a movie star's signature, coveted by many women and even copied by some with access to plastic surgery. Though David would never have approved, had he survived to see it, his daughter's adult face would be recognized around the world, adorning the covers of countless popular magazines.[2]

Della and her mother, Isabella, wanted to name the baby Annabel, combining Isabella's name with "Ann," the name of David's recently deceased mother, but the women lost out this time, to David. On one of his frequent trips by railroad to sell livestock, he'd taken a fancy to "Myrna," the name of a whistle-stop town his train clamored through. He insisted that his daughter be called Myrna. There was consensus about the baby's middle name, Adele, a version of "Della." Being named after a train station would turn out to fit the restless Myrna, who would travel widely and change her address often. "I don't like to stay very long in one place," she once told a reporter.[3]

Wanderlust ran in both the Johnson and Williams families. Seeking a better life, all four of Myrna's grandparents had crossed the Atlantic from Europe to the United States in the 1850s or 1860s: two came from Wales, one from Scotland, and one from Sweden. Myrna's personality, a writer for a fan magazine would claim, mingled the national traits of her forebears. "She has the reserve of the Welsh, and a good deal of the canniness of the Scot. Didn't Sweden produce Garbo, the exotic?"[4]

Myrna's wayfaring grandparents, ever on the move as they sought abundance on the western frontier, traveled by ocean steamer, covered wagon, stagecoach, freight wagon, ox train, horseback, riverboat, railroad, and even by foot before all four landed forty miles southeast of Helena, where the Bozeman-to-Helena stage road crossed Crow Creek at the gold-rush mining town of Radersburg. At the time they arrived, the sprawling Montana Territory—559 miles long along the Canadian border—was both isolated and "practically uninhabited. One could travel for miles without seeing so much as a trapper's bivouac. Thousands of buffalo darkened the rolling plains. There were deer, antelope, elk, wolves and coyotes on every hill." Before the 1883 arrival of the Northern Pacific Railroad, the railroad station nearest to Radersburg was more than six hundred miles distant, in Corinne, Utah, a stopping place for stagecoaches and freight teams.[5]

The population of Radersburg, located on the plains in the shadow of the snowcapped Big Belt and Bitterroot mountains, never amounted to much. At the peak of the gold rush, in 1869, it reached its high point: one thousand residents. This was the period when Myrna's grandparents arrived, joining other settlers descending on the boomtown from all over the map. The number of citizens in Radersburg had dwindled to 169 by 1880, the year Della was born, compared to three thousand in Helena. With a population of seventy in the 2000 Census, it seems well on its way to becoming a ghost town.[6]

To get to Montana Territory, Myrna's pioneer grandparents braved blizzards, rockslides, wind, rain, insects, sleet, and dust storms. They forded streams, coaxed rickety wagon wheels out of muddy ruts, and urged fly-plagued mule trains and recalcitrant livestock over makeshift bridges. They ascended mountain passes on treacherous trails, camped out on the open prairie, nursed sick children, and left behind injured or dead horses and cattle. On the overland trail they encountered Indians, both friendly and not. On a freighting trip to Montana Myrna's grandfather D. T. Williams "met friendly Indians at Campbell's Creek; they showed many scalps of white men on long poles." Williams and his party bowed their heads in prayer as they drove past gravesites marking recent burials. By the end of their journey each weathered immigrant surely knew, if he or she hadn't known before starting out, how to skin a buck, tan a hide, hitch a wagon, dress a wound, and fire a gun. Among the family treasures that Myrna still owned in the 1940s was a pair of pistols and a flintlock rifle.[7]

The adversity the new settlers faced once they arrived in Montana Territory began with the struggle to get water, which had to be hauled from

Crow Creek, "unless there came a drifting snow and one went to the work of melting it." They quickly built houses made of logs, with sod roofs and dirt floors. Eventually they constructed more substantial dwellings, where kerosene lamps or candles supplied light after the sun went down. Wood served as fuel and cost six dollars a cord, unless you felled the trees yourself. Chamber pots or the outhouse—not a friendly place when the temperature plunged below zero—made do as bathrooms. Unless you were a fearless rider with a good horse, or commanded your own buckboard, getting out of town could present a challenge. Roads were few, unpaved, and for many months in the year were buried under snowdrifts. The stagecoach from Bozeman to Helena stopped in Radersburg only three times a week. Hiring a livery to Helena would cost you a day's time and set you back thirty-eight dollars.[8]

Della's father, John Johnson, was a carpenter who hailed from Göteborg, Sweden. His first stopping place in America had been Chicago. In 1867, at age twenty-seven, he had walked the 150 miles to Radersburg from Fort Benton, where the Missouri River steamer from St. Louis had deposited him. He and his friend Albert W. Sederburg, also a Swede and a carpenter, gallantly gave up their seats on the stagecoach to two ladies in need; hence the long hike (*BB*, 7). John Johnson headed for Radersburg after gold had been discovered at the Keating and East Pacific mines, hoping for a lucky strike at a time when fortunes could be made with a flash in the proverbial pan.

John Johnson and A. W. Sederburg tried their luck in the gold-rich streams and quartz mines but soon settled for a surer way to survive. As partners they opened a cabinet shop in town, on the ground floor of a two-story log building they constructed, which also housed the Masonic temple. There they built and sold tables, dressers, bedsteads, washstands, chairs, and cedar caskets. John Johnson continued placer mining, too, during the warmer months and, when Della was only eight, made a habit of taking her along to the diggings.[9]

Myrna's paternal grandfather, David Thomas Williams, a rancher, died at age sixty-eight, the year before she was born. Known as D. T. Williams, he started out on a Welsh farm in Neath, near Swansea, sailing at age twenty from Liverpool to Philadelphia in 1856. If he'd remained in southern Wales, where coal mining, copper smelting, and the railroad were blackening the cities, he believed his scant resources and lack of education would have condemned him to a grim future. In 1880, twenty-four years after emigrating, he still could not read or write English, according to the U.S. Census. When he was new to American soil, he tried coal mining in Pennsylvania, then gold mining in Mason City, Virginia, and the California Sierras, before making his way to Austin, Nevada. There he met his future wife, Ann Morgan Davis, she of the auburn hair, tilted nose, green eyes, and freckles that Myrna would inherit. To convince Ann and her immigrant Welsh parents that he would make a trustworthy husband, Williams went into business hauling freight from Salt Lake City with two four-horse teams. Having impressed his future in-laws, he married Ann in Toole, Utah, but the couple did not linger there. After their first child was born, they switched from hauling freight to ranching and moved to Elk City, Idaho, where they raised cattle and horses and had a second child. The enterprising and tireless D. T. had his eye on the open range of Montana Territory, which offered cheap land for homesteaders, lots of it, and was booming. Now that gold seekers were flocking to the mining camps, they would need horses for transportation, herding cattle, and plowing. The newcomers would be hungry for beef and bread, as would the settlers at military forts and Indian agencies. Boardinghouses would need milk and butter. The recently arrived cowboys and farmers would be donning leather chaps, vests, and boots, all of which made horse and cattle ranching and wheat farming seem to him winning undertakings, despite the relentless toil and hardship they entailed. D. T. and Ann set out in 1870 for Montana's Crow Creek Valley, each driving a wagon. The pregnant Ann drove their two children and her blind mother, along with blueberry and gooseberry bushes and apple tree seedlings to transplant in Montana (BB, 4–5). When Myrna revisited the ranch a final time in the early 1980s, a few of Ann's gnarled apple trees were blooming in what used to be her orchard.[10]

Whenever Myrna recalled stories about her frontier forebears, she wondered at their grit, can-do spirit, resourcefulness, and courage. She did not share the scathing opinion voiced by her father's friend, the celebrated western painter Charles Russell, that the pioneer should be seen as a despoiler, a desecrator of virgin land who "traps all the fur, kills off all the wild meat, cuts down all the trees, grazes off all the grass." She hailed Grandfather Williams for his up-by-the-bootstraps rise from the poverty of his boyhood and for accumulating enough Montana land and stock to render him one of the wealthiest men in his county (which was Jefferson County first, then became Broadwater after 1897). Under the 1862 Homestead Act, which Abraham Lincoln had signed, in 1870 the newcomer D. T. Williams could and did acquire 160 acres of public Montana Territory land in the Crow Creek Valley, land that had long been a buffalo hunting ground for migrating Flathead, Shoshone, Blackfoot, and Crow Indians and, since the coming of Lewis and Clark to the Missouri River headwaters in 1805, had seen an occasional white trapper, hunter, fur trader, or mountain man. With the advent of the gold rush, farmers, other ranchers, and a few merchants and innkeepers were beginning to join the miners invading the area, the only valley of the Missouri River.[11]

To take title to the 160 acres, D. T. Williams had to "prove up." That meant he had to live on the land for five years and make improvements on it. He built a log house, chicken coops, a barn, corrals, and split-log fences. Fifteen years later, under the Desert Land Act, he bought another two hundred acres for twenty-five cents an acre, parts of which he had to irrigate with ditches, for despite the Crow Creek, the land was often dry. He planted acres of wheat, displacing wild grass, buffalo berry, brush, pine, cedar, and willow trees. Myrna boasted that by the time Montana became a state, in 1889, her grandfather owned fifteen hundred head of cattle, many horses, and most of Crow Creek Valley's acreage (*BB*, 6–8). He held stock in several mines, as well.

For all her pride in the prominence of D. T. Williams and the craft and industry of her Johnson grandfather, Myrna identified most with her grandmothers. "They've always been heroic figures to me," she said, "my two grandmothers, coming from protected childhoods in Wales and Scotland to a strange land, fighting like hell to make civilized environments for their men and children" (*BB*, 7).

Twice widowed by the age of forty-five, Grandmother Isabella Giles Wilder Johnson was the only one of Myrna's grandparents that she actually got to know, the other three having died before she came into the world. Grandmother Johnson rarely complained. "She never took anything as a hardship. She had a lusty, fearless joy in life, and hardships were a part of life and you took them standing up." Born in Largs, Scotland, Isabella had set out on a sailing vessel from Scotland in her teens. She traveled with an aunt, leaving behind her bereft mother and many siblings. In America Isabella married at age seventeen, but her first husband died in Iowa, where they had been living. She arrived in Radersburg as a widow with a four-year-old son, James Wilder (*BB*, 6–7). No doubt she hoped to be able to support James with what she gleaned from the diggings in Montana gold country. When she joined a wagon train to cross the plains, she brought along her cut glass and French china. Soon after arriving in Radersburg, she married the Swedish carpenter John Johnson, who with his partner, Sederburg, built them a house. The Johnsons would have three children, of whom Della was the youngest.[12]

Compared to Europe and the eastern states, the western mining frontier offered women greater independence, more social flexibility, and an opportunity to speak out. For a woman to work outside the home was not unusual in Montana. Myrna's Johnson aunt, LuLu Belle, became county treasurer, and Myrna grew up hearing spirited political talk around the dinner table. That an aunt sought and won public office is not surprising. The Williams family lived in a state that would follow the leads of other western states—Wyoming, Colorado, Utah, Washington, California, Kansas, and Arizona—in granting women the vote in 1914, six years before the Nineteenth Amendment enfranchised women nationally. Montana in 1917 elected Jeanette Rankin the first U.S. congresswoman. Myrna Loy always attributed her own political activism to the atmosphere in her home and home state. As she saw it, the scant number of Montana citizens made each voice count for more.[13]

Della's uppity spirit was a source of strife, contributing to a contentious marriage that survived several separations. David's quarrel with her about her picture on the magazine cover was neither the first nor the last of its kind. Though Della and David knew one another from childhood, they saw the world differently and often took opposite sides in an argument. He was a Republican, she a lifelong Democrat. The pleasure-loving, musical Della, an accomplished pianist, studied at the American Conservatory of Music in Chicago and, before marrying, had considered a career as a concert artist, but she said, "I had to abandon all thoughts of realizing that ambition when I married." She continued to enjoy performing on the piano and organ.[14]

David, though he shed his Presbyterian parents' unbending religious faith, clung to their straitlaced morality. He had little feeling for the performing arts and considered a woman's public display a step toward the gutter. Della, whose father carved and painted wood figures and crafted cedar furniture, identified with artists, while David favored practical, remunerative, and traditionally masculine pursuits: ranching, selling land and cattle, appraising farms for a bank, serving the community via his lodge. At his father's ranch during his younger days he wore a ten-gallon hat, rode horses, chowed down with cowhands, drove cattle, and roped steers. He lacked the long, lean good looks of his fellow Montanan, and future Hollywood cowboy, Gary Cooper—David's face was round and his build chunky—but in his youth he lived the rough-and-tumble outdoor life of a genuine cowpuncher. Later, in Helena, he sat on bank boards, but as an appraiser and seller of farmland he continued to spend time outdoors, often in the saddle. Della, too, rode a horse confidently, because a Montana woman simply had to. But in contrast to David, Della, after her father's early death, inhabited a cultured world of women presided over by her mother, who sang at the piano, read books, put up jelly, baked ginger cookies, and cultivated the tiger lilies and pansies in her garden.[15]

The friction between Della and David rarely erupted into open warfare, but it remained a constant during Myrna's girlhood. Myrna had no model of marital harmony. The screen's future Perfect Wife came out of a less than perfect union in which Della's role was neither consistently nor clearly defined. Della balked at being purely domestic yet lacked economic independence. Music-making showcased her skills, providing pleasure, an identity distinct from that of wife and mother, and activity, but no income. The compliant wife Myrna Loy sometimes played both in movies and in her real-life marriages was definitely not modeled on her mother.

When Della Mae Johnson and David Franklin Williams got married in Helena in March of 1904, twenty-four-year-old Della had completed her musical training in Chicago, and David, one year older than his bride, had finished school at the Commercial Department of the State Agricultural College in Bozeman. At age twenty-three, just a few years after finishing college, he'd been the youngest man ever elected to serve a term in the Montana legislature, representing Broadwater County as a Republican in 1903. His particular interests as a representative were education, agriculture, irrigation, and water rights. Just prior to their wedding David and Della had been living as single young people in Helena, sharing a lively circle of friends, but they returned to the Williams ranch in Crow Creek Valley after tying the knot. David, whose prosperous parents both died within months of his marriage, abandoned politics and took over at the Williams ranch, working as a stockman and farmer. He was not its sole owner, however, but a part owner with his two brothers and two sisters. His father's will had left the land in equal one-fifth shares to his five surviving children. Della, much happier in Helena, served reluctantly as a ranch wife, even though she was moving closer to her hometown. She knew how to cook but hated doing it. The ranch employed a Chinese cook. Holiday meals, according to Myrna, were always prepared by her father, who sometimes brought home from Chicago cracked crab on ice.[16]

The Williams ranch, called "The Home Place" in legal documents, had no electricity or outdoor plumbing. Water used for bathing, cooking, or laundry had to be pumped by hand and heated in a barrel. Ice that was needed to keep perishables fresh was stored in an icehouse and covered with sawdust to prevent it from thawing. Helena offered many more of the amusements, conveniences, and comforts that Della appreciated than did the remote Crow Creek Valley, about fourteen miles from the nearest train station. A photograph exists, too blurry to enable reproduction, that captures an idyllic moment of ranch life several years after Della and David settled there: Della, in trousers, white shirt, and sun hat, sits on a saddled dark-coated horse; Myrna, behind her (about five years old), rides a smaller white horse, and near both a dark filly with her colt grazes on sunlit grass.[17]

David and Della grew up on the raucous mining frontier after the gold rush had peaked. Big changes were afoot in the Montana Territory. When they were toddlers, in the early 1880s, herds of buffalo still blackened the plains, and the Battle of the Little Big Horn, in which Colonel George Custer and 120-odd other members of the 7th Cavalry died fighting Sioux and Cheyenne Indians fewer than two hundred miles southeast from Radersburg, was a recent memory. White settlers still talked about it, as they talked about Chief Joseph's dramatic 1877 attempt to lead his band of Nez Pierce to refuge in the nearby Bitterroot Mountains. Many of the white cattlemen held the Native Americans in contempt and, fearing attacks, demanded protection from the U.S. military, which established posts throughout the territory. By 1883 the buffalo had disappeared, wiped out by a combination of overhunting and disease introduced by cattle. The Indians, once dependent on the buffalo herds, moved onto reservations, but the vast reservations often had to cede portions of land to provide right-of-way to the builders of the Great Northern–Northern Pacific Railway.[18]

David managed to grow up without racial bigotry, and in his time at the legislature befriended fellow representative Frank Linderman, a hunter and trapper turned newspaperman and author who became fascinated with the stories told to him by Flathead, Cree, Crow, and Chippewa tribesmen he befriended. His well-known *Indian Why Stories,* a collection of tales with illustrations by Charles Russell, helped teach the white man something of the red man's traditions. Linderman was one of the non-Indians who joined with Indians pushing for a home for landless Crees and Chippewas. In his thirties David Franklin Williams joined that effort, which resulted in the 1911 formation of the Rocky Boy Reservation near Havre, at the abandoned Fort Assiniboine. This reservation was and still is owned by its occupants, not the U.S. government (*BB,* 8).

Della and David attended Radersburg's one-room grammar school on the hill, a wood-frame building that also housed the Methodist church. The town had only this one church—Della used to play the organ there—

but supported three saloons (one run by a woman), a liquor shop, and a brewery. Although many prospectors of gold and silver had moved on to what they hoped would be richer claims in other parts of the country, mining of some sort (for silver, lead, zinc, and iron ore after the gold had played out) continued in Radersburg into the early twentieth century, and despite the civilizing presence of the church, the school, a general store, and three lodges, frontier unruliness—the whoops that go with whiskey, high-stakes poker games, fancy ladies, and bucking broncos—lingered. The tiny town, once the Jefferson County seat, had its own jail and sheriff by the 1880s. Before that, a murderer or some other unfortunate transgressor might be found dangling from a rope extended from a beef scaffold. During the gold rush, robbery and claim jumping were common crimes. Nearby mining camps had been named Hog-Em, Cheat-Em, and Rob-Em. Although crime diminished by the 1880s, drinking, gambling, and disputes over claims continued to disrupt everyday life. Ranchers still had reason to complain about horse thieves and cattle rustlers. Gun toting was the rule, not the exception. The itinerant Methodist preacher, known as Brother Van (William Wesley Van Orsdel), had his work cut out for him. He rode into town on a white horse, always boarding with a different local family, which received him warmly. Brother Van enjoyed celebrity status in Radersburg and its environs. "The women were crazy about him," Della recalled.[19]

Social life in this rough but no longer booming gold-rush town revolved around dancing parties where a pistol-packing chaperone would expel anyone carrying liquor or a six-shooter. Group dances—square and circle—were favored, though couples might venture a Highland waltz or two-step. The women at the dances pinned up their long hair, donning floor-length skirts with pinched-in waists, bustles, and blouses with high collars and puffy sleeves. Their men put on freshly laundered blue jeans, pressed shirts, and polished boots. The dances could last all night, because the revelers feared that the roads were too dangerous to travel in the dark.[20]

During the school year Della participated in a literary society, led by the schoolteacher, which offered drama programs, too. On Saturday nights recitations of poetry took place, and pageants and tableaus were presented. Come spring there would be Sunday afternoon horseback riding parties after church. On the Fourth of July everyone flocked to a big picnic, where Old Glory would be unfurled and the Declaration of Independence declaimed. Della, who lived in town, participated enthusiastically in the community goings-on, but David, ensconced in the Valley on the Williams ranch, could join the fun less often. He liked parties, but he was needed for chores when he wasn't at school.[21]

The outdoor events Della enjoyed had to take place in spring or summer because the long, frigid winters could be, and often were, deadly. Cowboys had to put on "two suits of heavy underwear, two pairs of wool socks, wool pants, two woolen shirts, overalls, leather chaps, wool gloves under leather mittens, blanket-lined overcoats and fur caps." During the infamous winter of 1886–87, when the temperature plummeted to sixty-three degrees below zero, hundreds of thousands of Montana Territory cattle and sheep perished trying to find forage in the snow and ice. A similar freeze when Myrna was a year old made railroad tracks snap and sent starving cattle into the towns in search of grass. Humans died too. David's older sister Hattie succumbed in the brutal winter of 1887. Of David's ten siblings, only five—the five who would eventually inherit the ranch—survived into adulthood. According to Myrna (BB, 6) scarlet fever took several of them.[22]

Recollections of the severe Montana winters didn't taint Myrna's rosy picture of her early years at the Williams ranch. In her autobiography she speaks lovingly of the fragrant roses spilling over the split-log fence in front of the ranch house; her grandmother's apple trees in the back, which yielded bushels of apples in summer; and her grandfather's cottonwoods, whose leaves she tried to taste. She recalls playing with the baby lambs and the dobbin Dolly she was first taught to ride with no saddle, only a bridle (BB, 13). It's always spring or summer in her recollections.

Myrna would always regret that she never got to portray a frontier woman onscreen in a Gary Cooper western. Cooper, whose British parents settled in Helena, grew up playing cowboys-and-Indians and collecting arrowheads—activities that apparently escaped young Myrna, though in her Hollywood days she could still throw a lasso. She did play a Salinas Valley ranch wife in the 1949 film based on Steinbeck's The Red Pony. To most film lovers, though, news of Myrna Loy's Montana ranch background comes as a shock. Who pictures Nora Charles wearing cowboy boots, denim, buckskin, or calico frocks? In her screen heyday Myrna Loy embodied city-bred, martini-quaffing, chiffon-gowned elegance and sophistication.[23]

Myrna's earliest memory was of the endless acres of wheat fields where she wandered off on her own, losing her way, not to be found by anxious searchers until late at night. That trauma didn't curb her fondness for plunking herself down in the midst of a field of swaying brown-gold grain, looking up at scudding clouds and the expansive, mountain-framed sky, which might shift its color from blue to darkest gray in a matter of seconds. "I used to be alone most of the time—that's great for the imagination." The only other child around was her cousin Laura Belle Wilder, daughter of Della's sister Lu, but although Myrna loved her cousin, a five-year age gap separated them. From the start, Myrna tended to be a solitary dreamer, busy with her own thoughts and quite self-sufficient. Those traits would linger. Don Bachardy, who sketched her when she was close to seventy, refers to her "charming wistful vagueness" and "untragic aloneness." Because there were no playmates of her own age around the ranch, she frolicked with the animals or invented human companions. "I liked having friends nobody else could see," Myrna would say of herself. "Maybe that's the Welsh in me. You know how they believe in . . . the little people."[24]

If this young daydreamer prized stillness, she also loved to move. Physically adventurous, Myrna often scraped her knees while climbing trees, tumbling in the hay, or scurrying through a wheat field. In early spring she braved swimming in an icy stream. Surviving photographs of her in early childhood show her all dolled up in pretty dresses, with a locket around her neck and a ribbon in her hair. Della made sure Myrna looked her best for the camera. But on the ranch and later, in Helena, Myrna was known as a tomboy. She and her father were pals. He read her stories and would take her along for berry picking, horseback riding, or rabbit hunting. He never struck her. The only spanking she ever received was from the hired man, Ben Sitton, who had forbidden her to crawl through the wire around the ranch. "I did, so he spanked me."[25]

Ranch hands ate at a long kitchen table. In the same room, behind the potbellied wood-burning stove that provided heat, Myrna stored her slate, picture books, and child-size red chair. There she cuddled two gray kittens named after local plants, Timothy and Alfalfa. At night, after the candles were blown out, she could hear the howls of wolves and coyotes from her bed. More soothing was the sound of her mother playing Brahms's "Lullaby" on the piano, accompanied by Aunt Lu's violin. Thus comforted, Myrna would drift off to sleep.[26]

CHAPTER 2

Not Your Typical Helena Girl

When Myrna was five, her parents decided they'd had enough of ranch life. They pulled up stakes and moved to Helena, a former mining camp that had burgeoned into a thriving commercial center and, as Montana's capital, a political hub. Pitched against Mount Helena and Mount Ascension, with the Big Belt Mountains to the east and spurs of the Rockies poking the sky to the north and west, Helena offered sweeping mountain views and bracing air plus city amenities. Its clanging streetcars, bustling shops, imposing civic buildings, flourishing public library, and lively theater scene must have made it seem like a metropolis after the isolation of Radersburg and the Crow Creek Valley. Here the population exceeded twelve thousand! Even in Helena, though, horses remained essential to everyday life. Most homes of the day came with outdoor hitching posts, and the rich had carriage houses, soon to become shelters for newly available automobiles. On a pretty day the Williams family, which would soon acquire a Dodge touring car, might ride the streetcar to Central Park, where they'd find a beer garden, a dance pavilion, skating rinks, a zoo, and a merry-go-round.[1]

For Myrna, even going for a walk felt like an adventure, since the Helena streets zigged and zagged. Built at the bottom of a ravine, the city grew up along the course of a meandering stream. Miners had altered the terrain by digging tunnels under most neighborhoods, some of which were naturally hilly. The odd-shaped lots, furrows, and steep slopes, down which Myrna went bobsledding in winter, could turn the terrain into a child's oversized playground.[2]

The Williams family settled into a modest but comfortable house on Fifth Avenue, in a middle-class enclave east of Last Chance Gulch with none of the showiness of the elite west side, where gold barons, copper kings, and bankers of the plush 1880s had built ostentatious mansions with carved mahogany mantels, Tiffany stained-glass windows, and little stands on which New Year's Day visitors placed their printed calling cards.

Grandmother Johnson had cashed in her Radersburg mining claim, leaving behind the house John Johnson had built, and moved with her son Fred to Helena's Breckenridge Avenue, a few blocks from the Williams's new home. Myrna often spent weekends with her grandmother, whose front hall display of programs from touring plays starring the likes of Minnie Maddern Fiske or John Drew attested to her fondness for going to the theater (*BB*, 8). Also within walking distance was the grand Italian Renaissance state capitol, with its figure of the Goddess of Liberty astride the burnished copper dome and Charles Russell mural within, depicting Indians encountering Lewis and Clark. To this stately structure Myrna's father had reported for duty in the legislature in 1903, when he helped plan Montana's observance of the Lewis and Clark Centennial. Now, seven years later, David worked out of the less lofty Pittsburgh building, where the 1910 Polk's Helena Directory announced his occupation with one word, "Lands." His business card elaborated: "Specializing in small farms on easy payments."[3]

Helena had survived several disastrous fires and many economic ups and downs. The economy slumped with the lowering of silver prices in 1893; banks failed. With the coming of the twentieth century, prosperity returned as gold mining geared up in nearby Marysville, and Helena residents could find work constructing Canyon Ferry or helping to build two Missouri River dams in the area. The Williams family arrived as an upswing in population began, statewide. Electrical power plants and telephone lines began to sprout. Land values rose. David F. Williams, who soon began selling insurance and brokering loans, as well as offering farmland and other real estate, had chosen a potentially lucrative line of work.[4]

Della became pregnant soon after the move to Helena, and a son, another David F. (which in his case stood for Frederick, as in uncle Fred Johnson), came into the world in May 1911. Little David, a towhead, at once became his mother's darling, though he didn't share his sister's sunny disposition. Della spoiled him throughout his life, and Myrna did too, eventually. Initially, however, at least according to one account, she refused to even look at her newborn brother. A photograph of the boy with his six-year-old sister shows him with a dour expression and Myrna wearing a smile that appears less than spontaneous. But despite this she looks fetching. Even then, the camera loved Myrna. She could be shy around strangers but never around a camera. In every image of her with little David, both children are beautifully groomed and expensively dressed, like manikins in a store window. In one photo Myrna wears a sailor hat with a striped border and a pleated skirt over a long jacket that appears hand-sewn; David, who looks about a year old here, has on knit rompers, matching hat, and lace-up boots.[5]

When he was old enough to draw and mold figures, David displayed artistic talent and started his young adult life wanting to become a sculptor. As soon as he was old enough, Della set him up with lessons in art, which Myrna also studied. A nun at the local convent served as the teacher (BB, 16).

Myrna had an excellent eye, a good sense of form and design, and a talent for working with her hands. Guided by the art-teacher nun, she enjoyed both molding clay and drawing and would later excel both at homey crafts like knitting and at practical tasks like changing flat tires and fixing gadgets in need of repair. She studied piano, too, and learned two pieces for a student recital that she could still play in adulthood. She attended Central Elementary School, where English, history, and geography were her favorite subjects and arithmetic her bane. Gary Cooper, just a year older than she and then known as Frank, at times attended the same school, but Myrna didn't recall knowing him there. He claimed he remembered her pigtails and freckles, as well as her mother once bestowing on him a jar of apple jelly when he came by the Fifth Avenue house. Myrna would go sledding past the substantial home of Judge and Mrs. Cooper, Frank's English-born parents, who knew Myrna's parents (BB, 14–15).

In Helena the solitude she had known on the ranch gave way to a community-centered life filled with other children. Afternoons she made fudge with her girlfriends, went on excursions to the turreted brick library, and devoured books she had borrowed: *Little Women, Lorna Doone,* Tennyson poems. Well-liked and easy to get along with, Myrna nonetheless sensed that something set her apart. "I was not your typical Helena girl. For one thing, my parents were more liberal than most people from Montana." When a black family moved in across the street, bigoted neighbors ostracized them, but Della welcomed them, encouraging the children to play together (BB, 18).[6]

Myrna began to think about what she might want to be when she grew up. She knew she wanted to do something distinctive. Influenced by Presbyterian aunts and uncles, and by the convent art teacher, she went through a martyr period at around age eleven, when she hoped to become "a nun or nurse and spend my life doing good works." She soon became guilt-ridden for harboring aspirations she considered less noble: she now wanted to be a performer, perhaps a dancer or actress. From the time she could walk, she had the habit of sometimes standing on tippy-toes.[7]

As a budding actress she, along with her neighborhood friends, put on plays behind a makeshift curtain in the Williams cellar, near the neatly stored shelves of preserves in jars and as far as possible from the dank corner with the coal chute. For their production of "The Sleeping Beauty" Myrna was cast as the witch, doubling as the prince, and for the latter role wore a plumed hat and bloomers over black stockings. She stuffed the toes of a pair of oversized slippers with paper to make the toes curl up the way they did in picture-book illustrations of princes. She missed out on starring as the Sleeping Beauty because she didn't look like a storybook princess, lacking the long, golden curls that crowned the head of her angelic looking next-door friend, Amy. "She was a lace paper valentine, I was the comic variety. The boys made a great fuss over her. *I* carried my own books." Myrna saw herself as "a very plain little girl" with "carroty hair, freckles . . . and unpleasantly skinny. I was a tomboy, too. Grubby hands and knees, torn dresses." Not realizing that teasing can signal affection, she smarted when boys would yell, "Redhead, gingerbread, five cents a loaf." She'd run and cry, skinning her knees on the stairs. She claimed she never felt adored. "Never once did anyone ever hug me or pat my head and say, 'What a lovely, luscious little girl.'"[8]

Myrna and her mother played out a tug of war in which Myrna constantly turned up bruised, scraped, and torn, with smudges on her face, and the meticulous Della cleaned her up, vigorously applying washcloth, soap, and scrub brush. She braided Myrna's unruly red hair into two tight pigtails. Eventually, Della won this battle. Myrna learned to groom herself immaculately.

Myrna was cast more than once as a male character in her childhood amateur theatricals. When she and her friends dressed up as dolls for a living doll show, Myrna, as the Papa doll, donned a top hat and a man's suit jacket. She submitted to this casting decision but ardently wished that she looked more like a princess and got treated more like one. "I suffered agonies in silence," she recalled years later. "I always have been inarticulate when it comes to personal pain. I wanted, passionately, to be beautiful."[9]

Della became seriously ill with pneumonia after young David's birth and required home visits by nurses who supplied tanks of oxygen. With his wife still in fragile health some months postpartum, David senior encouraged Della to hasten her recovery by taking the baby and six-year-old Myrna with her to balmy Southern California rather than enduring another winter in frigid Helena. Della, Myrna, and babe-in-arms David Frederick took the train to San Diego, renting a house by the sea in La Jolla. There they remained through winter, spring, and then into summer. Della discovered that she loved both California's sunny climate and its relaxed way of living. She felt no isolation because she had friends from Montana who visited and other friends who moved nearby. For the first time in her seven-year marriage she experienced the freedom of living away from her husband and found that she rather liked it. Myrna, too, found the seaside enchanting. In La Jolla she befriended a kindly old naturalist, Dr. Kline, who owned the local aquarium and taught her to catch eels and hunt for shells on the beach.[10]

David senior came to visit in August, in time to join the celebration of Myrna's seventh birthday. The long sojourn in California, coupled with all the train fares, must have cost plenty, but there is no evidence that money was a major concern. At this point the focus was on Della's health and on getting to know an alluring part of the world. During his visit David senior resisted Della's entreaties to buy land in California, proclaiming himself a Montanan, by God (*BB*, 17). He and Della evidently quarreled. She fervently wanted the entire family to relocate and tried to convince David that he could make a good living selling real estate in the Land of Sunshine, which was attracting hordes of newcomers. He wouldn't hear of it, however, and dispatched his family to return home to Helena's Fifth Avenue. They did so in time for Myrna to resume her schooling in Helena in the fall of 1912.

Four years later, Della needed a hysterectomy, and she and the children returned to Southern California, this time to a shingled house in the Los Angeles area with a honeysuckle-strewn porch on Hart Avenue in Ocean Park, near Santa Monica. Across the street lived a friend who put them up when they first arrived. Della had persuaded David to allow her to undergo both the surgery and the convalescence in a healing climate. He indulged her by giving his reluctant consent. They remained long enough for Myrna, now almost eleven, to be enrolled in school in Ocean Park for several months and for her to take her first dancing lessons, which she loved. She formed a tight bond with a girl named Louella Bamberger (later called Lou MacFarlane), who lived next door and would remain a lifelong friend. Myrna, tall for her age, was already aware of boys and seemed quite worldly to the younger Lou. The two enjoyed Saturday afternoon dances for children at Ocean Park Pier. Myrna had taught herself the steps to popular ballroom dances, which she in turn taught her friend. At the Saturday dances Myrna and Lou would dance together (*BB*, 19).

Della recovered quickly from her surgery. Myrna remembered her mother enjoying parties, champagne, and the jazz orchestra at the Nat C. Goodwin Pier. Della didn't seem to be pining for home, Montana, or her absent husband. Whatever passion once existed between Della and David, both still in their thirties, had by now subsided.

Myrna did miss her father, and her beloved Johnson grandmother as well, but she flourished nonetheless beside the Pacific Ocean. While investigating barnacles beneath the pier, she got her first glimpse of movie stars cavorting at a private beach. The women wore bathing costumes with bloomers and tied their hair up in turbans. She viewed more actors at close range when Della took the children on a tour of Universal Studios, where they watched William Farnum (who would later appear with Myrna in *A Connecticut Yankee*) "shootin' it up with wranglers" under blue lights (*BB*, 18). That same day they also watched Dorothy Davenport and Jack Pickford at work. But what most entranced Myrna on her first visit to a movie studio was the filming of a sequence "in which a small girl broke out of a fancy egg and danced exquisitely." According to Della, "That inspired Myrna."[11]

All this California fun ended abruptly when David senior issued another edict for their return to Helena. Della complied, but once they were reinstalled in the family home, Myrna keenly sensed the friction in her parents' marriage. Her mother was certain she no longer wished to live full time in Montana. She wasn't saying she wanted to break up the family, only that she should cast the deciding vote on where they should pitch their tent. California, still smogless and without freeways, offered a healthier life for one and all, she insisted; the family should follow the sun. As he had before, David stood his ground. Now working for the Banking Corporation of Montana and serving as a member of the board, he was the breadwinner, the head of the household, and the son of pioneer Montana ranchers, whose tradition he honored. With the outbreak of war in Europe came a business boom that benefited the entire state. Prices were high for farmland; now was no time to leave. His roots were in Montana; his brothers and sisters all lived nearby, so in Helena they would remain.

By this time Myrna had developed a decided attachment to Southern California. But one of the compensations of being back in Helena was that now, at age twelve, she could begin taking Saturday morning ballet classes with Miss Alice Thompson. Grandmother Johnson further stimulated her love of dance by taking her to see a performance of Maurice Maeterlinck's *The Blue Bird*. Myrna was moved to choreograph her own version of a "Blue Bird" dance and was invited to perform it in a talent show following the annual banquet of her father's lodge, the Benevolent and Protective Order of Elks. The talent show took place on the stage of Helena's spanking new Marlow Theater. Looking every inch the princess she had long yearned to become, she leaped across the stage in a pale blue silk dress decked with blue ribbon bows. "Miss Williams, who is much admired for her grace and beauty, has received many compliments," reported the *Helena Record-Herald*. Her tomboy days had ended.[12]

Myrna's triumphant dance, witnessed by many Helena friends and relations, marks a turning point, a decisive step toward a future of creativity and performing. But as she took her bows at the Elks show, two notable absences tempered Myrna's joy. Her beloved maternal grandmother, Isabella Johnson, had recently died of cancer, at age seventy-four. And Myrna's idolized father, David, chose to be out of town on a business trip on the night Myrna was to perform for his lodge. David had agreed to fund Myrna's dancing lessons, Della recalled, because "he recognized that aesthetic dancing embodies the finest ideals of art and music." But he could not comprehend how a daughter of his could possibly want to cavort in public. Della reminded him that Myrna had two parents and that she, Della, happened to be one of them. She tried to convince him that there was nothing shameful about being an "artistic" dancer, but he insisted, "No daughter of mine is going to be a chorus girl." According to Della, "he fancied all professional dancers were . . . of questionable morals." David's disapproval stung all the more because, after Grandmother Isabella's passing, Myrna and he had been spending more time together, becoming even closer than they'd been before.[13]

Despite her father's opposition, Myrna held fast to her ambition to become a dancer but tried not to provoke. She disliked talking about her feelings and concealed from both parents the news that she had experienced her first crush, on a boy in her neighborhood, Johnny Brown. Johnny barely knew that she was alive, however. It was the blonde neighbor Amy he wanted as his valentine. Myrna, when she was grown but had not yet married for the first time, would look back on these first un-requited love pangs and comment, "I've always fallen in love with the wrong man—or with a man who didn't know the state of my feelings," a truth that remained with her throughout her life.[14]

Despite her silent pining, and the tensions in the household, there were still many joys to savor in Helena: dancing class, horseback riding with her father, frolicking in the snow with her brother, and holiday dinners with many guests and tables piled high with puddings and roasts. Her father's largesse and hospitality made Christmas a bountiful time. Myrna called him "a Santa Claus type of man" (BB, 14).

Going to the movies on Saturday afternoons became an eagerly antic-ipated treat. The habit got started in Ocean Park, California, where she and Lou attended Saturday matinees and serials like The Perils of Pauline. But movies were available in Helena, too. When the Williams family first moved there from Crow Creek Valley, moving picture shows had been confined to rowdy theaters in the saloon district, and the proper Williams clan had kept its distance. Not any more, now that the respectable He-lena Theatre on North Jackson, which seated eight hundred, was offer-ing "photo spectacles" appropriate to young viewers. After 1918, films could also be watched at the gleaming new Marlow. Myrna had favorite actresses. A fan of Marie Doro in Oliver Twist, she was also completely smitten with the image of Annette Kellerman as a mermaid who detaches her body from a fish tail to marry the hero in Neptune's Daughter.[15]

Because of her parents' interest in politics, Myrna from an early age developed an awareness of the wider world. The outbreak of the Great War heightened that interest. Her father, a "Teddy Roosevelt Republi-can," had been inclined to vote for prointerventionist Charles Evans Hughes against Woodrow Wilson in the presidential election of 1916. Wilson's reelection campaign slogan had been, "He kept us out of the war." Myrna, precociously siding with her Democrat, proneutrality mother, helped talk him into voting for Wilson, who ended up winning Montana. She, Della, and David senior also backed Wilson's campaign to establish the League of Nations.[16]

By April of 1917, when the United States entered the war, breaking from its earlier neutral stance and joining the Allied effort to defeat Ger-many, fanatical patriotism took hold in Montana as it did elsewhere in the nation. Neighbor turned on neighbor in Helena as it became a crime to speak German or to say anything "disloyal, profane, violent, con-temptuous or abusive" about government, soldiers, or the American flag. Of Montana's adult male population, 10 percent, nearly forty thousand men, enlisted in the military, the highest percentage in the country. Flags waved and trumpets blared as the 2nd Montana 163rd Infantry paraded down Helena's Main Street.[17]

David senior, at age thirty-nine, felt moved to enlist in the fall of 1918, not solely out of a sense of duty and genuine love of his country. Conflicts with Della fueled his desire to flee into the battlefield. Looking back, Myrna saw him at this juncture as agitated, unhappy, and close to a breakdown. She sensed her father's precariousness, without knowing exactly what caused it. The truth is that, though she had no inkling of this, David senior had more than the war, more than marital disharmony on his mind. He had plunged himself into financial hot water. To fund land-buying deals in various locations, he had borrowed money from banks and from friends (including Della's father's former business partner from Sweden, A. W. Sederburg) and from relatives, including his sister Emma Stonehouse and brother-in-law Fred Johnson. He had secured one promissory note "by chattel mortgage on 8 head horses, 4 sets harness, 2 drills, 2 red cows (1 dead), 1 drag harrow, 1 fourteen inch breaking plow." In 1918 he had fallen behind on his monthly payments for the family home in Helena and was facing possible foreclosure. Della's expenditures for travel to California in past years, and extravagantly long stays there, had surely contributed to the family's insolvency.[18]

In February 1918 David Franklin Williams, while in Los Angeles, wrote and filed a last will and testament that was witnessed by three Los Angeles residents. What was he doing in Los Angeles at this time? Was he looking around for real estate, reconsidering his stance on remaining in Helena? Did he decide to write a will in his thirty-ninth year because he recognized that he might die on the European war front after his contemplated enlistment in the military? If he survived that peril, did he foresee a separation from Della, or a divorce? Affirmatives to at least some of these questions seem likely.

Myrna recalled being at home in Helena, shortly after she turned thirteen, dressed up as a girl soldier with a cap and a khaki jacket, when, with a voice cracking with emotion, she tried to persuade her father to change his mind about enlisting. She wanted him home. He didn't yield to her entreaties. Should anything happen to him, he told Myrna, *she* should take charge of the family. "You're my little soldier. When I go, I'm leaving you to take care of things" (*BB*, 21). What an extraordinary thing to say to a schoolgirl who had just entered her teens, especially considering the financial hole he was in the process of digging. Myrna took her father's words to heart. They would shape her future role in the family and ultimately define her sense of purpose. She would become a person with a fierce work ethic, a young woman with ambitious goals for herself who at the same time shouldered responsibility for others.

The Spanish influenza epidemic prevented David's planned enlistment. Beginning in September of 1918, a virulent strain of the disease walloped the entire country. Almost a quarter of the national population contracted the infection, and out of every one thousand that fell ill, nineteen died. Army camps were decimated as more soldiers died from the flu than had fallen in the trenches. Calls for 142,000 draftees were canceled. In Montana entire homesteader families died in their beds, and children not yet stricken wore balls of asafetida tied around their necks.[19]

When Myrna, her brother, and Della all came down with the flu, David senior nursed them, aided by a professional nurse who came to their house for just one hour a day to administer medicine and pack them in ice. Myrna remembered waking from sleep to find her father sitting beside her, holding her hand. She also recalled a sleepwalking episode. Feverish and not aware of her own movements, she wandered out of her bedroom. Her father gently led her back to bed.[20]

When David himself contracted the disease, Myrna, who had recovered, went to stay with a neighbor. She learned of her father's death by overhearing a morning phone call and went to pieces. Recalling the moment to James Kotsilibas-Davis more than sixty years later, while working with him on her autobiography, Myrna again broke down.[21]

David Franklin Williams, not yet forty years old, died November 7, 1918, two days before Kaiser Wilhelm II abdicated and four days before Germany signed the armistice and hostilities ceased. "Funeral services for David F. Williams, who died at 8:30 yesterday morning from effects of influenza, will take place at 11 Saturday morning from Flaherty and Kohler chapel under the auspices of the Helena lodge of Elks," reported the *Helena Independent*. "The Rev. James F. McNamee of First Baptist Church will preach the sermon." David Franklin Williams's estate was billed $365 for funeral expenses, including "casket, box, services," the hearse, and five taxis. He was buried on November 11, to background noises of jubilation—drumbeats, bells, sirens, and shouts—as the rest of Helena celebrated the armistice.[22]

"I worshipped him," Myrna said of her father, whose death proved to be the determining event in her life. "I coped with his loss by accepting the responsibility for my mother and brother he had entrusted to me" (*BB*, 22).

CHAPTER 3

Life without Father

In asking Myrna to take responsibility for the family if he died, her father had cast a kind of spell, one that could not be broken. Myrna began to think like a parent instead of a child.

David's will reveals that despite his plea to Myrna, he had made other, more hardheaded provisions for the future of his wife and children, plans he hadn't shared with either Myrna or Della. The last will and testament that David Franklin Williams wrote, or at least put on public record, in Los Angeles in February of 1918 designated his married older sister, Nettie Williams Qualls of Helena, as executrix of his estate and guardian of the "persons and estates" of his two minor children, who were his named beneficiaries. David empowered Nettie, in the event of his death, to hold her deceased brother's property in trust for minors Myrna Adele and David Frederick, "to handle said property as though it were her own" until the children reached adulthood. As for Della Williams, who was, after all, his wife when he wrote the will and the mother of his children, David's will instructed Nettie to pay Della the sum of twenty-five dollars per month, so long as Della remained "single and chaste."[1]

David's estrangement from Della all but leaps from the pages of his final testament. His will indicates that when he wrote it, he felt some financial obligation to his wife but not much beyond that. It's the tribe started by his parents, D. T. and Ann Williams, personified by his trusted older sister Nettie, and continued by his two Williams children, his blood kin, that he calls his own. Nettie and his children represent "us," and Della, joined to him by law but not by blood, is "them." Myrna and young David are the ones for whom he wants to provide an inheritance. As for Della, even though twenty-five dollars a month, the equivalent of about $353 in the year 2009, was a far less paltry sum in 1918 than it is now, his carefully monitored provision for her attests duty, not love. Further, it lays bare David's wish to deprive his widow of true adult independence, since it binds her for subsequent years to the judgments, allotments, and ministrations of her sister-in-law Nettie Qualls. According to the will, if Nettie decides at some future point that Della has been "unchaste," she has the right to withhold Della's monthly stipend. She sits in judgment. Worse yet, from Della's point of view, by appointing Nettie guardian of Myrna and young David's "persons and estates," David senior undercuts, or attempts to undercut, his wife's authority over her own children.

The name Nettie Qualls doesn't appear a single time in Myrna Loy's autobiography, *Being and Becoming,* nor in any of the several interviews Myrna gave that touched on her early life. Nor is Aunt Nettie, a teacher, mentioned in the script of the May 1956 episode of the television biography program *This Is Your Life* that was devoted to the life story of Myrna Loy, though her father's younger brother, Myrna's uncle Elmer Williams, is. Uncle Elmer actually came to Los Angeles that May to tell the television audience about the Williams ranch and Myrna's Montana girlhood. It seems safe to conclude that neither Myrna nor Della felt close to the upright, Presbyterian, Montanan aunt/sister-in-law to whom they would long remain tethered.[2]

But Nettie Qualls deserves respect, and probably won at least a measure of it, for her steadfast and responsible attempt to honor her brother David's last wishes and to untangle and restore some credit to the confusion and debt, along with a considerable amount of property that he left. At the time of his death, David Franklin Williams had all of $138.11 in his bank account, less than $2,000 in current worth. His property—the land and personal effects (including that Dodge touring car) that he owned or was in the process of acquiring when he died—had to be sold to generate cash. His debts amounted to almost $12,000, and his assets eventually were assessed at just over that same amount. Because the estate was so strapped for cash, Nettie and her lawyer arranged with the court for the estate to pay only 10 percent of what David owed to creditors, not the whole sum. This left a small pool of cash from which she could in time draw. When, after more than two months following her brother's death, Nettie on behalf of the estate had not yet repaid a claim of more than $1,000 owed to the Bank of Boulder, that bank tried to have her removed as executrix. Nettie Qualls and her lawyer successfully defended her right to continue as executrix by arguing to the court that she was doing the best she could, considering her difficulties in sorting things out, and that she had been acting in the best interest of the estate's beneficiaries. Nettie Qualls explained to the Lewis and Clark County First District Court that her brother's estate provided little help in the way of official inventory, account books, or clear, readily accessible data about his business dealings and real estate holdings. She faced quite a daunting task trying to piece together the patchwork of estate obligations but did manage to eventually carry it off.[3]

Nettie also demonstrated an admirable sense of fair play, for she allowed Della to acquire for nominal sums property that David might have willed to her—the Fifth Avenue house they had occupied in Helena (the one burdened with several months of delinquent payments to the seller) and a portion of the Crow Creek Valley Williams ranch and land. The latter transfer of property didn't happen until 1942, when the estate was close to being finally settled, and it required Myrna's help, since she and her brother had inherited the rights to their father's share of Williams ranch land. Della acquired the equity in their Fifth Avenue house in Helena for the sum of one dollar in 1919, soon after her husband's death.

Della must have spent some sleepless nights worrying about her future ability to stay afloat financially even before David died, because in 1918 she briefly enrolled as a student at Helena Business College, a remarkable step for a woman who had never held a job for wages and whom everyone in the family considered impractical when it came to money. She clearly sensed the precariousness of her marriage and had to know that David, depressed and in an agitated state, had fallen behind in payments for their house and had accrued numerous other debts as well. She feared she might very well be faced with having to fend for herself and the children. Concerns about the Spanish influenza epidemic, and the war, surely alarmed her further. Death was in the air. As it turned out, in the tumult of 1918 she never finished business college. She would later earn some money by giving piano lessons, helping out in a dress shop, and for a brief period working as a clerk in a small company.[4]

Soon after burying her husband in Helena's Forestvale Cemetery, where her own ashes would one day repose in a plot right next to David's grave, Della decided to leave Montana and start a new life, relocating with the children to a place she'd long considered the land of milk and honey, Southern California. Although she would occasionally return for visits to her home turf, she wanted to leave behind those frigid Montana winters and put some distance between herself and her past life, with its entire cast of characters, including the now all-powerful Nettie. She made an exception of her sister Lulu Belle, Myrna's favorite aunt, persuading Aunt Lu to come to California, bringing along her daughter, Laura Belle, Myrna's older cousin, next to whom Myrna had sat at many a laden table at family Thanksgiving and Christmas dinners. Laura Belle's health was fragile—she had an unnamed degenerative neurological condition, possibly multiple sclerosis—and found walking increasingly difficult. Everyone hoped that the California sunshine might do her some good. The sisters, Della and Lu, could pool resources to run a household, raise the three children, and pay the bills. A boarder from Radersburg, old man A. W. Sederburg, once a partner in the cabinet-making business with Della's father, soon joined the household as its sole adult man, remaining for a year or so. According to Myrna, the lifelong bachelor, now in his sixties, had a lady friend and was not romantically involved with either Della or Lulu Belle. He functioned as a sort of adopted great uncle. Various Johnson women had been looking after him for years.

Della continued to own the family home in Helena, perhaps renting it out before deciding to sell it when it became clear after some months that they would not be returning to live there. The income generated from that house, together with a small insurance settlement, a few hundred dollars that Della inherited from her mother's estate, and the monthly stipend from Nettie, allowed her to buy train tickets and move the household into a pretty California bungalow. It was located not in La Jolla or Ocean Park, where she'd stayed in the past, but in the Palms section of Los Angeles, "city of sunshine, fruit and flowers," a block north of Venice Boulevard, the Culver City border.

For Myrna the move to California worked as a tonic. She continued to grieve for her father, but in this new, yet familiar, environment she felt the excitement of starting over in a household far more harmonious than the one she'd known in Helena. She had flourished during her childhood stays in Southern California and was glad to be back near the ocean, palm trees, and lush flowers she loved. She adored her Aunt Lu, who took on most of the cooking in the reconstituted household, much to Della's delight. Aunt Lu was close to Myrna and a warmer, more homey person than was Della, who always made Myrna's friends welcome in their home but tended to focus on the outside world of music, women's clubs, and community work on behalf of the arts. She immediately enrolled Myrna in dance classes and set about purchasing tickets for herself and both children to as many performances of classical music, dance, opera, and theater as she could find: Pavlova, Paderewski, Chaliapin, and Eleanora Duse were among the standout performers Myrna saw live and would never forget (*BB*, 29).

Della got to know the local classical musicians, befriending the impresario Lynden E. Behymer, who was involved with the newly founded Los Angeles Philharmonic, and joining the campaign to establish the Hollywood Bowl as a venue for outdoor summer symphony concerts. The stimulating new surroundings and interesting company that Della supplied helped Myrna to look forward, not back.

Although her father's death left Myrna with a sometimes suffocating sense of responsibility, and an enduring hunger for the security, support, and love a stable father might have provided, it also freed her, encouraging her to set her own goals and, with Della's help, to make her own way. In Helena Myrna's interest in performing had caused strife between her parents. Now, with her mother's encouragement, it could be indulged, unabated. To be sure, there were protests emanating from the Williams family in Helena. Aunt Nettie Qualls took a dim view of Della's expenditures for Myrna's dancing lessons and denounced the support Della continued to give her daughter's expressive, creative impulses. As Della once explained in an interview, "Her father's family was furious with me. They wrote, demanding to know why I was permitting Myrna to go ahead like this. I didn't pay any attention to them, for I sympathized with Myrna." In general, Della was kicking up her heels, exulting in a sense of independence and freedom. Along with other American women she won the right to vote in 1920, and the fervent Democrat surely exercised her franchise once she established residence in California, opposing Harding's "Back to Normalcy" campaign.[5]

In her autobiography Myrna reports that when the family moved, they resettled in Culver City, not the Palms section of Los Angeles. Her geographic confusion isn't surprising, since Delmas Terrace, the street on which they now lived, extended into Culver City and is named for a co-founder of that enclave. Della, after the move, quickly became active in the Culver City Women's Club, where she presided even after Myrna became well known and the family had moved to Beverly Hills. The transplanted Williams family, evidently unaware of just where the borderline between Los Angeles and Culver City fell, considered themselves Culver City-ites.

Their new neighborhood in California had been a farming and ranching area in the days before the Los Angeles Aqueduct opened and, in 1919, when the family arrived, had a small-town, bucolic, Edenic ambience. There were stretches of open bean fields, walnut orchards, orange groves, vineyards, and dirt roads, which in rainy season turned to rivers of mud. Horses with buggies were still in use by some auto-challenged families and local businesses, and Main Street in Culver City—which had been laid out in the middle of a barley field—maintained watering troughs for horses. Initially, according to the 1920 census, there were only twelve single-family houses on their block, with a Presbyterian church on the corner, where Myrna briefly taught Sunday school until she flubbed the answer to some biblical question and the minister, a Reverend O'Connell, who lived down the street, "breathed fire and brimstone all over" her (BB, 25). That ended that. Teaching Sunday school was as close as Myrna ever came to fulfilling her girlhood ambition to become a nun, although she held on to her ideal of service to a higher cause. Instead of offering selfless devotion to God or a religion, Myrna became an acolyte in the temple of art.[6]

Della worried that the Reverend O'Connell, the judgmental minister down the block, would catch a glimpse of Myrna dancing barefoot in a flowing Grecian tunic between the twin palms in front of their house and breathe more thunder. All bluenoses didn't live in Helena, after all, and they did not all have Williams as a surname. Plenty of stern finger-pointers could be found right here in California.

From the house at 7137 Delmas Terrace (which would now, since remapping, be number 3729) it was an easy streetcar ride on the Venice Short Line to Venice or Ocean Beach, where Myrna's special friend Lou Bamberger lived. Lou had become one of Della's piano students, and through Lou Myrna met another lifelong friend, Betty Berger (later Betty Black), who came from an Orthodox Jewish family. Della invited both girls to stay overnight at the Williams home, and a tight three-way friendship took hold. Betty remembered playing word games and spinning phonograph records in the Williams home. She recalled that Myrna in those days wrote poetry and plays; she'd sew the costumes for the plays herself, putting those deft hands to work. Myrna definitely had a practical side. She read and wrote poetry, true, but if the vacuum cleaner broke, she could take it apart and fix it.[7]

Downtown was also within easy reach on the streetcar. There Myrna took her weekly ballet lessons in the Majestic Building, and after class she would stop in at the Los Angeles Public Library, loading up with as many books as her arms could carry. She devoured them on the ride home and during the following week, replacing them with a new set on each return visit.

The streetcar also carried the book-laden Myrna to an elite private girls' high school, Westlake School for Girls, on Westmoreland. Wealthy acquaintances of Della's from Montana had sent their daughters there and recommended it to Della, who somehow managed to scrape together the tuition. Although most of the other girls at Westlake came from very affluent families with debutante aspirations, social cachet played no part in the choice of that school for Myrna. Della believed that the education provided at Westlake would be top-notch, and that was what counted. Far from being a snob about social class, she believed that no school could set the mark too high for her bright, responsive, and talented daughter and that Westlake would provide Myrna a solid foundation in culture and the arts. Since Della had taken a part-time job at a dress shop, which offered Myrna a big discount on clothes, Myrna always came to West-lake beautifully turned out (*BB*, 26). Myrna, who studied piano and French at Westlake with particular enjoyment, and danced in the school's May Festival, did not form enduring friendships there, but the rarefied atmosphere confirmed her already strong belief that she need not feel inferior to anyone. Never arrogant or socially assertive, Myrna nonethe-less held her head high, developing impeccable manners, a well modu-lated voice, and other signs of good breeding. In this respect she differed dramatically from her brassier future friend Joan Crawford, whose rough childhood and chorus girl past shaped her into an insecure young woman unable to shake the need to prove herself worthy.

Myrna's fond memories of her teen years at the Delmas Terrace house, which beckoned with a trellis bursting with roses and offered a back-yard full of orange, peach, and apricot trees, never dimmed. Della kept a goat in the yard, believing its milk to be curative to young David, who had what Myrna called "a touch of TB." Apparently the goat's milk—and the benign climate—worked because his tubercular symptoms soon vanished (*BB*, 25).

The rustic, Edenic feeling of their first months in California didn't last long. The entire Los Angeles area had been burgeoning since the end of the Great War, and mammoth changes were afoot. The movie industry, already the biggest business in town by 1920, helped draw tourists and settlers to the region because it provided jobs and because Hollywood films and their attendant publicity advertised Los Angeles to the wider world. As the film industry flourished, the increasingly popular and avail-able automobile required paved roads, and developers' subdivision of agricultural land soon ruled the day. Where grain fields had recently stretched, banks, hospitals, churches, stores, schools, hotels, restaurants, and newly built homes sprouted. Real estate was needed for the hordes swarming in to settle in the city and its environs at the rate of more than 350 per day. The population of Los Angeles grew from nine hundred thousand in 1920 to more than two million a decade later.[8]

Along with the throngs, Prohibition had arrived, and nightspots began to open where fun seekers, many of them employed by the nearby Culver City motion picture studios—Ince, Goldwyn, Hal Roach—gathered after work to dance, dine, and drink bootleg liquor. Because it had a lax police department and a location close enough to the waterfront to be handy for bootleggers, staid Culver City became, paradoxically, a center for vibrant, often illicit, nightlife. Raucous Washington Boulevard clubs like the Kit Kat Club, the Doo Doo Inn, the Monkey Farm, and the Green Mill kept the neighbors awake after hours. In 1922 Culver City's local government, in a none-too-successful attempt to keep the lid on, passed a resolution prohibiting dancing in cafes and restaurants after 11:00 P.M.

Della harbored no fear that Myrna would fall under the spell of the hard-drinking, jazz-loving nightclubbers and dance-crazed flappers thronging to Washington Boulevard. She had the opposite concern: that her daughter wasn't having enough fun. Myrna didn't often go out on dates with boys but continued her old pattern of getting crushes and worshipping from afar. "I was a wallflower," Myrna would say of herself years later. "I tried to console myself by being an overwhelmingly arty character. It was the Era of Wonderful Nonsense, [but] I didn't reap much of the fun I saw around me." Artistic, bookish, serious-minded, and shy, Myrna steered clear of flapperdom in her early and midteens. She had a few good friends but otherwise preferred to be alone or with her family. She danced, but not the Black Bottom. The dreamy-eyed high school student preferred Chopin to jazz, and when she pranced on the grass in bare feet, she donned wisps of draped chiffon, not sequin-spangled sheaths with fringed hems that swayed to the beat. Ethereal, but at the same time purposeful and grounded, she wore her curly hair loose and flowing, like a model for a Pre-Raphaelite painting, not bobbed in the latest jazz-baby mode.[9]

Myrna had fallen under the spell of Ruth St. Denis, who with her husband, the dancer Ted Shawn, had founded Denishawn, an innovative, highly influential Los Angeles–based school of interpretive dance, and a well-known concert dance company that toured around the country, drawing huge audiences at venues like the Greek Theatre in Berkeley and Lewisohn Stadium in New York. Denishawn, which attracted Martha Graham and Doris Humphrey as students and company dancers, also had links to the world of motion pictures. Several current and future Hollywood actresses, including Lillian Gish, Carmel Myers, Ruth Chatterton, Constance and Joan Bennett, and, most famously, Louise Brooks, took classes at Denishawn, Brooks at the company's New York studio. A number of cinema dancers also studied at the Los Angeles Denishawn School, for example Margaret Loomis, who as an exotic dervish entices a crowd of Arabic men with her swirling scarves and bare midriff in the casino scene of *The Sheik*. When a film director sought a dancer who could deliver seductive harem dances before the camera, or peer kohl-eyed through veils of Babylonian decadence, Denishawn could show the way.[10]

Ruth St. Denis, a white Protestant American, became enchanted with the traditions of the East as a young woman, and in particular with a series of exotic goddesses she portrayed. Her "Egypta" choreography came into her head when she saw a poster of the goddess Isis in an ad for Egypta cigarettes. Her "Radha," danced to the music of Delibes, set in a Hindu temple, and based on the story of Krishna, required the use of brown body paint. Her "Green Nautch" was inspired by Indian temple dancing, and her "O-Mika," about a courtesan who becomes a goddess, grew out of her exposure to traditional Japanese dancers and her study with former Japanese geishas. St. Denis's adaptation of Asian ritual dancing became wildly popular in private salons and public theaters in America and Europe, complementing the Orientalism—harem pants, turbans, incense burners, patterned Turkish carpets, and embroidered cushions in dimly lit boudoirs—that had come into vogue in the late nineteenth century and that by the 1920s had become well entrenched.[11]

Born Ruth Dennis on a New Jersey farm, "Miss Ruth" moved to Los Angeles in 1915 after marrying the much younger Ted Shawn, a fellow dancer who was equally drawn to all things beautiful, spiritual, and otherworldly. Once a skirt dancer in vaudeville, after touring Europe with David Belasco's acting company and seeing performances by the famed Japanese dancer Sado Yacco, Ruth Dennis morphed into the spiritual Ruth St. Denis and became a groundbreaking soloist whose work incorporated motifs from ethnic dance. Like San Francisco–born Isadora Duncan, she saw dance as an expression of both nature's divinity and the unshackled soul. St. Denis, like Isadora, had studied ballet, rejecting its rigid European formality, its artificiality, and its insistence on toe shoes but retaining some of its physical rigor. Miss Ruth taught her students to control and discipline their bodies, but at the same time she encouraged them to be individualistic and, above all, natural and free in their movements.

She taught many of her California classes outdoors. Students danced in bare feet, draped in flowing, Grecian-style garments that left the legs uncovered. To puritans this near nakedness was scandalous. Proper young ladies were supposed to fully clothe their bodies in public. But the definition of feminine propriety was changing fast in these postwar years, as skirts got shorter, corsets disappeared, and waistlines dropped, or vanished altogether. St. Denis and Duncan, both American New Women, were at the cutting edge of female dress reform, and Myrna, who didn't need or own a corset, went right along with them. Both St. Denis and Duncan promoted health-enhancing gambols in fresh air, and no one ever caught either one of them in the sort of constricting, waist-cinching, high-collared shirtwaist and floor-length skirt that Della had worn for a family portrait just a few years back.[12]

Della, responsive to the coupling of the aesthetic with healthful outdoor living, approved Ruth St. Denis as the right dancing teacher for Myrna. Her friend, the impresario Lynden Behymer, served as manager of the Denishawn Company.

An actress as well as a dancer, St. Denis created elaborately costumed dance productions that blurred the line between drama and dance. Each of her dances focused on a central character, usually danced by St. Denis herself. Known for her poise, flowing movements, and the precision of her gestures, she choreographed dances that, aided by atmospheric sets, lighting, and costumes of her own design, evoked subtle moods and a spirit of place—whether China, India, Egypt, Japan, or Java.

Her training in the Delsarte method of expression guided her. François Delsarte, a French music and dance teacher who died in 1871, developed a system of "scientific," body-based expression and pantomime that was much in vogue in nineteenth- and early twentieth-century dramatic circles. The catalogue for summer 1918 at the Denishawn School lists a class in "Dramatic gesture based on the system of François Delsarte." Delsarte exercises, which American actors in training rehearsed, tried to match a performer's role in a scene with an appropriate, individual way of moving, standing, or emoting; each character had to find her or his own rhythm and, for each emotion, a corresponding gesture. Appropriateness, control, and relaxation were key. Myrna, who as a screen actress would excel at timing, restraint, and mastery of subtle nonverbal cues such as the deft shrug of a shoulder or arching of an eyebrow, learned her Delsarte gestures indirectly, by watching the work of actors experienced in his method, and via Ruth St. Denis, with whom she studied. She was taught how to maintain the erect posture and queenly bearing that became part of her signature. She learned pantomime, which would serve her well as an actress in silent film. She also was shown exactly how to sustain a still position, for posing in the Delsarte tradition was essential to Denishawn training. "If dancing is essentially the music of motion," Ted Shawn claimed in an article he wrote for a health magazine, "it is also true that there is action even in a perfectly still position." Ruth St. Denis herself taught Myrna the "Water Lily" pose, and Myrna in turn taught it to her friend Lou.[13]

Myrna and her friends sometimes snuck over the fence into the Culver City Goldwyn studio and practiced posing there, snapping photographs of each other in front of standing movie sets (BB, 26). All this studied attitudinizing enhanced her readiness for both the still and the movie camera, a few years down the line. In the 1926 film The Exquisite Sinner, produced at MGM and directed by Josef von Sternberg, as Myrna Loy she played a Living Statue. She was one of four extras who posed naked, covered with white body makeup and holding a bit of strategically placed drapery.[14]

St. Denis's impact on Hollywood didn't come by way of a direct implant. Since she trained so many actresses, and was seen by such a large audience, it was more a matter of osmosis, of an influence that seeped in. She had far more respect for, empathy with, and genuine curiosity about Asian and Middle Eastern ethnic dance traditions than did Hollywood, which trafficked in stereotypes and made little distinction between Chinese, Arabic, Javanese, Spanish, or East Indian temptresses. Hollywood borrowed from St. Denis, nonetheless, merging her exotic "look" and some of her characteristic undulating movements with those of other Oriental and Arabic stock types, including Theda Bara favorites like Salome and Cleopatra.

Myrna took only about a year of classes with Miss Ruth, along with classes in Spanish dancing that Della sponsored. But Ruth St. Denis had an impact on young Myrna that went beyond their actual hours together as teacher and student. Myrna kept a scrapbook with meticulously art nouveau–style hand-decorated borders she drew and colored herself with pastel crayons. She called her scrapbook "Angels of the Dance," and held on to it over the years, through all the changes of address. It has survived and is filled with clippings that Myrna, between the ages of fifteen and twenty, cut out of newspapers and magazines. She pasted in images of her personal angels—Pavlova, Isadora Duncan, and Theodore Kosloff, the dramatic Russian dancer who appeared in DeMille films, had a studio in Los Angeles, and had been the lover of Natacha Rambova, the dancer-designer who became Rudolph Valentino's wife. Myrna included in her "Angels of the Dance" scrapbook a copy of a Richard Le Gallienne translation of a poem, "Omar's Lost Love Song," another testament to her susceptibility to the romance of the atmospheric East. But the chief angel in Myrna's scrapbook is Ruth St. Denis herself. There are more images of and about St. Denis than of any other. Myrna gave a place of honor to a highlighted quote from Miss St. Denis that mirrored her own thoughts: "Beauty is a spiritual quality, and must prevail."[15]

Ruth St. Denis's cult of beauty, her quiet exoticism, her esteem for the crafts of set and costume design, her belief that all the arts are interrelated, and her emphasis on being both natural and restrained when performing fused with Myrna's own impulses, which Della had helped to mold. In California, free of David's moralizing constraints, Della was doing her best to turn Myrna into an "aesthetic" performing artist, a version of what she might have become if she'd had the chance. "If her father had lived," Della said of Myrna, "I doubt very much if she'd have had this [performer's] life." Della's goals for Myrna, in these first California years, harmonized with those Myrna developed for herself. As Ruth St. Denis, whose own mother played a key role in the dancer's formation, once told a class filled with mostly young female dance students, "A talented girl is the result of a mother who has been repressed and into whom goes all that mother's ambition and culture."[16]

Della had started Myrna with downtown ballet classes at Madame Matilda's École de Choréographie Classicet [sic]. There Myrna practiced her pliés, pirouettes, and arabesques and threw herself into the discipline of barre work. But Mme. Matilda, who had danced professionally at La Scala, took it upon herself to inform her Montana-bred pupil early on that she would never become a professional ballet dancer because she didn't have the kind of arched feet or short toes that adapted well to work *en pointe*. Myrna may have felt momentary disappointment, but giving up ballet for modern interpretive dance came to feel exactly right.

Myrna had a definite aim and the ambition to match it. She fervently wished to become a professional interpretive dancer with a studio and her own company, just like Ruth St. Denis. When she confessed this, in her sophomore year, to the two headmistresses at Westlake School for Girls, the headmistresses chastised her, informing Myrna that for a Westlake girl, who'd been given every advantage and trained to enter Society, a future career as a dancer was unsuitable. It simply would not do. The head-mistresses bought into the entrenched view that for females all professional performing was low class and morally suspect. When Myrna reported this snooty outburst to her mother, Della agreed that Myrna should leave Westlake and its finishing-school atmosphere after her sophomore year and transfer to a more sympathetic school, one that did not look down on artists. As Myrna put it, "I decided that since I already was familiar with the correct fork use, I really didn't need the school. I wanted more from life."[17]

Myrna transferred to a public school—the free tuition was another plus—near the beach, Venice Union Polytechnic High, and at once preferred it to Westlake. Venice High offered classes in sculpture with a well-known sculptor and teacher, Harry F. Winebrenner, and a chance for Myrna to study drama and elocution, as well as English, at which she excelled. She did poorly, as she always had, in math but was able to learn the role of Ophelia when she served as understudy in a school production of *Hamlet*. To help her develop and expand her performing skills, she signed up for lessons downtown in singing. Socially, she remained quite isolated from her fellow students. Since she entered Venice High School as a junior, she found herself an outsider, excluded from cliques and friendships that her classmates had already formed. Venice High, unlike Westlake, had boy students, but according to Della, "High school boys were too carefree to hold her interest. She admired men who had an aim in life. . . . Myrna has always been attracted to older men." Myrna did nurse a secret crush on a football player and went out a few times with a neighbor, a young actor from Mississippi named Truman Van Dyke, who appeared in movie serials. Truman took her tea dancing at the Montmartre Café on Hollywood Boulevard (*BB*, 37). An older man, a photoplay title writer named Howard Buffum, corresponded with her. In a letter, he complimented her for her determination to help her mother, who was ill at the time, and referred to her relationship with Truman Van Dyke. "Your friendship with Truman I am watching," he wrote, "hoping it will unfold beautifully."[18]

It didn't. The chaste Myrna, although she was blossoming into a beauty who would be chosen her school's Queen of the May, was far more interested in her artistic pursuits and her few close girlfriends than in having a serious beau. Della surely helped to orchestrate this state of (no) affairs. She encouraged Myrna's independence and nurtured her talents and friendships, so long as they posed no threat to her own supremacy or ambitions on Myrna's behalf. She was no conventional stage mother, breathing down her daughter's neck and arranging her calendar. Myrna, a good planner and organizer, handled her own date book, and when bookings began to arrive, she set them up herself. But Della loomed large in the background. When Myrna got an opportunity to audition or perform as a dancer, Della would accompany her at the piano. Della also played the piano for them when Myrna and her friends Lou and Betty performed together at a women's club, and yet again when the three girls appeared as dancers on a Chautauqua program. The dancer who preceded them on the latter occasion had broken a string of beads, which then noisily rolled all over the stage. The stage crew, if there was one, failed to pick up the fallen beads before the next number ensued, to the chagrin of the three dancing girls waiting in the wings. Betty and Lou tried to persuade Myrna that they should bow out, that they would hurt their feet if they tried to dance barefooted on the hard beads, but Myrna, who had set up the booking, insisted that they must go on, bruised feet or not, "for art's sake." They danced, and they suffered the consequences.[19]

By the time Myrna approached her seventeenth birthday, Della had begun to invest her hopes in her daughter's future earning capacity. Money from the sale of the Helena house was gone, and Della's income as a piano teacher and sometime shopkeeper remained meager. She does not seem to have tried to become a bigger earner, perhaps believing she could not shoulder a full-time job. Her sister, Lu, couldn't work either; she had to stay home to care for her now bedridden daughter, Laura Belle. David junior was still in grade school. Della looked to Myrna as the family's best financial hope.

Myrna took several part-time jobs while still in high school, and she immediately turned over any money she made to her mother. She earned twenty-five dollars a month teaching a children's dance class at the Ritter School of Expression in Culver City. During the summer she briefly replaced an acquaintance who worked as a film splicer at the David Horsley laboratories. This was her first employment in a movie-related job, but at the time movies had not yet captured her imagination. "I was a *danseuse*" (BB, 37).[20]

One job for which Myrna wasn't paid in money, but that reaped rich benefits of another sort, was modeling for her Venice High School sculpture teacher, Harry Fielding Winebrenner. A sculptor who had studied in Rome and at the Art Institute of Chicago before becoming primarily a teacher, Mr. Winebrenner was creating an allegorical group sculpture for the school's grounds, a "Fountain of Education" to be placed before the outdoor pool. Winebrenner looked for students to serve as live models for his three abstractions, selecting a football player to embody the Physical, a pretty girl who got good grades to personify the Mental, and Myrna Williams to stand for the dominant spiritual figure, Inspiration, "a prismatic refraction of intelligent understanding, beauty and grace." In the completed sculpture Myrna's slender, loosely draped figure stands highest, with face uplifted and one arm extended in front of her, the other reaching behind, a vision of purity, grace, youthful vigor, and aspiration that caught a reporter's attention. "Southland Produces Venus," ran the headline for an article about the group sculpture in the *Los Angeles Times*. The other two models were ignored.[21]

Because of the sculpture, Myrna Williams's name appeared in the newspapers for the first time, and it would appear again, along with a photograph of Myrna's portion of the statue, a year later when the sculpture of her was separated from the other two figures and transported aboard a battleship, the *Nevada,* for a Memorial Day pageant (directed by Thomas Ince) at Venice Beach. Two other battleships, it was announced, would fire salvos, seven airplanes would strew flowers in tribute to the war dead, and a wreath from President Harding would be dropped into the sea. A *Los Angeles Times* news story promised that "Miss Myrna Williams, a Venice high school girl who posed for the statue, will take part in the ceremonies aboard ship." For many years the figure of Myrna presided over Venice High from its pedestal near the flagpole in front of the main building. Constructed in cement, it was vulnerable to weather and repeated vandalism and was removed in 2002. An alumni-led fundraising campaign made it possible to duplicate the original and this time cast it in bronze. The new statue was unveiled at a ceremony in front of the high school in April 2010.[22]

By the time the original statue was put on display, in May of 1923, Myrna had dropped out of high school to go to work and help her family. Her father had counted on her, and that was fine with Della. Leaving school was difficult but didn't feel like a huge sacrifice, because Myrna knew she wanted to perform and was eager to get started on her career. When she heard that dancers were being hired, she auditioned, along with hundreds of other girls, and was selected to join a chorus to dance in prologues to movies at Grauman's Egyptian Theatre. The pay was thirty-five dollars a week—nothing to sniff at. Her reason for taking the job might have surprised Sid Grauman: "I never wavered," Myrna explained, "in my conviction that I was the man in the family."[23]

CHAPTER 4

Enter Myrna Loy

You wouldn't know it to look at her, but at eighteen Myrna Williams was a walking battlefield. Opposing impulses tugged at her. The wistful-eyed dreamer contended with the practical, levelheaded miss who learned to drive during her teens and could change a flat tire with dispatch. The withdrawn poetry lover did battle with the striking beauty with fierce ambition to succeed, a need to express herself artistically, and an urge to show off onstage. Her friend Betty Berger, two years younger and still in high school when Myrna began her first professional dancing job, found it remarkable that Myrna felt comfortable wearing a skimpy, revealing costume onstage if her role demanded it. Still not sexually active herself, Myrna had a sophisticated air and seemed free of prudish concerns about what was proper or modest. Her exposure to the world of professional dancing, her reading, and her independent travel around Los Angeles had all contributed to her apparent worldliness. She matter-of-factly informed Betty, who came from an overprotective Orthodox Jewish household and had been approached by a woman on a streetcar who tried to pick her up, that not all women desired men; some desired other women. Betty had never heard of lesbians before. Myrna also advised Betty, who looked up to Myrna as a fount of wisdom on intimate matters, that conventional views about sex and morality should not be held sacrosanct.

Betty had a cherished steady boyfriend who was not Jewish—Bob Black, the man she would marry. Her parents disapproved, urging Betty to find a Jewish beau, but Myrna encouraged Betty to stand her ground

and stay with Bob, if she truly loved him. Why care about obeying out-
dated and constricting rules set by others? What mattered was being true
to one's own heart (*BB*, 36).

Daring with her advice to Betty, Myrna was often tongue-tied among
those she didn't know well. Many of the colleagues she worked with
over the years sensed her reserve, which could work either for or against
her. There would be directors, producers, screenwriters, and probably
fellow actors, who pushed for her to release those emotional brakes, to
let herself go. More often her tendency to underplay, her way of subtly
evoking feelings without clobbering the point, won favor. But there was
another Myrna altogether—the tangle-haired free spirit. Anyone who
has seen her cut loose on the screen as a gyrating, bare-midriffed native
girl or as the gypsy vixen who drives men mad knows her shadow side,
the wild-eyed, barefooted siren who can seduce a man with a slink, an
exposed shoulder, and a come-hither glance. It was this confounding
mixture—Myrna's mysterious face, her lithe figure, and sensual movements, joined to a deep strain of palpable repression—that riveted peoples'
attention and got her started as a dancer on one of Hollywood's most visible stages.

Grauman's Egyptian Theatre might have been built as a set for a D. W.
Griffith or Cecil B. DeMille extravaganza. Sid Grauman, an instinctive
showman who owned a chain of movie palaces, built it in 1922 as a kind
of dream structure. (His opulent Grauman's Chinese Theatre, a few blocks
to the west on Hollywood Boulevard, would open in 1927 and allow
stars to immortalize their footprints in cement.) Grauman hired the ar-
chitects Mendel Meyer and Gabriel Holler to design a templelike Egyptian Revival sanctuary on Hollywood Boulevard, an $800,000 palace
of movie worship that would ride the crest of Egypto-mania triggered
by Howard Carter's 1922 excavations at the tomb of Tutankhamen. The
theater's mammoth scale, its 1,760 seats, its sunburst ceiling, its long courtyard adorned with a striking sculpture of a man with a dog's head and
an ornamental carved elephant, the huge scarab above the proscenium,
the wall adorned with hieroglyphics, the massive columns at the main
entrance, and the monumental carved heads on pillars flanking the heavy
wooden door were all designed to inspire awe.[1]

When Myrna joined the troupe dancing on the Egyptian's stage in
1923, there were Middle Eastern shops along the forecourt, and each time
a show was about to begin, an actor dressed as an Egyptian sentry trod
the ramparts, calling out the title of the feature in stentorian "Hear Ye,
Hear Ye" tones that could be heard from afar. Attending a movie at the

Egyptian Theatre was no casual outing; it was something to plan and to remember with a souvenir program, a genuine, capital-*E* Event, especially for those lucky enough to get a seat at the October 18, 1922, premiere of Douglas Fairbanks's *Robin Hood*. This was the first-ever Hollywood opening night gala and the film that opened the Egyptian Theatre. Tickets could be reserved two weeks in advance at a cost of five dollars each. "We approached amid the glare of a hundred spotlights," an on-the-scene columnist told her readers, "worked our way across the street between a thrilling jam of Rolls Royces, Nationals, Pierce Arrows." That was Ruth Roland she spotted, in person, resplendent in sable, and behind her Blanche Sweet in silver lace and sealskin. Megastars Charlie Chaplin, Gloria Swanson, and Pola Negri, all diminutive in stature, loomed large as they took turns smiling and waving to the crowd of gawkers gathered on Hollywood Boulevard. *Robin Hood*'s star and producer Douglas Fairbanks failed to make an appearance; he and his wife, Mary Pickford, were away.[2]

The lavish, elaborately costumed twice-a-day dance prologues, some gathering as many as a hundred performers onstage at one time, lasted almost as long as the featured film. Accompanied by a live orchestra, each prologue focused on a theme related to the picture being shown, and some included in-the-flesh appearances by costumed members of the movie's cast. The public came to see the live shows as much as the movies that followed.

To get herself hired, about eight months after the *Robin Hood* premiere, Myrna had to audition for a well-known brother-sister team known as Fanchon and Marco, in charge of prologue production at the Egyptian. Their real names were Fanny and Mike Wolff, and they were the musical offspring of a Los Angeles clothier. As children they used to entertain at lodge parties and picnics. When they got older, as skilled ballroom dance partners they began appearing in dinner shows at nightspots such as Tait's, in San Francisco. Before long they switched hats. Assuming the functions of promoters and producers, they hired and trained other performers, finding a ready market for their brief live musical revues that were designed for movie theater stages. Their Los Angeles studio on Sunset Boulevard became "a factory for producing fifteen-minute shows." Fanchon and Marco supplied costumes and set designs, as well as the choreography and the talent—dancers, announcers, and musicians—for the productions they rehearsed. Fanchon eventually led several companies of female dancers called the Fanchonettes and directed dances for movies. Janet Gaynor, Joan Crawford, and Bing Crosby are just three of the many celebrated artists who, like Myrna Loy, once trained and trod the boards for Fanchon and Marco. Myrna remembered the couple as "marvelous dancers and hard taskmasters" (BB, 33).[3]

Myrna was paid thirty-five dollars a week to dance twice a day at Grauman's Egyptian. In the prologue to DeMille's *The Ten Commandments,* as one of the Dancing Favorites of the Pharaoh, she and the other dancers in the Egyptian Ballet wore halters and headdresses, made angular hand movements copied from Egyptian wall paintings, and took deep kneeling bows, their arms extended on the floor in front of them. "Fanchon had us doing so many salaams," Myrna told David Chierichetti, "that I've had trouble with one of my knees ever since." A few months later, the elaborate prologue to *The Thief of Bagdad,* another Fairbanks fantasy, found her among sixteen Dance Maidens executing a barefooted East Indian Nautch dance à la Ruth St. Denis. In the prologue to *The Gold Rush,* clad in wintery white and silver, she represented the Spirit of Ice. Myrna's movements tended to be languid, and Fanchon sometimes had to prod her to "Snap it up!"[4]

Between the matinee and the evening shows she and some new friends from the troupe would get together for dinner at one of the nearby restaurants, perhaps at the Musso & Frank Grill. Feeling adult and independent, Myrna moved with three of the other young dancers into a rented house in Hollywood but—not quite ready to make the break—soon returned to Della, David, Laura Belle, and Aunt Lu on Delmas Terrace. Della liked her daughter to be near, and Myrna found it convenient to return home. While renting, she'd been burdened by household chores, which her roommates were happy to leave to her, the mature, responsible one in the group.

The entire company of Grauman's Egyptian Theatre prologue dancers went over to Paramount to appear as bacchantes in an orgy scene in a film directed by Raoul Walsh called *The Wanderer* (1926). "I was acting my head off," Myrna remembered, "drinking and hanging over the couch" holding a wine goblet (BB, 37). But since she was an anonymous member of a large group, she didn't consider this her true debut in pictures, which would soon take place.

A photograph of her dancing with two others from the Egyptian Theatre troupe led to her first screen test. After a performance, a Hollywood portrait photographer named Henry Waxman went backstage at the Egyptian and approached Myrna, telling her that he wanted to take pictures of her. As Myrna told it, "I chanced, that night, to be the central figure in the dance numbers. [When Waxman] offered to photograph me

I was flattered and accepted the very kind offer, which was to be without cost to me. No one had ever wanted to photograph me before." Fanchon and Marco allowed Myrna to go to Waxman's studio on Sunset Boulevard, an old, abandoned streetcar that he had fixed up as a workspace. Wearing a flowing dress, bare feet, and untamed tresses that photographed black, she went before the camera in several group poses from a Prologue, staying on for some solo shots. After the long photo session Waxman told Myrna that he thought she had something special. He found her remarkably photogenic; maybe she'd be movie material. Waxman then mounted several of the developed and enlarged pictures of the dancing girls, displaying them both in the courtyard of the Egyptian Theatre and on his studio walls.[5]

During a visit for his own portrait sitting, Rudolph Valentino took notice. Focusing on Myrna's dramatic and kinetic image, he asked, "Who's the girl?" Waxman told him that her name was Myrna Williams and that she danced in prologues at the Egyptian. Valentino prided himself on his ability to spot talent. Like Waxman he sensed that the striking young woman might have a future on the screen. After watching Myrna dance and visiting her backstage at the Egyptian, he immediately wanted her to be seen by his designer wife, Natacha Rambova, because he knew that Natacha, too, would be taken with the young dancer.

It may be that Valentino and Natacha Rambova (née Winifred Shaughnessy of Salt Lake City) became socially acquainted with Myrna, who liked Waxman and was spending some off hours at his studio, helping him with developing negatives and printing. Valentino and Rambova, who these days were not getting along very well, were on friendly terms with Waxman, too. According to Myrna, Rambova was far more exotic looking than her sweet, boyish, celebrity husband. Tall, with a fine complexion and a habit of walking like the ballerina she had once been, with her spine straight, head held high, and toes pointing out, Rambova was the most beautiful woman Myrna had ever seen. She usually covered her dark coiled braids with a turban and often wore dangling earrings, clunky necklaces, and calf-length velvet or brocade skirts (BB, 37). Her eyes were heavily outlined in kohl, and she favored dark red lipstick.

Sometime in the spring of 1925, the year of his separation from Rambova, Valentino offered Myrna a screen test for a role in his upcoming film Cobra, for Ritz-Carlton Pictures. He was looking for an actress to play the role of a demure secretary named Mary, the love interest in that movie for both Valentino's character, the Italian Count Rodrigo Torriani, and the count's American boss and best friend, Jack, who by the end of the movie has married Mary. In the screen test Myrna was to enter a drawing room, lift a book from a table, first registering interest, then surprise, then amusement. Myrna's lack of acting experience told on her during the test, which was conducted in a portable dressing room at Paramount. She tested poorly, appearing "stiff, absurd, ugly," and it didn't help that the cameraman had shot the scene at the wrong speed, making her movements appear jerky. She looked gaunt onscreen even though Valentino himself had spent time expertly applying makeup to her face before the test was shot, and Natacha Rambova, who hadn't yet stopped serving as her husband's professional partner and adviser, lent her the clothes she wore for the test. "Rudy himself made me up," Myrna recalled to Gladys Hall in 1935, "and to this day I think there has never been an hour so terrifying, so thrilling, as that hour when Rudy's hands worked on me, when Natacha brought me her own clothes to wear. [They were] so friendly, so kind."[6]

The excitement and hope inspired by the planned screen test turned into a major trauma for Myrna once it was over. Knowing she had flubbed the biggest opportunity of her young lifetime, she came home and cried for hours, taking to her bed and staying there for two weeks. Valentino, she remembered years later, "was looking for a leading lady, and I was just a skinny kid." When she got the news that another, more practiced, actress, Gertrude Olmstead, had been chosen to play the secretary in *Cobra*, Myrna was hardly surprised, since she had seen the test onscreen and found herself awful in it. But anticipating the bad news didn't protect her from it. The fact that the Valentinos had been so welcoming to her made the sting of their professional rejection all the more hurtful. Her withdrawal put her job at the Egyptian Theatre—which she'd held for two years—in jeopardy and alarmed Della.[7]

When Myrna emerged from this period of sustained and uncharacteristic despondency, she found her resolve strengthened. Instead of giving up on herself, she now had a renewed determination to succeed. She thought she might try to earn enough money to go to New York and attempt to get work on the stage there. Though her plans could change from one day to the next, she had revised her wish to be a dancer, adding a new ambition: she might become an actress, too. Her recent exposure to a stage performance by the great Italian actress Eleanora Duse had reminded her that acting could be high art, worthy of her aspirations.

Back in the world after her retreat, Myrna quit her dancing job at the Egyptian Theatre, which she believed had taken her as far as it could. Gaining stage experience in New York might have served her career well, but she simply didn't have the money for the cross-country trip. Instead, she decided to pursue opportunities in her own backyard. She began haunting the casting office at Metro-Goldwyn-Mayer, the powerful, recently formed studio that was an amalgam of Metro Pictures Corporation, Goldwyn Pictures, and Louis B. Mayer Pictures. MGM's huge lot, behind high white walls on Culver City's Washington Boulevard, was within walking distance from her home, part of a very familiar local landscape. In her first years in California she and her friends had climbed the fence at what was then Goldwyn Studios and posed for snapshots near the sets. The Ritter School of Expression, where Myrna had taught children's dance classes during high school, was right across the street. Myrna knew a few people who worked for MGM. She had a musician friend, Hazel Schertzinger, whose brother, the composer Victor Schertzinger, had directed several Metro-Goldwyn (pre-MGM) films. He promised to help Myrna get bit parts at the studio from which so many cinematic blessings seemed to flow. It wasn't her connections, however, but her looks and persistence that got Myrna through the door.[8]

The spring and early summer of 1925 brought several movie career breaks, all in a cluster. Myrna went before the motion picture cameras in three different productions, two of them at MGM. The first of these was *Ben-Hur*, the elaborate biblical spectacle, based on a novel by Lew Wallace, that cost close to $4 million to produce—the most expensive Hollywood film up to that time. *Ben-Hur* shooting dragged on and on, bleeding money. Production in Rome had begun in 1923 as a Goldwyn picture, under Charles Brabin's direction. With the merger of Goldwyn, Metro, and Louis B. Mayer Pictures, it had become an MGM project, and the original director, screenwriter (June Mathis), and leading man (George Walsh) all had been replaced. Ramon Novarro now starred, under the direction of the veteran Fred Niblo, and early in 1925 the entire company had been summoned back to the States from Rome, to complete shooting in Culver City.

Myrna briefly thought she might land the part of the Virgin Mary, but that didn't happen. In these earliest days of her film career she became all too familiar with setbacks and disappointments. *Ben-Hur*'s casting director, Bob McIntyre, "the god in the grille," had spotted her, looking forlorn and possibly undernourished, outside the MGM casting office, and her hopes soared when he opened the grille and told her to put on a costume Kathleen Key was supposed to wear in one scene. It turned out to be the costume they were initially interested in shooting for a color test, not Myrna, and the costume in question was decidedly unglamorous, the garb of a leper. "They did not want *me*," said Myrna. "They wanted a body. Any body weighing less than 120 pounds on which to drape the leper costume Kathleen Key was to wear" as Ben-Hur's sister, Tirzah. "That was my grand entrance into motion pictures!"[9]

After the makeup artist Lillian Rosine removed the garish makeup Myrna had applied to her own face and replaced it with a professional makeup job, Christy Cabanne, who was working as a second-unit director, took another look at her and did a double take. What a remarkable and photogenic face and form! He told her she had a crack at playing the Madonna, nothing less than the mother of Jesus. Again Myrna's hopes soared as she put on a blonde wig and white robes. She tested well this time, but the powers at MGM—either the chief of production Irving Thalberg or the director, Niblo—decided instead to go with a "name" actress for the part of the Virgin. Lillian Gish was mentioned as a possibility, but in the end the role went to the actress who had played Peter Pan to great acclaim, Betty Bronson, who looked suitably virginal, as Myrna believed she herself did not. Bronson was a safe choice for the studio, but Myrna was crestfallen.

She did get a bit part in *Ben-Hur* but one that was quite a comedown from the role she'd hoped to get. Wearing a black Medusa wig, she played a hedonist in a box at the chariot race, one of the mistresses of a wicked senator portrayed by Hank Mann. The shot was subsequently cut from the film and survives only in a still. Despite the disappointments, Myrna did find it exciting to be standing around the *Ben-Hur* sets during shooting of big scenes. Of the star Ramon Novarro, later her friend and costar in *The Barbarian,* she said, "He was poetry, walking."[10]

As a consolation prize Metro offered Myrna a dancing role in *Pretty Ladies,* a backstage drama described as a jazz picture (although silent) that had been modeled on the lives of dancers and comics in *The Ziegfeld Follies.* Actors played thinly disguised versions of Will Rogers, the dancer Frisco, and the singing comic Eddie Cantor. Norma Shearer, not yet married to "boy wonder" Irving Thalberg, had a small part in it, wearing a dazzling costume designed by Erté. Leading lady ZaSu Pitts was cast as a plain-looking, brokenhearted comedienne. Monta Bell, soon to direct Greta Garbo in her first American film, sat at the helm. Set in New York City, *Pretty Ladies* was shot on the cheap in Culver City. The New York City shots looked fake. A rooftop view of New York's lit-up theater district was simulated by what was "obviously a curtain" and didn't fool anyone familiar with the real thing. There were plenty of elaborately staged dance numbers for the chorus line. Scenes displaying "living chandeliers and undressed ladies, usual revue adjuncts, are to be seen," reported *Variety*.[11]

Two of the scantily clad chorines who made up the living chandelier were Myrna Williams (uncredited) and a new girl in town, listed in the credits as Lucille Le Sueur, who would soon be publicly rechristened "Joan Crawford" in a *Movie Weekly* "name the starlet" contest. In one *Pretty Ladies* scene, Myrna remembered, she and Lucille/Joan "were supposed to look serene while sitting on blocks of ice" wearing "little balls of marabou." Far more aggressive, sexually available, and publicity-hungry than Myrna, the magnetic Lucille/Joan poured her heart out to her new friend. "I remember how she would lie on the floor, her head in my lap, in her dressing room, and worry and cry," Myrna told Gladys Hall. Joan, who had a beautiful figure, a determined jaw, and a dramatic slash of a mouth, "always worried terribly." The MGM producer Harry Rapf had been chasing Joan, apparently with some success, and she worried about the consequences if she brushed him off. "I [worried] too," admitted Myrna, "but I never showed it." The two screen novices formed a friendship that stuck, although they didn't see much of each other socially after Crawford's career took off in a rapid ascent to stardom. She had an overwhelming will to succeed, "more willpower," Myrna said, "than anyone I ever knew." Following *Pretty Ladies,* Myrna and Joan, the "hey-hey" girl, posed as pinups together, wearing shorts and vamping, for *Art and Beauty* magazine. Although Joan Crawford remained the subject of tattletale gossip for most of her long career, Myrna's loyalty to and affection for her never wavered.[12]

Heavily made-up, intense, and a terrific dancer, Crawford, aided by her handlers at MGM, worked at being spotted and photographed around town at hot spots like the Vernon Country Club, the Ship Café in Venice, or Hollywood Boulevard's Club Montmartre. She won trophies at Cocoanut Grove Charleston contests and posed at a sales conference as Miss MGM. Pictures of her with a variety of male escorts, most of them handpicked by publicists, turned up regularly in fan magazines and the press. Crawford also frequented popular restaurants with girlfriends, one of whom might have been Myrna if Myrna had been willing. "Joan Crawford used to ask me to go to the Ambassador for tea with her or to the Biltmore for dinner," but aloof Myrna had no taste for such outings. "Things like that bored me," she explained in an interview. "I never had much small talk. Now and again I went out dancing with Don Alvarado [an actor, also known as Don Page] and one or two other boys.

I went, really, because my mother worried about me." Della did voice concern that Myrna's all-work-and-little-play pattern wasn't healthy, though when the time came for Myrna to pull away and declare her sexual independence, Della would object, tugging hard on the maternal cord.[13]

Joan Crawford had long since broken free of the supervision of her own mother, a hardworking, much-married, less conventionally respectable and less educated woman than Della. With two broken marriages behind her and two kids to support, she once ran a laundry in Kansas City and trained her daughter to be an expert at ironing shirts. Myrna and Joan both *had* to work. Each had a mother and brother who depended on their incomes. Crawford showed none of the indulgent affection for her brother, Hal, that Myrna felt for David; she actively resented Hal, calling him "a parasite and a drunk." Both Joan and Myrna became the family breadwinner by age twenty. Joan, whose father abandoned them early in the game, learned to dance by dancing, not by taking ballet lessons or studying with Ruth St. Denis. Joan's stepfather ran an Oklahoma vaudeville house, and Joan, then called Billie Cassin, caught the show-business bug there. She never attended a ritzy high school like Westlake School for Girls. She did enroll in one school where she was supposed to be a helper in the dorm but was actually corralled into cooking and cleaning for thirty, and she was brutally beaten by the headmaster's wife when she failed to measure up. She briefly attended Stephens College, leaving school for a chorus line job in a Chicago show. That led her to a Broadway chorus line, where MGM's Harry Rapf spotted her and gave her a screen test. Myrna's opposite number when it came to feverish hoofing in nightclubs, bed-hopping, and seeking the spotlight, Crawford readily accepted the crown as one of Hollywood's reigning hard-living, fun-loving flappers and would soon sign a contract with MGM.[14]

Content to maintain a low social profile, Myrna pursued her professional goals with single-minded determination. Wounded by the way *Ben-Hur* had turned out for her, and frustrated by the whimsical habits of casting directors, she picked up the phone and called Natacha Rambova. Considered a cold fish by many in Hollywood, Natacha genuinely liked Myrna, and Myrna could sense their rapport. Although very different in personality and background (Natacha's mother had married money and sent her daughter to be educated in Europe), Myrna and Natacha were both dancers; both were arty, ambitious, and cultured; and both were considered exotic looking and standoffish. Rambova's private life had ruptured since the time of Myrna's *Cobra* screen test. Her term as the wife of Rudolph Valentino was about to come to a painful end, with bitter consequence for Rambova's career as a designer of movie sets and costumes. *The Hooded Falcon,* an ambitious film about Moorish Spain that she and Valentino had hoped to make together, never got off the ground because of budget problems. Now, under financial pressure, Valentino had signed a new contract with United Artists and had verbally agreed to exclude Natacha Rambova from working with him or even putting in an appearance on the set. Rambova had played a prominent behind-the-scenes role in several past Valentino films, and she was habitually baited in the press for "wearing the pants" and being a haughty dominatrix. The marital split left her professionally high and dry. Feeling betrayed by Hollywood, and angry, she would soon leave for Paris and file for divorce. But before she left California, Rambova had decided to produce, with financial help from Valentino to the tune of about $50,000, a film of her own, which would show what she could do and at the same time serve as her Hollywood swan song.[15]

When Myrna telephoned her, Natacha told her at once that the *Cobra* test was not the total disaster Myrna believed it to be. "She told me it wasn't bad—that it must have been the projection machine that made it seem so jumpy." Rambova then offered Myrna a role in the picture she was producing, to be titled *What Price Beauty?* The title echoes the name of a tremendously popular Broadway play from 1924, *What Price Glory?* Written by Maxwell Anderson and Laurence Stallings for a Broadway production produced by Arthur Hopkins, the World War I drama had been a success in New York before being adapted for the screen and turned into a major 1926 Fox film.[16]

After a single screening, *What Price Beauty?* was pulled and would not be officially released and distributed by Pathé until 1928. Though the reasons for the delay can only be guessed at, Valentino's sudden death in 1926 surely had something to do with it, since his estate was being contested. He had financed the film via his manager and estate executor, George Ullman, and the production ran way over budget. Just who owned the rights may have been unclear. Rambova's unpopularity in the Hollywood movie world must also have played a part. She had trouble finding a distributor while she was still in Hollywood. After their very public divorce, and Valentino's sensational demise, no major studio wanted to get near the work of his former wife, a reputed harridan. Following Valentino's death, the press mocked Rambova's film, in most cases before even seeing it.

But publicity for *What Price Beauty?* brought it some positive attention in the summer and fall of 1925, before the Valentino divorce and near the time of the actual shooting of the picture. The *Los Angeles Times,* in an article that included pictures from the production, called the movie "a rather adroit answer to the critics who have made the assertion that Miss Rambova has been influencing too much the career of her husband. It is . . . her declaration of independence." And what a resounding declaration it was. "Some of the sequences," reported the *Times,* "incline to be quite ultra and fantastic."[17]

With Parisian taste, a penchant for the avant-garde, and the experience of designing the outré sets and costumes for Nazimova's *Salome* behind her, Rambova decided to indulge her adventurous proclivities to the hilt in this picture, her sole independent cinematic venture, which unfortunately has not survived. The designer Adrian Gilbert, later known simply as Adrian, had come to Hollywood with the Valentinos to create costumes for their failed project *The Hooded Falcon,* but he stayed on to work on *What Price Beauty?* He would soon be launched as a rising star among Hollywood designers. Natacha gave him carte blanche on her picture, which she wrote as well as produced. A satire of the beauty industry, *What Price Beauty?* starred Nita Naldi, the voluptuous, flashing-eyed, dark-haired veteran of many temptress roles, as a vamp who vies with a country girl for the love of the manager of a beauty parlor. In a dream sequence the heroine dreams she's in a surreal beauty parlor where she must choose among several different types of women, represented by different models wearing various wild Adrian getups. Myrna played the "intellectual vamp." Natacha supplied a wig, giving her a short blonde "do" with bangs that formed points on her forehead, pixie style. Adrian created turtlenecked, formfitting red velvet pajamas for her tall, slender form, adding a sarong at the waist, long sleeves, and a fur-trimmed train. Natacha also oversaw Myrna's makeup. "She slanted my eyes and—unquestionably—that bizarre role was the beginning of my artistic career."[18]

Although Myrna's part in the dream sequence was small, media attention now came her way. Images of her wearing her *What Price Beauty?* costume, captured in still photos taken by Henry Waxman, became the basis of a picture spread in the September 1925 issue of the fan magazine *Motion Picture.* "There's a great buzzing and roaring in our ears," ran the copy that accompanied the photos. "It's thousands of readers asking 'Who . . . is she? Who Is She?' " Describing Myrna as "piquant, elfin, boyish, lithe, the essence of grace," the anonymous fan magazine writer seemed all in a dither over this new screen discovery. "You don't know whether she's innocent or sophisticated; whether she's a low-brow or a high-brow," he or she sputtered. "But you know that she is very, very young and very, very fascinating." The article quotes Natacha Rambova heralding Myrna as "the 1926 flapper model." It advises all "breezy, tomboyish flappers" from 1925 to "practice changing your type, or on New Year's Day you'll find yourselves frightfully out of date." For the first time, but not the last, Myrna was touted as the prototype of modern young womanhood.[19]

The *Motion Picture* magazine article referred to this fascinating, streamlined young actress by a new name, not Myrna Williams but Myrna Loy. Myrna let herself be persuaded that Williams was simply too prosaic a surname for her, and besides, there were already plenty of Hollywood actresses around with the name "Williams"—Kathlyn Williams, for instance, also of Welsh descent and also from Montana. A poet friend, Peter Rarick, probably aware of the modernist poet Mina Loy, came up with the name "Loy." When discussing the name change, Myrna never mentioned Mina Loy. She told Gladys Hall that Peter Rarick, an avantgarde sound poet who was part of a group of artists she befriended, had visited Henry Waxman's studio once when she was there. "He told me that I should change the name of Williams. It was a very good name, he said, for a little girl from Montana, but it didn't fit the pictures Henry had made of me. It wasn't exotic enough." Myrna said she believed that "he got the name Loy from a book of Chinese poems." She immediately signed the Waxman photos with her new, exotic name, and used it from that point on. When Myrna was told decades after choosing the name "Loy" that the word means "to float" in Thai, she was delighted with the information.[20]

Myrna sometimes missed her real name and the family history it conjured. People she knew of Welsh descent, like Richard Burton, would insist on addressing her as "Miss Williams," and she rather liked that (*BB*, 42). Myrna Loy knew that the real Myrna was a freckle-faced, auburn-haired girl from Crow Creek Valley and that Williams fitted very snugly "the girl who walked to and from work because she didn't have any other means of locomotion, the girl who helped with the dishes and pressed her own clothes." But Natacha Rambova had fashioned her as Myrna Loy and pointed her in a new direction, facing east.[21]

By July of 1925, that all-important year, a month before her twentieth birthday, Myrna Loy had signed a contract with Warner Bros.

CHAPTER 5

Warner Bros.' Exotic Vixen

There are at least two versions of the story explaining how Myrna Loy came to be signed by Warner Bros. Myrna's autobiography credits her first contract as the coup of Minna Wallis, older sister of the studio's publicist and future producer Hal B. Wallis. Minna, a single woman who got around in social Hollywood, served at the time as private secretary to Jack Warner but would soon become a talent agent representing Myrna Loy, as well as Clark Gable and George Brent. She had an office on Sunset near Bronson, close to Henry Waxman's photography studio, and Waxman eagerly showed her the pictures he'd taken of Miss Loy, suggesting to Minna that she set up a screen test for his discovery. Minna agreed to try to get the photogenic dancer a Warners contract, but she believed that a screen test would not show her to best advantage. Instead, she simply snuck Myrna into a scene in a Lowell Sherman movie called *Satan in Sables,* whose director, James Flood, happened to live on Delmas Terrace right across the street from Myrna and her family. During shooting, Minna seated Myrna beside, then on the lap of, the rakish Lowell Sherman in a banquet scene, making sure that in a close-up of Sherman, Myrna's face would show up distinctly in the frame. In *Satan in Sables,* a lost film, Myrna Loy turned up in more than just the banquet scene. "I was the trollop," said Myrna, "who lured [Sherman] to parties, broke champagne glasses and was the hell-cat in general." The ruse worked. Jack Warner, after seeing the rushes, asked, "Who's that next to Sherman?" His next words were, "Sign her" (*BB,* 43).

Another explanation comes via an unpublished interview with Alma Young, who worked as a script supervisor at Warners for decades, beginning in 1923. Young described Myrna Loy at the time she arrived at Warners as "tall and thin," with eyes that "had a regular slant." She believed that Myrna and Irene Rich were brought to the Warner Bros. studio at the urging of the debonair, mustachioed investment banker Motley Flint, a major financial backer of Warners as it expanded and a close friend of Jack Warner. Alma Young hinted that Motley Flint promoted Myrna Loy because he had a romantic interest in her. That's easy to believe, but since he was forty years older than Myrna and not divorced (although separated from his wife), his interest was almost certainly not reciprocated by Myrna. At this point she was still very much the good girl in her private life, "the only good girl in Hollywood," John Ford would call her, because she didn't sleep around (*BB*, 58). Motley Flint, a bon vivant with deep pockets, often hosted lavish parties attended by Warner Bros. players and executives. Although not a big partygoer, Myrna surely attended some of them. She makes no mention of him in her autobiography, not even noting Flint's role in the notorious Julian Petroleum scandal of the late 1920s, involving the bilking of small investors, or the rather spectacular fact that an aggrieved purchaser of overissued Julian Petroleum stock who held Flint responsible for his financial ruin murdered Flint in court in 1930. Although Flint may have encouraged Jack Warner to hire Myrna, it was Minna Wallis who made the contract happen.[1]

"Myrna Loy has been signed by Warner Bros. because of her distinctly unusual and Oriental type," the *Los Angeles Times* reported, a few months after she had actually signed her seven-year contract in July of 1925. Warners' publicity department touted its new find as the Oriental type before she had played a single exotic role. Even though *What Price Beauty?* had not yet been officially released, and only a few people had seen it, Jack Warner, the youngest of the four Warner brothers and the one in charge of day-to-day production at their Sunset Boulevard studio, was apparently among those who had. Without access to the movie, a wider public *had* seen the spread on Myrna Loy in *Motion Picture* magazine with the Henry Waxman photographs of her, clad in body-hugging pajamas designed by Adrian, and it associated the slinky young starlet with Rambova, the dark-haired, kohl-eyed beauty who had cast Loy in *What Price Beauty?* Popular opinion held that Rambova's "entire life was motivated by the distant ringing of temple bells and flavored by the fragrance of incense." In Myrna Loy, fans were led to believe, "Rambova's Svengali" had created "a Trilby who retains the best features of Theda Bara," the celebrated screen vamp of the 1910s who had supposedly been born in the shadow of the Sphinx, "and Sadie Thompson," Maugham's tawdry fallen woman in the play *Rain*, based on his short story.[2]

During the silent era, typecasting based on an actor's physical traits was common, and there were just so many types available to young screen lovelies. Shapely, intense, dark-haired actresses like Nita Naldi tended to be cast as vamps. Colleen Moore and Clara Bow, soon to be joined by Joan Crawford, had dibs on flapper roles: peppy, flirty, modern, and all-American. Rambova had cast Myrna Loy as the "intellectual flapper," but that label didn't stick in the way the association with Rambova did. The name *Loy*, which sounded Chinese, provided another clue to her exotic status. Myrna's sophisticated air ruled out ingénue roles, in any case. She didn't have the girlish, blonde, virginal quality of a Mary Pickford, who wore "a kind of halo," or of Warners' newest star, the blonde, angelic-looking Dolores Costello, who was still in her teens.[3]

Myrna, a reed-thin, redheaded dancer who photographed as a brunette and whose makeup concealed the freckles that might have qualified her to play country bumpkins, possessed widely spaced almond-shaped eyes. Her brows could easily be shaped to look Asian, the effect enhanced by whitening her ample eyelids. "Myrna Loy never looks like anyone else," ran the caption under a photo of her published in the *Los Angeles Times*. It claimed, "She is able to achieve an oriental atmosphere with the slow lift of her eyelids." She seemed destined to be seen not as an American girl next door but as a foreign outsider and a temptress, often one who lives in a city and traffics in sin.[4]

In *Across the Pacific*, her first Asian role, she donned a sarong, put a flower in her long dark tresses, and did her best during shooting in Malibu to convey seductiveness tinged with menace. This hardly original combination was a cliché of the Yellow Peril thinking rampant in 1920s America. Released in October 1926, *Across the Pacific* cast her as a spy, a Philippine "native love girl" who tangles with the American soldier Monte Blue during the Spanish-American War, trying to lure him away from the white woman (Jane Winton) he really loves. Critics took note. Edwin Schallert of the *Los Angeles Times* wrote, "Myrna Loy is a revelation. If there is a more sinister type than she on the screen I do not know who she might be. The charm of her personality is that for all its seeming menace it remains alluring." Carl Sandburg, at the time a film critic for the *Chicago Daily News,* seemed smitten. "This here Myrna Loy is the star player," he averred. "She is the subject of a thousand poems and stories of the orient" (quoted in *BB*, 45).[5]

In *Crimson City* (1928), a "lost" film recently rediscovered in Argentina, she was a Chinese love slave in a Shanghai waterfront dive, "where crime is curtained behind glamorous silks." She ends up stabbing her Chinese keeper, saving the white man she loves, but sacrificing herself by jumping off a boat. Said Myrna, who almost drowned after leaping from that boat, "Nobody thought of me as the virgin, I guess. I had these slinky eyes and a sense of humor." The sense of humor would go unnoticed by producers and directors for a while; for now her eyes, "look," and body type set the tone.[6]

When *Photoplay* included Myrna Loy in a picture story on the current crop of fetching new starlets, it photographed her in a brief sarong, a lacy see-through top, with a long, trailing silk scarf cascading from her hip. Despite her piano legs and thick ankles, which would later prompt sniping in the trade papers, the article called hers "the most beautiful figure at Warner Studio" and claimed she was "modeled like a statuette." To judge by this and other publicity shots of Myrna at age twenty, the formerly highbrow *artiste* had morphed into a pinup girl adept at cheesecake poses. She showed up in a black bathing suit in newspaper photos, spunky, pert, outdoorsy, and svelte, tossing a beach ball to another pretty girl. The trailing mass of curls had vanished; in its place came a stylish flapper mop, curly as ever but now bobbed to look altogether modern. The straight, lanky, well-proportioned figure that became exotic when draped in a sarong or mandarin-collared sheath could easily sport a knee-kissing fringed dress just right for kicking up your heels to the Charleston.[7]

Myrna was thrilled to find herself a contract player at Warner Bros., but she soon learned that her job amounted to slave labor. Working under banks of Cooper-Hewitts, hissing sun-arcs, and blazing Klieg lights was hot, exhausting, and dangerous to the eyes. She had to rise at 5:30 six days a week in order to be camera ready by 9:00, and she sometimes had to work through the night. Because she portrayed so many characters with brown or yellow skin, her makeup regime took an especially long time. She got to know the makeup crew well, and her dyed and greased body made her feel anything but erotic under the lights. Often she worked on two or three films at one time.

Not yet a major studio, Warner Bros. specialized in low-budget, quickie productions turned out at breakneck speed. It spent roughly half as much money as MGM did on an average production and made a big success of its extremely low-budget Rin Tin Tin films, starring a German Shepherd dog. In these days, before there was a Screen Actors Guild, film actors could be and were summoned to work at any hour of the day or night and for any length of time. Vacations, breaks for meals, sick leaves, or days off were not mentioned in contracts. The studio owned the exclusive rights to the player's acting services, as well as to her or his photo sessions and personal appearances. Myrna could work for another studio only when Warners chose to rent her out, not otherwise. Illness or physical disability alone might excuse her from the set, and the studio reserved the right to investigate the alleged cause of any absence. She had to agree to repay the producer for any financial losses incurred by her absence. At the studio's discretion she could be (and was) laid off without pay for periodic two-week intervals. The pay, most of the time, was good. She began at only seventy-five dollars a week but got a raise every six months, with each renewal of her contract. By 1927 she was earning $500 a week and had purchased a house and a car. By 1929 her salary was $700 a week.[8]

Myrna continued to hand over her money to controlling Della, who allotted her small amounts for spending money. Myrna's reluctance to take charge of her own finances would remain a lifelong trait. In some ways this let-someone-else-do-it attitude liberated her, but in others it served her poorly. If she'd had more of a Mary Pickford–like hard head for business and money management, she would have exercised far more control over her career. Perhaps her avoidance of handling her own money had something to do with her father's wild spending and a fear that she might go the same route if she had the chance.

Soon after signing with Warners she took an apartment in Beverly Hills so that she wouldn't have to commute far in the wee hours. Della, Aunt Lu, and young David remained on Delmas Terrace but without cousin Laura Belle, who had died at the age of twenty-six. (She is buried in Radersburg.) Myrna soon returned to Delmas Terrace, but after her brother graduated from high school in 1929, she bought a Beverly Hills home at 221 North Crescent Drive. Della sold the Delmas Terrace house, and the family moved in with Myrna. Her attempts at independent living never lasted for long.

Despite the grueling pace at Warner Bros., Myrna Loy initially felt upbeat and excited to find herself working at full tilt as a movie actress. "I was having a ball" (BB, 48). The exotic roles were initially fun to play, and she took them seriously, attempting to get beyond stereotypes by reading up on the customs of China, Java, and the other countries whose women she portrayed. Everything felt new to her, and she relished the chance to learn while doing. Eager and uncomplaining, with a sturdy constitution she once likened to that of a peasant, she was a quick study who believed that she'd lucked into her main chance. Since Myrna had no stage experience as an actress, and had not studied acting except in high school, Warner Bros. would provide her apprenticeship. There were plenty of talented people around from whom she might pick up pointers, although no single person took charge of tutoring or mentoring her.

The cigar-chomping dynamo Darryl Zanuck, who walked around carrying a sawed-off polo mallet, created many of her roles. A lowly screenwriter who was only twenty-three at the time Myrna was hired, he penned so many Warners scripts that he invented a slew of pseudonyms to hide behind: Melville Crossman, Mark Canfield, Gregory Rogers. A shrewd, hard-driving Nebraskan who'd been on his own from the age of thirteen, Zanuck had an instinct for both action-packed, tabloid-style storytelling and the marketplace. He would soon take control at Warners as head of production and become a major force in Hollywood, going on to found 20th Century Pictures, which in 1935 would merge with the Fox Film Corporation to form 20th Century–Fox.

Zanuck wrote the script or story for nine of Loy's early vehicles, including *Across the Pacific,* which a few critics singled out for praise because of Myrna Loy's exotic charm. Zanuck must have been impressed, so much so that he continued to confine her to similar sarong roles, relieved only by the occasional excursion into the equally marginal world of American big-city crime. He had a definite impact on Loy's career, but because at Warners he couldn't picture her as anything but an exotic temptress or a gun moll, she came to see that impact as a negative one. She believed he limited her. Myrna once caught him, a married man, at the studio with a starlet on his lap, and she always wondered whether the rift she felt existed between them had anything to do with that. But Zanuck's numerous infidelities were no big secret. Even his wife, Virginia Fox, a former actress in Buster Keaton comedies, seems to have been aware that her husband played around, although she was spared the particulars. Zanuck, despite his many talents, apparently had all the emotional maturity of a frisky fifteen-year-old. He and his office mate, the director Roy del Ruth, drilled holes in the office wall so that they could spy on the screenwriter Bess Meredyth next door.[9]

Zanuck, who would later produce gritty Depression-era underworld dramas such as *The Public Enemy, Little Caesar,* and *Baby Face* as vehicles for the likes of Jimmy Cagney, Edward G. Robinson, and Barbara Stanwyck, tried to squeeze Myrna Loy into the tough-girl mold, with little success. He wrote the story for 1928's *Midnight Taxi,* "about cheating cheaters, rum runners and plain crooks," where Loy, looking smashing in furs, played Gertie, the wife of a bootlegger, and for the same year's *State Street Sadie,* where she was a Chicago policeman's daughter who pretends to be pistol-packing gangland cutie Sadie in order to avenge her father's murder. "I'm on the other side of the law again," Loy joked to the *Los Angeles Times.* "I have had an almost steady job carrying a .38 and dodging machine gun bullets." *Variety* found her miscast as Sadie. "Myrna Loy, with her exotic style, doesn't suggest the daughter of a policeman." The movie acknowledged her essentially ladylike quality by providing her an out: she's really a well-bred girl, only pretending to be bad. The same trick had been used in Loy's first venture into gangland, 1927's *The Girl from Chicago,* where she was a southern belle masquerading as a crook's girlfriend to save her wrongly imprisoned brother. Archie Mayo, director of *State Street Sadie,* called her "the dual personality girl," an actress who could vamp it up in one sequence and play "the demure home girl" in the next. The tough-girl roles never carried much conviction. Gum chewing didn't come naturally. As Delight Evans put it in a fan magazine, Myrna Loy is "caviar, not corned beef and cabbage."[10]

Zanuck also wrote the story for *Ham and Eggs at the Front,* a racist "Negro comedy" requiring Loy and all the other white actors playing blacks to wear blackface makeup. Spoofing *What Price Glory?,* it was set in France during the Great War and concerned an all-black American regiment. Myrna's role as Fifi, a Senegalese waitress spying for the Germans, caused her profound embarrassment and regret when she looked back at it.

Several directors who were or would become celebrated—Ernst Lubitsch, Lewis Milestone, Howard Hawks (at Fox), and Michael Curtiz—helmed movies in which she appeared, but in every case she played a small role and was rarely singled out for special directorial attention. Lubitsch cast her as a plain-looking maid in *So This Is Paris.* He instructed her on the proper way to lightly knock on a boudoir door, but that was it. In *The Caveman* Lewis Milestone also cast her as a maid, this time an enticing French soubrette in a black uniform and a frilly white apron and cap, whose lines (given in the intertitles) include such gems as "ze lunch ees sairved." Warner Bros. movies tended to be class conscious, and *The Caveman,* adapted by Zanuck from a Gelett Burgess story, fits that description: a bored Park Avenue debutante, deftly played by Marie Prevost, transforms a crude coal heaver into a gentleman by scrubbing him down, barbering his hair, teaching him elementary manners, and dressing him in tails and a top hat. Myrna Loy had little to do in the film beyond answering the phone, responding to the doorbell, and serving drinks while looking adorably saucy. She wasn't a vamp in this picture, but *Variety*'s reviewer nonetheless named hers "one of the best vamp bits yet revealed. She is tall, has a provocative face."[11]

Although she continued to be singled out in the press, at Warners she still sometimes played parts so insignificant she didn't even merit a listing in the credits. Harry O. Hoyt wrote and directed her first outing with star billing, the 1927 melodrama *Bitter Apples,* which was set on the high seas but was in fact shot by photographer Hal Mohr on a boat plying the waters between Los Angeles and San Francisco. Here she played another in a long list of evil beauties, this one part Sicilian and bent on revenge. Determined to torture the man she holds responsible for ruining her banker father and prompting his suicide, she marries him, but guess what? After a shipwreck, she and her victim husband (Monte Blue) fall in love. Warners advertised *Bitter Apples* as "A Stupendous Dramatic Spectacle of Realism—Elemental Passion—Daring Heroism—Torrential Force—and Vengeance on the High Seas."[12]

Most of her coplayers in her early movies—Warners regulars such as Clyde Cook, John Miljan, the comedienne Louise Fazenda, and Patsy Ruth Miller—ranked as team players rather than shining stars. An exception was Conrad Nagel, a popular leading man featured in four of Loy's Warner Bros. films and one of the founders of the newly formed Academy of Motion Picture Arts and Sciences. Myrna admired his acting skills, honed on the stage, and appreciated his patience with her as she learned her craft on the job. But when it came to status, no actor in any of her films held a candle to John Barrymore.

Along with the recently imported German director Ernst Lubitsch, John Barrymore stood out at Warner Bros. as a prestige talent hired by a company scrambling to upgrade its image and badly in need of class acts. The most admired stage actor in the English-speaking world, and among the theater's most commanding presences, Barrymore came to Warners on the heels of his stage triumph in New York and London as Hamlet. Dashing, swashbuckling, and worthy of his moniker "The Great Profile," he had starred in 1924 in Warners' *Beau Brummel,* filmed in New York, and during shooting had become the lover, at age forty-two, of Mary Astor, an eighteen-year-old ingénue with a dictatorial, exploitative father. Although Astor's parents controlled her every move and pocketed her every dollar, they allowed her, during filming of *Beau Brummel,* to visit Barrymore's Manhattan hotel for daily coaching sessions on acting, interspersed with lovemaking. When Barrymore moved to California after signing a lucrative three-picture contract with Warners—he would receive at least $76,250 for each picture and had the right to approve each script and each costar—Mary Astor expected to resume their romance in Hollywood, where her career was flourishing. But shortly before shooting of *The Sea Beast,* he fell in love with another eighteen-year-old, his chosen leading lady, Dolores Costello, who according to Myrna was so lovely she looked more like an orchid than a person. On the set of *Don Juan,* a costly costume drama, Mary Astor sensed immediately, despite Barrymore's insistence to her that Dolores Costello was "just a chicken," that she'd been unceremoniously dumped.[13]

Barrymore's habit of scanning the cast list for the most delectable female morsel and springing for her was standard operating procedure for a major male star, a ranking producer, or a director who happened to be vehemently heterosexual. In her autobiography the actress Gloria Stuart describes being goosed by a buzzer—to much hilarity on the set—on her first-ever day of shooting. The man with the buzzer turned out to be her director, Archie Mayo, also Myrna's director in *State Street Sadie, Crimson City,* and *Beware of Married Men,* all from 1928.[14]

Myrna had a chance to observe the Barrymore-Astor backstage melodrama at close range because she had a role in *Don Juan,* in which the brokenhearted Mary Astor played pure and lovely Adriana Della Varnese opposite Barrymore's flamboyant Don Juan. During the shooting of that film Myrna, costumed as Lady-in-Waiting to Estelle Taylor's Lucretia Borgia, stumbled into Dolores Costello's dressing room one day and was astonished and chagrined to find not Dolores, who didn't appear in this movie, but a weeping Mary Astor, surrounded by Dolores Costello's collection of photographs of John Barrymore (*BB,* 50).

Barrymore was a busy man during the shooting of *Don Juan.* While courting Dolores Costello (whom he would marry in 1928) and doing his best to avoid Mary Astor, except when he had to kiss her passionately on camera, he also made a play for Myrna. In his cups he would call her late at night from some watering hole in Culver City, saying, "This is the ham what am" and inviting her to join him. At the Warners studio he teased and tormented her. She had tested for the large role of Lucretia Borgia in *Don Juan,* and while she wore the costume for the test, Barrymore had kidded her for being too skinny and flat-chested. Insisting that she needed more padding, he asked the seamstress for pins and began sticking pins into the padding that was in place, telling the seamstress, "You've got to fill her out." On another occasion he swore at Myrna in the middle of a scene because she chose to listen to the director, Alan

Crosland, instead of obeying Barrymore's improvised instructions for changes in the blocking. Myrna responded by walking off the set, a daring move for a novice, and Barrymore subsequently apologized (*BB*, 40). Barrymore might have taught Myrna a lot about acting, but what he mainly taught her was to watch her back.

Don Juan, an overblown extravaganza with a diffuse script by Bess Meredyth, provided Barrymore the opportunity to match his onscreen lovemaking talents to those of Valentino and to pit his athletic prowess against Douglas Fairbanks's. Publicity put out by Warners claimed that he bestowed 191 kisses in the course of the movie. (Myrna Loy may be the only lovely woman in the picture he did *not* kiss.) He portrayed his own father, seduced countless gorgeously gowned ladies, leaped from balconies, swung from vines, escaped from a prison tower into the Tiber, fended off the advances of scheming Lucretia Borgia, dueled with the villainous Donati (Montagu Love), rescued an innocent maiden from torture, and galloped off with her on a white steed. Mary Astor, who portrayed the maiden, called it a "turgid, rambling melodrama." She said that the director, Alan Crosland, a drinking buddy of Barrymore's who took on the assignment after Lubitsch turned it down, lacked the spine to hold the large company of players together. "He'd walk around, brushing a waxed mustache with a finger," trying to tame the crowds of noisy extras. "The sets were dark, gloomy, smoking with torches; the costumes . . . elaborate and heavy."[15]

Myrna Loy, as Lucretia Borgia's "chief poisoner" (*BB*, 49), made an appropriately sinister display of Hollywood-style Roman decadence, lurking under balconies to spy, casting sideways glances, and "slinking around with vials of this and that." With a hood over her hair and a curl on both her lip and her forehead, she rides a horse onscreen for the first time. Her performance garnered praise from the playwright Robert E. Sherwood, at the time the movie critic for *Life* magazine.[16]

Despite its excesses, *Don Juan* has secured a place in film history as the first movie feature with a recorded soundtrack. It had no audible dialogue, but it did have sound effects and a synchronized Vitaphone sound-on-disc musical score, recorded at the Manhattan Opera House by the New York Philharmonic Orchestra using technology Warners developed in partnership with Western Electric. *Don Juan*'s New York premiere on August 6, 1926, followed a program of short Vitaphone films, including one in which the film czar Will Hays, head of the Motion Picture Producers and Distributors Association, cleared his throat and then spoke in lifelike audible tones. "No story was ever written for the screen as dramatic as the story of the screen itself," he intoned. The six subsequent Vitaphone shorts delivered concert performances, mostly of weighty classical music interpreted by esteemed musicians and designed to impress. The program put Warner Bros. on the map as the cinema studio at the forefront of sound technology. "Vitaphone Stirs as Talking Movie," ran a *New York Times* headline the day after the much ballyhooed *Don Juan* opening at the Warners Theater on Broadway, at the time the only theater in the world equipped to screen movies with synchronized sound. "New Device Synchronizing Sound with Action Impresses with Its Realistic Effects" ran the review's subtitle. "Vitaphone Bow Is Hailed as Marvel," *Variety* concurred. The first five *Don Juan* screenings brought in almost $14,000, and the value of Warner Bros. stock soared. A film that had cost $546,000 to produce would earn more than three times that and become Warner Bros.' most profitable film to that time.[17]

Not to be outdone by New York, Grauman's Egyptian Theatre was fitted with wires, speakers, and turntables for playing wax discs, in preparation for the Hollywood *Don Juan* premiere two weeks later. The crowd outside the theater stretched for two blocks in each direction on Hollywood Boulevard as John Barrymore trod a path strewn with rose petals to enter the theater and searchlights on the roof of the Egyptian beamed an electric rainbow. All the stars and supporting players in the picture came out, among them Myrna Loy. Warners' radio station KFWB broadcast the voices of the formally attired actors as they entered the courtyard.[18]

Radio preceded sound pictures at Warner Bros. Responding to the current craze for broadcasting, the studio had installed radio station KFWB on its premises early in 1925, mounting two radio towers in front of the lot. The idea was that radio would help to publicize films and film artists to an audience of millions. Sam Warner, the brother most interested in technology, ran the station, and he was the one who persuaded his brother Harry, the money man in New York, to see and hear a demonstration of a test film made by Bell Telephone Labs, a subsidiary of AT&T. In it a man talked, and a jazz orchestra played. Sam Warner's idea originally was to use the new technology to create canned music for films, relieving theater exhibitors of the expense of hiring live house musicians to play before and during screenings. When Sam reminded Harry that spoken dialogue as well as music could now be electronically wedded to the movies, Harry's oft-quoted response was, "Who the hell wants to hear actors talk?"[19]

Myrna Loy had a bit part as a curly-headed chorus girl in Warner Bros.'

next pioneering experiment in sound, *The Jazz Singer,* the musical starring Al Jolson that told the story of a Jewish boy who defies his cantor father to become a Broadway singer. *The Jazz Singer* catapulted the underdog studio to a top position, surpassing giants Paramount and MGM, even though this first talkie feature only talks some of the time. *The Jazz Singer* is partly a silent film, with most dialogue indicated by the traditional intertitles. Loy's single line, "He hasn't a chance with Mary," comes via a title card, and she speaks it in a nightclub scene to her ruffle-collared twin in the frame, Audrey Ferris. But this full-length film included sound sequences, folding in the throbbing voice of Al Jolson singing "Toot, Toot, Tootsie," "Mammy," and four other songs and adding a few hundred words of spoken dialogue, some of it ad-libbed by the star. Jolson actually had uttered the famous lines "Wait a minute, wait a minute, folks. You ain't heard nothin' yet" in his vaudeville act and on film in an earlier Vitaphone short, "Al Jolson in a Plantation Act," but this time the spontaneous-sounding words became indelible. They were a cinematic shot heard round the world, heralding a new era.[20]

Myrna, who along with other secondary players had permission to stand by on the sidelines of the new soundstage and watch Jolson sing as his voice was being recorded, found him mesmerizing. But "nobody realized that we had entered a whole new age" (*BB,* 52). In fact, Hollywood was filled with naysayers like Louella Parsons, who predicted that sound movies would soon be forgotten. "I have no fear," she wrote, "that scraping, screeching, rasping sound film will ever disturb our peaceful motion picture theaters. The public has no intention of paying good money to be so annoyed." MGM's production chief, Irving Thalberg, also believed that sound was just a fad that would soon pass.[21]

Sound, however, made Warner Bros. It allowed the studio to rake in $8 to $9 million in profits in 1928 and to buy up First National and take over its Burbank spread. But it also sent Hollywood into a tailspin. "Articulate films will knock this joint agog," predicted *Variety*'s Jack Conway, and he was right. Just as the artistry of silent movies peaked, almost everything about moviemaking had to be reinvented. Films temporarily lost their fluidity. Cameras became immobile; because they whirred they had to be encased in soundproof booths called "iceboxes." Actors fell victim to "mike fright." They had to play to a hidden microphone, perhaps planted in a flowerpot, not to one another, and at first all dialogue sequences had to be shot indoors. Another problem was that scenes with sound could not be edited. The Vitaphone sound-on-disc system required each scene to be recorded without any break from beginning to end. As Hal Mohr, the cinematographer who shot *The Jazz Singer* and many other Warner Bros. films, remembered: "It was impossible to cut the scenes," and each scene had to be shot "in one operation" lasting (no longer than) eleven minutes. When shooting a short scene, the cameraman would try to stretch it to "make it last long enough to get enough film onto the projector to permit the projectionist to have enough time to thread the other projector machine."[22]

Sealed soundstages were erected at great cost. Warners had five of them by fall of 1928, each carrying a price tag of more than $200,000, and the new king on the set became the soundman. New lighting technology was required, in part because of the space taken up by the enclosed cameras. If several of these cumbersome boxed cameras were operating at once, there would be little space left for lights. Moreover, the old arc lights buzzed, and the microphones picked up their sound. Quiet incandescent globe lights had to be introduced, and they entailed film that was panchromatic (sensitive to all colors) instead of orthochromatic (sensitive to green and blue light). The newly installed globe lights produced heat so intense it wilted the actors as they performed their scenes and forced them to keep changing clothes and refreshing their melting makeup.[23]

Movie theaters had to be completely renovated to show Vitaphone pictures, a process costing between $16,000 and $25,000 per theater, depending on its size. Operators had to be trained to handle both a projector and a turntable, and to coordinate the two. They demanded, and got, pay increases. Three or four men now worked in the projection booth, where one or two had sufficed before. If a stylus skipped or if a stretch of film happened to be damaged or missing, the resulting discontinuity produced hilarity in the audience. Because Vitaphone's cumbersome discs could only be played a limited number of times before they wore out, and because they broke easily, bulky extra discs had to be shipped with each Warners sound film.[24]

Despite the expense of renovations, exhibitors took the plunge. Talkies had tremendous drawing power. By midsummer 1928 three hundred American theaters had been wired for sound; by fall of the next year eighty-seven hundred had been. Movie attendance reached an all-time high in 1929, the year the stock market crashed. By that time Warners no longer monopolized the talkies, and Vitaphone was being displaced by an optical technology developed by Fox that put sound directly onto film. By 1930 silent movies were just about finished. Only Chaplin continued to carry the banner for the art of filmed pantomime.[25]

As Hollywood producers scoured Broadway in search of actors with trained theatrical voices, silent players panicked, fearing they would be dropped—and many were. The foreign accents of Emil Jannings, Vilma Banky, and Pola Negri became liabilities, while the stock of a stage-trained American actor such as Conrad Nagel shot way up; MGM signed him at $5,000 a week. Uncertain about how Garbo's voice and accent would go over, MGM postponed her debut in talkies until 1930. Clara Bow's stammer and Brooklynese added to her list of woes, but Ann Harding, imported from the Broadway stage, was heralded as "the girl with the million dollar voice." Audiences laughed at the stilted lines spoken by John Gilbert in his first talkie. Actors with British accents, such as Ronald Colman, enjoyed new stature. Diction coaches flourished, but jobs for even the most articulate screen actors became scarcer. Since production expenses had doubled for talkies, fewer movies were being made. One consolation to multilingual actors was that they might be hired to appear in a foreign-language version of a popular talkie.[26]

Those actors who successfully maneuvered the leap into talkies had to get used to working in silence. Silent movie sets had been noisy operations, alive with clamor. Directors used megaphones to call out instructions, musicians played background music to create a mood, and carpenters working on sets sawed and hammered away. Now, according to Frank Capra, "all of a sudden you had to work in the stillness of a tomb. If you belched, or if you coughed, you'd wreck a scene."[27]

Myrna recalled her first experience with a microphone, on the set of *State Street Sadie:* "Jack Warner took me and Conrad Nagel back to the back of his stage, and they had this room blocked off with a lot of black curtains hanging all around, and there was this thing hanging in the middle of the room, this microphone—a most terrifying object. He said, 'Say something.' " Although she was petrified, Myrna's silky voice recorded well. It had a pleasing lilt, a built-in smile. Not a big voice, it had personality, class, and great clarity. Myrna could boast of exemplary diction. Ten years down the road, when she was making a film with Spencer Tracy, Tracy's deaf son Johnny, visiting the set, focused on Myrna as she spoke her lines because he could understand her best (*BB,* 154).[28]

During the transition to talkies Myrna appeared in several mongrel films that added sound dialogue sequences, sound effects, and musical scores to movies that, like *The Jazz Singer,* were essentially silent. One of these was the lavish epic *Noah's Ark,* which slapped on awkward, poorly integrated lines of dialogue that sounded like "little more than audible spoken titles." The *New York Times* critic Mordaunt Hall complained that "when these utterances are heard, they frequently border on the ridiculous." Directed by Mihaly Kertesz, a recent arrival from Hungary who had helmed epics in Austria and whose name had been Americanized to Michael Curtiz, *Noah's Ark* cost more than $1 million to produce. Because of the many calamities that occurred during its shooting—star Dolores Costello contracted pneumonia, Curtiz broke a leg while demonstrating how to fall down the steps of a temple, thirty-eight ambulances had to be called, an extra lost his leg, and possibly more than one extra was killed—Dolores Costello called *Noah's Ark* "Mud, Blood and Flood."[29]

Most of the injuries occurred during filming of the tumultuous flood sequence, in which spill tanks dumped thousands of tons of water to destroy a temple with columns a hundred feet high. The photographer Hal Mohr tried to talk Curtiz and producer-writer Zanuck into using process photography, shooting in a way that would wreck the set but spare the people. "My contention was we could get better results without endangering anyone." Zanuck and Curtiz overruled him, both men bent on doing it their way—"for real." They made a bad situation worse by using extras, not stuntmen, to navigate the cascading floodwaters. An outraged Mohr quit in protest, and shooting stopped for several weeks while a substitute cameraman, Barney McGill, was found and brought in. Meanwhile, according to Mohr, "a couple of people were injured to the point that they never did recover." No one ever made the injuries or casualties public, and the Warner Bros. Archive file on *Noah's Ark* contains no report or legal brief on accidents.[30]

Three years in the making, *Noah's Ark* imitated earlier film epics such as Griffith's *Intolerance* and DeMille's *Ten Commandments* by telling parallel stories, one biblical and the other set in modern times. Every credited cast member played dual roles, one a contemporary of Noah, the other from the era of the Great War. Myrna Loy is both a slave and a Broadway dancer. Dolores Costello, the female lead, portrays both a German chorus girl and a handmaid in the household of Noah. Costello's modern and biblical-era characters are both in love with male counterparts played by George O'Brien, the male lead. With two major stars, sensational train wrecks and floods, a Vitaphone score, and a cast that included hundreds of animals, among them rare single-striped zebras and sacred oxen from India, the film made money despite mediocre reviews.

Michael Curtiz, who became the hyperactive contract director responsible for more than 150 films, including *Casablanca,* wanted to star Myrna in a film version of *Madame Bovary,* but Warners blocked the project, fearing that a movie about adultery would never get past the censors (*BB,* 49). Instead, Curtiz used her in an inane Technicolor western musical, *Under a Texas Moon* (1930), starring charmless Frank Fay as a singing Mexican lothario pursuing cattle rustlers in Texas and featuring Myrna, in one of several Hispanic roles she played, as flirty Mexican spitfire Lolita Romero. It didn't help that Curtiz and Frank Fay were not on speaking terms during shooting. The picture's sole distinction was its outdoor color photography, made possible when the sound engineer used a new Western Electric sound truck equipped for recording discs on location.

When she played a character who spoke English with a foreign accent, Myrna had to fend for herself; dialect coaches had yet to be called onto the back lot. For the role of Azuri, the treacherous half-caste native girl in 1929's *The Desert Song,* she improvised, taking a cue from the actress she'd seen in a stage version of the Sigmund Romberg operetta. "It was a kind of French Moroccan patois, some awful thing. I made it up, really. I used to make up all kinds of foreign accents." She speaks such lines as, "Azuri, she don't forget," and "Vere ees Pierre?" For the latter line Myrna received much ribbing from friends "who would come to me, give me a strange look and say, 'Vere ees Pierre?' "[31]

Thanks to Darryl Zanuck, she had to fight to play Azuri in *The Desert Song,* a prominent role in the first-ever sound operetta on film, and Loy's first all-talking picture. The operetta had enjoyed a long run on Broadway, and for the screen version theater veterans John Boles and Carlotta King were cast in the major singing roles. Although Loy had already spoken lines in several talkies, had appeared in more than thirty films, and had been at Warners for close to four years, Zanuck, now head of production, insisted on testing her before allowing her to play Azuri. "I'm not sure you can handle this," he told her, threatening to remove her before the picture was completed if she didn't measure up. "I'll take the chance" (*BB,* 57), she insisted, refusing to be cowed, and when the cameras rolled, she proved herself, excelling in a wild nautch dance where the crowd throws coins at her as she tosses her hips, eyes flashing, her feet and midriff bare.

Loy's seductive Azuri resembles her gypsy hellion Nubi in *The Squall.* Directed by Alexander Korda, who was making his first talkie, the film was set in Korda's native Hungary but shot at night in Burbank. This is the story of an intruder, a tempestuous dark-skinned beauty with tousled black hair, dangling earrings, and an off-the-shoulder blouse, who disrupts the serenity of a farm family that had been living harmoniously before she arrives, pounding on the door seeking shelter during a storm. They allow her to join the household as a servant, and before long she has seduced every single male within reach, from the hired man to the son to the father, robbing, conniving, and deceiving each between tumbles in the hay. Her foil is the sixteen-year-old Loretta Young, who plays Irma, the pure, naive fiancée forsaken by Paul (Carroll Nye), the son of the house. He was a dutiful student devoted to Irma before falling under the spell of the spitfire Nubi and stealing money to buy a pearl necklace to win her favor. "Nubi, she give you kiss for every pearl," but Nubi, "she not love anyone."

Loretta Young would play an innocent good girl to Loy's experienced femme fatale in two more films, *The Devil to Pay* and *The Truth about Youth*, both from 1930. Offscreen she considered Myrna mysterious and gorgeous, and looked up to her, but found her aloof. She got a kind of "stay away" feeling from her. They later got to know each other socially but never became close friends.[32]

Although *The Squall* has laughable lines ("How long have you been tangled up with that strumpet?") and a murky soundtrack, Myrna Loy's work in it carries an electrical charge, a vibrancy that attests to a new self-confidence and an ability to both enjoy and kid the excesses of her role. Nubi, the quintessential home wrecker, typifies the sort of character associated with the name Myrna Loy in her prestardom days. The screen's future "Perfect Wife" started out as the perfect Other Woman whose bewitching allure drove decent men to stray.

The more third world temptresses Loy played, the less likely it became for her to get a chance to try anything else. Azuri and Nubi paved the way to a loan-out to Fox for *The Black Watch*. For this film, based on the Talbot Mundy novel *King of the Khyber Rifles*, the director, John Ford, requested Myrna Loy to play Yasmini, the Joan of Arc of India. He admired her performance as Azuri in *The Desert Song* and thought she would bring exotic beauty to the costarring role. Yasmini leads a Khyber Pass rebellion against British rule at the time of the Great War in Europe. A woman warrior who sees herself as a new Cleopatra, she conducts herself with far more dignity than either the half-caste Azuri or the gypsy Nubi. She sometimes wears a veil and never appears partially clothed—although her nipples are clearly visible in one of her sheer costumes. Usually she is draped in billowing yards of white fabric from head to toe. In our first glimpse of her she is asleep behind a net curtain. A servant pulls the curtain back to reveal Loy's face in close-up. A movie camera has never before lavished so much doting attention on her arresting visage, which both Ford and the cinematographer, Joseph August, clearly appreciated. As Yasmini, who is worshipped as a goddess, she moves and speaks slowly, with stately majesty, addressing even the man she loves as "thou" in an oracular tone. Loy's performance feels stilted. It's as if she's been shot with a tranquilizer dart.

One of the reasons for this lack of animation and integration with the rest of the spirited film is that after John Ford had completed shooting *The Black Watch,* dialogue scenes scripted by James K. McGuinness were added. These extra dialogue sequences, coached and supervised by a British actor and stage director named Lumsden Hare, have a wooden, tacked-on quality. Ford found them "really horrible—long talky things" that had nothing to do with the story. No wonder a critic for the *Los Angeles Times* complained that Ford failed to knit together the film's disparate elements, calling *The Black Watch* "an unwieldy combination of *The Green Goddess, The Big Parade,* and a generous helping of Dante's *Inferno.*" The same critic sang the praises of Myrna Loy's melodious speaking voice and predicted, "The role should establish her as a favorite of the talking screen."[33]

The British-born Victor McLaglen gives the film whatever coherence it has. A former boxer and Irish fusilier who appeared in many John Ford films and would win a 1935 Academy Award for his work in *The Informer,* he plays Captain Donald King, who is torn from his bagpipe-playing Scottish regiment, the Black Watch, as it embarks for Europe after the outbreak of the Great War. He wants to join his fellow Scots in battle, but because he was raised in India and speaks Indian dialects, he's chosen by his commander to be posted to India on a secret mission: he must prevent holy war by deposing Yasmini, the worshipped rebel leader. The moment Yasmini sets eyes on Captain King her fate is sealed. Passion overtakes her, womanly love for a man displacing her supposedly mannish love of power. She receives King in her chamber, declaring from a reclining position, "It is sweeter to be a woman to one man than goddess to thousands." Because the Hays Office had proscribed miscegenation, she must assure King that she is really a white woman, a descendant of Alexander the Great, no less.

McLaglen has a gruff, commanding presence, and when he removes his shirt to fight a Pashtu in the seething Cave of Echoes, we can understand why Yasmini's eyes widen with admiration. But in the love scenes with Yasmini he is hopelessly inhibited. Even when Ford had the couple try embracing in McLaglen's dressing room, the actor balked, complaining, "Myrna, she's just a child" (*BB*, 56).

Ford thought he'd directed high drama, but in movie theaters, McLaglen's Captain King elicited unintended laughter when his pronunciation of the name "Yasmini" sounded like "Yes, Minnie," and the audience howled. Myrna's friends took to calling her Minnie, a nickname that stuck.

Attracted to Myrna, Ford enjoyed teasing her. When *The Black Watch* was completed, he invited her to a party at his home, which turned out to be a stag party. Myrna was the only female present, although Ford's wife, Mary, was somewhere in the house and had opened the door for her. After recovering from her initial shock, Myrna stayed and enjoyed herself. A young, shy John Wayne (still known as Marion Morrison), who'd served as prop man on *The Black Watch* set, stayed in the background (*BB*, 58).

During Myrna Loy's later years at Warner Bros., reviewers and fan magazine reporters protested that she was not getting a fair shake. Under a full-page portrait of her in a cloche hat, *Photoplay* commented, "Hollywood is wasteful of beauty. Myrna Loy, for instance, has something to contribute to Art. But, for the most part, she is relegated to the ungrateful task of vamping in modern operas." A critic for New York's *Outlook and Independent* wrote that Myrna Loy "has never had a chance to do anything but run around in Oriental costumes and talk Pidgin English. . . . Myrna Loy has intelligence and it's high time someone gave her a decent part."[34]

By 1929, though, she was at least drawing some serious attention. *Screenland* magazine in August singled out her work in *The Squall* and *The Black Watch* as the best performances of the month. *Photoplay* profiled her in September as "The Siren from Montana," characterizing her as a quiet home girl offscreen who had never been further east than Montana. "Myrna doesn't make whoopee in the Hollywood meaning of the term. She smiles when she says perhaps she makes whoopee in her own way. She doesn't like to go to parties because bad gin has its after effects. She rides and swims and goes often to the theater. When she isn't working she models statues, but she is working most of the time. . . . She lives with her mother and younger brother, who graduated high school this year."[35]

Myrna recognized that she could appear haughty. When Joan Crawford offered to teach her how to dance the Black Bottom, she told Joan no thanks, partly because Myrna feared she wouldn't dance it well but also because "I had airs and thought of myself rather above a dance called the Black Bottom."[36]

An earlier *Photoplay* article reported that she was "going with" the young actor Barry Norton, a native of Buenos Aires who appeared in *What Price Glory?* and many Spanish versions of Hollywood films, and whose real name was Alfredo Carlos Biraben. The article hints that marriage might be in the offing. In her autobiography Myrna calls Barry Norton a "perpetual male ingénue" who was "one of my more serious flings" (*BB*, 54). She was a bit more revealing in an interview with Gladys Hall, where without naming him she referred to Norton as her "first adult love," someone she was drawn to because, like her, he disdained small talk and partying. She added that as a man he fell short of her heroic ideal. "Not a man yet, still a boy." Was he a failure as a lover? Apparently Norton was in the process of defining his sexuality. According to Ramon Novarro's biographer, André Soares, Norton later came out as gay.[37]

The failure of her relationship with Barry Norton may have contributed to a bout of the blues that Myrna suffered as the 1920s drew to a close. Working at Warners no longer gave her much gratification, for as the studio soared on the wings of sound to its economic zenith, she felt left behind and professionally stymied. Her fame was growing, yes, but her range as an actress was not. She couldn't break out of the exotic vamp straitjacket. She felt touched, but also depressed, when a Chinese man in San Francisco wrote to propose marriage to her, sweetening the offer with a promise to take her back to China, "their" shared native land. Even in a light, though interminable, 1929 musical revue, *Show of Shows*, there she is in the "Chinese Fantasy" number, made up as a Chinese doll, dancing a pseudo-Chinese number before a pagoda, surrounded by chorus girls in coolie hats who twirl parasols while Nick Lucas croons a song named for her character, "Li-Po-Li." The repetitiveness of her roles, combined with their lack of subtlety, began to feel stifling. "What depressed me was the sense of a barrier between the audience and myself, which I tried to penetrate, but couldn't. . . . When you were a heavy, by George, you were a heavy. Not a saving grace; no chance of adding a little white to the black."[38]

The artificiality of these roles rankled, especially when she was assigned to impersonate an Asian character in a cast that included actors who were actually Asian American. Next to Anna May Wong, with whom she appeared in *The Crimson City*, Myrna said, "I looked about as Chinese as Raggedy Ann" (*BB*, 52).

She didn't want to be limited to one type of part, but she did want to keep acting in pictures. When Darryl Zanuck called her into his office one December day to tell her that Oriental roles were going out of style, that they didn't have much call for her type any more, and that Warners would not renew her contract into the new decade, her blue mood turned to black. Zanuck would later tell an interviewer that his failure to discover Myrna Loy was the worst error of his career.[39]

CHAPTER 6

Breakthrough

Myrna began the 1930s at a low ebb. At age twenty-five she still lived in a modest Beverly Hills home with her mother, brother, and aunt, and she remained very much under Della's thumb. Although Myrna supplied the money to buy it, the house they lived in legally belonged to Mother, not Myrna. Clinging to her maternal identity, Della had turned down a marriage proposal because she wanted to "devote herself to her children," but Myrna had begun to wish that some of her mother's devotion would find other outlets. Balking at the tightness of Della's grip, Myrna tried to persuade her mother to allow her younger brother, David, who'd recently finished high school, to study art in Europe, but Della wouldn't hear of it.

Myrna continued to support her family, doing so with a growing sense of insecurity as the Depression took hold. The ranks of the unemployed swelled, and breadlines formed in cities all over the country. Banks were failing, businesses closing. As Broadway theaters went dark in New York, more and more stage actors and vaudevillians flocked to Hollywood seeking work, just as studios reduced the number of contract players they employed. "Los Angeles is a good place to stay away from for those who must work to eat," *Variety* warned its readers. Warner Bros. had given Myrna Loy the boot around the time it signed on Jimmy Cagney, Joan Blondell, and Edward G. Robinson, stars with Broadway credentials who would help define that studio's gritty, crime-driven, street-smart, and slangy style, custom made to fit the Depression. Myrna had no new studio alliance and no contract.[1]

She did have an agent in her corner, however—Minna Wallis, who now ran a talent agency in partnership with Ruth Collier. With Minna's help Myrna continued to freelance as a screen actress, sometimes working for obscure Poverty Row studios such as Sono Art or Chesterfield, and she despaired of ever getting beyond hackneyed, bad-girl roles in B pictures. Her dance background helped her stay afloat. In 1930's *The Truth about Youth* she was Kara, known as "The Firefly," a shady cabaret entertainer who sashays seductively with a practiced air but whose singing had to be dubbed. The same year, in the Technicolor operetta *Bride of the Regiment,* she donned a blonde wig and gyrated with abandon on a banquet table to win back Walter Pidgeon's affection. "The directors could see me as a dancing girl or a heavy, but never as an actress."[2]

She jumped at the chance to play the suicidal wife of a gigolo violinist in *Cock o' the Walk* because her leading man would be an actor she admired, Joseph Schildkraut. Newly divorced, Schildkraut took her out a few times, dazzled her with stories about his Berlin days with Max Reinhardt, and made a pass (*BB,* 60). *Cock o' the Walk* was universally panned, but Loy's performance opposite Schildkraut won her plaudits from *Variety,* which proclaimed, "Myrna Loy makes a dumb and passive role look graceful and seem real."[3]

In *Renegades,* a burning-sands action picture directed by Victor Fleming for Fox, she played Eleanore, a European spy of the blackest dye determined to destroy the Frenchman she once loved, Deucalion, portrayed by Warner Baxter. Exactly why she hates Deucalion goes unexplained; it's a case of motiveless malignancy. Betrayed by Eleanore, who sold his secrets to the Germans during the Great War, Deucalion becomes a deserter of the French Foreign Legion and along with three fellow deserters joins the Riffs in Morocco. He kidnaps Eleanore and forces her to serve as a camp follower. She'll go with any man, even the Arab Marabout (played by Bela Lugosi), who keeps her in his harem. This clear violation of the newly articulated Production Code edict prohibiting miscegenation got by the censors, who were not yet rigorously enforcing the rules. In the end Deucalion resumes his allegiance to the French and turns his weapons against the Arabs. Pretending to cozy up to him in the sand dunes for a climactic clinch in the violent finale, Eleanore shoots him dead with a machine gun as the camera closes in.

Although Loy's Eleanore had white skin and spoke English without a foreign accent, this was a role she'd often played before, another slinky and exotically costumed vixen, an all-too-familiar menace devoted to seduction and treachery. Myrna's own comment on Eleanore suggests that she had been reading about psychoanalysis. "Eleanore is a complex of complexes," she told an interviewer. "I'm afraid she's a case for international psychology. To enumerate her psychoses would break down the combined vocabularies of Brill and Freud."[4]

Shot in three weeks in the blistering heat of the Mojave Desert, *Renegades* tested the mettle of both cast and crew. Crawling in the dunes, drenched in sweat while clutching a machine gun, Myrna got sand in her teeth, and her makeup kept melting away. Warner Baxter remembered that it was so hot "they had to keep the cameras packed in ice-bags like a fever patient, so the celluloid wouldn't catch fire." Myrna liked and respected Baxter, a high-salaried (because he'd won an Oscar for his work in 1928's *In Old Arizona*), competent, and darkly handsome but rather stiff and bland Ohio native with whom she would appear in three more pictures, and she no doubt enjoyed being the much doted upon sole female in the cast. After the film was released, the critics complained justly about the confusing plot and absence of motivation in Jules Furthman's screenplay, but they succumbed to Myrna Loy's allure. One confessed, "Her strange eyes start heat waves dancing in the Moroccan desert for me."[5]

Her work in *Renegades* elicited a slam from Louella Parsons, who snidely commented, "Miss Loy is one of the best-looking girls on the screen, and maybe one of these days her acting will match her looks." But the same performance prompted Fox to sign her to a six-month contract at $750 a week in the fall of 1930, a drop from the $850 a week she commanded for her work in *Renegades*. "This brings to an end a long period [it was actually less than a year] in which [Loy's] fate hung in the balance," a Los Angeles daily reported. "She was gaining prominence at Warners when the movies found their tongues. For a while it appeared as if she might fade away with a number of other silent favorites. Recently, however, she has had several good roles." "Good" here means prominent rather than high quality.[6]

Myrna signed with Fox during a time of turmoil at that studio after its founder, William Fox, had been forced out. He'd borrowed more than $40 million to purchase Loew's, Inc., but a Justice Department antitrust suit prevented the merger. In addition to his financial woes, William Fox was recovering from serious injuries suffered in a 1929 car crash. Although under its founder the Fox Film Corporation had pioneered sound-on-film technology, had broken ground with its Movietone newsreels, had attracted top directors such as John Ford and F. W. Murnau, had built a new all-sound studio in Westwood, and in 1930 controlled more than five hundred theaters, a new mogul, the utilities magnate Harley Clarke, now sat at the helm. Clarke's tenure lasted only a short time. He left Fox in 1931, a year that saw movie ticket purchases drop by 40 percent, contributing to what was called "the worst year financially in the history of pictures." Fox profits plummeted, the studio losing more than $4 million. That year Myrna Loy, too, would part company with Fox.[7]

While at Fox, Myrna became more socially confident and more visible than she'd previously been, turning up at gala movie premieres, at a filmed reception for Fanchon and Marco, and at an Embassy Club dinner where she sat at Jack Warner's table, along with Clark Gable, William Powell and Carole Lombard (who would soon marry), Jimmy Durante, and the screenwriter Gene Markey. Ira and Lee Gershwin invited her to an A-list party at their home, where Oscar Levant bestowed on her a red rose from a vase as she shyly walked by the piano. The European-born stage actress Elissa Landi, who made her Hollywood screen debut in a 1931 World War I film called *Body and Soul,* in which young Humphrey Bogart played an air force pilot and Myrna Loy had a small role as a sexy spy, was her hostess at several cocktail parties where guests from all over the world shared wide-ranging conversation. Myrna found Landi "lean and bright, with wonderful humor" (*BB,* 62). They would work together again, further down the road.[8]

Fox and Myrna Loy were not particularly well matched. The studio was known for its folksy, down-home style, while Myrna was still associated with sin and exoticism. Fox's biggest female star at the moment was the sincere, all-American, no-frills Janet Gaynor, and the top-earning king of the set was the gently satiric, aw' shucks Oklahoman Will Rogers.

Myrna had a chance to get to know Rogers when she played Queen Morgan le Fay to his time-traveling Yankee in *A Connecticut Yankee* (1931), a box-office winner with rentals of $1.3 million and among the *New York Times*' ten best films of the year. In this adaptation of the Mark Twain novel, Fox's second go at the story, most of the laughs come via anachronisms, the jarring juxtaposition of things medieval and things ultramodern. Radios, helicopters, cars, telephones, factory time cards, and a reference to *Amos 'n' Andy* invade storied Camelot, with its turreted castle, massive banquet tables, dark dungeons, and jousting knights. Will Rogers starts out as a small-town radio mechanic, Hank Martin, braving a stormy night drive to deliver a battery to a spooky mansion. These are hard times, and Hank needs the business, "if they pay cash." At the mansion, knocked on the head by a suit of armor, Hank wakes up in the court of King Arthur, where he earns the title "Sir Boss" by making fire with a cigarette lighter and then successfully predicting an eclipse of the sun with the invocation "Prosperity, Farm Relief, Freedom for Ireland, Light Wines and Beer." Impressed by Sir Boss's ability to make the sun vanish and the kingdom go dark, King Arthur (William Farnum) asks him if he's a magician, and Rogers replies, "I'm just a Democrat. You have to be a magician to make a living these days."

As the lavishly gowned Morgan le Fay, sister of King Arthur, Myrna Loy is once again an evil beauty, this time a sexual aggressor with a yen for Will Rogers's laid back, lasso-throwing Sir Boss. In the scene where she comes on to Sir Boss and plants a kiss on him, he protests, "I ain't used to messin' around with any queens," and blushes a deep crimson. The film was shot in black and white, but for this scene hand tinting was used to show Rogers's face going red. According to Myrna, Will Rogers truly was a shy man, ill at ease in love scenes. Off camera, though, he gently flirted with her, whistling and hollering in her direction whenever he caught a glimpse of her as he drove by (BB, 63).

Because she says she saw only more vixen roles in her future if she remained tied to Fox, Myrna reports in her autobiography that she broke her contract to begin freelancing once again. Press accounts reported that it was Fox that failed to pick up her option. What really happened is that Fox dropped its option on her initial contract, which would have raised her salary; it did offer to keep her on for another six months at her starting salary of $750 a week, and Myrna rejected those terms. She felt she could do better, perhaps at a studio with deeper pockets, and her agent, Minna Wallis, must have encouraged her to go independent.[9]

Leaving Fox after one year proved far less traumatic than leaving Warners after five years had been. Myrna now had enough self-assurance to trust she could cut a swath in the movies, with or without the backing of a single studio. The ensuing months would find her frequently back at Fox as a freelancer, in addition to working twice for Goldwyn, once for Paramount, and once, as Becky Sharp in a low-budget, modern-dress Vanity Fair, for the obscure Allied Pictures.

She was hired on a picture-by-picture basis by the smallest major studio, RKO, where Irene Dunne was being heavily promoted as the top female star. In Consolation Marriage (1931), the first of two RKO pictures Myrna made featuring Dunne, Irene Dunne's name appears above the title and Myrna Loy is billed fourth—a situation not calculated to promote warm feelings on Myrna's part toward the star. Myrna continued to view Irene Dunne, a brilliant, justly celebrated comic actress, as a rival who often got parts she wished she could have landed for herself. In later years they had political differences, too, and never seem to have bridged the gap.

The chance to appear in a film quite different from any on her list of previous credits arrived with a role in a Samuel Goldwyn production, *The Devil to Pay.* The man who cast her was Arthur Hornblow Jr., an urbane, impeccably tailored ex–New Yorker who had a Columbia University law degree. Initially hired as a screenwriter, Hornblow had come to Goldwyn's attention as the adapter and Broadway producer of a scandalous French play about lesbians called *The Captive.* He now held a job as Goldwyn's chief of production. Hornblow was married to the stage actress Juliette Crosby, a frequent visitor to the *Devil* set, and they were expecting a baby. They lived a few blocks away from Myrna, on the very same street, North Crescent Drive in Beverly Hills.

Hornblow was friendly with the French-born director of *The Devil to Pay,* George Fitzmaurice, brought in by Goldwyn to replace the original director, Irving Cummings, after two weeks of shooting, and with the star, Ronald Colman, Goldwyn's dashing, British "King of Romance." The Hornblows, Fitzmaurice, and Colman, as Myrna remembered it, were "all very chummy" (*BB,* 62).

The first time they met, Hornblow greeted Myrna by telling her straight off that she'd been absurdly miscast in the past, that she was no China doll. "You don't look anything like those silly parts they've been giving you" (*BB,* 62). For *The Devil to Pay* he awarded her the delectable part of Mary Crayle, a glamorous London actress and mistress of the charming and profligate nobleman's son, played by Ronald Colman.

The Devil to Pay is a talkie that really talks. It introduced Myrna Loy to a screen milieu she would make her own, the comic world of upper-class urban sophisticates who converse in breezy, literate dialogue and seem to live on air. This sort of drawing-room high comedy had its roots in theater. Although the British playwright Frederick Lonsdale created the script for a motion picture, his background was in writing for the London dramatic stage and musical theater. One of his best-known plays is *The Last of Mrs. Cheyney* (1925). Arthur Hornblow Jr. had introduced Lonsdale to Goldwyn and brought him to California to work on *The Devil to Pay.*[10]

Myrna's role isn't large, but she comes across—British accent and all—with great flair and aplomb. For a change her character isn't menacing. She's an alluring woman of the world, affectionate, fun-loving, and light-hearted, who yields gracefully when informed by the man in her life,

Ronald Colman's Willie Hale, that he's become engaged to another (Loretta Young) and must stop meeting her for romantic midnight suppers. Louella Parsons praised her performance as "the best and most natural Miss Loy has ever given." Naturalness in acting mattered now in a way it hadn't during the silent era and the earliest days of the talkies. Myrna Loy was finding her element.[11]

Myrna's dissatisfaction with her previous roles implied an argument with characterization by formula and with simplistic moral distinctions. She disagreed with the binary thinking behind movies that divided people into one of two categories: good or bad. Although she'd already appeared in plenty of sound pictures that depended on exaggerated, one-note character types, she believed that talkies were evolving in a direction that allowed for a truer, more nuanced, view of humankind, a broader outlook. In *The Letter,* she pointed out, "Jeanne Eagels wasn't a good woman, neither was she bad. She was a victim of circumstance." The more varied and shaded possibilities afforded by talkies would offer her salvation as a screen actress. "It was only when I spoke lines that I persuaded directors to give me a chance to play roles of a less stereotyped nature."[12]

Myrna considered her role in *Transatlantic,* a visually spectacular melodrama set on a luxurious ocean liner bound for Europe, another breakthrough. Partly, this was a matter of her new screen identity as a soignée, respectable, and wealthy American wife instead of a scantily clad foreign hussy; partly it was about being showcased in an important film. Displaying "a restraint and poise that she has not touched before," she brought class to the role of Kay Graham, the sympathetic and forgiving wife of a successful banker (John Halliday) who is openly carrying on a shipboard affair with a sexy Swedish dancer (Greta Nissen). Loy, to her relief, at last plays a lady sinned against, not sinning. "Myrna Loy, who has wrecked hundreds of homes in the movies," wrote Louella Parsons, "occupies the other place this time."[13]

Transatlantic had a high profile. It opened at the Roxy in New York and Grauman's Chinese in Hollywood, and it was widely reviewed. With a cast that included Edmund Lowe as a rakish gambler and Jean Hersholt as a European-born lens grinder, it boasted lavish art deco sets by Gordon Wiles that would garner an Academy Award. It also benefited from the controversial cutting-edge photography of James Wong Howe, who made innovative use of deep focus. Howe and Wiles clashed often on the set, arguing about lighting and the size of the sets. "I wanted ceilings to give the claustrophobic feeling of a ship," Howe recalled. "[Wiles] did full ceilings and half ceilings for me, and I used special lights in the engine-room to give an illusion of depth." Not everyone liked Howe's avant-garde shooting techniques, but Myrna did. She said at the time that she found the opening sequence, for which Howe used a long tracking shot and montage to show passengers boarding as the boat smokestack belches steam, "one of the most thrilling things I've ever seen," adding that she recognized that throughout the picture "the people in the story are not as important as the boat." Howe shot most of the picture using a wide-angle lens, which he said "pushes everything back, scatters everything," but not for the scenes involving Myrna Loy or Greta Nissen. "Of course, women couldn't be photographed with a wide-angle lens," Howe remembered. "It distorts, and they don't like that."[14]

Because *Transatlantic* created quite a buzz, Myrna's good notices counted for something, and she believed that her director, William K. Howard, respected her in a way previous directors had not. She also worked well with James Wong Howe, who would photograph her in a total of seven films. Howe considered her a very savvy screen actress whose "cleverness is that she knows just as well as I do what effects to get. Unlike the many sudden upstarts in Hollywood, she has had long experience, and she meets a cameraman half way."[15]

A newspaper reporter, Hal Wiener, interviewed Myrna after the opening of *Transatlantic,* and the resulting article emphasized how American she looked in the flesh, with fair skin and titian colored hair. "Myrna Loy, as I met her on this particular afternoon, typifies the American girl. . . . When I met her she was garbed in a tennis outfit—white sweater and skirt and green tennis shoes." She told Wiener she had said good-bye to all those previous roles as a home wrecker and had turned a corner. No longer would she labor to keep the sin in cinema. "I have lured other women's husbands away from their happy homes. I have been the cause of suicides. . . . But that is all past now. *Transatlantic* was the turning point of my career. I have reformed. The scarlet woman of the screen is a thing of the past for me."[16]

She spoke too soon. In three of her next four films she was back to stealing husbands, and in the one exception, *Skyline,* she did her best as a sophisticated society blonde to seduce the boyfriend of sweet, pure Maureen O'Sullivan.

In *Rebound* she makes off with Ina Claire's husband during his Paris honeymoon, no less. In this comedy of manners, based on a Broadway play by Donald Ogden Stewart, the champagne-quaffing upper-crust players trade quips as they flit between New York mansions and Paris hotels. They choose their marriage partners as casually as if they were arranging a whirl around the dance floor. Loy's Evie Lawrence has married a rich man she doesn't love, leaving her steady beau, Bill (Robert Ames), in the lurch. On the rebound Bill marries Sara, Ina Claire's arch and witty character, and off they trot to Paris. There Bill takes up with Evie again. The selfish Evie and the obtuse Bill flaunt their liaison, and Sara only estranges Bill further when she shows him her pain, weeping openly and begging for his love. When she asserts herself and decides to divorce him, though, Bill claims he wants her back and forgets Evie. In his autobiography Donald Ogden Stewart, author of both the screenplay and the play *Rebound,* reveals that as playwright he'd allowed Sara to express his own hard-won conviction that a balance of power must be maintained within a couple; one lover should never surrender power by kneeling as a supplicant before the other.[17]

Edward H. Griffith, one of Myrna's favorite directors, had to sneak her into the picture just a few days before shooting began. Florence Eldridge had been signed to play Evie and had to be bought out of her contract. Ina Claire didn't want Myrna at all, and Claire ranked as a star who commanded $30,000 to play Sara, in contrast to Myrna's $750 a week. After watching Myrna's screen test, Claire dismissed Myrna as "Sunbonnet Sue" and proclaimed, "That woman could never take a man away from me." Thirteen years older than Myrna, recently divorced from John Gilbert, and far better known to theatergoers than to movie fans, Ina Claire found Myrna's fresh beauty a threat, and she shared with many other stage actors an unabashed condescension toward mere screen players.[18]

Rebound is a dialogue-driven movie, not terribly cinematic and very much a filmed theater piece. RKO's gamble that Depression-era audiences would flock to an escapist romp with the smart set didn't pay off in this case, and the company lost $215,000 on the film. Myrna, however, believed that the role of Evie helped prepare her for her future in comedy. "I had a part that was not exactly comic, but [Evie] was the naughty girl in it, . . . and she had a very funny drunk scene." It didn't hurt that she came off as a credible rival to the accomplished Ina Claire, and that her name in the print credits appeared just slightly smaller than the star's.[19]

Although earthbound and heavy-handed, her next RKO film, *Consolation Marriage,* shares with *Rebound* a preoccupation with the pull former lovers can exert on a married pair. When their true loves marry richer mates, castoffs Irene Dunne and Pat O'Brien console each other and decide to wed but agree not to expect fidelity. Myrna, of course, was cast as the vain, unfeeling former girlfriend. Arriving at the home of married ex-beau Pat O'Brien, she steals into the garden for a kiss while O'Brien's wife, Irene Dunne, sheds stoic tears in the baby's room upstairs. This film at first seems to daringly condone marital permissiveness by placing Dunne and O'Brien in an open marriage, but it backs away in the end, attempting to prove that such unconventional arrangements can't compete with the traditional comforts and rewards of fidelity, hearth, and cradle. Loy's character, Elaine, ends up rejected and, at least for the moment, alone.

Again in *Arrowsmith,* a Goldwyn film based on the Pulitzer Prize–winning novel by Sinclair Lewis, Loy is the alluring other woman who entices a happily married man away from his wife. She plays Joyce Lanyon, a worldly New York divorcée visiting the West Indies, where her wealthy father owns a plantation. During an outbreak of the bubonic plague, Dr. Martin Arrowsmith (Ronald Colman), temporarily parted from a self-sacrificing wife, meets Joyce, coolly elegant even in the tropics, when she offers her white arm to be inoculated after many black arms have been similarly offered. Soon Martin is bunking at the plantation, and Joyce is offering the idealistic doctor more than her arm. What we see of their adulterous relationship onscreen is far less explicit than what was written into the script by the adapter, Sidney Howard, but cut. Joyce's words addressed to Martin Arrowsmith, "I have fallen terribly, insanely in love with you. . . . I'm not a child. I've been married," were removed, as was Dr. Arrowsmith's response, "You make my life seem suddenly rather empty. But terribly exciting." Publicity stills show Martin Arrowsmith and Joyce embracing, but no such scene made it to the final cut. All we see are two adjacent bedrooms, Joyce's and Martin's. In one Joyce spreads out her negligee on a bed. In another Martin sits on his bed and ponders. We're shown the light under the door of Joyce's room, and left to fill in the blanks. John Ford may have feared that showing more would subject his film to cutting by the censors, even in this supposedly permissive pre-Code era. It is also possible that cuts were made at the last minute, without the director's consent.[20]

Produced by Samuel Goldwyn, with Arthur Hornblow Jr. as the uncredited executive producer, *Arrowsmith* was nominated for four 1931 Academy Awards, including one for Best Picture, and elicited stellar reviews. Mordaunt Hall of the *New York Times* tipped his hat to Goldwyn for leading the public rather than following it and for producing an "intelligent and forceful film." Some critics thought that the very British Ronald Colman, although a fine actor, had been miscast as an American midwesterner. They were right. Everyone applauded Helen Hayes's moving performance as the nurse who becomes Dr. Arrowsmith's doomed, adoring wife. Sinclair Lewis himself endorsed the film as true to the spirit of his novel. He attended the Los Angeles premiere and admitted that he had wept throughout the screening.[21]

Myrna sensed Arthur Hornblow's growing interest in her during the filming of *Arrowsmith*. She returned his admiring glances, but they held back, not acting on their mutual attraction until after Arthur separated from Juliette Crosby.

John Ford, too, made known his own special yen for Myrna. Before retakes he abruptly left the set after a dispute with Goldwyn. Ford sent a telegram to Myrna, putting her in the position of being the only one who knew his whereabouts at a time when everyone involved in the production was desperate to locate him.

Helen Hayes also thought that Ford was attracted to *her*. "He got stuck on me a little," she reported, and he kept phoning Hayes after the day's shooting. Edgy and conflicted, he was looking for a liaison outside his marriage and, according to his biographer, Joseph McBride, was acting out his personal conflicts on the *Arrowsmith* set.[22]

MGM, the richest and most prestigious Hollywood studio, and the one that was best weathering the Depression, signed Myrna Loy to a five-year contract in the fall of 1931. It was Minna Wallis who accomplished this feat. She was friendly with Norma Shearer, Thalberg's wife, and had attended their wedding. Minna was well aware that Shearer had become one of MGM's A-list romantic leading ladies, going head to head with Joan Crawford and with Garbo, who occupied a tier of her own. Minna knew that the studio renowned for employing "More Stars Than There Are in Heaven" was a place where an actress could soar. She showed Irving Thalberg, the youthful and talented vice president in charge of MGM production, a clip from *Skyline*—a Fox film about builders of New York skyscrapers in which Myrna looks ravishing but has little to do in the way of acting—and Thalberg was sold. According to one Los Angeles daily, however, it was her performance in *Transatlantic* that had really impressed him.[23]

Myrna's arrival at MGM felt like a homecoming of sorts. She had grown up in the shadow of the Culver City studio and had taken baby steps into the movies with an extra's part in *Ben-Hur* and a bit as a dancer in *Pretty Ladies*. She felt certain that the strides she had made as an actress over seven years and sixty films were finally being acknowledged. But the elation she initially felt quickly dulled. "All the heartbreak I'd endured before was nothing compared to what I felt when I learned why they had signed me. I made a silent test for a picture and they liked it. Then they gave me the dialogue and asked me to make a vocal test. I said, 'To whom am I supposed to be speaking?' And then it came out. I was supposed to be speaking to a dwarf, and the picture was to be called *Freaks*. I said, 'No, gentlemen, I'm sorry.' "[24]

Myrna had made it clear in interview after interview that she'd had her fill of playing venomous outsiders. She simply wanted the studio officials to regard her as a human being, she insisted. "I'm tired of being a freak." Arthur, who advised her on career matters and whose opinion counted for much, was telling her that she must no longer allow herself to be typed as a one-note menace. She should try to play women more like her real self. "The screen was turning to naturalness and humor."[25]

Directed by Tod Browning and featuring a cast of sideshow circus performers with various disabilities and deformities, *Freaks,* although opposed by the studio head, L. B. Mayer, went ahead as a Thalberg production intended to be MGM's answer to Universal's *Frankenstein,* a tremendous hit. It would have cast Myrna Loy as Cleopatra, a sinister trapeze artist who couples with a dwarf. Publicity posed the question, "Can a full grown woman love a midget?" When Myrna balked, the role of Cleopatra went to Olga Baclanova, "The Russian Tigress."

Myrna accepted a role in the Marie Dressler vehicle *Emma* without protest, but playing a spoiled, grasping, and snobbish rich girl in her first MGM picture didn't exactly make her jump for joy. Dressler, whose performance would win her a 1932 Academy Award nomination, portrays the title character, a greathearted nanny in a motherless household who eventually marries her widower boss (Jean Hersholt) and after he dies is accused by three of his four grown children—the very children she has lovingly raised—of being both a fortune hunter and a murderer. In her sixties now and a wildly popular, beloved star whose pictures made more money than Garbo's, the homely, overweight Dressler inspired Myrna's admiration and devotion. Myrna prized her warmth and generosity, as well as her acting skill. She listened when Marie, after hearing Myrna's complaints about her unsympathetic role, cautioned her to be patient. Just wait, Dressler advised. "You've got the whole world ahead of you" (*BB,* 71).

CHAPTER 7

Cutting the Veil

Out of the blue one day Irving Thalberg summoned Myrna to his office. She'd been at MGM for about a year, and she knew that Thalberg, the most powerful and respected producer in Hollywood, didn't give away his time lightly. She barely knew him, having met him only in group situations, but realized this private meeting had to be about something important. Her anxiety, mounting while Thalberg kept her waiting, escalated into anger when he finally showed up and from behind his massive desk, which was raised on a platform as a way of compensating for his slight stature, addressed her without looking at her. He instead focused his gaze out a window, his back turned. She chided him for his rudeness; where she came from, a gentleman did not turn his back when speaking to a lady. Registering surprise at her outspokenness, Thalberg swerved his chair so that he now looked her squarely in the eye. A sensitive-looking man who weighed only 122 pounds, he had an intelligent, fine-featured face that Myrna considered handsome, even beautiful. He had dark, comprehending eyes and spoke both softly and calmly, "as if his words were a sort of poetry." Everyone in Hollywood knew that Thalberg suffered from a heart condition and was physically fragile. He concealed a row of prescription pills in bottles behind his office dictograph. Thalberg also had a reputation for astuteness, bringing together a rare combination of nice-Jewish-boy-from-Brooklyn bookishness and Hollywood whiz-kid ambition and practical savvy about making movies. Anybody with that much power had to have a ruthless side. Robert Montgomery considered him money-crazed and a tough, cold operator. "Thalberg was a sweet guy," the studio manager Eddie Mannix once said of him, "but he could piss ice water."[1]

Myrna was unprepared for the intimate tone Thalberg now took. "Myrna," he told her, "you're terribly shy," and your shyness is hurting you, "putting a veil between you and the audience." He urged her to cut through the veil and make a grab for something more. The public was already beginning to adore her. She was beautiful and was progressing at MGM, inching her way to star status. But she must no longer allow constraint to hold her back (*BB,* 79).

Myrna had yet to appear in a lead role in an important MGM film, though she never stopped working. In addition to her turn as the mean-spirited daughter in *Emma,* she'd portrayed a calculating cabaret hostess in the Prohibition melodrama *The Wet Parade,* based on an Upton Sinclair novel. She'd been Robert Young's charming American neighbor in a Paris boardinghouse in *New Morals for Old,* a part much reduced from the one originally planned in the script. She'd worn Adrian-designed outfits once again and had relished the chance to work alongside talents like Walter Huston and Jean Hersholt, but still she had not been asked to show her stuff as an actress. MGM's photographers, designers, and makeup crew made sure she always looked ravishing before the cameras, but—as at Warners—the producers imprisoned her in roles with little emotional range. She kept to the familiar punishing schedule, rising at 5:30 on weekdays to arrive at the studio for makeup by 7:00 and be camera-ready by 9:00. She'd study her lines under the hair dryer. MGM, rushing her from set to set, rarely allowed time for her to catch her breath, let alone for rehearsal or for learning a script in advance. Thalberg's summons was confirmation that at least someone with clout had been paying attention.

Thalberg's advice didn't magically transform Myrna Loy into a brassy extrovert or an emotional volcano, but it did have an impact. It boosted her self-confidence and persuaded her that MGM had plans for her. It empowered her to fight harder for the roles she wanted. And it may have helped nudge her out of her mother's household. Soon after the meeting with Thalberg she finally, at age twenty-seven, laid claim to the life of an independent, sexually active woman who happened to be in love with the producer Arthur Hornblow Jr.

Before their relationship caught fire, Myrna and Arthur hadn't seen one another since *Arrowsmith* closed production. Some months later they met by accident in a drugstore, and the next day Arthur, now separated from his wife, Juliette, sent an array of gorgeous roses with a dinner invitation enclosed. After that they were rarely apart.

Arthur was eight years older than Myrna, worldlier, and far better read than she. The transplanted New Yorker was not just Myrna's lover but also a kind of guru and teacher who was helping to mold her. Arthur had a musical Polish Jewish mother and a literary British father who had moved to New York and there become the founding editor of *Theatre* magazine. The younger Arthur, fluent in French after serving in counterintelligence in France during World War I, felt at home among Europeans, particularly those who worked in the theater. He advised Myrna on what to wear in front of the camera (Adrian's creations were too fussy for her, he counseled) and on which roles to pursue or avoid. He gave her books to read, introduced her to his cultured, successful, and usually famous friends, and exposed her to the pleasures of the *New Yorker*. Arthur served both as Myrna's sweetheart and the father she had done without since the age of thirteen.

Della put up a tremendous fight when Myrna at last declared independence. She didn't want Myrna to leave, nor did she give her blessing to her daughter's growing intimacy with Arthur. Fleeing with just a suitcase, Myrna rented an apartment in Beverly Hills and then sent her friend Lou MacFarlane to fetch the rest of her things from North Crescent Drive. In a fit of pique Della soon took off for a year in Europe, financed of course by Myrna. During the next several years Myrna would change addresses numerous times, renting digs now in Beverly Hills, now in Santa Monica, now in Hollywood. All the flitting around gave her a delicious footloose sensation and lent credence to the official line that she lived alone, but, in truth, most of the time she was bunking with Arthur. In addition to paying her own rent, she continued to support her mother, aunt, and brother, David, the latter now hoping to make headway as a commercial artist but not getting very far.

Mad about Arthur, Myrna wanted nothing more than to marry him. "I believe in LOVE," she told Gladys Hall, "the love of the poets, the love of a lifetime. When that love comes to us, genuine and four-dimensional, infidelity is impossible. Love is one body indivisible and cannot be broken into fragments." To Myrna, love on this scale entailed the merging of two bodies and souls, plus the security and commitment that a wedding ring promised. But Arthur kept stalling, telling her that Juliette refused to give him a divorce. That was a way for him to buy time. He wanted to be with Myrna, and assured her that he loved her alone, but was in no rush to acquire another wife. Arthur's feelings toward Myrna seem to have been more ambivalent than hers for him, from the get-go. He ran hot and cold. And although a brilliant man who cultivated the art of living well, he lacked Myrna's greatness of heart.[2]

Myrna's joy at being coupled with Arthur was enormous but less than total. It gnawed at her that her lover was still a married man. Readers of the February 1932 issue of *Vanity Fair* were treated to an Edward Steichen portrait of the sophisticated-looking Mr. and Mrs. Arthur Hornblow Jr. Brunette Juliette Crosby, smiling and attractive in a print dress, sits beside smiling Arthur, shown in profile and looking quite French in a black beret. Arthur and Juliette no longer lived together by the time the photo was published.

The first Mrs. Hornblow, Juliette Crosby, briefly resumed her stage career by appearing opposite Walter Huston in a dramatization of *Dodsworth*. Arthur brought Myrna to see the play at the Biltmore Theater, then took her backstage to meet Juliette. Myrna would later see this introduction of the new love of Arthur's life to his discarded wife as an unfeeling, even cruel, way for Arthur to treat Juliette, but at the time she withheld any harsh judgment (*BB*, 77).

In the spring of 1932 Myrna went on loan to Paramount, the studio to which Arthur Hornblow would soon be moving after years of close association with Samuel Goldwyn. Arthur appears to have played no part in arranging this particular loan-out, however; it was the work of Myrna's friend and admirer, the innovative director Rouben Mamoulian. Mamoulian, who trained at the Moscow Art Theater, made his name directing theater in New York and caused Hollywood to sit up and take notice with his inventive use of the camera in *Applause*, his first venture as a film director. Mamoulian wanted Loy to appear as the man-hungry Countess Valentine in *Love Me Tonight*, a comic operetta in the Lubitsch mode, which Mamoulian was producing and directing. Based on a French play, with a glorious Richard Rodgers score and Lorenz Hart lyrics, it was a musical fairy tale set in France. It starred two big-ticket players, Maurice Chevalier and Jeanette MacDonald, and was photographed by Victor Milner. Mamoulian conceived the film as a stylized exercise in rhythm and rhyme. From the movie's magnificent opening, where the city of Paris awakens to a basso continuo of chimes, hammer strikes, knife grindings, and the sweeping strokes of a broom caught in a tracking shot, *Love Me Tonight* sustains a beat.

Mamoulian had escorted Myrna to the opera and theater a few times;

he obviously enjoyed her company. He saw a twinkle in her eye that other directors had managed to miss and that he wanted to capture on the screen. He told her that although her Countess Valentine part was not written into the script, and Paramount saw no need to include her, he knew she had a place in *Love Me Tonight* as a witty foil to Jeanette MacDonald's dreamy, nose-in-the-air princess. Every few days he would hand her lines typed on blue interoffice memo paper. Countess Valentine, an aristocratic temptress who thinks of nothing but sex, suffers from ennui. She has no function at court other than to lounge around the chateau taking naps, waking just long enough to change her Edith Head–designed gown, flirt briefly with whatever attractive man she encounters, or deliver a naughty bantering line. When asked, after the princess faints, "Can you go for a doctor?" she responds, "Certainly, bring him right in!" When Jeanette chides, "Don't you think of anything but men, dear?" Valentine ripostes, "Oh yes, schoolboys." Preview audiences roared at these less than earth-shatteringly clever quips. Hearing their delighted response gave Myrna her first heady whiff of her own comedic powers.

Although she was later supportive of Myrna, at the time that Jeanette MacDonald worked with her in *Love Me Tonight,* competition prevailed. When Myrna appeared in a pink frock for the formal hunt ball scene, MacDonald demanded for herself, and was given, the dress Myrna wore. Even though this film was shot in black and white, colors still mattered to actors and to photographers. Myrna substituted a black velvet low-backed gown that contrasted elegantly with her white powdered wig and with the pale pastel shades adorning all the other ladies at the ball. Countess Valentine steals the scene.

Maurice Chevalier, the film's other big star, simply ignored Myrna. Although she sometimes rode with him in his car to shooting locations in the San Fernando Valley, he kept to himself, saving the fabled smiles and exuberant Gallic charm for his moments in front of the camera. "His gaiety is put on and taken off with his makeup," observed Jack Grant in *Photoplay.*[3]

Censors, who made plenty of cuts even in pre-Code Hollywood, eliminated a few of Countess Valentine's risqué lines. She would not be allowed to offer Maurice a private moonlit showing of the "virgin spring." Myrna sang a chorus of "Mimi" in the film, her sole venture doing her own singing onscreen, but before the film was reissued to American theaters in 1949, a time when the Code was being enforced, the scene was cut because of the revealing silk nightgown she wore in it. In European prints it stayed in.[4]

Even though *Love Me Tonight*, which cost almost $1 million to produce, failed to make money in the United States, Myrna loved working on the picture and felt extremely happy during production. She formed a lasting friendship with Richard Rodgers, who enjoyed teasing her about her relationship with Arthur (and who would soon write a song for another Loy picture, *Manhattan Melodrama*). She knew that it would be hard to top the talent of *Love Me Tonight*'s cast and crew, and she was aware that she had contributed something buoyant, spicy, and delicious to the picture. Her performance shimmers. Mordaunt Hall in the *New York Times* found her "easy and graceful" as Countess Valentine.[5]

Her next two roles reprised the bad old days of lurid ethnic stereotyping, but Myrna threw herself into them with over-the-top abandon. Aided by exaggerated makeup in RKO's *Thirteen Women*, as the hypnotic, half-Javanese and half-Indian Ursula Georgi, she terrorizes a group of white former schoolmates who once banished her from a sorority, predicting their doom in a series of mailed horoscopes. One piercing stare of her basilisk eyes is enough to torpedo a life. Only Irene Dunne's character, Laura Stanhope, fights back, enlisting the aid of a police detective, played by Ricardo Cortez, to protect her young son from Ursula's murderous talons. The film was put together so hastily and haphazardly that only ten women, not thirteen, figure in the plot. Characters that were to have been played by Betty Furness and Phyllis Fraser were dropped, and Myrna herself was a replacement for the originally cast Zita Johann. Two days after the film's opening, one of the actresses in it, British-born Peg Entwistle, captured headlines when she committed suicide by leaping from the enormous "Hollywoodland" sign on Mt. Lee. To the cast of *Thirteen Women* it must have seemed as if Ursula Georgi's power to kill with a hypnotic stare extended into real life. The film came and went so quickly that—aside from the tabloid attention to Entwistle's suicide—it barely made a blip on the consciousness of the moviegoing public. Nevertheless, as an example of campy, unintended hilarity, it is great fun to watch.

Back at MGM Myrna appeared in her first Metro picture since her conversation with Thalberg. As the sadistic and sensual dragon lady daughter of Dr. Fu Manchu in *The Mask of Fu Manchu*, she played her last exotic temptress with a flourish, reprising the broad, scenery-chewing acting style she'd honed during her years in silent pictures. The director, Charles Brabin, was a veteran of silent films who had directed the celebrated vamp Theda Bara in her last two movies and become her husband. He knew a thing or two about sinuous, dark-haired screen vixens equipped with fatal gazes.

Although the setting was mostly Hollywood's version of China, the narrative begins in England, and in *The Mask of Fu Manchu* Myrna was surrounded by Brits: Brabin, Loy's coplayer Lawrence Grant, and the film's star, Boris Karloff, were all British born, and the plot involved archaeologists from the British Museum. Karloff, fresh from his triumph in *Frankenstein*, was borrowed from Universal to portray the nefarious Harvard-educated Chinese scientist bent on the destruction of the white race, a fictional creation of the novelist Sax Rohmer.

MGM seems to have started this production without a clear sense of where it wanted the film to go. According to Karloff, in the original script, which was incomplete on the first day of shooting, his character sometimes spoke flawless Oxford English and sometimes pidgin. Three days into production, the original director, Charles Vidor, was replaced by Brabin, and the screenwriter, Courteney Terrett, yielded to a team of writers that at one time included five names and eventually reduced itself to just three. Boris Karloff decided that the only way to approach his maniacal role would be to kid it, and Myrna followed his lead.[6]

The absurd plot pits two sets of explorers competing against each other in the Gobi Desert as they search for the sword, mask, and tomb of Genghis Khan. The group from the British Museum has virtue and the British Empire on its side. Pitted against them, Fu Manchu and his henchmen exult in evil, seeking nothing less than world domination, "to kill the white man and take his women." Each side enlists the support of a young, alluring woman. On the English side is Sheila Barton (Karen Morley), a blonde, always dressed in white, who dons a pith helmet and insists on joining the Gobi expedition after her archaeologist father has been kidnapped and tortured by Dr. Fu Manchu. Sheila's opposite number, played by Myrna Loy, is Fu Manchu's dark-haired, sexually ravenous daughter, Fah Lo See. She keeps a pet python and wears elaborate tall headdresses (one of which looks a lot like a fringed art deco lampshade) and floor-length, high-collared embroidered gowns designed by Adrian. Appropriately, her face, lit from below, is often cast in shadows. Sheila's boyfriend, Terrence Granville (Charles Starrett), for the moment serves as Fah Lo See's preferred object of lust. After his capture by Fu Manchu, Fah Lo See orders him to be stripped and whipped. She looks ecstatic as she urges those doing the whipping to go "Faster! Faster!" At least she didn't have to do the whipping herself, as had been proposed in an earlier draft of the script. Terrence is manacled, laid out on a divan, and injected with a serum distilled from a mixture of Fu Manchu's blood, dragon blood, and reptile organs that will render him passive; he will do as he is commanded.

MGM went all out on lurid effects, introducing a pit of snapping crocodiles, a bell torture, electrical shocks, and walls of metal spikes to the indignities his enemies face at Fu Manchu's headquarters. A reporter for the *Los Angeles Record* noted that "the picture is so packed with underground passages, electrical death machines, snakes, tarantulas, . . . hypnotizing serums, daggers in the back, trap doors, screams, smoking fluids, mummies coming to life, and all the other gasp accessories that the audience was unable to do anything but laugh."[7]

In her next movie Myrna again, as she had in *The Devil to Pay* and *Rebound*, spoke literate lines that originated in the theater. She considered her work as Cecelia in *The Animal Kingdom* another landmark in her career, a "final break with the exotics" and her first straight dramatic part "of sufficient importance to really attract attention." Based on a sophisticated Philip Barry play that in its Broadway run starred and was coproduced by Leslie Howard, the movie adaptation, made when Myrna was again loaned to RKO, was chosen to launch the new thirty-seven-hundred-seat RKO Roxy Theater in New York. That, along with its appeal to worldly, upper-crust moviegoers, qualified it as a prestige picture. But Myrna might easily have missed out on the experience, and the wide exposure, because it seems that David O. Selznick, head of production at RKO and bent on making quality "adult" pictures that scored with a select few rather than grade-B programmers pitched to the masses, appreciated her beauty but wasn't yet much impressed by her acting. Even though Loy had been considered for the role of Cecelia on Broadway, refusing it only because MGM wouldn't grant her time away from Culver City, Selznick opposed casting her; he favored Karen Morley, another actress borrowed from MGM, for the role of Cecelia.[8]

Selznick may have been aware that his new protégée at RKO, Katharine Hepburn, had designs on *The Animal Kingdom*. Hepburn learned the part of Daisy Sage, an artist who is Cecelia's free-spirited rival, for the Broadway production, from which Leslie Howard, in his capacity as coproducer, fired her while it was still in rehearsal. Not one to let go without a fight, Katharine Hepburn even used a scene from *The Animal Kingdom* in her first movie screen test, her debut on celluloid.[9]

Leslie Howard had wanted Hepburn fired from the Broadway production because she towered over him and he couldn't bear her mannerisms or "insufferable bossiness." Now, in the movie version of *The Animal Kingdom,* Myrna Loy would be cast as Leslie Howard's wife. Maybe Hepburn, still smarting from Howard's rebuff, resented Myrna's ability to get and keep a role opposite Leslie Howard. Hepburn issued a left-handed compliment, saying that Myrna got the Cecelia role "because she's beautiful"—as if her looks were all she had going for her (*BB,* 76).[10]

Selznick and his extremely bright and socially influential wife, Irene Mayer Selznick, daughter of MGM mogul Louis B. Mayer, were long-time friends of Arthur Hornblow Jr. The Selznicks and the Hornblows, during the time when Arthur was still living with his then-wife Juliette Crosby, were close enough friends that when newborn Terry Hornblow left the hospital in his mother's arms in January 1931, Irene Selznick drove the baby and Juliette home. Irene, who described Arthur as "crisp and debonair" and "a man of taste in wine, women, and letters" who was "the ultimate cosmopolite," never even mentions Myrna Loy in her memoir. If she ever had an interest in Myrna, it was only as an appendage to Arthur.[11]

Myrna had an advocate, though a far less influential one than David O. Selznick, in the RKO director Ned Griffith, who had directed her in *Rebound* and who had scored a hit with another film based on a Philip Barry play, the 1930 version of *Holiday.* Griffith prized Myrna's talent and potential, and he wanted her to play Cecelia in *The Animal Kingdom.* Dubious, Selznick wouldn't even agree to allow Myrna to test for the role. Her screen test opposite Leslie Howard had to be conducted on the sly, at night (*BB,* 76). Although Leslie Howard, a persnickety vegetarian, could smell garlic sausage on Myrna's breath, the test went very well. Selznick liked it and agreed to give Myrna the part.

The Animal Kingdom is an example of the adult fare Selznick wanted at RKO. Its premise was so daring that attempts to reissue the film in 1935 and 1937 were denied by the Production Code Administration. The script questioned the sanctity of marriage, suggesting that a union of true soul mates—the characters played by Leslie Howard and Ann Harding—trumps any other kind of marriage and can thrive without legal or religious sanction. Harding's Daisy Sage, the artist and ex-mistress, speaks the naughty line, "I'm a foolish virgin—well, foolish anyway." It's clear that Daisy and her best friend, Tom Collier, the prominent New York book publisher played by Leslie Howard, have been longtime lovers. When bohemian Daisy goes off to Paris on assignment, debonair Tom becomes engaged to Myrna's Cecelia Henry, a gilt-edged knockout whose beauty masks the reality that she's a far less interesting and more conventional, manipulative, and mercenary woman than independent-minded Daisy. Tom's moneybags father wants him to settle down and encourages him to marry Cecelia. When Daisy returns and Tom tells her of his engagement to Cecelia, he tries to persuade Daisy that they must continue their friendship, but, heartbroken, Daisy turns him away. Now married to Cecelia, and living an isolated and comfortable suburban life in Connecticut, Tom submits to the tarnished values of his wealth-obsessed father and wife. He compromises his integrity by becoming a publisher of the kind of lucrative pulp fiction he used to scorn. Cecelia has encouraged this lowering of his literary standards, and she generally disdains Tom's previous life.

When Daisy finally meets Cecelia at a birthday party for Tom, she tells Tom that she feels pity for him. She has caught Cecelia embracing Tom's lawyer, and she has read one of the trashy novels Tom is publishing, pronouncing it tripe. In the past Tom has found Cecelia sexually irresistible. Myrna plays her as bitchy but very alluring in the frothy negligee she wears in the bedroom scene. But after she locks Tom out of their bedroom because he won't agree to move into town and live with his rich father, he finally sees Cecelia as the greedy schemer she is. He leaves her, telling his butler that he's "going back to my wife." Tom's true wife, according to Philip Barry, is Daisy, the woman he can talk to, not the one who wears the wedding ring.

Plenty of behind-the-scenes drama accompanied the production of *The Animal Kingdom*. Myrna quickly fell under Leslie Howard's spell, as he did under hers. The sensitive, responsive, and easy-to-get-along-with Myrna appealed to him far more than had the commanding, angular, and contentious Katharine Hepburn. As for Myrna's reaction to Howard, she found his combination of passion and fine British manners hard to resist. "We grew very fond of one another on that picture," Myrna remembered. "I mean, it could have been a real scrambola—if I'd allowed it to be." Leslie Howard appeared to be upper crust, but that wasn't his background. Born Leslie Steiner to middle-class Jewish parents in London, the popular actor began his stage career after experiencing shell shock in World War I. He had a loyal wife and two children but proved very susceptible to his leading ladies. He'd apparently had a fling with Marion Davies and later would have an affair with Merle Oberon. Known for his restraint as an actor, in the flesh he proved impetuous. While Arthur was away in New York, he came to Myrna's rented house, pressing her to run away with him. She was tempted but managed to hold back (*BB*, 77).[12]

Myrna would later freely admit that Leslie Howard almost drove her to stray from Arthur. While Howard was still alive (he would be killed when his plane was shot down by the Luftwaffe in 1943), she stayed mum. But, never naming names, she once told an interviewer that sometimes a love relationship needs to be threatened by a third party if it's going to endure. "It takes three to make a love affair," she maintained. "When a girl isn't truly in love with John Doe, she finds that out after meeting John Roe. But when a girl's truly in love with John Doe, even a temporary infatuation for John Roe only makes her realize how much she loves the first one. . . . Not that I recommend the method—it's too chancy!" Her devotion to Arthur kept her on the straight and narrow.[13]

Several reviewers praised Myrna's performance as Cecelia. *Variety* said she "made a vivid figure as the Lorelei wife." Mordaunt Hall in the *New York Times* wrote that Miss Loy as Cecelia "does capital work. She speaks her lines nicely and suits the action to the words, and some of her best scenes are with Mr. Howard." Jerry Hoffman, in the *Los Angeles Examiner,* went all out, declaring, "Myrna Loy, as I've been yelling for seasons, is one of the most greatly underrated actresses on the screen. She is no one type. She hasn't a marvelous background of stage training. But this young lady has a feeling for character portrayal equal to the best and most famous of our recognized stellar actresses."[14]

David O. Selznick must have appreciated what Myrna accomplished in *The Animal Kingdom.* He borrowed her from MGM again for *Topaze,* another RKO film that treats adultery with utter casualness and would be denied permission for a reissue by the PCA in 1936. Based on a Marcel Pagnol play and voted Best Film of 1933 by the National Board of Review, *Topaze* had a Ben Hecht script and starred John Barrymore as Professor Auguste Topaze, a naive but principled schoolteacher who loses his job when he refuses to alter the failing grades of one of his students, the obnoxious Charlemagne de La Tour-La Tour, whose parents are a wealthy baron and baroness. Auguste Topaze then goes to work for the baron, who has a business manufacturing soft drinks. Professor Topaze appears in an ad endorsing the baron's product, and the baron names the drink Bubbling Topaze, which becomes the rage. Topaze trades in his beard, pince-nez, and threadbare morning coat to become a natty, affluent man about town, winning the affection of the baron's mistress along the way.

Myrna Loy is Coco, the baron's elegant mistress. In the opening scene we see her, clad in Chinese silk pajamas, conversing with the much older baron before a sitting room fireplace in a cozy domestic scene that is interrupted when the baron leaves to go home to his wife and son. Later, thrown together in the lab of the baron's chemical company, Coco and Topaze are increasingly drawn to one another, but the sexual nature of the attachment is only suggested. They escape together to racy movies with titles like *Man, Woman and Sin*. Although the Coco role provided many opportunities for Myrna to seduce the camera, the formulaic part didn't provide much of an acting challenge.

John Barrymore did fine character work as Dr. Topaze, a scholarly, soft-spoken man without any of the preening vanity or swashbuckling dynamism of his 1926 Don Juan. Myrna found him sadder and quieter than the man she remembered from six years earlier. She concluded that things at home were not going well for him, because when she asked him about Dolores Costello and their two children, he would change the subject. Repeating a scene from their days at Warner Bros., he walked right by Myrna, failing to recognize her, on their first day on the *Topaze* set. When the director, Harry d'Abbadie d'Arrast, brought this social blunder to his attention, Barrymore apologized to Myrna, blaming his slight on an alcohol-induced haze (*BB*, 78).

One reason MGM was so willing to rent or barter Myrna Loy's services to other studios was that even though Metro would report profits of $9.3 million in 1932, a rigorous attempt at cost cutting was under way. Movie theaters across the country were closing at an alarming rate, and cuts in actors' salaries were attempted—usually under protest. Even L. B. Mayer and Irving Thalberg submitted in July 1932 to 35 percent pay reductions. Enforced pay cuts for all actors who made more than fifty dollars a week went into effect, though only for a short time, in March of 1933 after the newly inaugurated President Franklin D. Roosevelt closed the banks. Soon the federal government started making noises about the unseemliness of paying a screen star $2,000 a week at a time when American labor was fighting for a minimum wage of forty cents per hour. Government-enforced pay cuts for movie actors, mandated by the National Recovery Act, seemed imminent. In response to this threat, and also because most actors believed that the Academy of Motion Picture Arts and Sciences was a producer-dominated, antiunion organization and did not speak for them, the Screen Actors Guild was founded. Although colleagues Robert Montgomery, Boris Karloff, and Frank Morgan were among the founding members, Myrna herself did not join until 1937.[15]

The leadership of MGM changed radically after Thalberg had a heart attack late in 1932 and left for a rest in Europe. His once close relationship with L. B. Mayer had grown competitive and shaky, and there was speculation that he might even sever his connection with MGM altogether. In his absence David O. Selznick departed RKO to become producer for his father-in-law at MGM, taking on powers no one but Thalberg had been allowed until then. Rough and tough Eddie Mannix, a former bouncer and "an Irishman with the face of an English bulldog," took on new responsibilities as production manager. When Thalberg returned, he became the head of just his own unit, rather than of all MGM production.[16]

MGM finally saw fit to cast Myrna Loy as a leading lady in an elaborate production opposite Ramon Novarro, but the film, *The Barbarian,* was a throwback to the days of Rudolph Valentino in his silent Sheik roles and Novarro's own earlier turn as *The Arab.* The screenwriter Frances Goodrich, who, with her husband, Albert Hackett, did a few days' work on the script before Anita Loos and Elmer Harris replaced them, couldn't bear the creakiness of the assignment. She complained to her agent that writing about sheiks and ladies in distress in California in 1933 felt completely phony. "It was all so false, all hooey." Goodrich got it right, and she and Hackett bailed out, but Myrna was stuck with the assignment.[17]

The Barbarian, originally titled *Man of the Nile* and shot partly in Yuma, Arizona, was a vehicle for a once top-ranked leading man, Ramon Novarro, whose star was now fading, though he was still highly paid. He portrayed Jamil, an Egyptian dragoman or desert guide who, of course, turns out to be actually a prince. As a suitor who tries to win Myrna Loy's camel-riding character, Diana, a name lifted whole from *The Sheik,* away from her stodgy British fiancé, played by Reginald Denny, Jamil shows himself capable of both romantic savoir faire—he serenades Diana and drops orchids on her as she sleeps—and caveman-type savagery. He kidnaps Diana, deprives her of water, forces her to walk the desert sands, and embraces her against her will. She in turn humiliates him, striking him with a whip and throwing water in his face during a marriage ceremony in his village. They end up floating in a boat down the Nile as newlyweds. Their union avoided another potential clash with the PCA rule against miscegenation because Diana has confessed to Jamil that her mother was an Egyptian, making her half-Arabian.

The 6.4 magnitude Long Beach earthquake on March 10, 1933, shut down production of *The Barbarian* for part of the day and sent the back lot into pandemonium. As the earth heaved and rumbled, power went out, arc lamps tumbled, and palm trees doubled over outdoors. Cast and crew fled the soundstages in panic. The quake killed 115 people in the

Los Angeles area. Losing half a day of shooting and scaring the pants off people seemed like minor calamities compared to the lost lives.

Back on the set, Myrna appeared in a scene showing her afloat and apparently nude (she actually wore a flesh-colored body stocking), in a pool strewn with rose petals. "Tits and sand sell tickets," MGM producer Hunt Stromberg once judiciously observed. The suggested nudity provoked the wrath of the censors and had to be cut to eliminate "all shots in which the girl's body is visible through the water." *The Barbarian* made a profit of $100,000 but was added to the list of movies denied permission for rerelease on moral grounds after strict enforcement of the Code began in 1934.[18]

Ramon Novarro and Myrna became chummy during production of *The Barbarian.* She found him a "gentle, quiet man" whose company and musical talent she enjoyed. She attended a musicale he gave in his own home theater at which Thalberg, John Gilbert, the set designer Cedric Gibbons, Jeanette MacDonald, Randolph Scott, and Cary Grant also turned up. She stayed in Novarro's house when he went to Europe to give more vocal concerts. When MGM's publicist Howard Strickling decided to promote the friendship as a torrid romance, the usually compliant Myrna balked. She hated the Hollywood gossip mill and resented being forced to be fodder for it. She succeeded in getting Strickling and his publicity department to cease and desist but not until after a flurry of newspaper and fan magazine articles with titles like "A Secret Wedding for Myrna and Ramon" had been published. How ridiculous, Myrna insisted. "Ramon wasn't even interested in the ladies" (*BB,* 80).[19]

Loy played her first career woman, the novelist Mary Howard in *When Ladies Meet,* but here she's no self-sufficient pillar of feminine strength. Her working-gal status in *When Ladies Meet* counts for less than her tangled love life. She has a devoted journalist boyfriend, played by Robert Montgomery, but is in love with her married publisher, portrayed by Frank Morgan. The surprise twist in the plot comes with an extended, potentially disastrous encounter between Loy's character and the publisher's wife, played by Ann Harding, during a rainy weekend in the country. Just by coincidence, Mary is completing a novel about a woman in love with a married man, and without realizing she's speaking to her lover's wronged wife, she solicits Harding's opinion on what a wife should do when her husband strays. In the end Mary must face the reality that the publisher she thought would love her forever just wanted a short-term romp in the hay and that she's been painfully deceived. The pain doesn't last too long, however. She has dreamboat Robert Montgomery waiting in the wings and ready to offer both a wedding ring and undying devotion.

Robert Montgomery, who would appear in two more pictures with Myrna, had a lot in common with her. Here were two attractively slim sophisticates good at playing society high hats, two MGM actors who each had a way with elegant attire and a witty line. Each could summon the kind of champagne-bubble effervescence one would hope to find at a ritzy dinner party or, more likely, at a screen version of one. For some years Loy and Montgomery were political allies and fellow partisans of FDR, but that changed in the postwar era as Montgomery veered to the right. When they worked together on *When Ladies Meet,* though, Loy and Montgomery became quite friendly. Alice Brady, who played a dithery older woman in *When Ladies Meet,* would get together with the two of them after work, forming a spontaneous and affectionate trio primed for a good time.

Myrna Loy's performances were being regularly singled out in reviews as the harbingers of stardom. The *Hollywood Reporter* hailed her work as Mary Howard in *When Ladies Meet* as "another shining milestone in what promises to be a brilliant career."[20]

Her work as shady lady Gertie Waxted in *Penthouse* prompted a chorus of raves. Gertie was different from the characters Myrna had previously played at MGM. Finally, the studio allowed her to smile, crack wise, crinkle her nose, and show off her party clothes. In this movie she's neither a high-hat snob nor a menacing she-devil. She's a likable dame, the warm-hearted mistress of a gangster. That liaison doesn't hold her down; Gertie makes it clear that she's available to other men and doesn't expect to be punished for her sins. At a nightclub she frequents, where socialites rub elbows with thugs sporting fancy suits, she meets the lawyer Jack Durant (Warner Baxter), the man she'll go home with that night. Durant has already learned that Gertie isn't the sort who would mind sleeping over in the penthouse of a man she hardly knows. "She'll come to dinner, and she won't give you an argument if you ask her to stay for breakfast," Nat Pendleton grins when he's about to present Gertie to Durant. She wears a big black bow on the bodice of her white gown, as if she's a walking box of chocolates waiting to be unwrapped and sampled. Censorship concerns mandated that she and Jack Durant don't actually get into the sack together, but she does borrow his pajamas and spend the night at his place. She's a tough cookie, capable of slugging the butler, but smart and sassy enough to engage her wealthy host in spirited repartee *and* to help him elude a murder trap set by her nasty underworld boyfriend.

Writing for the *New York Herald Tribune*, Richard Watts Jr. extolled the "lovely and distinctive humor" that Loy brought to the role. *Variety* gushed: "Myrna Loy reveals new skill in the management of light scenes—light on the surface but with the inference of tenseness in the background. This actress has progressed in command of technique with each picture she has done until she now stands as one of the most serviceable femme leads in the Hollywood lists, one who has escaped from a limited type to a broad range of leading roles."[21]

In *Penthouse* Loy was directed for the first time by W. S. ("Woody") Van Dyke, a man who would sit at the controls for seven more of her films, including the best of the *Thin Man* pictures, and whose backing was key in boosting her to stardom. A former child actor and assistant to D. W. Griffith on *Intolerance,* Van Dyke was also an expert navigator, radio buff, and wireless telegraph aficionado. He had made his name directing outdoor adventure pictures such as *Trader Horn* and *Tarzan, the Ape Man,* as well as various westerns. Nicknamed "One Take Woody," he was known for the speed and economy of his productions. Prizing spontaneity, he avoided rehearsals and repetitions, convinced that the first take was the best. Van Dyke didn't allow his actors to think things over, and he was a master of the setup. He did his editing with the camera, not bothering to shoot "protection footage." Pauline Kael referred to him as "the whirlwind."[22]

Van Dyke said of his own shooting style: "The reckless pace at which I work has a little more behind it than mere desire to get through and save money. The heightened tension and lack of dreary rehearsals . . . gives a crisp, vital quality to the final production." He never explained to actors how a scene should be played, and in this respect, according to Selznick, he was the opposite of the painstaking George Cukor. Related to his breakneck pace was a zany cowboy streak that could spur violent mayhem. "In his Western days, he shot up country hotels for fun. There were few to challenge his reputation as the toughest guy and the hardest drinker in Hollywood." On the *Trader Horn* set he poured enough Scotch into a baboon to make the primate stagger.[23]

Myrna saw Van Dyke's swift efficiency as a by-product of his ability to cut and edit film in his head. "He always knew his shots." She also thought that his hard-charging directing mode emanated from an electrifying personality. He made you feel "good about things most of the time." But inside, she thought, "he was probably a very sad man." Renowned on and off the set for his vast drinking capacity, Van Dyke was one of those rare imbibers who managed to get drunk at night and still show up clean, shiny, and primed for work early the next morning. He expected no less of his drinking companions. Loy also connected his customary velocity and economy with his being a captain in the U.S. Marine Corps Reserves. His buzz-cut hair, lean build, and fondness for wearing boots proclaimed his quasi-military style.[24]

Van Dyke was exciting to work with but not exactly easygoing. Myrna complained that she felt worn out and needed a rest, not just from Van Dyke but from screen acting in general. "I've had too much to do," she told a reporter. She'd appeared in fourteen films since signing with MGM, some of them on loan-out. She yearned for a vacation, but the roles kept coming, with no break in sight. The only time off she took during these first years on the MGM assembly line was a brief visit to Hawaii to see her dear friends Betty and Bob Black early in 1934. Even if her MGM contract had entitled her to relax now and then, Myrna herself feared that if she stopped working so hard, the career momentum she was building might be lost.[25]

Van Dyke took over as director of Myrna's next film, *The Prizefighter and the Lady*, after Howard Hawks left the set. Hawks, who stayed on long enough to guide the novice actor Max Baer through his opening scenes, had expected that the leading man in this film would be Clark Gable, an experienced actor and a man he liked. Gable was originally supposed to be playing opposite Norma Shearer. By the time Hawks entered the picture, the casting gears had shifted again, and he was expecting to direct Gable and Jean Harlow. Hawks balked when the story refocused and heavyweight boxer Max Baer, a six-foot-four Goliath who'd pulled off nineteen knockouts in a row, replaced Gable. As far as Hawks was concerned, this was one casting change too many. Baer wasn't even an actor, although American prizefighters had been jumping the ring's ropes into show business for decades. Louis B. Mayer got on the case, precipitating Hawks's exit. Hawks had managed to get behind schedule in his shooting, and that wouldn't do. Hawks was out.[26]

Three months before *The Prizefighter and the Lady* began shooting, the Jewish Baer had defeated German heavyweight Max Schmeling at Yankee Stadium. The Nazis, who had claimed Schmeling as a symbol of Aryan superiority, interpreted his defeat by an American Jew as a worldwide humiliation. Germany would ban *The Prizefighter and the Lady* as a provocation to "national socialist feeling" that glorified Baer, "a Jewish Negroid type."[27]

Baer's character, Steve Morgan, is supposed to be vain and cocksure, traits he didn't have to stretch too hard to conjure, but the actual Max Baer, according to Myrna, was "an unsophisticated baby at heart," a man "as unprotected as a white rabbit." Before they played any scenes together, the assistant director Earl Haley informed Myrna that Max was terrified to come near her. "He'd seen me on the screen and imagined I was too grand for words." The script required Myrna's character, Belle Mercer, a nightclub singer, to fall for the fighter and marry him after a single night out on the town with him. She gives up her singing career, dons an apron, and forgives her husband's catting around—all for love.[28]

Myrna recalled the love scenes with Max Baer as "simply delicious. It was like the first kiss of a boy who had never kissed a girl before when he kissed me. He was positively reverent and so naïve." Eventually, Max Baer, a natural actor who delivered a better performance than anyone had a right to expect, came to view Myrna as a kind of big sister to whom he confided his heartaches. Among those was his guilt about his boxing past; he'd inadvertently killed, by means of his knockout punch, one of his opponents in the ring. His $3,000 a week MGM salary, as well as his heavyweight championship, depended on his brutish strength, but he revealed to Myrna that he feared that very power might make him kill again. He also, most likely, confided some of the complexities of his love life. Myrna's "unprotected white rabbit" prowled around quite a bit. Newly divorced, he was being sued for breach of promise by one cutie on his list of bedmates just as his most recent conquest, Jean Harlow, sidetracked him. Ads for the film promoted him as the new "It" man of the screen, but because MGM wasn't willing to match the high salary he thought he was worth, Baer never made another picture there, though he acted for other companies.[29]

Practical jokes were the order of the day on the set of *The Prizefighter and the Lady*. Van Dyke handed Myrna an exploding cigarette. Jack Dempsey, who played himself as the referee in the big fight between Baer and the heavyweight champion Primo Carnera, wired Max Baer's chair. During the fight scene Myrna released a toy mouse into the ring, causing Baer, who had a mouse phobia, to leap into Carnera's arms.[30]

The climactic fight scene, a prelude to the real-life 1934 heavyweight championship bout in which Carnera would lose his title to Baer, was filmed on an MGM soundstage that replicated the ring in Madison Square

Garden. Celebrities from the worlds of movies and prizefighting turned out to watch filming of the extended match, which ends in a draw. According to *Variety,* Carnera only agreed to the no-win situation after MGM added $10,000 to his original fee of $35,000.[31]

Although Baer snared all the publicity, MGM awarded Myrna Loy top billing on *The Prizefighter and the Lady,* an indication of her rising favor. *Variety* duly noted how she had "come along-in her last few pictures." Another sign was the professional company she kept. MGM included her in the all-star lineup for *Night Flight,* along with Clark Gable, John Barrymore, Helen Hayes, Lionel Barrymore, and Robert Montgomery. Cramming a great many stars into one movie became the vogue after the success of Thalberg's 1932 production of *Grand Hotel* and Selznick's *Dinner at Eight.* Although she is up there with big names, Myrna Loy practically disappears in *Night Flight,* which lists her character in the credits as "pilot's wife." She and Helen Hayes, another pilot's wife who at least merits a name, spend their time waiting anxiously for the return of their flying ace husbands and living for news of them when they take to the skies. As *Variety*'s astute Cecelia Ager put it, "a flyer's mighty fortunate to have Myrna Loy for a wife, the way she asks no questions, the way she accepts his arrivals and departures, . . . but above all the way she looks warm, gentle, yielding." This wouldn't be the last time Myrna Loy would find herself playing the little woman.[32]

When MGM cast her in *Men in White* opposite Clark Gable, its hottest ticket among leading men, giving them equal, above-the-title billing, the studio seemed to be telling the world that Myrna Loy had arrived.

Clark Gable's handsome face and devil-may-care grin, his he-man build, palpable virility, and easy swagger had pushed him into the top ranks of stardom after several years of rejected screen tests. On presidential election night in November of 1932, Will Rogers commented after listening to the early returns, "Clark Gable is leading Hoover and Roosevelt both." Hollywood had quickly pegged Gable as a muscular brute who proves he's sexy by refusing to shave and slapping women around. He was the man, Thalberg said, "every woman wanted and every man wanted to be." Offscreen, Gable's interests ran to boozing, hunting, cars, motorcycles, and women. He never let the fact that he had a wife stand in the way of a steamy affair, or the promise of one. His overheated liaison with Joan Crawford, "the affair that nearly burned Hollywood down," might have derailed both their careers if Crawford's thenhusband, Douglas Fairbanks Jr., had named Gable in their divorce. Gable, called on the carpet by Louis B. Mayer, knew he couldn't pretend his affair with Crawford concerned them only. Mayer, he said, "would have ended my career in fifteen minutes. And I had no interest in becoming a waiter."[33]

MGM kept a tight lid on the information fed to reporters, and Mayer, his operations chief Eddie Mannix, and Howard Strickling, head of publicity, constantly intervened and tried to manipulate the private lives of stars. The attitude was, MGM made you, and therefore MGM owns you. Backed by a morals clause in every actor's contract that threatened termination if a player did anything that might "shock, insult or offend the community," Mannix snooped, copying every single message, incoming and outgoing, in an actor's box. Privacy didn't exist, except on the fly in a bungalow or dressing room. The head of the story department, Sam Marx, recalled, "Phone calls to the players were screened, escorts provided, romances promoted or destroyed, and marriages arranged or rent asunder."[34]

Although she had a reputation for being a cooperative team player, Myrna balked at any attempt by columnists or MGM publicists to shape or intrude on her personal life. Her outrage at the planted stories romantically linking her and Ramon Novarro marked her most strenuous protest to date at the studio. Posing for publicity photos was one thing, dispensing inside information about what she did off the set quite another.

Despite her hostility to prying eyes, an occasional reporter got wind of her relationship with Arthur, still legally married to Juliette Crosby, and hinted about it, as well as other possible liaisons, in gossip columns. A *Photoplay* photographer sneaked a picture of Myrna and Arthur at a party—they look most unhappy about being caught by the camera—and the published caption refers to them as companions. "At the moment," ran a bit in the *New York Daily Mirror,* "Miss Loy has an actor, a producer and a prominent business man on three separate strings. And the producer attachment, which is of long standing, is liable to cause her a lot of embarrassment any minute." But a Los Angeles newspaper columnist praised Myrna's friendliness to the crew on the set, her sense of humor, and her well-scrubbed good looks, going on to say that Myrna had managed to stay out of the publicity limelight. She was called "the most voluptuous and least accessible beauty of the cinema world."[35]

Myrna didn't simply shut out intruders from the press who tried to scope out her private life; she also refused to spread stories about others. Her good breeding and tact didn't allow her to acknowledge in her autobiography that MGM's alabaster foundations were almost shattered, soon after she arrived at the studio in 1932, by the scandal created by producer-writer Paul Bern's mysterious and bloody shooting death at the home he shared with his wife, Jean Harlow. Almost certainly a suicide, Bern's death rocked Hollywood, dominating newspaper front pages for weeks.

Considering her reluctance to gossip, it matters that Myrna did tattle on Clark Gable in her autobiography. She and Gable had the same agent, Minna Wallis, with whom Gable was close. It was Minna who arranged for Loy and Gable to meet for the first time at the annual Mayfair Ball, a formal dinner dance at the Ambassador Hotel. Myrna greeted MGM's most valuable male star by cracking, "My ears stick out too." Big ears were a no-no for movie stars who played romantic roles. Whenever she was in a Selznick production, Selznick instructed the makeup crew to glue Myrna's ears close to her head, which she hated, especially when the glue began to melt under the lights and had to be reapplied. MGM usually handled the ear problem simply by giving her a hairdo that covered the ears or by making sure she was shot from a flattering angle. Gable, who had no patience with fuss and artifice, balked at having his "flaps" pinned against his head with fish-skin tape. Now that he had clout at MGM, he could assert himself, insisting that the ears came with the rest of Clark Gable, but when he was trying to break into the movies, his ears almost stopped him cold. Before Gable ever appeared in a movie, Howard Hughes, after seeing him in a play, dismissed him. "He'll never get any place, this guy," he augured. "With those ears he looks like a taxi cab with both doors open."[36]

At Warner Bros., where Gable worked before Thalberg snagged him for MGM, both Darryl Zanuck and Jack Warner had decided the ears made Gable look like an ape and sent him packing. Myrna's remark about their shared ear problem was her way of trying to establish buddy-ship, nothing more.

At the Ambassador, Myrna and Clark danced together to "Dancing in the Dark," an experience she remembered as "divine." After the ball they were driven to their respective homes in the same chauffeured car. According to her account in *Being and Becoming,* Myrna, Gable, and his socially prominent wife, Ria, several years older than he and somewhat matronly in appearance, shared the backseat. They'd all had plenty to drink, but Myrna was clearheaded enough to become unnerved when Gable started sidling up close to her. He got out of the car to accompany her to her door and as she fiddled with her keys, grabbed her and planted a love bite on her neck. She responded with a shove, and he fell back a few porch steps into the hedge (*BB*, 84).

Myrna once said of Gable, "He believed his own publicity, that he was irresistible." She must be the only woman who ever wrote for publication about spurning him, though there were a handful of movie colony women—Mrs. Basil Rathbone was one—who privately said they considered him coarse and "not my type." Most of the countless women he approached, and millions more who only worshipped from afar, got weak-kneed in his presence. Joan Crawford confessed that in a scene in *Possessed* where Gable had to grab her roughly, "his nearness had such an impact [that] if he hadn't held me by both shoulders, I'd have dropped." Joan Blondell reported that she and Barbara Stanwyck both had to sit down to steady themselves the first day he showed up on the set of *Night Nurse*. That was the kind of response that Gable expected. *Photoplay* called him "a caveman with a club in one hand and a book of poetry in the other." He kept the poetry part under wraps, fearing it would tarnish his superman image.[37]

Gable could be moody. During the shooting of *Men in White* he repaid Myrna's rebuff by ignoring her as much as he could, walking past her to offer coffee and cakes to the English actress Elizabeth Allan, who played a student nurse in the picture and with whom he was smitten. Not until their next film together would Gable and Loy develop a warm, relaxed camaraderie.

Based on a Pulitzer Prize–winning play by Sidney Kingsley that was still on the boards in New York when the film opened in Chicago, *Men in White* ran into trouble with the Hays Office even before shooting began. The problem was that an abortion figures prominently in the story about a young Dr. Ferguson (clean-shaven Gable), who, although engaged to Myrna Loy's character, Laura Hudson, has an affair with the student nurse played by Elizabeth Allan and gets her pregnant. The nurse attempts an abortion and develops peritonitis. The young doctor operates on her, trying to save her life, but she dies as the intern adjusts her bed to ease her pain. Gable showed a new side here, disclosing what *Variety* called "a tenderness wholly foreign to the rough stuff he has been doing."[38]

After reading a synopsis of the plot, James Wingate of the Hays Office wrote to Eddie Mannix that the story "presents grave danger from the standpoint of the Code and censorship." Cuts were ordered to make the cause of the young woman's death more ambiguous. References to peritonitis were deleted, as if that solved the problem. But the implied illicit intimacy between nurse and doctor, and the resulting pregnancy, stayed in, and not surprisingly after the Legion of Decency came into being in 1934, it declared the film unfit for public exhibition.[39]

Myrna's role was an unsympathetic one for most of the film. Her rich, socially ambitious, Laura Hudson resents her fiancé's demanding profession because it interferes with their social life. She wants him to abandon his plan to study with the idealistic Dr. Hochberg (Jean Hersholt) and leave his job at a metropolitan hospital for a posh private practice on Park Avenue. After touring the hospital, fainting during a witnessed operation, and holding the hand of the dying nurse, she's allowed to show a new empathy that leaves room for a possible reconciliation with Gable's character. She has learned—and we in the audience are meant to applaud her for it—that a woman must put her future husband's career first.

The release of *Men in White* had to be delayed in New York and Los Angeles because the producers of the play didn't want to have to compete with the movie version in cities where the live play remained on the boards. As a result, the film had a longer than usual run and was still playing in movie theaters in the spring of 1934, when the surprise Frank Capra hit *It Happened One Night* was also making the rounds. Gable's performance as Peter Warne, the waggish reporter who romances a runaway heiress played by Claudette Colbert, added to his already considerable luster. He and Colbert would both be honored with Academy Awards. When he removed his shirt in a tourist cabin he shared with Colbert, revealing some bare flesh and a pair of brawny shoulders, the swoons could be heard round the world, and undershirt sales plummeted. *Men in White* benefited at the box office from an epidemic of Gable fever.

Clark Gable, who'd made *It Happened One Night* on loan to Columbia Pictures, would be back at MGM opposite Myrna Loy in her next film. Myrna had blown it when she turned down the role of heiress Ellie Andrews in *It Happened One Night* because the script—not yet revised in the version she saw—seemed weak but also because she was working so hard she couldn't see straight. What advice Minna Wallis provided when Myrna was considering the script that got away isn't known. Myrna became very defensive about what proved to be a serious error in judgment, never acknowledging that it was one. But she knew she didn't want to blow it again. In her upcoming film she would once again appear opposite Clark Gable. This time she would also be working with someone she hadn't met yet, a dapper actor new to MGM by the name of William Powell.

CHAPTER 8

Mr. and Mrs. Thin Man

"Myrna Loy and William Powell are the ham and eggs, the peaches and cream, the salt and pepper of the movies," an MGM scribe commented as their fourth of six *Thin Man* films was being released. "They go together naturally as night and day." The screen marriage of this matched pair of lithe bodies and insouciant spirits outlasted any of Myrna's off-screen couplings and for their fans has never lost its luster. Powell and Loy made fourteen films together between 1934 (the year they first worked together, in *Manhattan Melodrama,* and also the year of *The Thin Man*) and 1947. Their connubial bliss seemed so perfect that fans found it hard to believe that in real life they were never married to one another. During their heyday Loy regularly received fan mail seeking marital advice because of the obvious happiness of her union with Powell. When the couple came to San Francisco to make *After the Thin Man* in the mid-1930s, the St. Francis Hotel management, unaware that Jean Harlow, also in San Francisco, was Powell's main squeeze at the time, booked Loy and Powell into its honeymoon suite. Receptionists at the hotel, no doubt wearing red faces, promptly corrected the gaffe. Since proprieties had to be observed and scandal avoided, Loy and Harlow ended up rooming together in the luxe quarters, while Powell growled about being consigned to a room the size of a large closet (*BB,* 142).[1]

Powell and Loy's breezy teamwork as Nick and Nora Charles in *The Thin Man* seemed pitch-perfect. Dressed to the nines and armed with quips that amuse but don't inflict wounds, they live in the moment. They savor each teasing barb as they relish one another, always poised for the next clue-chasing adventure in detecting or martini-lubricated good time at some chic nightspot.

Their constant drinking onscreen, which never produces seriously slurred speech or any other aftereffects more repellent than a severe headache, raised a few hackles in 1934. The Production Code's chief censor, Joseph Breen, wrote to MGM's Louis B. Mayer to advise that "drinking at the bar should be held down to that necessary for character and plot." After the film's release, a few letters to Breen and to fan magazines expressed horror at the amount of alcohol the characters in *The Thin Man* consume. Hollywood's strict enforcement of the Production Code was just about to begin, but the edict mandating a Production Code Administration seal of approval before a movie could be distributed, and instituting stiff fines for erring producers, was still a few months in the future when the film premiered.[2]

The Legion of Decency had already shaken up the entire American film industry with its well-organized and financially damaging film boycott, and everyone in the business knew a more serious crackdown was just around the corner. Producers were trying to stave off government censorship by orchestrating their own in-house cleanups.

Anticipating the tough rules on morals that would soon be rigidly enforced, the designers of *The Thin Man* put married Nick and Nora into twin beds with a veritable canyon between them. Nick and Nora are a sexy pair, constantly finding excuses to touch, falling into one another's arms once in a while, and lolling around in silk, satin, and mink in the parlor on Christmas morning. When he's about to face danger in his warehouse search for the missing inventor Clyde Wynant, Nora's voice quivers when she tells Nick to take care of himself. "I do believe the little woman cares," says Nick before they kiss and clinch. At the very end of the movie they seem to be about to make love in the bottom bunk bed on the train taking them back to California (Asta, the dog, coyly covers his eyes with his paw to avoid watching). Most often, though, Nick and Nora show their affection via mutual ribbing. "Nicky, I love you because you know such *lovely* people," says Nora as one thug after another joins their party. When Nora asks him if he goes for a particular type of girl, Nicks answers, "Only you, darling—lanky brunettes with wicked jaws."

Nick and Nora rarely speak a straight line, so much do they love verbal and physical pokes in the ribs. But in the privacy of their hotel bedroom they never seem to have sex; they just dodge bullets, converse, recover from hangovers, and now and then try to catch forty winks. Mostly, Nick drinks.

About the nonstop alcohol consumption in *The Thin Man*, and its potentially dire influence on public morality, a concerned woman, possibly a theater manager, wrote to the Production Code Administration's Joseph Breen to observe, "It seems to me what has been taken out in vulgarity has been put back in drinking." By the time *After the Thin Man* began production in 1936, even stricter censorship was in place, and Breen balked again at the "excessive amount of drinking." He itemized eight scenes on eight different script pages in which "liquor is exhibited or consumed, or characters are shown under the influence." In an attempt to comply, MGM toned down some of the drinking, but one hardly notices.[3]

Breen and his fellow bluenoses lost the first round. *The Thin Man*, like Dashiell Hammett's best-selling novel, came right out of the Prohibition mind-set. Published immediately after the 1933 repeal of Prohibition, the novel is a shrine to the martini that does double duty as a primer on cures for the hangover. The movie picks up that cue. According to the screenwriter and biographer Gavin Lambert, the film's director, W. S. Van Dyke, came to work with a flask of gin in his pocket, from which he regularly sipped and which would be refilled a few times during the day.[4]

Our introduction to Nick and Nora comes about eleven minutes into the film, in a posh Manhattan hotel bar. Nora's entrance required her, elegantly turned out in a jaunty black hat and Dolly Tree–designed fur-collared suit, and laden with just-purchased Christmas packages, to charge in on Christmas Eve, calling "Asta" to the eager white wire-haired terrier who's yanking her on a leash as he sprints toward his goal: Nick. At the bar Nick has been demonstrating the proper way to shake a martini ("always shake to waltz time"). Dragged along by Asta, Nora tumbles to the floor, falling flat on her face in a perfect three-point landing, and then slides several feet as the packages go flying. Helped to her feet by two gallant men who rush to her aid, the unflappable Nora stands upright and approaches Nick without missing a beat. Her makeup still intact, she looks perfectly put together when Nick greets her with the words, "Hello, Sugar." Van Dyke shot this sequence unrehearsed and in one take, with the camera on the floor. To prepare Myrna, he'd merely asked her if she knew how to fall by tripping herself. Sure of her poise and trained dancer's grace, she allowed as how she could, even if she'd never done slapstick. She hit her mark with her chin on the first try (*BB*, 89).

A few minutes later Nora, who will wear an icepack on her head the next day, orders "five more," so she can match Nick in number of martinis consumed. "Line 'em up," she tells the barman, playfully indicating to Nick that she's not going to let him show her up. There's an element of cheerful rivalry between them.

The Thin Man has a witty script by the married screenwriters Albert Hackett and Frances Goodrich that allows Nick and Nora to spar and sparkle, introducing a buoyant romantic comedy dimension that the Hammett novel doesn't have. On the printed page Hammett's fictional hard-boiled sleuth and his heiress wife are plenty smart-mouthed, hard-drinking, fast-living, and with it, but they occupy rooms more dimly lit—more noirish—than their screen incarnations. In the novel they don't dress as stylishly, host as many parties, or go in for as much horseplay as MGM's Nick and Nora, though in the movie they're equally devoted and prone to the same affectionately sarcastic mutual needling, some of it directly quoted dialogue from the book. The movie script, though it closely follows the original, adds laugh lines (such as Nick's "he didn't come anywhere near my tabloids") and gives Asta the dog (who's not a terrier but a schnauzer in the book) more prominence. The movie tones down, but doesn't eliminate, the vicious sadism of the villainous Mimi (Minna Gombell), ex-wife of the missing Clyde Wynant; in the book she's prone to beating both of her adult children black and blue. And the Hammett novel lent Nick Charles an ethnic identity that got lost in Hollywood. The original Nick is a Greek-American whose real surname, Charalambides, had been whittled down by an Ellis Island immigration agent.[5]

The novel, not being subject to the restrictions of the Hays Office, is also racier, with Nora at one point asking Nick if he "got excited" when tussling with mendacious Mimi. Hammett's novel makes perfectly clear what is only vaguely hinted at in the film—that Nick and Mimi were briefly lovers some years back when they "killed" a couple of afternoons together, presumably in the sack. Nora's ability to shrug off Nick's casual extramarital philandering has discreet echoes in the movie script. When she catches Nick embracing young, pretty Dorothy Wynant (Maureen O'Sullivan) to comfort her, all Nora does is act surprised and make a face at him. Nora knows that Nick doesn't view her as the only attractive female on the planet, but in the movie she has less to forgive.[6]

The Hacketts, a witty, stylish pair of New Yorkers who lent to Nick and Nora much of their own dash and affection for one another, wrote scripts for the first three *Thin Man* pictures. Frances Goodrich's nephew David Goodrich makes the case that "the real" Nick and Nora are the

Charles-like Hacketts, but Hammett said he based the character of Nora on his own relationship with the playwright Lillian Hellman. Hammett had been a detective in San Francisco, and he was a notorious boozer, so there may be more than a little of Hammett in Nick. Hammett and Hellman were lovers, political allies, and drinking companions who liked to kid one another, and Hellman, like Nora Charles, often had urged her mate to return to working as a detective. Of course fictional and dramatic characters can come from diverse sources and are seldom photographic copies of actual people. They're composites. Lillian Hellman herself confessed that when Hammett gave her the manuscript of the novel *The Thin Man* to read and told her she was Nora, she first felt "it was nice to be Nora, married to Nick Charles. . . . But I was soon put back in my place. . . . Hammett said I was also the silly girl in the book [Dorothy Wynant] and the villainess," manipulative, lying, money-greedy Mimi.[7]

The Hacketts were initially underwhelmed by the prospect of adapting the novel *The Thin Man,* which had gone through six editions since its 1933 publication and had been serialized in *Redbook* magazine. Despite the book's popular success, Frances Goodrich wrote to her agent that she hoped the producer Hunt Stromberg would decide to scrap the idea of doing it as a movie. "I hope so. It stinks." She and Albert Hackett nonetheless completed a sterling script in three weeks, a script some consider even better than the novel. Van Dyke had told the Hacketts he wanted them to focus on the interplay between Nick and Nora, not the complicated plot about the missing inventor, Wynant; his engaged daughter, Dorothy; shady girlfriend, Julia; and grasping ex-wife, Mimi. "I don't care anything about the story," he told them; "just give me five scenes between those two people."[8]

Powell and Loy's light touch and flair helped the movie adaptation, which had been budgeted as a B picture and which no one at MGM expected to go anywhere, become a surprise smash hit. *The Thin Man* was nominated for Academy Awards for Best Picture, Best Actor, Best Adapted Screenplay, and Best Director; earned initial profits of more than $700,000; and became one of the most celebrated films of 1934. Although Myrna Loy was ignored in the nominations for the Oscar, she wasn't ignored by adoring fans, who took both Nick and Nora to their hearts and tended to think of Loy and Powell as two sides of the same shimmering coin. Theirs was a marriage that may have been "made in Culver City," as one observer put it, but it "played like heaven."[9]

Aware and considerate, Powell and Loy shared a droll sense of humor. There was plenty of joking on the *Thin Man* set. According to Loy,

"We got into the habit of clowning around, having a good time." Myrna claimed that the memorable scene where Powell shoots Christmas ornaments and party balloons with his new air gun began as off-camera antics. Powell often made jokes at his own expense. He pointed out, for instance, that he could never have become a for-real sleuth because "I have never been able to solve anything in my life, not even high school algebra. I have to call in the entire household to help me find a collar button. I am absolutely no good as a detective without a *Thin Man* script."[10]

Powell loved practical jokes. When Loy turned thirty-five, he sent her a funeral wreath for her birthday, adorned with a ribbon that read, "Be brave, dear." When fans elected her Queen of Hollywood, consort to Clark Gable's King, Powell sent what looked like a florist's box of long-stemmed roses; it turned out to contain bunches of sour grapes and dry leaves, accompanied by a note that offered "Love from William the Fourth," because Powell had come in fourth in the popularity poll conducted by Ed Sullivan that Gable won (*BB,* 146). On the day they were scheduled to plant their footprints in cement in the forecourt of Grauman's Chinese Theatre, Loy and Powell alarmed Sid Grauman by showing up on Hollywood Boulevard laughing, each sporting a pair of floppy swim flippers large enough for Bigfoot. Powell said they wanted to make a big impression.[11]

Quips were in style, on the screen and off. Whether it was a Cole Porter lyric, a Mae West zinger, or a Noel Coward witticism, catchy phrases and rapid repartee ruled during this golden age of both radio and high comedy. Without a script Myrna Loy wasn't much of a quipster. She was a laugher whose whole face lit up a room when she registered amusement. At times she felt intimidated by Arthur's witty friends—they included Dorothy Parker, George S. Kaufman, Herman Mankiewicz—fearing she couldn't keep up with their conversational volleys. With Powell, who became part of their social life, she could relax. She didn't feel called on to perform when off camera. She could simply enjoy his company.

The fact that Powell and Loy never got into bed together offscreen may help explain the durability and warmth of their professional partnership. As Myrna pointed out, if they'd become lovers or spouses, they inevitably would have fought now and then. As friends, they never did.

They did disagree on politics. Loy was a dedicated liberal Democrat and Powell a conservative Republican, when he was political at all. That they voted for different candidates didn't matter. They savored working together and missed one another during the sometimes-long gaps between films that paired them. He called her "Minnie" or "little Myrna," even though she was five-feet-six, and he knitted those thick brows over some of her more dubious career decisions. She called him Bill. In general Powell was more of a worrier than Loy. Prone to bouts of depression, he fretted about the possibility of losing fans by turning Nick and Nora into parents, which didn't happen until the third *Thin Man* outing, 1939's *Another Thin Man*. Powell thought the addition of Nick Jr. would remind fans of the passage of time and might spoil the devil-may-care magic between Nick and Nora, making them seem staid or stodgy. He knew that part of their appeal to Depression-weary Americans came from their aura of complete abandon. They live in a hotel suite, where they call room service when they want food, or in a mansion staffed by servants. Nora knows nothing of household drudgery. In *After the Thin Man,* suddenly hungry, she talks Nick into getting out of bed in the wee hours to cook her scrambled eggs. Well-heeled, high-living Nick and Nora obviously didn't have to worry about having another mouth to feed, and in the first two *Thin Man* movies they could shut the door to their posh Manhattan hotel apartment or palatial San Francisco digs whenever the spirit moved them and take off on some new chase, without having to first leave instructions for the nanny about when to feed the baby.

An actual marriage involving stars in Hollywood faced tough odds. Myrna, still single in the spring of 1934, when *The Thin Man* was shot, was twenty-eight years old and enmeshed in a passionate and stormy love relationship with Arthur Hornblow Jr. She wanted to be his wife but couldn't be until he divorced Juliette Crosby. Arthur felt comfortable living in sin; it was the thought of remarrying that made him break into a sweat.

Powell, forty-one, had lived through two divorces, the first of these quite difficult because it involved a son, Powell's only child. He blamed the failure of his brief second marriage to Carole Lombard on the competing pressures of two high-powered acting careers. During his current reversion to bachelorhood he was carrying on a prolonged, intense love affair—which the press called an engagement—with the gorgeous platinum blonde Jean Harlow. Harlow, who herself had three marriages behind her by age twenty-three, wanted nothing more than to wed Powell. He returned her affection but was wary of tying the knot with another young, ambitious, and much-in-the-spotlight Hollywood star so soon after his marriage to Lombard failed. It wasn't hard to come up with additional examples of derailed marriages between stars.

Loy and Powell became an established romantic comedy team because

The Thin Man hit the jackpot. MGM executives heeded the clamor for more Powell-and-Loy movies for one reason only: their pairing paid off at the till. "Is your cash register on a diet?" asked an ad in *Variety*, pitched to theater managers, that MGM ran immediately post–*Thin Man*. "Get ready for FAT box-office for Mr. and Mrs. *Thin Man*, the public's adored couple." Since Powell and Loy were stuck with each other for as long as they remained at MGM, it's a good thing they got along so well. They celebrated many birthdays together, since his fell on July 29, hers on August 2, and seem never to have exchanged a cross word.[12]

With all their gifts, neither Powell nor Loy suffered from swelled-head syndrome. Although Myrna wanted to be paid and esteemed as much as her costar, and in 1935 went on strike against MGM to prove it, her stance was "me too," not "me first." But if these two lacked selfishness or preening vanity, they possessed self-assurance. They came before the cameras as veterans, each of whom had served time during the silent era playing wicked foreigners. They each conveyed professionalism and complete ease. And why shouldn't they? By the time they took the cinema world by storm playing Nora and Nick Charles, Myrna Loy had appeared in eighty-one films and William Powell in close to sixty. These were two seasoned pros.

If the first big surprise about *The Thin Man* was how well it fared at the box office, the second had to do with the way the words *Thin Man* in the title were understood. In the Hammett detective novel and in MGM's early publicity for the film, they referred to quirky Clyde Wynant, played by Edward Ellis in the movie, who goes missing. The cinematographer James Wong Howe's shot of a scary elongated shadow of the walking Wynant, and a still of that long, menacing sidewalk shadow silhouette of a walking man in an overcoat and tipped fedora became an emblem of the film for MGM's *Thin Man* publicity campaign. Howe and Van Dyke quarreled about how many shadowy shots the film should have. Van Dyke and art director Cedric Gibbons wanted shadows everywhere, but Howe favored a naturalistic look and thought that the signature sidewalk silhouette lost impact if surrounded by countless other shadows. He said, "I wanted it stripped of shadows, except for one effect when [Wynant] walks and casts a long thin shadow on the sidewalk." The result was a compromise, with more shadows in the picture than the artful, independent-minded Howe wished but not as many as Van Dyke wanted.[13]

Despite the intended focus on Wynant, in no time the public began to assume that the Thin Man of the title referred to William Powell's slender, fedora-sporting Nick Charles, not Wynant. The studio ran with that assumption. In all the subsequent *Thin Man* films the title refers to Powell, and Myrna Loy's chicly slim Nora became Mrs. Thin Man. '

The Thin Man was the second film Loy and Powell made together, a rematch. They met while shooting *Manhattan Melodrama*, a Woody Van Dyke quickie completed in just over three weeks for $355,000, in which they play a couple who marry but almost part because of conflict over a friend, an imprisoned gangster played by Clark Gable. Produced by Selznick, *Manhattan Melodrama* became a big moneymaker for MGM and scored an Oscar for best story. The fact that "Most Wanted" gangster John Dillinger was gunned down by FBI agents outside Chicago's Biograph Theater after attending a screening of the picture no doubt helped it cash in at the box office. MGM was not above bragging in ads, "Dillinger Died to See This Picture!"

Manhattan Melodrama and *The Thin Man* shared a New York City setting and traded on that city's grit and glitter. They both featured tough guys, crime, and gold-digging dames, along with high-living swells. James Wong Howe, renowned for his mastery of low-key lighting, which creates moods by emphasizing the contrast between dark and light, shot both pictures. Woody Van Dyke directed the films in rapid succession in the spring of 1934. Originally scheduled for production before *Manhattan Melodrama*, *The Thin Man* in the end followed it by just a few weeks. Both were released in May of 1934.

When *Manhattan Melodrama* begins, Loy's character, Eleanor, is still involved with Blackie Gallagher, the high-rolling, gun-toting gambler played by Gable. Powell plays Blackie's lifelong friend Jim Wade, the upstanding lawyer Eleanor will marry. The camera tracks Eleanor and Jim on election night in New York City, when Wade wins his race to become district attorney. Eleanor, at the time of this Loy-meets-Powell scene, is the longtime mistress of Blackie. She has made it clear to Blackie that she's getting tired of life with a gangster. She'd happily trade the Cartier diamonds he has draped on her for a less flashy life on the straight and narrow. On this raucous night of celebrating Jim Wade's election, Eleanor bounds into Jim's moving sedan and nearly crash lands on Powell's lap. Powell exclaims in character, "Pardon me if I seem to intrude." Off camera, seconds later, his first-ever words to the actress who would prove to be his ideal costar and long-term movie mate were a courtly, mocking echo of Stanley greeting Dr. Livingstone: "Miss Loy, I presume?"

From that initial scene together, Powell would remember, "a curious thing passed between us, a feeling of rhythm, complete understanding, an instinct for how one could bring out the best in the other." Powell had shared the screen with several actresses—he was too much the gentleman to name names—who *didn't* connect with him, actresses who, he said, "seemed to be separated from me by a plate glass window" (*BB,* 88, 92). With Myrna there was instant connection, no plate glass.

Manhattan Melodrama is the only film William Powell ever made with Clark Gable, who'd been at MGM since 1930 and had established himself as a major box-office draw, especially among women. He was *the* male sex symbol of the 1930s, occupying in that decade the spot vacated by Rudolph Valentino with his untimely death in 1926. Gable and Powell got along just fine. They shared off-camera laughs while *Manhattan Melodrama* was being filmed, but they were congenial colleagues rather than close friends. As individuals and male types they couldn't have been more different. Unlike Gable, Powell didn't consider himself a lady-killer. After playing a gigolo in *Ladies Man* in 1931 he demurred, "Someone like Valentino should have played this part. Not Bill Powell." His tastes were more highfalutin than those of rough-and-ready Gable, a high school dropout who'd worked as an oil-rigger and telegraph linesman. Powell admitted that he had a reputation around the studios for being "a bit of a fuss pot," someone who "always wants to dot every 'i' and cross every 't.'" He'd been known to lavish time on the just-right arrangement of a silk square in a chest pocket.[14]

Powell saw himself as a pigeon, not a peacock. He believed his God-given looks were nothing special and that he had to make up for that deficit by donning what he called "fancy tail feathers." He wouldn't dream of making an appearance without a tie, much less without a shirt. Powell's best male friends tended to be other stars, fellow film actors with whom he'd worked. The elegant, theater-trained Brit Ronald Colman was a Powell buddy, as was the sleek-haired former D. W. Griffith favorite Richard Barthelmess. Gable, an outdoorsman, preferred hanging out with men not connected with the film world who'd go hunting or fishing with him. When it came to palship within the Hollywood movie industry, he picked athletic, motorcycle-riding Victor Fleming, who'd directed him opposite Jean Harlow in *Red Dust.*[15]

Powell and Gable would end up competing for 1934's Best Actor Academy Award, Gable for his work as Peter Warne in *It Happened One Night*—made when MGM agreed to loan him to Columbia Pictures, possibly to bring him down a peg—and Powell for *The Thin Man.* Gable won.

As Louis B. Mayer saw it, Gable and Powell were opposites who wouldn't usually attract the same woman. Gable was the square-shouldered hunk, an instinctive man of action, with an untamed cowlick and a waggish grin enhanced by dimples and recently installed false teeth. Louis B. Mayer once told a writer who was scripting lines for Gable to "write a story from the neck down. Action only. . . . He doesn't have to say anything that means anything." Compare cerebral, white-collar Powell, a man of many well-chosen words; a skinny six-foot beanpole; a slope-shouldered, citified, and silver-tongued baritone. (Gable spoke with a mid-western twang in the tenor range.) A sophisticate who'd been to Paris and took to it, Powell had a bit of the dandy about him. With Gable the whole idea was to make his most ardent fans imagine him in the raw.[16]

Loy's talent for partnership allowed her to draw on one side of herself when she faced Powell, another side with Gable. She excelled at picking up and answering cues, falling into step, "listening" with her entire body. As a kid she'd practiced social dancing in the living room, sometimes being led by her friend Lou, sometimes taking the lead herself. In *Manhattan Melodrama*, when she and Gable have a scene together, Gable dominates, while keeping his emotional distance. Love scenes with him were difficult to act, Loy claimed, because Gable was so protective of his macho image that he was afraid to show any feelings that could make him look soft or vulnerable (*BB,* 88). His character, Blackie, likewise shrugs off his girlfriend's rejection, never revealing that he hurts. He's more visibly pent-up in his two-shot scenes with Powell, especially the concluding death chamber sequence with Blackie gamely marching off to his own execution, than he ever is with Loy's Eleanor.

Loy also maintained that since Gable liked for-real, tough women (he was pals with unaffected Harlow but couldn't bear the diva airs of Jeanette MacDonald), when facing him onscreen, she had to play it rough. But her feistiness isn't evident in her early scenes with Gable in *Manhattan Melodrama*. Here she's mostly willing to accept his rules, asserting herself only when she decides she's an old-fashioned girl after all ("Maybe I want to wear last year's hat"), ready to trade in her life as a gangster's moll for stability sealed with a wedding band and a home. Blackie, she eventually decides, is just "a little boy playing with a big box of matches," and she wants a crack at settling down with a more grownup mate. Powell's Jim Wade fits that description.

With Powell and Loy there is more equality, more emotional connection, and a buoyant sense of improvisation. At their corner table at the Cotton Club, pounding mallets on the table to celebrate New Year's Eve, they display some of the spontaneous and infectious playfulness that would become their trademark as a team. Parties and celebrations keep turning up in their films, but in this outing Powell has many somber, thoughtful moments. He had a dark, "black Irish," side, perhaps, Myrna conjectured, inherited from his mother, which gets full play in his impersonation of Jim Wade.

While directing *Manhattan Melodrama*, Van Dyke picked up on the chemistry between Loy and Powell. The way they lit each other up made him think these two natural celebrants might click as Nick and Nora Charles in *The Thin Man*, a picture Powell had agreed to play in before jumping from Warner Bros. to MGM.

Van Dyke, convinced that "a murder mystery could be turned into laughable entertainment," brought Hammett's detective novel to the attention of Sam Marx, head of MGM's story department, who bought the rights for $22,000. Van Dyke believed the movie would awaken the public "to the truth that romance actually can exist happily between a man and wife who aren't newlyweds."[17]

Making daily married life look like fun, and romantic fun to boot, hadn't happened before in movies, which in the past had depicted spouses, wives in particular, either as colorless, hemmed-in drags or embattled victims, vexed by cheating, jealousy, and other forms of misery. A wedding often provided the finish point to a story—usually a story about lovers younger than Nick and Nora, as it did for Myrna Loy and Ramon Novarro at the conclusion of *The Barbarian*. Showcasing a couple who've been married a while but who remain loving, sexually interested in each other, and delightful company to boot broke conventions both cinematic and literary. It also pleased the censors, since the Production Code pushed marriage, banning illicit sex from the screen. But having married protagonists worried producers. When a happy and legally wed couple gets the spotlight, the thinking went, where was the conflict supposed to come from, and how could the pair be made compelling to an audience? In *The Thin Man* the mystery of Wynant's disappearance and the subsequent murder of his mistress, Julia Wolf, supply some of the crowd-pleasing answer, but the appeal of Loy and Powell provides the lion's share.

Van Dyke championed Loy's casting as Nora Charles, but Louis B. Mayer had his doubts. He didn't see Myrna Loy as a comic actress. Van Dyke told Mayer that he'd auditioned Myrna for the role of Nora by pushing her into his Brentwood swimming pool, and she'd aced the test, displaying the game spirit he wanted for Nora (*BB*, 88). Since he'd previously directed Myrna in *Penthouse* and *Manhattan Melodrama,* he didn't really need to push her into the pool. He already knew she had what it took. The swimming pool story was probably a bit of embellishment used to persuade Mayer, and it worked. Mayer gave in, telling Van Dyke he could go ahead and use Loy in the Hammett picture so long as she'd be free to start her next film three weeks later. "One-Take" Van Dyke won MGM's gratitude by bringing in the low-budget film in record time. From the first scene to the final shot, Van Dyke recalled, he managed to complete *The Thin Man* in just sixteen days; most films—those not directed by Van Dyke—took about a month to shoot. The head of operations at MGM, Eddie Mannix, reported it took eighteen days, which is still amazing, at a bargain-basement cost of $231,000.[18]

Van Dyke eased Myrna's ascent to MGM's upper ranks by telling Mayer that the studio had been misusing Miss Loy, that she was headed for stardom if assigned the right parts; she should be playing characters closer to her real self: fun-loving ladies, endearing, flirtatious, and well bred. Van Dyke had first directed Loy in *Penthouse,* where as Gertie Waxted she starts off as a crook's kept woman who admits, "I'm not even a lady." But by the closing frame she *is* a lady, has in fact become the wife of a rich lawyer. Loy had spent the first part of her career playing exotic vixens and wanton hussies. *Penthouse* marks the exact point where in the eyes of MGM she rises, elevating both her social position and her mood. *The Thin Man* takes her even higher. She's an heiress who can fund cross-country train trips and long-term hotel stays for both herself and Nick. She decisively joins the enviable ranks of high comedy's bantering swells. Because of her identification with the Nora role, she will most often be cast as a well-heeled bantering *wife*. Here she'll make it big, and here she'll mostly remain. At MGM her upper-class status, once established, became set in concrete. When she once went to Louis B. Mayer with the idea of playing a household drudge based on a character in a book she'd read and liked, Mayer told her that he'd never consent to such casting: "You're a lady in my book, Myrna, and you always gotta be a lady," he insisted; no floor scrubbing for the new, improved Myrna Loy (*BB,* 116).

Because Nora brought the money to the Charles marriage, the balance of power tilts in an unorthodox direction. Her father bequeathed her stocks, a lumber mill, and a narrow-gauge railroad. It's Nora's wealth, which Nick manages, that has freed Nick to give up being a New York detective and for the past four years to devote himself to a life of leisurely drinking, high spending, and generally living it up in California. When

Nora urges him to resume his career by taking on the Wynant case when they are visiting New York, he tells her, "I haven't the time. I'm much too busy seeing that you don't lose any of the money I married you for." It's been a sweet life, and he's in no hurry to give it up to return to his old job as a gumshoe, though he's still on friendly terms with lots of hoodlums he once helped nab. They have names like Face or Stutsy and toss around lines about being sent up the river or spending time in stir. Nora is always politely amused at these plug-uglies, receiving them at the Charles's hotel apartment with good-humored hospitality. Joseph Breen and the PCA had protested the presence of so many con and ex-con characters. He was trying to discourage films that glorified gangsters and complained after reading Hammett's book that its "general tone is one of crime, deceit and sexual immorality. The characters are a heterogeneous collection of criminals and psychopaths." If Breen had a problem, Nora didn't. She wasn't a snob or a moralist, and she found the "dese" and "dem" crowd entertaining.[19]

Nora doesn't just urge Nick to take on the Wynant case; she wants to be a partner in helping him solve it. She likes the adrenalin rush detective work provides and can't bear being left out of the action. One scripted scene that was either cut or never filmed had Nora disguise herself as a man so that she can sneak into Wynant's plant and help Nick find the murdered Wynant's body, or maybe score by finding it herself. A still photo of Loy in drag, costumed for this scene, is in the MGM photo files. A scene that got both shot and retained shows her trying to horn in on Nick's act when he and police detective Guild (Nat Pendleton) get into a cab that will take them on an exploratory mission and Nora tries to join them. Instead, Nick tricks her into boarding another cab, telling the driver to take her to Grant's Tomb. Here, giving her the slip, Nick treats Nora like a pesky kid. She shrugs it off. The accepting, uncomplaining movie-Nora doesn't explode in anger the way Hammett's Nora does in the novel, when Nick belittles her theories about the murderer: "Don't be so damned patronizing," she snaps.[20]

Nora has a strong personality and a mind of her own that urges her to go off alone occasionally, but she's essentially a partner, not a soloist, and she avoids confrontation. She is defined by her relationship to Nick. The offscreen Myrna Loy, like Nora, tended to be a man's woman, content to let others manage her money and reluctant to scold. The all-important difference was that Loy had focused on a performing career since her teens and from age eighteen had paid her own way. She didn't need a man to support her, but her private emotions now concentrated on her cherished

Arthur and her consuming desire to marry him. Referring to the elusive prize of marriage, she told Gladys Hall, "Santa Claus hasn't put that priceless gift in my stocking yet." Marriage had become the Holy Grail, the fulfillment, she thought, of her dreams. No matter how often she'd played the Other Woman in movies (most recently in *When Ladies Meet*), in her heart, she revealed, "I am all on the side of the wife."[21]

She continued her long-term friendships with Betty Black and Lou MacFarlane, which dated from school days; both were now married. At MGM she was surrounded by a staff of female helpers to whom she was most loyal, generous, grateful, and affectionate; she paid for their hospital stays if they got sick and bought their babies layettes. Her stand-in, Shirley Hughes, went to Hawaii with her and was for a time dating Myrna's brother, David. And she got along well with Maureen O'Sullivan, who played Dorothy Wynant in *The Thin Man* and also had appeared with Myrna in *Skyline* and *A Connecticut Yankee*. But these days Myrna wasn't investing her deepest emotions in friendships with other women. She even made the astonishing statement, in a newspaper interview, that only men had helped advance her career. She was clearly thinking of directors who gave her breaks, like Van Dyke, Ned Griffith, and Mamoulian, or even of her fellow actor Lowell Sherman, who allowed her to sneak into that first Warner Bros. frame on the set of *Satan in Sables*. Women in the movie industry, she implied, were rivals competing for the best roles rather than helpmates. She made an exception for Natacha Rambova, who provided her first movie part. But that was it, by her reckoning. "If women had banded together to help each other, the story of Hollywood might have been different," she concluded sadly. But what about her early palship with Joan Crawford when they were thrown together as nearly anonymous chorines in *Pretty Ladies*? What about Minna Wallis, who got Myrna that all-important first contract at Warners?[22]

Loy and Powell hit their stride playing smart New Yorkers, but in 1934 Myrna Loy had yet to set foot in Manhattan. Powell as a young man had lived there for several years as a drama student and stage actor, but he spent his teens in the Midwest and had to be tutored in elocution at drama school in order to shed his Kansas City pronunciation.

Thirteen years older than Loy, Powell began his life in the 1890s and never lost his hybrid air of an aesthete who grew up on alternating doses of Shakespeare and Mack Sennett. Self-mocking, courtly, and a touch fey, he was at the same time an inspired physical comedian in the slapstick tradition. An adroit tennis player, he learned fencing in high school and could negotiate a mean pratfall. During comic high jinks in which Loy sometimes played the straight man, he often ended up on his rear. Those tumbles he took in movies never dented his reputation as a worldly gentleman. He conveyed upper-class, British-inflected gentility, even if Powell's background was solidly middle class and American. His careful attention to the niceties of grooming; his perfectly tailored suits, spotless cuffs, and collars; his orotund voice curled around well-turned phrases; the deferential way he bowed his head slightly when being introduced— all would have helped him gain entry at any elite, leather-chair-and-brandy-snifter men's club.

Born in Pittsburgh, he moved with his family to Kansas City and attended high school there, playing Malvolio in the drama club's *Twelfth Night.* Powell's accountant father and musical Irish American mother wanted their only child to attend law school, but acting Shakespeare and the experience of working as an usher at the Kansas City opera house had infected him with theatrical fever. His parents, however, refused to back his ambition to become an actor. A great aunt came to his rescue after he dropped out of college, agreeing to provide a loan to help finance his attendance at the American Academy of Dramatic Arts in New York. After that, Powell launched his stage career in touring stock companies and on Broadway, where, now a married man with a young son, he came to the attention of the film director Albert Parker.[23]

When he began appearing in movies in 1922, Powell was considered not handsome enough to qualify as a romantic leading man. Instead, he played heavies: a henchman of Professor Moriarty in *Sherlock Holmes* or the evil Tito in *Romola,* a 1924 Lillian Gish film for which nineteen-year-old Myrna Williams, just before she entered movies and changed her last name, danced in a prologue at Grauman's Egyptian Theatre. Powell's flexible and cultivated baritone became his calling card in talkies and helped him move out of bad-guy roles and start playing heroes. He came to be associated with sophistication. *Suave* was an adjective so often applied to him that he got tired of hearing it. Several years before he scored as Nick Charles he had become renowned for portraying another debonair detective, Philo Vance, first at Paramount and then Warner Bros.

Two Selznicks, sons of the movie man Lewis Selznick and both movers and shakers in 1930s Hollywood, helped Powell become a star: the agent Myron and his younger producer brother, David O. The brothers' pooled intelligence, drive, and savvy expedited Powell's climb to the top rung, a stratospheric ascent Myrna Loy had yet to achieve. Even after costarring

with Clark Gable and being cast as Nora Charles, Myrna was still officially listed as a featured MGM actress rather than a star and was being
paid accordingly.

Myron Selznick, a driven, two-fisted, usually inebriated character who
after a spell as a producer became Hollywood's first "power agent," nego-
tiated the $6,000 salary for Powell at Warner Bros. When slumping ticket
sales forced Warners to cut that figure down to a mere $4,000 a week,
Powell said no dice. Warners freed him from his contract, and Myron
wheeled and dealed on Powell's behalf, signing him to work for David O.
Selznick's unit at MGM.[24]

David Selznick brought Powell to MGM at a time when the studio
badly needed to enlarge its pool of leading men. Loew's executives had
to be persuaded about the wisdom of hiring him, since the brass in New
York, in particular the head honcho, Nick Schenck, considered him a has-
been. But both Selznick brothers believed in Powell's potential value to
the Culver City giant, and they prevailed. Powell's deal with MGM came
through in time for the opening days of shooting *Manhattan Melodrama*
in March of that all-important year, 1934.

Powell had to take a further cut in pay, to a mere $3,000 a week, when
he moved to MGM, but what he temporarily lost in salary, he would
gain in prestige, since MGM, with its stable of top stars, its twenty-two
soundstages, and its reputation for gleaming, gorgeously mounted productions, ranked highest among all the studios. Powell quickly redeemed
himself, winning a ten-film, $500,000 contract. He would remain a star
at MGM for the next twenty-five years, retiring from that studio at the
top of his game in 1953, with a fat pension.

Less lucky in career matters, undervalued, and not as much of a fighter
for contract perks as Powell, though she was every bit as winningly expressive, just as hard working, and more beautiful to boot, Myrna Loy
would leave MGM and begin freelancing in 1945. Only *after* playing
Nora Charles did she part company with Minna Wallis, the beloved but
less powerful agent who got her started in pictures, and move up to become the client of Myron Selznick, the actors' representative whom the
big boys recognized as one of their own. Arthur had introduced Myrna
to Myron Selznick, and Minna, gracefully bowing out, had agreed that
Selznick would best serve her. Loy's salary, for which Minna Wallis had
fought hard, was $1,500 a week, half of Powell's $3,000. A year after
The Thin Man, her annual salary was still only $34,208 (about $530,000
in 2009), compared to Powell's $66,666. Mae West at Paramount took
in a whopping $480,833, making her not only the highest paid star in

Hollywood but the highest paid woman in America. When it came to salaries, Myrna Loy in 1934 wasn't even a contender.[25]

The producer Hunt Stromberg joined Van Dyke in Myrna's corner. Producers held the power cards at MGM in the 1930s, and Stromberg, a Kentucky-born former sports writer and publicist, headed the unit that produced most of Myrna Loy's MGM pictures, including *Penthouse,* four *Thin Man* pictures, *The Prizefighter and the Lady,* and *Wife vs. Secretary.* Tall and tousled, with thick hair, "restless blue eyes," and glasses with round, black-rimmed lenses, Stromberg didn't waste time fussing with his appearance. "One could tell his luncheon menu by looking at his tie," Sam Marx cracked. But fussing over casting choices—that he did. He also enjoyed an excellent rapport with his writers, a group that at various times included the Hacketts, F. Scott Fitzgerald, Anita Loos, and Dorothy Parker. The Hacketts reported that "with Stromberg, you had a real participation in casting," and you also enjoyed a respect rarely accorded screenwriters in Hollywood. Stromberg honored the words writers had put on the pages and would go to the mat to resist the attempts of others to revise them.[26]

Frances Goodrich and Albert Hackett, like Nick and Nora, had a low tolerance for boredom. After writing three *Thin Man* scripts, they felt they'd milked the characters to the max and wanted out. "We were getting morning sickness then, and crying in the typewriter, so we just left and went back to New York." In order to keep from being tempted to create yet more sequels, they even proposed killing off Nick and Nora at the end of the first sequel, *After the Thin Man,* but Hunt Stromberg wouldn't hear of that. The producer knew a cash cow when he saw one.[27]

Powell and Loy had created icons. On Nick and Nora's enduring appeal their own futures—their salaries, opportunities, and fame—would partly rely. But they, too, felt that without the Hacketts and Van Dyke, the series headed downhill. Once Nick and Nora became parents, Nick started calling her "Mommy," and she ceased to be the carefree Nora of *The Thin Man.* The fifth in the series, *The Thin Man Goes Home,* endowed Nick with conventional and proper small-town American parents whose disapproval of his drinking temporarily converts him into an imbiber of apple cider. By 1947, when the last of their Thin Man films, *Song of the Thin Man,* was shot, they knew that the series had lost its fizz. The original spontaneity had long since evaporated. Tired jokes about martinis and an obnoxiously cute Asta in the last of the series made a flat substitute for the original effervescence, although the film does have some passable 1940s jazz and a steamy performance by Gloria Grahame. MGM was slow to realize, but finally did, that the war had changed everything, including tastes and modes in comedy.

Woody Van Dyke, whose directorial chops had made all the difference on the first runaway hit, and who helmed the next three, died in 1943, at the age of fifty-three. "Van Dyke certainly didn't take care of himself," writes Rudy Behlmer, who edited Van Dyke's journal. "He was a chain smoker, a consumer of endless cups of coffee during the day and of many glasses of gin during the evenings." Commissioned as a captain and later a major in the marines, Van Dyke was crushed when told in the early 1940s that he no longer qualified for active duty. Myrna felt that MGM worked Van Dyke to death (*BB*, 115). He'd directed thirty-two films between 1930 and 1940, and his whirlwind shooting style had become obsessive.[28]

Hunt Stromberg, the distinguished, high-salaried, workaholic producer of the first four *Thin Man* films, and of more than a hundred additional MGM films, had begun taking morphine because of chronic back pain, but the drug was prescribed by an unscrupulous doctor. Stromberg became addicted, quarreled with Mayer about his contract, and left MGM in February of 1942. "We couldn't work with him when he was on drugs," the Hacketts privately revealed. He continued producing independently, with United Artists distribution, for another decade, raking in the bucks. He lived until 1968.[29]

Dashiell Hammett, who started it all, burned out early. His drinking, gambling, and carousing took their toll. He had trouble writing fiction—*The Thin Man* was his fifth and final published novel—and by May of 1938, when he was trying to complete the outline of the story for *Another Thin Man,* suffered a breakdown in his suite at the Beverly Wilshire Hotel. He had lost a great deal of weight and grown ill and weak. Frances Goodrich, by then a close friend, helped him pay his hotel bill and, with her husband, put him on a plane to New York. Lillian Hellman met it with an ambulance, which took him to Lenox Hill hospital.[30]

The Hacketts had been stalled in their efforts to complete the screenplay for *Another Thin Man* because Hammett was in no condition to provide the plot situations and motives they needed to move forward on their screenplay. They ultimately had to finish without him. Although Hammett had made a lot of money in Hollywood, he'd gone through most of it and was in debt. At the end of 1938 MGM suspended Hammett's contract.[31]

A few years earlier, Myrna had spent an evening with Hammett and others after he, she, and Powell all took part in a broadcast of excerpts from *The Thin Man* on a radio program hosted by Louella Parsons. After the show, Powell, Jean Harlow, Hammett, and Myrna gathered at Arthur's place, where Hammett quickly got drunk and, while speaking constantly of Lillian Hellman, made a pass at Myrna, "lunging and pawing" at her until Arthur informed him that he was looking ill and might want to go home (*BB,* 123).

MGM subsequently rejected Hammett's proposal for a *Thin Man* sequel based on the character Herbert Macaulay, the murderer in the novel. Hammett was proposing that in this sequel Macaulay would get out of prison and return to San Francisco—in drag—in pursuit of Mimi and her strange son Gilbert. MGM wouldn't touch it.[32]

Hammett sold the rights to the characters of *The Thin Man* to MGM for $40,000 in 1937. For him Nick and Nora had long since lost their magic, though they continued to pay some bills. Hammett would revisit them to write scripts for many episodes of the two-year television *Thin Man* series, which began in 1957 and starred Peter Lawford and Phyllis Kirk. Those reliable meal tickets, Nick and Nora, by now really got on his nerves. He wrote of them to Lillian Hellman: "No one ever invented a more insufferably smug pair of characters."[33]

The public disagreed. Nick and Nora Charles, a.k.a. Powell and Loy, took on a mythic life of their own. To devotees of Hollywood's Golden Age they are as indelible and as inseparable as Mickey and Minnie Mouse. Onscreen they still launch helium-balloons of delight.

CHAPTER 9

Myrna Loy vs. MGM

A Hollywood columnist named Robbin Coons visited the set of *After the Thin Man* in November of 1936. By then, Myrna Loy was nearing the peak of her popularity. A *Motion Picture Herald* survey had placed her box-office drawing power above that of Irene Dunne, Marlene Dietrich, and John Barrymore but well behind the likes of Garbo and Mae West.[1]

At the time of Coons's MGM visit the press kept whispering that William Powell and his constant companion, Jean Harlow, might be tying the knot sometime soon. Because of Harlow's closeness to Powell, Myrna had gotten to know her well. Myrna treasured her. Like most people who became acquainted with Jean Harlow by spending time with the actual person rather than the celluloid image, she responded to Jean's combination of innocence and frank sensuality, her unaffected manner, humor, and warmth.

Much of *After the Thin Man* was filmed on location in San Francisco, where Powell, Loy, and Harlow all stayed at the St. Francis Hotel, but the particular sequence being filmed when Coons visited—the movie's opening scene showing Nick sneaking drinks in their Pullman drawing room compartment while Nora packs her lingerie before getting off the train in downtown San Francisco—was shot on the MGM lot in Culver City.

"On stage 12 today William Powell and Myrna Loy are taking up where they left off nearly three years ago [in *The Thin Man*]," Coons wrote for the benefit of his Hollywood-besotted readers. "Detective Nick

Charles and wife have returned to San Francisco for their first scene to find their home a New Year's Eve bedlam. Nick, so thoroughly at home in New York, now is in a hot-bed of in-laws," a reference to Nora's San Francisco kin, a tribe of boring, snobbish, dilapidated blue bloods Nick can barely tolerate. Coons continued:

> [Director W. S.] Van Dyke signals a move over to Stage 24. He finds that his set isn't there yet. It is being utilized for some tests for *Parnell.* . . . Van Dyke yells to production manager Arthur Rose: "Hey, Rose, where's my set?"
> Through the great stage door a truck backs in bearing an open section of a sleeping car drawing room on a portable platform. Eight men strain to pull the camera up an incline to position; property men dash in with the Charles' luggage.[2]

The blow-by-blow account was meant to add to the orchestrated buzz MGM's publicity department wanted to create about *After the Thin Man.*

At MGM the vogue of *The Thin Man* meant that engines immediately began revving for a sequel reusing Dashiell Hammett's seductive mix of hard-boiled characters, wit, and mystery. The second Thin Man movie, which took several years to mount, would ideally boast another script spiked with Hackett and Goodrich's zingers, propelled by Van Dyke's full-speed-ahead directorial style. Most important, the sequel needed the sparks kindled onscreen by Hollywood's reigning make-believe Mr. and Mrs. America, William Powell and Myrna Loy, who simply had to be tailed by Asta, the scene-stealing white wired-hair terrier first portrayed by a dog named Skippy. (There were several Astas over the years.) The threesome—elegant, bantering couple plus winsome, mischievous dog—had become emblems of a brand, like Coca-Cola. Their likenesses, on display everywhere, could not be escaped, unless you stayed home day and night with the shades drawn.

Skippy, whose name was changed to Asta, had become a star in his own right and would soon be fought over as "Mr. Smith" by warring screwball spouses Irene Dunne and Cary Grant in *The Awful Truth* and as "George" digging up dinosaur bones in *Bringing Up Baby.* Asta's favorite fireplug, however, was banned in 1936 from subsequent *Thin Man* movies because Joseph Breen objected to all the dog toilet jokes in *After the Thin Man.* Well, he had a point. Not that moral sensibilities are outraged, but rather that the repeated cute joke overstays its welcome.[3]

For Myrna Loy, who had certainly appeared in urbane, dialogue-driven comedies prior to *The Thin Man,* but whose celebrity as Nora Charles sealed and embossed her claim on lead parts in such pictures, the hunt was on not just for additional Nora Charles outings but for more roles that showcased her now-acclaimed gifts both for acting in light comedy and for portraying likable wives.

Her stock, if not her paycheck, had risen at MGM, partly owing to her own soaring popularity and partly to flukes. She now rated a deluxe dressing room with her name painted in gold on the door. Two leading Metro actresses had departed the studio, creating vacancies at the top level. Marie Dressler died, leaving a big hole in many hearts, including Myrna's. And Marion Davies, along with the rest of Cosmopolitan Productions, decamped for Warner Bros. when head honcho William Randolph Hearst, Davies's lover and protector, had a falling out with L. B. Mayer over who would play Marie Antoinette in an upcoming Thalberg production. (Norma Shearer won the part.) Mayer went on the lookout for properties that could become "Myrna Loy pictures," especially any with the potential to be William Powell vehicles as well.

Of course, even a studio capable of producing films with the assembly-line speed, precision, and efficiency of MGM's Culver City plant couldn't come up with product right away. Scripts had to be written, budgets planned, contracts signed, talent lined up, sets designed and built; the calendars of much-in-demand players and crew had to be cleared of rival commitments before the cameras could roll on *After the Thin Man*. Powell, milking his immense fan base, signed a loan-out agreement with RKO, while in-demand Loy costarred with Spencer Tracy, Warner Baxter, Cary Grant, Robert Montgomery, and Clark Gable, as well as with Powell in two non–*Thin Man* features before reprising her role alongside him as Nora Charles.

After the Thin Man wouldn't be released until December of 1936, almost two and a half years after the original *Thin Man* opened. MGM backed it with a huge ad campaign and spent wildly on this spin-off: $673,000 compared to $231,000 for the first *Thin Man*. The studio was doing all the things it hadn't bothered to do for the original, which had self-ignited in its relatively low-rent corner nonetheless. *After the Thin Man* would yield profits of more than $1.5 million, doubling the grosses *The Thin Man* achieved on its first run.

In *After the Thin Man* the Hackett and Goodrich script and Van Dyke's direction succeed in completing the action set in motion back in 1934, as if they were finishing a sentence that had been left hanging in midair. Even Asta's leash matches the one in the last scene in *The Thin Man*. The Hammett story zeroes in on the already-established class difference between Nick and Nora, emphasizing Nora's swanky but desiccated aristocratic roots and Nick's preference for the far more colorful and down-to-earth company of boxers, boozers, and ex-cons. A boyish-looking Jimmy Stewart was put to work playing a villainous cad who's in love, in a twisted way, with Nora's cousin Selma (Elissa Landi). The character actor Sam Levene, fresh from his Broadway stage outing in *Three Men on a Horse,* installed himself as a series fixture playing Lieutenant Abrams, head of the homicide squad.

To film on location, Powell and Loy arrived in San Francisco on the Sunset Limited, accompanied by Jean Harlow, who according to the *San Francisco Chronicle* announced that she was serving as the official chaperone. She denied that she and Powell were on their honeymoon. Every detail of the stars' appearance merited comment: "Miss Loy's costume was a navy blue tailored suit, a dusty pink blouse, a saucy little blue hat, and sables. Miss Harlow wore a sports outfit of a lighter and more vivid blue. Her hat, gloves, bag and shoes were bright yellow suede, her furs a double . . . fox scarf. Powell wore tan slacks and a checked coat." The Southern Pacific train depot at Third and Townsend, the paper announced, would serve as the location for the next three days of moviemaking.[4]

San Francisco, where Dashiell Hammett had worked during his days as a private eye, came through as a picturesque backdrop, providing the requisite fabulous views, a few of them contrived. Nob Hill mansions don't really overlook Coit Tower, but never mind. Making the most of the scenery, Van Dyke at the same time had to battle low-hanging fogs that played havoc with his lighting. He contended with crowds of noisy, overly enthusiastic locals who came to gape during shooting on the steps of the de Young mansion on California Street. "We did succeed," Van Dyke remembered, "in filming most of our exteriors up and down San Francisco's throbbing streets and around its historic landmarks, with the mighty Golden Gate [still under construction at the time] and the [just completed] San Francisco–Oakland Bay bridges, symbols of the new and greater San Francisco, constantly in the background."[5]

After the Thin Man does the best it can, which is pretty well, considering that it's a sequel. But as Woody Van Dyke knew, first tries generally win any freshness test. "There is no formula by which a true natural can be duplicated," agreed Otis Ferguson in reviewing *After the Thin Man.* The humorist Irvin S. Cobb uttered what may be the final words about the inevitable deficiencies of sequels. "A sequel," he told Myrna, "is like a second helping of casaba" (*BB,* 142). If only MGM had been listening.[6]

Myrna already had completed principal shooting on one film, *Stamboul Quest,* which was ready for editing and retakes just as *The Thin Man* made the rounds for its first run. *Stamboul Quest* is no romantic comedy, though it provides romance aplenty, and in it Loy portrays a single woman, not a wife. Supposedly based on the memoirs of a drug-addicted former World War I–era German spy known as Annemarie Lesser, who, according to Myrna, was still alive and residing in a Swiss sanatorium when the film was made, *Stamboul Quest* turned Myrna Loy into the mysterious, possibly sinister, and definitely German Fräulein Doktor who falls in love with an American medical student, improbably played by the jowly thirty-five-year-old Irishman George Brent. *Stamboul Quest* was MGM's attempt to cash in on the popularity of previous hits featuring star actresses portraying glamorous shadowy ladies: Greta Garbo's spy turn as Mata Hari and Marlene Dietrich's secret agent picture *Dishonored*. Loy's Fräulein Doktor prowls around Constantinople in a black cape and a huge slant-brimmed hat. "Look for the woman spy in the most popular of luxury cafes," Cecilia Ager teased in "Going Places," her *Variety* column. "She will always be the most conspicuous lady in the joint. It is a fallacy, the spy picture explains, to think that a spy wants to go unnoticed." George Brent, borrowed from Warners, made a satisfactory but uncharismatic leading man, and the estimable Herman J. Mankiewicz, screenwriter for *Dinner at Eight* and later coauthor of the script for *Citizen Kane*, got credit for penning the formulaic screenplay. Donald Ogden Stewart wrote a treatment for it in 1933 that seems to have gotten lost in the shuffle.[7]

Stamboul Quest did fairly well at the box office, earning a profit of $235,000 and winning markets both foreign and domestic, although a movie theater manager in Nampa, Idaho, provincially complained, "Not one person in 50 knows what Stamboul means, or gives a darn if you tell them. Not one person in two knows what Quest means. The producers should rediscover this United States, with its one hundred thirty millions who are not reading decadent novelists." So much for attempting to import to the Corn Belt cosmopolitan cloak-and-dagger types who sip Turkish coffee on the Orient Express.[8]

Loy and Powell were reunited in *Evelyn Prentice*, released seven months after *The Thin Man*. This film was also a reunion for Loy and the director William K. Howard, one of her favorites since *Transatlantic* made waves among the critics and turned Myrna Loy into an elegant and tony American wife. The melodramatic Lenore Coffee script used those old familiar standbys—adultery, blackmail, courtroom reversals, murder—as plot hooks. Except for one goofy scene wherein the Prentice family does leg lifts together on the carpeted floor, *Evelyn Prentice* submerged the comic gifts of the stars, asking them to play it straight as an upscale, workaholic lawyer and his lovely and loving but neglected Park Avenue spouse. This was Loy's first outing as a mother (to a daughter played by Cora Sue Collins), and the two generations act enough heart-tugging scenes together to qualify the film as a weeper.

Evelyn Prentice marked Rosalind Russell's movie debut. Russell played a wealthy femme fatale client of Powell's who, with the help of Powell's legal savvy, is acquitted of a manslaughter charge and then does her best to lure her willing-to-stray attorney, Powell, from the path of marital fidelity. In her autobiography, *Life Is a Banquet,* Russell wrote that during her starting days at Metro she was usually cast as a husband-stealer, making off with the spouse of a drop-dead gorgeous actress such as Joan Crawford, Loy, or (in *China Seas*) Jean Harlow. "There would be Jean, all alabaster skin and cleft chin, savory as a ripe peach, and I'd be saying disdainfully to Gable or Bob Montgomery, 'How can you spend time with *her?*' " In *Evelyn Prentice* Russell's attempt to steal Powell from Loy backfires, but it leads Loy's character, the eponymous Evelyn, into a disastrous intrigue that has violent consequences that appear to implicate her in a murder. Fear not. Everything's hunky-dory in the end, by which time Loy and Powell have both amply demonstrated that if called upon to emote and tug at heartstrings, they can.[9]

The antic Roz Russell, a total pro as an actress and full of beans on and off the set, quickly won the friendship of both Powell and Loy. The corny movie that brought them together squandered a bevy of talents, breaking most of its promises. *Variety*'s review got it right: "There's all the material here for a sock film, but it's unlikely to get that rating." The "strong sob yarn" and "money cast" failed to rescue a disappointing picture.[10]

Eager to correct her mistake in turning down *It Happened One Night,* Myrna accepted Frank Capra's next offer, which required her loan-out to Columbia Pictures. By now Capra occupied one of Hollywood's few seats as a director who qualified as a star in his own right. He wanted Myrna for the role of Alice Higgins, female lead in *Broadway Bill,* a horse-racing yarn based on a Mark Hellinger story and scripted by Robert Riskin, the celebrated screenwriter who'd worked with Capra to revise the *It Happened One Night* script, making both of its lead characters more appealing. Myrna had rejected it as just awful before the character of Ellie acquired her rebellious spunk.[11]

Most of *Broadway Bill* was filmed in San Mateo, south of San Francisco at the Tanforan Race Track and at a nearby ranch for thoroughbreds. It's the story of easygoing regular fellow Dan Brooks (Warner Baxter), a dissident member of the patriarchal J. L. Higgins family. Married to snooty Margaret (Helen Vinson), one of several Higgins sisters, Dan chafes at the arrogant self-satisfaction of his wife's father (Walter Connolly), who also happens to be his boss at the Higgins Paper Box Company. Old man Higgins pretty much owns the town of Higginsville, so to incur his wrath is to risk a lot. What Dan really wants is a rough-and-tumble, no-necktie life devoted to thoroughbred horses, rather than thoroughbred people. He quits his job managing the Higgins Paper Box Company to ready his horse, Broadway Bill, to compete in the Imperial Derby. Aided by his African American trainer Whitey (Clarence Muse) and by the tender ministrations of his wife's younger sister Alice (Myrna Loy), who sells her jewels to raise money for the race's entrance fee, he beats the odds and asserts both his independence and his determination to surmount adversity. Broadway Bill wins the race after a series of setbacks almost keeps him out of the running, but the horse dies of a burst heart at the finish line. Margaret ultimately divorces Dan, leaving him free to marry her warm-hearted younger sister, the unselfish, horse-savvy Alice, who, like Ellie in *It Happened One Night,* has rebelled against her stuffy family.

Myrna enjoyed the *Broadway Bill* shoot. She had worked previously with the solid if lackluster leading man Warner Baxter and grew fond of Capra, a man whose depressive tendencies were nowhere apparent during filming. She remembered Capra as a director with a sense of fun and an appreciation for detail. To convey the conformity of the Higgins family, Capra shows them all lifting their soupspoons to their mouths in synch at the dinner table. "He was able to put fantasy into real things that were going on, in a very charming way."[12]

Since *Broadway Bill* was a Frank Capra movie, it had to champion folksy and colorful everyday Americans, who, in this tale, are caught up in the excitement of betting on horses, scheming, grooming thoroughbreds, and cheering for them at the track. To build tension before the big race for the Derby, Capra's usual cinematographer Joseph Walker put together a montage of quick headshots of two-dollar bet-placers, secretaries, nurses, and other underpaid types using the phone to gamble on Broadway Bill, a horse rumored to have a shot at defeating the favorite. (A blonde Lucille Ball plays a bit as a telephone operator.) Some stock horseracing footage was used in the racing sequence, but the live footage shot by Joseph Walker throbs with a special energy. He mounted two cameras on a platform installed on the chassis of a charging Pierce-Arrow to photograph an actual race. Because there was a law on the books that prohibited racing the same horses twice in one day, there could be no retakes.[13]

Capra immediately antagonized San Francisco newspaper readers by hiring a few rich socialites, including the blue blood investment banker William H. Crocker, to play some of the four hundred three-dollar-a-day extra roles. California was still gripped by the Depression, and local papers showed a photo of the high-hat Crocker collecting a paycheck while unemployed would-be performers grimly look on.[14]

Broadway Bill has some funny and affecting moments, and Myrna Loy came through with a natural, wholly endearing performance. André Sennwald of the *New York Times* hailed her for reaffirming "our faith in her, both as a light comedienne and as a person." Her ease with horses contributes to the relaxed feeling she conveys; her early days on a Montana cattle ranch served her well here. But Capra didn't work hard enough against looming sentimentality, otherwise known as "Capra-corn." Alas, mawkishness taints the film.[15]

Capra had wanted Clark Gable to play Dan Brooks, but MGM didn't want to lend him again to Columbia Pictures. Why allow Columbia to cash in on the box-office appeal of a huge Metro star? Warner Baxter's Dan Brooks frustrated Capra because the actor was terrified of being bitten or kicked by a horse, especially one with its tail up. "As a result," Capra writes in his autobiography, some "warm scenes I had in mind between the man and his horse I could not do," and those he did shoot fell short. He vowed to remake the film one day using a male lead in love with horses, and he eventually kept his promise to himself. In the 1950 musical remake for Paramount, *Riding High,* Bing Crosby, in private life an owner and breeder of thoroughbreds, became the Un-Warner Baxter. Because of budget concerns, the remake used footage and a few of the same actors from *Broadway Bill.* For many years it was hard to find a print of *Broadway Bill,* which was pulled from distribution after *Riding High* was released. Capra turned the 1934 film into the disinherited black sheep of his family of Capra pictures, ignoring it in favor of the Crosby version, in which Crosby sang "Camptown Racetrack" and Coleen Gray played the role of Alice. There was no Myrna Loy in sight.[16]

Myrna had turned down a role in *It Happened One Night* partly because she was suffering from overwork and exhaustion, maladies that had plagued her since soon after she began her now-decade-long screen-acting career. In the spring of 1935, as she neared her thirtieth birthday, she took stock. By now she had appeared in eighty-six films, twenty of them since signing with MGM three years back. She still wasn't married to Arthur but passionately wanted to be. Stuck in what she considered a rut, she felt something had to change. She yearned for a breather, a chance to journey somewhere distant with the well-traveled, French-speaking Arthur. She had the itch to see parts of the world beyond Montana, California, Hawaii, or Mexico—the only places she knew firsthand.

Myrna was also becoming impatient with Louis B. Mayer, resentful of MGM's refusal to fully acknowledge and financially reward her new status as a bona fide star and as William Powell's equal. She considered Powell's higher rank and double salary profoundly unjust, although Powell had enjoyed star status far longer than she and had carried films on his own rather than as part of a duo. Her original MGM contract, signed in 1931, would not expire until 1937, but she felt entitled to new terms. Her chance to escape MGM and make her point came during shooting of a film called *Escapade.*

Escapade was a remake of the Viennese movie *Maskerade,* shown in the United States in 1937 as *Masquerade in Vienna.* "Story concerns a sophisticated young rake," to be played in the American version by William Powell, "who tumbles in love with an innocent sprite," to be played by Myrna Loy, *Variety* reported. The sprite, named Leopoldine Dur, was "a shy little person," companion to a countess, who becomes innocently drawn into a scandal concerning an adulterous wife who posed for a portrait while wearing little more than a mask and a fur muff. In the original Viennese version, an actress called Paula Wessely played Leopoldine. Myrna told writer Elizabeth McDonald that Wessely's performance in *Maskerade* was "so absolutely perfect that the studio wanted me to be as much like her as possible. I was to imitate another actress." The entire film copied the original, shot by shot.[17]

From the get-go Myrna felt unenthusiastic about the role and the slavish copying. Mayer cajoled her into accepting it, making her believe he only wanted the best for her and telling her, "Myrna, you're like one of my family. If you were my mother, my wife or my mistress, I could not be more sincere" (*BB,* 98). Recalling the unhappy episode, she said, "I knew *Escapade* was all wrong for me. I was supposed to be a little gamine flower girl who Bill [Powell], portraying an artist, discovers, and paints a portrait of, and you know that's not the right kind of part for mama." It drove her crazy that "they were copying every detail" of the German-language *Maskerade;* there seemed to be no chance for her to put her own stamp on the role. MGM had bought both the print and the script of the Viennese original and had Herman J. Mankiewicz, who knew German, write the adaptation.[18]

Since when was Myrna Loy the sort of actress you'd cast as an "artless, unsophisticated girl"? Since never. Her sophisticated air had followed her throughout her ten-year movie career, a link yoking the early exotic temptress roles to the fetching upper-class women she had played more recently. Myrna believed that the studio was purposely trying to humiliate her, but that seems unlikely. Executives were probably guilty of simple thoughtlessness, joined with their usual interest in the bottom line. For Mayer the only thing that mattered was promptly finding another Loy-Powell vehicle while the two were at a peak of popularity. Myrna also maintained, and here there is evidence to back her up, that after ten days of shooting, MGM, and, in particular, producer Bernie Hyman, really wanted her out of the picture, preferring to substitute the newcomer Luise Rainer, a German-born actress under contract at MGM but not yet put to work, as the ingénue. Max Reinhardt's son Gottfried, a director, writer, and producer, had recommended Rainer based on his knowledge of the work she'd done with his father in Vienna. Anita Loos also put in a good word for Rainer. A refugee from the Nazis, Rainer had a big talent, which quickly won her the enthusiastic backing of her *Escapade* colleague, William Powell. With a characteristic generosity of spirit, Powell insisted that Rainer be ranked beside him as costar, or he would "look like an idiot."[19]

Despite the scope of her acting talent, Rainer would turn out to have no knack for adapting to the ways of Hollywood, which she would soon come to consider crass, superficial, and artistically stifling. She would resent her lack of control at MGM, the studio's not allowing her to choose her own roles: "I was just a piece of machinery with no rights." Insisting that a psychologically acute performance had to come from the inside, from the actor's soul or psyche, she held Louis B. Mayer in contempt—and made no secret of it—for saying he could make an actress out of any "good looker." A cosmopolitan European, she bonded with Thalberg, a fellow book lover who was comfortable with writers, but felt at sea after his death in the fall of 1936. A few years down the line, after she'd won two Oscars in a row—one for her work in 1936 as Anna Held in *The Great Ziegfeld,* the second the following year for her star turn as O-Lan in *The Good Earth*—Rainer, by then tumultuously married to the writer Clifford Odets, broke her contract with MGM and left town after Louis B. Mayer told her, "We've made you and we are going to kill you." She quickly became a Hollywood has-been. But in early May of 1935, when she reported to the set of *Escapade,* she was still an eager newcomer at MGM, collecting a weekly paycheck until the studio found the right first Hollywood role for her.[20]

Myrna had made no secret of her discontent with her part in *Escapade,* but she knew the consequences if she simply quit without first ironing out the contractual implications of abandoning the set. It was her devoted hairdresser Eleanor who revealed to Myrna that she'd just done Rainer's hair for a screen test—for the very same *Escapade* role that Myrna had been unhappily and unsuccessfully trying to play (*BB,* 99).

Here the story gets even more complicated. The director Robert Z. Leonard apparently agreed with Myrna that she had been miscast. Ten days into shooting, producer Bernard Hyman and studio manager Eddie Mannix plotted to replace Loy, explaining to the public that she had voluntarily withdrawn because of illness compounded by exhaustion. Escorted by Hyman to Mannix's office, Myrna was informed that she no longer had a part in *Escapade.* Mannix advised her to go to Palm Springs and rest "until the whole thing blew over." Myrna told him no, she was not going to agree to plead illness. At that point, displaying a feistiness that came as a shock, she simply walked. That night, Myrna recalled, "I had dinner with my agent, Myron Selznick, and we hatched a plan. The next morning I went right back to the studio and told Eddie Mannix I was getting made up and would report to the set unless they gave me a legal release saying it was not my fault. They knew that I would upset Luise if I appeared on the set, so they rushed over with the release." Release in hand, with her MGM contract at least partially protected against future legal penalties for her absence from the set, Myrna felt free to leave town.[21]

One part of the *Escapade* saga that has not figured in any prior account needs attention here. Myrna had had an abortion a few weeks before reporting to the set to play Leopoldine. In addition to her issues with the role, she was contending not just with the loss of the baby she had conceived with the still-married Arthur but with even more devastating news. After the abortion she contracted a septic infection that rendered her sterile and ruled out future pregnancies. Myrna adored children and had eagerly anticipated motherhood. At the time of her crisis at MGM she was trying to come to terms with this private and painful new reality. She suffered enormous emotional turmoil, as well as physical exhaustion. She could not summon her usual resilience.[22]

The probable date of the abortion was early March 1935. *Escapade* went into production just a month later. The *Los Angeles Evening Herald Express* had reported that Myrna Loy was a patient at the University of California Hospital in San Francisco, "but the nature of her illness was not disclosed by her physician, Dr. Saxton T. Pope of Burlingame [who] indicated that the illness was of a minor nature." *Variety*'s "Chatter" column confirmed both the hospitalization and the secrecy, reporting only that "attendants at the University of California hospital decline to discuss ailment which confined Myrna Loy." *Photoplay*'s Dorothy Manners wrote of Myrna, "Several weeks ago she entered a San Francisco hospital for treatment of a bad case of nerves."²³

As soon as she could, after securing her release from MGM, Myrna took a plane to New York—her first-ever cross-country jaunt. Her seat mate on the flight, which included an Ohio stopover, was Leland Hayward, at present the partner of Myron Selznick at the Selznick-Joyce Agency in his professional life and in his private life trying to negotiate conflicting romantic alliances with Katharine Hepburn and the actress he was about to marry, Margaret Sullavan. Once in New York, Hayward, "a great charmer," accompanied Myrna on her town-car ride through the Holland Tunnel into Manhattan and on to her first view of Fifth Avenue, pausing at 59th St., where he deposited her at the stately and luxurious McKim, Meade and White–designed Savoy Plaza Hotel, adjacent to Central Park. The electric wattage of New York City seduced Myrna at once. She fell in love with Manhattan at first sight, and the metropolitan romance continued for the rest of her life (*BB,* 104).

Via Myron Selznick she let it be known that her breakaway from MGM might last a while; she was on the warpath, demanding better terms on her contract. MGM was, to put it mildly, displeased. The studio had given her a release from a specific picture, not permission to flee on an open-ended vacation. Eddie Mannix sent a telegram to her at the Savoy Plaza ordering her to report to work at the Culver City studio at 10 o'clock in the morning on Wednesday, May 15, 1935. MGM suspended her salary and, in her absence, cast Rosalind Russell as her substitute in *Rendezvous,* opposite William Powell.²⁴

Before she left New York, the *New York Times* reported that Myrna Loy, though new to Manhattan, toured it "with the gay assurance of a true cosmopolite," craning her neck to see the Empire State Building and sampling cocktails "from some of the better bars" but passing up the

chance to ride the subway. The columnist Ed Sullivan and famed hostess Elsa Maxwell were among the many Manhattanites who sought her
out, wining and dining her. Myrna was living it up.[25]

Her first excursion to Europe, via a restorative voyage on the SS *Paris*,
followed immediately. Arthur, already in London on Paramount business, had urged her to join him. He served as tour guide and companion, but since they weren't married, his presence by her side had to be
concealed from the press and the public. He sent her a radio telegram that
she read while still aboard ship: "Welcome Welcome Darling. Don't Mind
the Weather We Can Pretend Its Christmas. I Can Hardly Wait Bunty. A."
(*BB*, 105).

When she disembarked at Plymouth, England, she was with comedienne Polly Moran, not a close friend but someone who happened to be
crossing the pond on the same liner. At once Myrna rather startlingly announced to the waiting press that she was on the first lap of a holiday
from pictures and might never, ever return to acting in them. She would
rather live in London than California, she proclaimed with atypical abandon, because she preferred a climate with four seasons. In Southern California, with its eternal summer, "We don't die. We just wither up and
blow away." She didn't stay around to take questions. "Miss Loy soon
sped away mysteriously in a luxurious car. She refused to detail her plans
beyond saying she will stay in Sussex with Mr. and Mrs. Guy Bolton."
Arthur, who met her at the dock, sat beside her in the deluxe sedan as it
zoomed off.[26]

Guy Bolton, a prolific playwright and screenwriter who wrote the story
for *Transatlantic*, served as their British host. He lived with his wife not
far from London in Nutbourne, Sussex, at their Elizabethan "Thyme Cottage," where tipped-off fans and reporters soon "descended like a swarm
of hungry locusts on the idyllic peace of the Sussex Downs." Alfred Hitchcock, who lived nearby, came to pay his respects. (Myrna and Arthur
would meet him again in Beverly Hills, where, when she heard him describe his way of working with actors, Myrna privately decided that his
dominating methods on the set would clash with her own work mode,
and she hoped Hitchcock would never put her to the test by hiring her.)
Less-well-known acolytes had no trouble getting wind of her whereabouts, since the MGM publicity machine had swung into gear. The studio may have wanted to spank her for bad behavior, but why not get a
little free publicity on the side? Fans who read the newspapers followed
Myrna wherever she went, and hikers surrounded the Bolton cottage.
When the time came for her to depart Sussex, two young men on bicy-

cles followed her car in drenching rain all the way to London, hovering so close to the vehicle en route that "I was terrified every moment that they would be knocked off and killed."[27]

At London's Savoy Hotel five suitcases of fan mail awaited her. She rushed off to a reception at the Empire attended by three hundred people. Britain clearly adored her, and Myrna found it difficult to convince her throngs of admirers that "there's nothing sensational about me."[28]

London also provided the opportunity for her to meet Arthur Hornblow Sr. for the first time. Long a resident of New York City, where Arthur Jr. grew up, he'd returned to London after the American magazine he'd founded and edited, *Theatre,* folded in the mid-1920s, and was living with his Scottish second wife in Golders Green. They had a son, Herbert. The senior Hornblow was a cultivated man, once the Paris correspondent for the *New York Herald,* whose interests in theater, books, and all things French his namesake son shared.

Within six weeks Myrna and Arthur touched down in cobblestoned Paris, where they bunked at the Hôtel de Crillon. They were whisked away to be feted by Lady Mendl, the former Elsie de Wolfe (step-aunt of Natacha Rambova), at her Versailles chateau. Stops lasting a few days each in Switzerland, Hungary, Austria, Germany, and Spain, some of these destinations reached by train and others by car, followed. Everywhere they went, they dined in style, and Arthur, who'd been posted in France during the Great War, and who tended to fuss about food and drink, hunted down and ordered the choicest wines he could find to accompany their four-star meals.

In Budapest they ran into Robert Sherwood, the Pulitzer Prize–winning playwright, film critic, former *Life* magazine editor, and scenarist. A future Franklin D. Roosevelt speechwriter who would create the script for *The Best Years of Our Lives,* the tall (6'6.5"), unassuming Sherwood was traveling with the woman he was trying to marry, the former silent screen actress Madeline Hurlock. She had recently divorced the playwright Marc Connelly, once Sherwood's good friend. Legal snafus delayed their wedding plans, but they did manage to marry quite soon after their Hungarian encounter with Arthur and Myrna. The foursome—two as yet unwed couples stealing a premature honeymoon—lingered for a few days together in romantic, cosmopolitan Budapest, where Myrna was astonished to be recognized as Myrna Loy by an elderly Hungarian passerby who spoke no English but managed to pronounce her name properly (*BB,* 109). Myrna kept being reminded that her fame extended far beyond American shores.

During her European tour Myrna often felt she was living in one of her movies. The steamship she'd sailed on reminded her of the one in *Transatlantic,* and when she boarded the Orient Express en route from Paris to Budapest, "I had to pinch myself to realize it wasn't a scene from *Stamboul Quest.*" The delights of Paris, and the fun of being feted at a French chateau, must have made her think of *Love Me Tonight.*[29]

Back in New York in mid-July, Myrna immediately got down to career matters. With a New York law firm now advising her on how to get what she wanted from MGM, she pushed her argument with the studio powers up one notch. She publicly demanded a new contract, one that would give her full marks for being a star whose movies brought considerable money to the coffers of MGM. In the past, she pointed out, before she clicked with the public, she had waived an increase in salary at option time; now the studio owed it to her to make amends. "The gentle manner of Myrna Loy conceals a will of steel," one observer wrote.[30]

She held one powerful card in her hand: her partnership with Powell. *After the Thin Man,* already in the planning phase, required her participation. Rosalind Russell might do just fine in some pictures demanding a smart, wry brunette; and Ruth Hussey, a new hire who could play sardonic ladies, would work in others. But only Myrna Loy would do as Nora Charles.

Nick Schenck, head of Loews, Inc., the parent company of MGM, worked from a New York office, and Myrna believed that he disliked her; she certainly had no use for him. "He expected all actresses to be whores, and treated them accordingly." She found him merely crude, in contrast to the wily and theatrical L. B. Mayer. A shrewd and pragmatic businessman, Schenck realized despite his contempt for actresses in general that Myrna Loy had significant value to MGM. Her legal team in New York had convinced him she meant business and was not about to back down without concessions on the studio's part. He got on the phone to urge Mayer in Culver City to negotiate peace with her, *now.* Mayer at once called Arthur at Paramount, inviting him to breakfast to discuss the Myrna crisis (*BB,* 115).

"Myrna Loy Abrogates Contract" ran a front-page headline in the *Los Angeles Examiner.* Her New York attorney, Bill Saxe, claimed that he'd discovered a contractual breach on MGM's part that invalidated her present contract, which she wanted to see revised rather than totally destroyed. Making it clear that she hoped to return to MGM on her own terms, or at least better terms than those currently accorded her, she issued a statement widely carried in newspapers all over the country: "I was given the customary assurances [that my contract] would be adjusted if I achieved stardom," she stated. "I have also begged for stipulations such as the right to have an occasional holiday. The manner in which I have been handled finally led to a near breakdown. After fifteen pictures in two years—three times the normal number—I felt the time had come for fair treatment." Even though she hadn't even become a member of the Screen Actors Guild as yet, Myrna Loy became a poster girl for actors' rights.[31]

In her autobiography she indicates that she believed herself to be a trailblazer in taking on the Hollywood studios. It's true that Jean Arthur's fight with Harry Cohn at Columbia and those of Bette Davis and Olivia de Havilland with Warner Bros. had yet to happen. But she was forgetting that way back in 1922 Rudolph Valentino had gone on strike against Paramount, with what ultimately proved to be disastrous consequences for his career. Still, she showed courage and initiative, standing her ground and getting expert counsel until she prevailed.

Some members of the press corps whispered that the previously sunny and uncomplaining Myrna Loy had suddenly transformed into a demanding, temperamental diva. But *Variety*'s Cecilia Ager jumped to her defense, assuring readers that Miss Loy "was never a field mouse" and had not become a prima donna. "She is not quarrelling with Metro," Ager wrote after an interview with the woman kicking up all the dust. "Metro, alas, is quarrelling with her. Miss Loy speaks of Metro in respectful, guarded and friendly terms," while maintaining that though she may have been soft-spoken in the past, she "has always been, she says, an independent creature in her funny little way."[32]

That independent spirit announced itself with still more vehemence when her representatives revealed to the world that Myrna Loy had just thumbed her nose at MGM by signing a rival contract with Ben Hecht and Charles MacArthur, writers who together headed their own unit at Paramount's Astoria Studios, writing, developing, directing, and producing their own films. A press release announced that she was going to appear in a movie scripted by the successful Hecht-MacArthur team, coauthors of *The Front Page* and *Twentieth Century,* to be titled *Soak the Rich.* Myrna had visited MacArthur and his wife, Helen Hayes, at their Nyack, New York, home, and the idea of announcing the contract offer from the irreverent team, jokingly dubbed the Katzenjammer Twins, was hatched during that visit. Word went out that for her appearance in *Soak the Rich* Loy would be paid $75,000 for five weeks' work, $15,000 more than she received for a forty-week period at MGM.[33]

It turns out that though there really was a Hecht-MacArthur film in the works called *Soak the Rich* that would be released in 1936, no one ever believed that she would appear in it. "Some executives at Metro profess to see in the Hecht-MacArthur action one of the pranks for which the pair are noted," observed the *New York Times*. The announcement of the pending deal was a ploy, a maneuver concocted by the pranksters Hecht and MacArthur out of a desire to stick it to Louis B. Mayer while simultaneously aiding Myrna Loy's cause. Hecht and MacArthur disliked Mayer and had no qualms about taking him on. The prospect filled them with glee.[34]

The ploy worked. In no time the headline "Actress Mends Studio Quarrel" ran in the *New York American* and other newspapers. Although terms of the settlement with MGM were kept under wraps at first, all who were following the story heard that Myrna Loy had flown back to Los Angeles, patched things up with Mayer, and would soon be back at work. In a face-saving (and contract-protecting) gesture, Mayer maintained that Myrna Loy would still be getting the same pay that she was receiving before she went on strike. In other words, it appeared that she had not violated or changed her existing contract. The front page of the *LA Times* screamed, "Myrna Loy Back on Lot at Old Pay." What wasn't made public was that she was paid a bonus lump sum of $25,000, the equivalent of about $400,000 in 2009, and that when her contract came up for renewal in 1937, she would be given a significant raise to $4,000 a week.[35]

Was the one-woman strike worth the risk? By almost any measure, it was. It resulted in a professional victory for Myrna Loy and allowed her to take a breather and visit New York and Europe for the first time. It yielded a sorely needed sense of renewal.

CHAPTER 10

Mrs. Arthur Hornblow Jr.

"The Arthur Hornblows represent one of the happiest, most devoted couples in Hollywood," readers of the fan magazine *Motion Picture* learned in the fall of 1936, a few months after Myrna Loy and Arthur Hornblow Jr. tied the knot. And that "happiest, most devoted" label was just for starters. The picture-book newlyweds—a busy Paramount producer clad in Savile Row suits, and his charming movie star wife—were building a dream house. "While awaiting completion of the grand new house," the article continued, "they are spending their honeymoon at Palos Verdes, the swank colony at the shore."[1]

After years of nail-biting over Arthur's "I love you, but" attitude, Myrna's quest for commitment at last reached consummation. The wedding happened a year after their trip to Europe, on June 27, 1936, the very day that FDR delivered his "Rendezvous with Destiny" speech when accepting the nomination at the Democratic National Convention for his second term. Not giving too much thought to FDR's presidency at the moment, Arthur and Myrna wed hurriedly in Ensenada, in Baja Mexico, described in another of the passel of fan magazines attempting to track Myrna Loy's every move as a "sleepy, quaint" sun-and-sand-soaked town about seventy miles south of the border. The bride "wore a high-neck dress that buttoned up the back, beige crepe with hand-blocked flowers," and a brown taffeta hat, detail-hungry fans were told. A Mexican judge officiated, and the bride and groom were attended by two friends they'd brought with them from Los Angeles to serve as maid of honor and best man: Shirley Hughes and Ray Ramsey. Shirley, Myrna's stand-in at MGM, by now had become her close friend. Myrna and Arthur both liked Shirley's fiancé, the MGM cameraman Ray Ramsey. Neither Della nor Myrna's brother, David, had been asked to join the party. Myrna tended to keep the different spheres of her life quite separate, and any event involving Arthur usually excluded Myrna's family.[2]

Douglas Fairbanks Sr. hired a "cloud clipper" to fly down for the nuptial dinner at an Ensenada inn. Fairbanks was an old friend of the Hornblow clan, dating from the time when Arthur Hornblow Sr. edited *Theatre* magazine in New York. Fairbanks had been the subject of an interview Arthur Jr. published in New York right out of law school and long before he moved to California. Arthur's father, who wrote a monthly column called "Going to the Play," had known him back in the 1910s, when Fairbanks trod the boards as a Broadway actor. Fairbanks and Lady Sylvia Ashley, his newly acquired British wife (the former Edith Hawkes, who would one day become the fourth Mrs. Clark Gable), were the only Hollywood luminaries present other than Arthur and Myrna themselves. After the ceremony, and the celebratory dinner that immediately followed, the Hornblows drove north to Palos Verdes, California.[3]

The long-awaited wedding came as something of an anticlimax, since the high drama between Arthur and Myrna had peaked weeks before. The turning point came in late May of 1936, immediately after Arthur's divorce from Juliette Crosby was finalized in Reno. From the time four years back when they realized they were in love and wanted to stay together, Arthur had been telling Myrna that his hopes of becoming her husband were being repeatedly dashed, because Juliette wouldn't agree to a divorce. Juliette would decades later tell Myrna, with whom she became friendly, that this tale amounted to little more than an Arthurian legend, pure fiction. Arthur had *not* been pestering her for a divorce; she had *not* stood in his way (*BB*, 95).

Whatever the case regarding Arthur's truthfulness in the matter, it is certain that once Juliette obtained the divorce, on grounds of incompatibility, Arthur, at last free to marry, continued stalling for several weeks. Hurt and angry at the perceived rejection, Myrna took leave of Arthur's Bel Air house, where she'd been staying, though she always maintained an independent address. It's easy to imagine doors slamming. Accompanied by two protective women friends, Betty Black and Shirley Hughes, Myrna headed for the hills: her rustic cabin at Lake Arrowhead, a mountain ski resort above San Bernardino where many other film professionals also escaped to vacation retreats. Myrna had recently upgraded the simple Lake Arrowhead cabin, hiring a decorator to help her fix it up to meet Arthur's exacting standards. A canopy now adorned the double bed, and she installed a private ski jump outdoors. After spending a forlorn week in Bel Air without a word from Myrna, Arthur sent a message to her that amounted to waving a white flag of surrender. Life without you isn't worth living, the message said. Let's get married right away (*BB*, 127).

Arthur had become a prominent, well-paid Paramount producer whose 1935 film *Ruggles of Red Gap* was nominated for a Best Picture Academy Award. His $71,375 salary for 1935 would be worth roughly fifteen times that now, and he also got a percentage of profits from the films he produced. Known for his cosmopolitan taste and New York–by-way-of-Europe sophistication, he wore many feathers in his professional cap. For instance, Arthur had been responsible for bringing Ronald Colman to Goldwyn and to talkies. He had also negotiated directly with Sinclair Lewis for the film rights to *Arrowsmith*. He'd worked with some titans and had come to think of himself as one of the film community's anointed.[4]

This is not to say that every film produced by Arthur Hornblow Jr. rated five stars. Like most studio-contract producers, he turned out his share of routine programmers, including one Paramount dud, *Wings in the Dark*, pairing Myrna Loy with Cary Grant for the first time. It's unfortunate that the well-read Arthur wasn't able to put his own abilities and some sterling players to work on a stronger vehicle. This one stumbled on a truly absurd Nell Shipman–Philip Hurn script that required Grant to portray a pilot who loses his eyesight but flies blind, guided by the sure hand of Myrna Loy, the selfless stunt aviatrix who loves him. "High altitudes have a tendency to make scenarists just a trifle giddy," André Sennwald dryly commented in his *New York Times* review.[5]

Cary Grant and Myrna Loy became friendly during shooting, but *Wings in the Dark* wastes their talents and prompts an unintentional laugh fest. It does boast some accomplished aerial photography by Dewey Wrigley, and it allowed Myrna Loy to meet Amelia Earhart when Earhart visited the set as a consultant. She and Myrna posed together for the still camera, but Earhart couldn't rescue *Wings in the Dark*. No one could.

At Paramount, where he'd been producing films since leaving Goldwyn's employ in 1933, Arthur had met the wealthy banker Frank Vanderlip, a former assistant secretary of the treasury and president of National City Bank. Vanderlip became a Paramount bondholder and then chairman of the board after it went into receivership as a result of Depression-related theater closings and lagging ticket sales. The patrician investor, who lived primarily on the East Coast, owned a magnificent spread on a bluff overlooking the Pacific at Palos Verdes's Portuguese Bend. He named the estate Villa Narcissa after his impressively unnarcissistic wife, Narcissa Cox Vanderlip, a mother of six who was a former suffragist and advocate for women and children. Mrs. Vanderlip had worked with Eleanor Roosevelt on progressive reform campaigns and had been a founder of the League of Women Voters in New York.

The Vanderlips leased Villa Narcissa, a copy of an actual Roman villa, to newlyweds Arthur and Myrna. There they stayed for some months, their prized tranquility often interrupted by the screeching of the Vanderlips' outdoor flock of resident peacocks and by the quieter indoor voices of people gathered around a table at animated planning sessions. The Hornblows were meeting with the architect Roland E. Coate and with landscapers, an interior decorator, and builders, laying out blueprints for the design of an ambitious Beverly Hills estate on a wild, secluded, deer- and coyote-inhabited five-acre lot off winding Hidden Valley Road in Coldwater Canyon. Arthur didn't think small. He and his new wife intended to create for themselves something grand but understated, a home and grounds that expressed the style, refinement, and attention to detail that Hollywood had come to associate with the name Arthur Hornblow Jr. Myrna joined in the planning, but Arthur took the helm here, as he tended to do in general.

Arthur and Myrna entertained often on weekends during their idyllic time at Palos Verdes, hosting luminaries of the movie world. In this social sphere there weren't many degrees of separation among the participants. Everyone had worked with, had an affair with, or had married everyone else at one time or another, or was kin to someone well known in the movie colony. If not literally the case, it seemed that way.

Ernst Lubitsch might head over and dive straight into the Pacific. Myrna already knew the famed Berlin-born director who did so much to change the map of American film comedy and who had briefly served as Arthur's boss during Lubitsch's single year as Paramount's head of production. During Myrna's early days at Warner Bros., which coincided with Lubitsch's debut directing assignments at that studio, he'd given her a bit part in the Frenchified marital comedy *So This Is Paris*. Alas for Myrna, she never worked with him after that, but she got to know him socially. Hosting him at Palos Verdes, she'd spot him emerging from the sea, his abundant wet, black body hair clinging to his skin and making him look "like some mythical monster" of the deep (*BB*, 131). In his street clothes, with his perennial cigar drooping from his mouth like an extra tongue, his gnome's face, and his short, chubby frame, Lubitsch in appearance fit the stock comic roles he'd once played in German cabarets and silent two-reelers.

Loretta Young, now in her radiant twenties and under contract at 20th Century–Fox, had known Myrna since their starlet days at Warner Bros., when Young played the innocent good girl to Loy's oversexed gypsy vixen in *The Squall*. They'd renewed acquaintance at Goldwyn, vying on the screen for Ronald Colman's love and attention in the film that introduced Myrna to Arthur, *The Devil to Pay*. Young would arrive at Villa Narcissa on a Sunday morning on the arm of Eddie Sutherland, a London-born director who'd served back in 1923 as Chaplin's assistant and had once, also in the 1920s, been married to Louise Brooks. Sutherland collected wives. As Albert Hackett said of him, "He married a lot. Not in groups— one at a time."[6]

Sutherland had recently directed the Arthur Hornblow Jr. Paramount production of *Mississippi,* a musical set on a riverboat. *Mississippi* showcased Rodgers and Hart songs, but despite this bonus the production foundered. The film's star, Bing Crosby, kept disappearing from the set, and the riverboat captain, played by W. C. Fields, according to biographer James Curtis, harbored "genuine disdain" for Arthur Hornblow, though he could console himself with the company of Eddie Sutherland, the film's director and an old friend. The friction on the *Mississippi* set didn't interfere, however, with the bonhomie between Arthur and Sutherland. As for Sutherland's Sunday date, Loretta Young, she attested that when she and Sutherland visited the Hornblows at Villa Narcissa, she felt welcome and well looked after (*BB*, 132). Myrna would arrange for Loretta, a devout Catholic, to be driven to a nearby Paso Robles church to attend Mass.[7]

Another director with whom Arthur had worked in the past and would work again, Mitchell Leisen, turned up often at the Vanderlip spread. A former costume designer and art director for Cecil B. DeMille, the bisexual Leisen usually arrived at the Hornblows' accompanied by fellow costume designer Natalie Visart, his on-again, off-again lover and intimate friend over many decades. They could never marry because Leisen was divorced and Visart an observant Roman Catholic.

Leisen had deep roots in the silent era, unlike Arthur, who came to Hollywood from Broadway to help Goldwyn find and develop material for talkies. Leisen had designed costumes for *Robin Hood* and *The Thief* of Bagdad, two important Fairbanks vehicles, and for DeMille's *Madam Satan,* where Natalie Visart also worked as a designer. Natalie had attended the Hollywood School for Girls with Katherine DeMille, adopted daughter of Cecil, and remained close to her. That connection, plus Natalie's talent, led to her hiring as a DeMille designer and her professional collaboration with Mitchell Leisen.

Fascinated by dreams and renowned as a designer of dream sequences, Leisen saw a psychiatrist regularly. Myrna, who would later enter psychotherapy, had long been drawn to matters psychological and had done some reading on the subject. Like many of her acting peers, she linked insightful performances with psychological astuteness. As for Natalie Visart, she too had an interest in what made people tick and would converse with Myrna about complex relationships, her own passionate, troubled, and unlikely bond with Mitchell Leisen providing plenty of grist. Leisen, who was also enmeshed in a love affair with the dancer and choreographer Billy Daniels, had a breakdown in 1937. Visart would subsequently, in the 1940s, become pregnant by Leisen and suffer a miscarriage. Natalie Visart, who after her marriage to the writer Dwight Taylor became Natalie Taylor, remained Myrna's enduring ally and confidante.[8]

The agent Collier Young, a favorite within the Hornblow circle, attended weekend gatherings when visiting from New York. He would continue to move in Myrna's orbit over many years and many matings, since he was also pals with Arthur's good friend and Myrna's future husband Gene Markey. "Collie," a perpetually charming and youthful man who became a Hollywood writer, story editor, and producer, was a Dartmouth graduate like both Arthur and Gene.

When he visited the Hornblows at Villa Narcissa, Collie Young arrived with his wife, Valerie, a former actress. He would later wed Ida Lupino, then Joan Fontaine, then Meg Marsh. A waggish cutup who drank too much and told funny stories, he provided the kind of ebullient company that other party animals found irresistible. In her autobiography Joan Fontaine called him "a perennial Peter Pan, a wit and a wag whose avocation was writing and producing. Give him a lampshade and he'd wear it." She pronounced him her favorite ex-husband.[9]

Arthur's and Myrna's first years of marriage were for the most part harmonious and upbeat, if hectic. They worked nonstop six days a week, reserving Saturday nights and Sundays for one another and friends. If they lucked into a few days to play, they'd drive north to San Francisco or south to Mexico. They conversed endlessly during their times alone about what each was doing professionally. "I'm interested in Arthur's work and he's interested in mine," Myrna told *Photoplay*'s Lee Harrington shortly after she and Arthur moved into their white, rambling, newly completed Coldwater Canyon dream house. She added that music mattered a lot to both Hornblows. "He's mad for Debussy and so am I." They also liked Mexican songs. They owned a pear-wood Steinway piano, on which Myrna occasionally practiced pieces she'd learned as a girl, and the turntable on the Capehart phonograph in their music room got plenty of use. Often Myrna studied the lines she had to learn from a shooting script as music played.[10]

Myrna did everything she could to measure up to Arthur's standards and to please him. Theresa Penn, her African American maid, reported that when Myrna overcame her impatience with shopping and went off to buy clothes at a fancy shop, she would return to the store any garment that Arthur vetoed, though Arthur "never tells her not to keep something." He didn't have to tell her; Myrna knew whether or not he approved. But the perfect wife standard she set for herself came from society at large, not just from Arthur. She wanted to look beautiful for him. She strove to put his needs first. She tried to run the household efficiently. She would be to Arthur the unselfish, giving, and sympathetic wife her mother had refused to be for her father.[11]

Because Myrna was so seldom at home, she had limited time to devote to the traditional domestic role, but she did plan—always keeping in mind Arthur's food preferences—daily dinner menus for Sergei the cook to prepare, sometimes cutting out magazine recipes for his use. On the cook's night off, Myrna told Gladys Hall, "we have a few friends in and we all go in the kitchen and each one makes his or her 'specialty.' And Arthur always turns out something fit for the gods. [My specialty is] chef's assistant! I'm a wonderful potato-peeler, lettuce washer and carrot-dicer." Her willing assumption of the sous-chef role in the kitchen stands in for her position in other rooms. Not that she considered herself in any way a victim during the early years of her marriage to Arthur. She had almost everything she'd ever wanted.[12]

Despite being a two-career couple, with both partners working long hours at an exhausting clip, the Hornblows were doing what they loved to do on and off the lot. Arthur relished the role of host. He liked nothing more than selecting the food and wine for a gathering of illustrious friends. He went in for "wines at the right room temperature, exotic imported foods, flowers chosen to match the colors of Myrna's gowns and guests picked to match the mood of the host." At their first big party at their new home, guests included the Basil Rathbones (Mrs. Rathbone, the former actress Ouida Bergere, was now a celebrated Hollywood hostess), Mr. and Mrs. Ernst Lubitsch, Rouben Mamoulian, Loretta Young, and Joan Crawford, now a top star at MGM and currently married to Franchot Tone.[13]

Myrna had once been noted, and sometimes chastised, in the film colony for her love of privacy and disinterest in the high life. As recently as August 1935 *Photoplay* published an article by Dorothy Manners that pronounced Myrna Loy "the shyest person I have ever met" and concluded, "If Garbo's isolation has earned her the title of Hollywood recluse, then surely our own Montana-born Myrna is the authentic Miss X of Hollywood, the provocative unknown quantity." Clearly those days were over for the present. As Arthur's wife, Myrna emerged into the social limelight, and the press took note of the change in her. "Myrna Loy, once known as a Hollywood recluse, has become a regular gadabout after her marriage," read the caption on a news photo of the Hornblows dressed in style for a film premiere alongside Mitchell Leisen and Natalie Visart.[14]

Myrna attended a lunch given by Merle Oberon, along with Marion Davies, Marlene Dietrich, Charles Boyer, the quicksilver Constance Bennett, and her equally stunning sister Joan Bennett, with whom Myrna would later become quite close. Constance and Joan Bennett were two among three actress daughters of Adrienne Morrison and Richard Bennett, an illustrious stage actor who also worked in films and had appeared with Myrna in *Arrowsmith*. Both Constance and Joan Bennett had thriving movie careers. Each had adorned the covers of dozens, maybe hundreds of magazines.[15]

During her blonde phase Joan Bennett had acted (rather vacantly) in *Hush Money,* one of Myrna's early crime dramas at Fox, and had costarred opposite Ronald Colman in his first talkie, *Bulldog Drummond,* a Goldwyn picture that introduced her to Arthur. More recently she'd attracted notice playing Amy in George Cukor's *Little Women* and was Bing Crosby's love interest in *Mississippi.* Known for the ladylike manner she'd acquired at a Swiss finishing school and a cameo-like beauty, Joan Bennett had a sardonic wit matched by an efficient, independent spirit. That grit developed quickly when she found herself a divorced mother with a child to support at age nineteen. For several years Joan Bennett had been married to the screenwriter, novelist, and sometime producer Gene Markey, and they had a daughter together, Melinda, born in 1934. Since Arthur saw a great deal of Gene at this time, Myrna got to know him and, to some extent, Joan Bennett as well.

Gene Markey had the gift of gab. Well educated, droll, and socially polished, he shone in company. Catnip to women and a collector of beauties, he had dated Gloria Swanson and Ina Claire; he would later add Lucille Ball's name to his list of conquests. After his 1937 divorce from Joan Bennett he would marry Hedy Lamarr. He and Myrna would wed in 1946. But during her marriage to Arthur, Myrna and Markey were not romantically involved.

At a dinner party in honor of Dashiell Hammett Myrna met George Cukor. Although he had directed some scenes in *The Animal Kingdom,* Myrna never appeared in a George Cukor film, something they both regretted; they were fans of one another's work. Cukor found Myrna's face both wise and witty, "the kind of wit that amuses me—underplayed and very, very subtle" (*BB,* vii). They saw each other from time to time but never approached the closeness Cukor shared with Katharine Hepburn, whose career he'd helped create and mold. After a visit to his home decades down the line, Myrna would write to thank Cukor for his hospitality. "You certainly know how to handle a woman. . . . You are a wonderful host and a great director and I am delighted to be your friend. Even as a Dress Extra, you have *class.*"[16]

Another friend with class, William Powell, became a regular caller at Hidden Valley Road and contributed an orange tree to its orchard. According to Cary Grant, Myrna prized it so much that she took it with her and replanted it after she no longer lived with Arthur. Powell and Jean Harlow often joined the Hornblows to make a social foursome, going off together for high-spirited weekends at Lake Arrowhead.

Arthur didn't make much room in his life for people without social cachet, fame, or status. An unapologetic elitist, he preferred the company of bright, talented, high-profile members of the entertainment community. Richard Rodgers, Jerome Kern, and George Gershwin all accepted frequent invitations to the Hornblows', each in turn making a beeline for the beautiful Steinway. Myrna remembered Kern as a diminutive imp who once crawled into and then got stuck in a large ornamental ceramic jar on the Hornblow premises. He had to be carefully eased out by Arthur, Myrna, and several servants enlisted for the task. Richard Rodgers, who'd composed songs for two Myrna Loy movies, *Love Me Tonight* and *Manhattan Melodrama,* and who would later collaborate on Arthur's movie version of *Oklahoma,* always played his own songs, competing with the other composers for the prized seat in front of the keyboard. Myrna remembered Gershwin, shortly before his untimely death in 1937, as a man who didn't converse much but who couldn't stop playing the piano and hated to go to sleep (*BB,* 138). Myrna and Arthur attended a dance in Gershwin's honor at the Blue Room of the Trocadero following his concert at Philharmonic Auditorium. Jerome Kern, Cole Porter, Kurt Weill, Sigmund Romberg, and Fred Astaire attended as well.[17]

Being partly British himself, Arthur reserved space at his table or on his tennis court for members of the Hollywood British colony: Chaplin (Myrna found him self-centered but fascinating), Basil Rathbone, David Niven, Nigel Bruce, Ronald Colman, Alfred Hitchcock, Elsa Lanchester, and Charles Laughton. Arthur had produced a Charles Laughton picture, *Ruggles of Red Gap,* and took a shine to him and Lanchester, his equally amusing character-actress wife. Laughton told Myrna after their first meeting that she reminded him of "Venus de Milo in a traffic jam."[18]

Although Arthur had little use for Myrna's family and received them with reluctance, Myrna continued to see them regularly and to support Della, providing her with a maid, a car, and a chauffeur. When Myrna once attempted to take shelter under Della's roof after she and Arthur had a quarrel, Della sided with Arthur and told her she must go home to her husband at once. This from a woman who twenty years back, in Helena, had seldom yielded an inch to her own husband. Della remained consistent in her ability to extract all she could from Myrna while at the same time withholding emotional support when a crunch came. Myrna remained overprotective of her talented but spoiled younger brother, David, who wanted a career as an artist or designer but didn't give either effort much push. Myrna, who was still helping him pay his bills, hired him to decorate her MGM dressing room, and he got his picture in the papers.

According to Betty Black, Arthur also cold-shouldered most of Myrna's old friends, making an exception of Betty and Bob Black because Bob had rank. A physician, he was an officer in the navy and later chief of the Medical Corps.[19]

Arthur did invite his elderly father to come from London for a visit on Hidden Valley Road, and he and Myrna also hosted Arthur's former nanny, Mrs. John Popper of New York. "Mrs. Popper is out on a two month's vacation with all expenses paid by the Hornblows and is occupying the guest suite at the Hidden Valley ranch. She was almost overcome when Myrna took her on the *Too Hot to Handle* set and introduced her to Clark Gable."[20]

Myrna and Arthur were hardly a typical married couple. They lived large, though they tried to avoid Hollywood's most glaring sins of ostentation on the home front. "[We have] no ballroom, no game room, no projection room, no elaborate bar." Their grounds did include servants' quarters, a curved swimming pool whose irregular contour was meant to conjure a natural lake, a tennis court cut out of the side of a hill, and extensive plantings. The garden and orchard filled with lime and other fruit trees constituted Myrna's special domain. She had dearly wanted, and got, a bathhouse built at the orchard's edge, an idea she said had been "lifted bodily" from her memory of the Williams cattle ranch of her childhood. "We had a small white milk house, where the milk was stored and churned," which the architect for the Coldwater Canyon house copied. Both the Montana milk house and its California copy had green shutters and a draping of rambling, fragrant honeysuckle. The rose garden supposedly boasted a hundred different varieties of blooms, and the vegetable garden allowed them to eat homegrown carrots, lettuce, or green beans. For her birthday a few months after they moved into their house Arthur gave her a gold charm bracelet; among the charms was a tiny gold horn (signifying Hornblow) and a miniature wheelbarrow, in honor of the garden.[21]

For an at-home interview with *Photoplay*'s Dixie Willson, Myrna greeted the reporter in the garden, wearing no makeup and a sweater and skirt, "a peasant handkerchief tied under her chin." Willson wrote that she considered Myrna Loy's glamorous movie-star image to be a contradiction of her offscreen naturalness. "What a pity that so young, so completely without artifice, she should be so clever an actress that in roles of fashion and sophistication we suffer a loss of the enchanting Peter Pan Miss Loy actually is." MGM wanted its stars to look like stars at all times, to live up to the fabulous images created by still photographers like George Hurrell and Clarence Sinclair Bull and by the costumers and cinematographers who created their screen images. In public—at restaurants, elegant parties, or premieres—Myrna complied, feeling that she had a responsibility to look glamorous. But on her own turf, unless she was dressing for one of Arthur's formal dinners, Myrna preferred to be casual. She was no Joan Crawford, known for wearing heavy makeup and trying out several outfits before picking the right one for an interview. Myrna confessed, "I hate clothes. I'm dressed to the nines all day every day on the set, every detail perfect, every hair in place, a mirror poked under my nose every time I turn around. I'm tired of clothes. I'm tired of 'looking my best.' I loathe the very mention of shopping. In the isolation of Coldwater Canyon I can wear slacks [although she favored skirts] and shuffle along in slippers."[22]

The Hornblows employed a large staff, which included Helmut, the

German chauffeur; Sergei, the Russian cook (who specialized in borscht and lamb sashlik); and Jim, the head gardener. There were seven gardeners in all and a trainer for Arthur, an excellent tennis player and a fitness buff. They had several maids, including one devoted exclusively to laundry and another, Theresa Penn, who cared for Myrna's clothes and helped in the kitchen. Theresa adored Myrna. "She never bawls you out or orders you around." Myrna took Theresa to MGM once, explained the cameras and mike cables to her, and introduced her to William Powell, Penn's favorite actor. Powell, who knew of Penn's admiration for him, told the flustered woman, "Theresa, no actor thinks you're fresh when you pay him a compliment. He thinks you're smart."[23]

Myrna remained grateful to Theresa over the decades and remembered her in her will with a bequest of $1,000 and a pair of antique rose diamond ear clips.[24]

Like most women of her generation, Myrna had been programmed for wifehood. "I wanted marriage, we all did," she says in *Being and Becoming* (123). But not until her late twenties did she unlock her mother's grip and move in with Arthur, settling into a love relationship she couldn't fully enjoy until it became official. Now she had legitimacy, but she couldn't quite match the picture of domestic bliss in her head to her current situation. She'd always wanted children. She loved them and had a knack for taking care of people. (Pets too. She had a series of dogs.) But the possibility of bearing children of her own had been closed off after her premarital abortion. Loy acknowledges the abortion in her autobiography but not the sterility; she obviously considered that revelation too intimate for public disclosure, cutting too close to the bone. She admitted she'd had moments of yearning for a child but conceded that perhaps, considering her dedication to her craft and career, and the failure of so many other Hollywood actresses to make a success of motherhood, it was for the best. For the same reason, and no doubt because of Arthur's wariness, she didn't pursue adoption.

The pain of her lost pregnancy and subsequent barrenness lingered. The scene in *To Mary—with Love* where Mary (Myrna Loy), after losing a baby, with characteristic understatement silently turns her head away on her hospital bed pillow, carries a particular poignancy and truthfulness. She avoids her husband's direct gaze, never breaking down in sobs. As the picture's producer, Kenneth MacGowan, told Myrna decades after she created that moment, "You turned your face to the wall and it was devastating" (*BB*, 126). In that scene she paused midsentence as she spoke memorable words from the Richard Sherman script: "They say the movies should be more like life; I think life should be more like the movies."

Arthur's young son Terry provided an outlet for Myrna's maternal bent. He lived mostly with his mother in Virginia but would visit California, spending every other summer with Arthur and Myrna. Myrna showered him with affection and at least once took him along to the studio with her, allowing him the fun of riding in her chauffeur-driven black limo and visiting the set. (When she could, Myrna preferred to drive her own roadster.) While his mother, Juliette, was in Reno obtaining her divorce, Terry had stayed with his father and Myrna in Bel Air. Myrna went out of her way to be kind and attentive to the somewhat lost and fragile five-year-old boy. She brought home six ducklings for him to keep and cuddle, and she put them into his bed with him; they promptly soiled the sheets. Terry responded to Myrna's warmth and ease with him. When he was just learning to hold a pencil and to form letters into carefully printed words, five-year-old Terry wrote to her from Warrenton, Virginia: "i am sorry I went away from you. How is Blackie." Myrna saved this touching child's version of a *billet doux*. Terry and she remained close for the next six decades.[25]

Terry found his father, by contrast, a formidable opponent. Formal in demeanor, demanding, and harsh, Arthur aroused fear and, at times, loathing. Arthur made few spontaneous gestures of affection to Terry. When Terry rode with him in his car, he issued directives to his chauffeur via a microphone installed in the backseat of the car, rather as if he were the Wizard of Oz projecting commands from behind a screen. After a separation of months, Arthur would greet his visiting son with a handshake, not an embrace, and once Terry was installed in the house on Hidden Valley Road, Arthur would stand at the threshold of Terry's room rather than enter it. When Terry misbehaved in some egregious but now forgotten way when he was eight years old, Arthur decreed that by way of punishment, no one in the household, including the servants, should speak to him. For lesser infractions he was given black marks on a sheet of paper.[26]

Arthur was dutiful and financially responsible, never missing an alimony payment to Juliette and regularly doling out funds for the elite private schools Terry attended, which didn't come cheap. Though very bright, Terry had a chip on his shoulder and could act out. He didn't shape up as a student until quite late in his academic career, eventually completing medical school and training further as a neurologist. He started prep school at age ten at the academically rigorous, socially traditional Allen-Stevenson School in New York City ("An Allen-Stevenson boy is a Scholar and a Gentleman"), then attended Deerfield Academy in western Massachusetts for three years. At Deerfield he was caught drinking and smoking, unforgivable breaches of campus rules. Terry completed high school at Cheshire and then got into Columbia College, but he flunked out his freshman year. Arthur's advice to his son when he was beginning Columbia, Arthur's alma mater, had been, "Always wait for the green light." He offered another maxim: "Keep your fly zipped up."

Terry was an angry kid and rebelled against his father's rigid personality and social elitism. He didn't trust Arthur's tendency to surround himself with famous people and to this day disdains celebrity culture. Terry valued Arthur's Jewish side, associating being Jewish with the warmth of his nurse Nana, and he gives Arthur credit for acknowledging his part-Jewish heritage during the Hitler era. Arthur wrote to Juliette, whose distinguished father had served as the assistant secretary of the treasury under Woodrow Wilson, to tell her he didn't want Terry, then in prep school in the East, to grow up believing himself to be 100 percent Anglo-Saxon and Protestant.

In fairness to Arthur it should be said that to his stepson Michael he proved a very different, much kinder, and less judgmental paternal figure than he was to Terry. Michael, born to Arthur's third wife, Leonora Schinasi Morris, during her brief marriage to her first husband, Wayne Morris (a Warner Bros. actor, friend of Ronald Reagan, and later, navy pilot and decorated war hero), was a gentler, more compliant boy than Terry, a darling instead of a rebel and a good student who did everything right. Michael saw little of his biological father and bonded readily with his stepfather. He proved to be easier for Arthur to love than the problematic Terry, who must have reminded Arthur of his failings during his first marriage. Arthur legally adopted Michael, and Michael, encouraged by Leonora, dropped the surname Morris to become a proud bearer of the Hornblow moniker.[27]

Myrna's closeness to Terry wasn't something she shared with the press, but the fans certainly knew she had a husband. Despite this, men all over were being encouraged to entertain their own fantasies about settling down with filmdom's Perfect Wife. "Must Marry Myrna" clubs began forming around the United States, and she had at least twenty fan clubs in Great Britain. Myrna's fan mail, according to the *Los Angeles Herald*

Express, included around seventy marriage proposals a month. "It is curious to note the fact that the marriage of a movie queen affects not at all the number of letters she receives proposing marriage." The state of denial about Myrna Loy's availability carried over to the MGM dining room, where Jimmy Stewart went around saying, "There ought to be a law against any man who doesn't marry Myrna Loy" (*BB*, viii), and Spencer Tracy installed himself at the We Hate Arthur Hornblow table.[28]

MGM, meanwhile, had every intention of milking Myrna Loy's talent for wifehood for all it was worth.

CHAPTER II

Wife vs. Mistress

Asked in 1960 to survey past movie trends, Myrna zeroed in on the changing ways Hollywood had pictured married couples over the decades. "When I began playing leads," she told the columnist Dorothy Manners, "the troubles and pleasures of the hero and heroine took them right up to marriage, but never into it. Then there was the phase, which lasted a number of years, in which the theme of many pictures was that it was possible to be happy and content, though married. I think *The Thin Man* established this school of thought. Now we seem to be in a cycle showing how to be miserable, though married." It's clear she thought that by 1960 the movies had taken a step down since their (and her) glory days in the mid to late 1930s.[1]

If not every film career fits this marriage-centered template, Myrna Loy's certainly does. Pre–Nora Charles, she'd played the Other Woman repeatedly and, as talkies came into their own, a few wives, too: the wronged but forgiving wife of a philandering banker in *Transatlantic;* the sexy but unsympathetic wife of publisher Leslie Howard in *The Animal Kingdom;* the district attorney's at first content, then troubled, spouse in *Manhattan Melodrama.* Post–Nora Charles, she still occasionally got assigned the role of a romantically available single woman, and in *Parnell* (1937) she even managed to be cast as a politician's mistress; but now it was the wife parts that defined her. Although she didn't choose to be branded again with a type, typed she was, this time as somebody's quick-witted and usually upper-class other half.

The wife label took hold before Myrna had wed Arthur in her private life, but by becoming the very social Mrs. Hornblow, often photographed with her producer husband at movie premieres, fashionable restaurants, and A-list parties, she reinforced her glamorous married-woman image. To her fans she remained someone to like, adulate, or desire, even if she'd become unavailable to the legions of men who indulged fantasies about wedding her. Myrna's friend and fellow actor Robert Ryan claimed that the widespread male desire to marry Myrna Loy helped to boost the marriage rate in the 1930s, but, in fact, during the Depression American couples were postponing their weddings, waiting for less financially strapped times.[2]

The enormous popularity of *The Thin Man* and the success of Loy's partnership with Powell sealed her fate. In 1936 alone she appeared in three movies with him, twice as his wife: *The Great Ziegfeld,* a musical extravaganza and biopic in which Powell portrayed impresario Florenz Ziegfeld and she played his second wife, Billie Burke; *Libeled Lady,* a multistar screwball comedy featuring Jean Harlow and Spencer Tracy, as well as Loy and Powell; and *After the Thin Man,* released around Christmas time.

Her screen union with Powell held fast, but theirs was an open marriage that allowed them to reunite periodically after taking off for cinematic escapades with other marital or romantic partners. If she couldn't appear onscreen as William Powell's partner, she'd be some other actor's desirable mate. Over the years after 1934, in addition to Powell she was paired, as either sweetheart or wife, with Clark Gable, Robert Taylor, Warner Baxter, Robert Montgomery, Cary Grant, Spencer Tracy, Franchot Tone, Don Ameche, George Brent, Tyrone Power, Fredric March, Shepperd Strudwick, Clifton Webb, Melvyn Douglas, Walter Pidgeon, Robert Ryan, Charles Boyer, Adolphe Menjou, and (in a made-for-TV film) Henry Fonda. It's quite a list.

Somehow she missed becoming the screen wife of Spencer Tracy, but she does fall for him—she's an unlikely jewel thief and he's a G-man— in *Whipsaw,* her first movie to be released after she went on strike against MGM in 1935. Tracy, recently arrived at MGM from 20th Century–Fox, was at this stage a lesser star than she; her salary was slightly higher. He initially considered her standoffish, because of her habit of studying the script between scenes, but they were soon "on ribbing terms." As she watched him work, Myrna concluded that she and Tracy shared a similar approach to acting. They both sought naturalness, but each at the same time thought through all the details and planned every move. What appeared spontaneous was usually carefully choreographed (*BB,* 151).[3]

Despite having both a major drinking problem and a wife, Tracy chased women. He carried a torch for Myrna offscreen, trying repeatedly, without success, to set up dates with her (*BB*, 122). Faithful to Arthur, Myrna kept Tracy at bay, but being desired by a man as gifted, attractive, and complex as Tracy pleased her. She felt a pang of disappointment tinged with jealousy a few years down the road when Tracy told her he had found the woman he wanted to be with: Katharine Hepburn. "As selfish as it sounds, I liked having a man like Spence in the background, wanting me" (*BB*, 154). Over the years Hepburn landed many prizes that Myrna would have liked to claim, down to costarring with Henry Fonda in *On Golden Pond*. After Tracy's confession about Hepburn's place in his affections the door shut on what had been an ego-stoking flirtation with the man she called Spence.[4]

During her post–*Thin Man* heyday at MGM, Myrna Loy never carried a movie on her name alone, nor did she often take on roles conveying overwhelming womanpower or female autonomy. "In most of my pictures I complemented the male character, who usually carried the story," she explains in her autobiography, drawing a distinction between her signature partner roles and Bette Davis's powerhouses or Rosalind Russell's female executives. "This often meant that my roles were subordinate, but that's the way I wanted it." Loy didn't feel comfortable in command position, preferring an identity that Ethan Mordden defines as "consort rather than ruler." She considered herself miscast in her role as a magazine's crisply efficient executive editor in 1940's *Third Finger, Left Hand* and said that her leading man, Melvyn Douglas, an actor whose comic style blended well with her own, had to help her "get through" that one (*BB*, 164).[5]

Unlike Bette Davis, Katharine Hepburn, Marlene Dietrich, or Norma Shearer, Loy never wore a crown onscreen, although many thought her regal in bearing; and in *The Black Watch*, back in 1929, she'd played the Joan of Arc of India. Fans elected her Queen of Hollywood at the end of 1937, when readers of newspapers around the country cast their votes, choosing Clark Gable king. The syndicated *New York Daily News* columnist Ed Sullivan presented the royal couple's tinsel and purple velvet crowns at the packed El Capitan Theatre in Hollywood as millions of radio listeners tuned in to hear the coronation on a nationwide hookup on NBC. "I am presenting these crowns on behalf of 20,000,000 readers," announced Ed Sullivan at the microphone.[6]

After that, Clark Gable nicknamed Myrna "Queenie." When Gable,

Myrna, and Spencer Tracy appeared together in 1938's *Test Pilot*—MGM had reunited Gable and Loy partly to cash in on the Ed Sullivan–generated publicity—Tracy would tease Gable on the set with catcalls of "Long live the King!" (*BB*, 152). Myrna held on to her flimsy crown, and savored her moment of glory, but she didn't allow herself to get carried away. Yes, she wanted her talents to be recognized, put to good use, and financially rewarded, but she kept her stardom in perspective. Being a movie star never defined her as it defined a Joan Crawford. Myrna understood that fame was fickle, and she guessed that her days of stardom might be numbered. She spoke of retiring from the movies while still young.

The closest she ever came to a superwoman role was in *Double Wedding* (1937), where as Margit Agnew, a bossy control freak of a fashion designer / shop owner, she micromanages her sister Irene's love life, pays the bills for both Irene and Irene's milquetoast boyfriend Waldo, and acts like a five-star general in any situation. But even in that movie, love trumps power. After encountering the chaos principle in the person of Bohemian artist and acting coach Charles Lodge (William Powell), who sports a beret and lives in a trailer, Margit in the end gives up her independence, yielding even her consciousness—she's knocked out by an Oscar statuette—to become a bride. Usually it's Powell who gets to do the physical clowning, but here Loy has a go at it, too. Charlie's refusal to be cowed by Margit, his willingness to take her on, guarantees that he's the man she'll fall for. Too bad *Double Wedding* isn't a better movie. It's contrived and flatfooted, and neither Loy nor Powell enjoyed making it, despite its bang-up finale: a free-for-all wedding featuring two brides (Margit and Irene), two grooms, a confused preacher, quite a few drunks from the bar next door, and a maximum of commotion—all crammed into Charlie's tiny trailer in a Capra-esque crowd scene. Even this witless farce succeeds at fulfilling Myrna Loy's MGM destiny by leaving her true to type, as Powell's adoring bride.

A few famous screen actors—Boris Karloff and Mae West for instance—actually liked typecasting. They liked having a niche, being associated with a single role or kind of character—the Quipster Hussy, the Monster Man. An actor with a type owned a kind of work-insurance. She or he always had a safe place to go and could bank on being called on to play similar characters over and over again. Repeating an exaggerated and predictable type had once been the norm for vaudeville performers, for many stage players, and for scores of silent film actors too. Being typed helped both to define you and to sell your talent to the public, which seems to love what it already knows. Eugene O'Neill's father, James, played the same character in *The Count of Monte Cristo* on the stage more than six thousand times, to his undoing; but the family ate. Being associated with a single type or character fit into a marketing strategy related to advertising slogans, logos, and brand names. It was a way to telegraph your professional identity and invite the audience to get familiar.

Myrna liked being a partner, but she wasn't among those who enjoyed the safety and simplifying built into typecasting. Although she initially accepted the Perfect Wife moniker, and played along with it in multiple films, most of them produced at MGM, by the end of the 1930s she came to resent being pigeonholed and to tire of the predictability it brought to her career. After a few years of being locked in, continuing to occupy the wife niche started to feel like wearing manacles. Loy hoped to be known as an actress who could handle a range of roles, in drama as well as comedy: sad women as well as happy, virtuous or flawed, married or single. She didn't want to keep trading on her past successes. "I'm sick to death of playing those women—those . . . sweet wives—who have been crowding in on me with a vengeance in recent years," she said in 1939. "I aspired to them once. I'm anxious to retire from them now."[7]

The problem was that even after the studio finally upgraded her status and started paying her $4,000 a week on a new contract, MGM, the studio with the most stars, the largest plant, and the biggest budgets, found it easier to continue casting her as a congenial wife than to seek out fresh ideas. Loy was making money for Metro. Quigley's Annual List of box-office leaders in *Motion Picture Almanac* named her one of the ten top-earning actors in Hollywood in both 1937 and 1938, and there seemed to be no incentive to change a winning formula. Innovative in the way it managed star publicity, coordinated multiple elaborate productions, pooled its talent, and showcased the art director Cedric Gibbons's gleaming set designs, MGM marched to a conservative beat and tended to play it safe. Committed after 1934 to what we now call family values and to making "happy pictures about happy people" (the words are Louis B. Mayer's), the studio avoided risk when it came to hot-button social issues or politics.

Mayer himself, a staunch Republican and enemy of FDR, was the father of two overprotected daughters. He once told the writer Frances Marion, "I'm determined that my little Edie and my little Irene will never be embarrassed. And they won't [be], if all my pictures are moral and clean." Mayer, who started out in the junk business and once owned a burlesque theater, was no saint. He recognized the importance of sex, on the screen and off, and in pre-Code days seems to have had no problem with Jean Harlow's bombshells, Garbo's steamy love scenes with John Gilbert, or Myrna Loy's exotic nymphomaniac kinkiness in *The Mask of Fu Manchu.* He hosted annual alcohol-drenched orgylike Christmas parties at the MGM plant, plied visiting salesmen with starlet "dates," and permitted himself some extracurricular romances during the waning years of his long first marriage, which ended in divorce. The dissonance between what he advocated and the way he actually behaved does not seem to have cost the wily, capable, and highly theatrical Mayer many sleepless nights. Appearances concerned him, the things the public could see, more than what took place behind the curtain.[8]

Casting Myrna Loy repeatedly as The Wife spelled safety, both because it fulfilled audience expectations and because it conformed to the enforced Production Code, which decreed, "The sanctity of the institution of marriage and the home shall be upheld." Adultery, once a prime mover of Hollywood plots, now had to be skirted, shunned, or, if depicted, punished. According to the Code, "adultery must not be explicitly treated, or justified, or presented attractively." Divorce, too, was ruled off limits; it couldn't be shown in what Breen and his compeers considered to be a favorable light. Abortion, of course, was completely out of the question.[9]

To Mary—with Love, a melodrama made when Myrna was on loan to 20th Century–Fox, is a film about a marriage. It tracks the first ten years in the tumultuous union of Mary (Myrna Loy) and Jock Wallace (Warner Baxter), wed in 1925. As it follows them through the decade, the movie tests the Code's moral boundaries. It touches on both adultery and divorce, and while it doesn't show an abortion, it does include the intimate, emotionally devastating aftermath of a stillbirth. Joseph Breen made a laundry list of objections to the script, and some of the required cuts and revisions were made by 20th Century–Fox, which was paying Myrna $3,000 a week but was giving Metro $9,000 a week for the privilege of borrowing her. Despite Breen's initial protests, much of the redlined material stayed in the completed film, which still managed to win a purity seal. In *To Mary—with Love* adultery threatens to unmoor the Wallaces. Mary starts packing to leave Jock immediately after she finds another woman's compact in the couple's bedroom, but Jock, repentant, persuades her to stay. The lady with the compact (an ironic Claire Trevor) makes it clear, though, that she'd happily run off with Jock, given the chance. Mary, too, has encountered temptation but resists the professed love of an old friend with a yen for her.[10]

The much-tested Wallace marriage just barely stays afloat, buffeted by economic ruin after the crash of 1929, unemployment, a period of living on Mary's scant earnings as a candy store clerk, Jock's boozing, the shared heartbreak of a stillbirth, and a string of divorce threats. Punctuated with newsreel clips that recall such actual events as the Tunney-Dempsey fight and Lindbergh's welcome-home ticker-tape parade, the Richard Sherman screenplay does a meager job with both characterization and structure. John Cromwell's haphazard directing doesn't help. The seemingly endless sequence of highs and lows, fights and reconciliations, lean years and fat lacks focus and becomes wearying. *Variety* had reason to slam *To Mary—with Love* as a "hash-over of the semi-realistic glamorized Hollywood approach to unemployment and tough times," tagging it condescendingly as a movie that "will please women, but it will make men restless with its meandering triviality and lack of action." But the most telling response to this film comments not on its dubious success as a movie but rather on the institution of marriage. The reviewer for the *London Observer* wrote of *To Mary—with Love*, "It begins where most pictures end, with confetti; it ends where all marriages end, with compromise."[11]

With adultery banished, sex within marriage became the thing. Myrna considered her role as Linda Stanhope, wife of the publisher Clark Gable in *Wife vs. Secretary,* one of her sexiest. She and Gable are constantly smooching. "That woman had one foot in the bed through the whole story," Loy told David Chierichetti. But the Breen office objected even to married love when shows of affection became too overheated onscreen. Warner Baxter's kiss on Loy's bare shoulder in *To Mary—with Love* elicited an outcry from the Production Code Administration, although that particularly erotic bit stayed in the movie. Breen filled his notes with warnings to cover up. The exposed flesh married couples displayed in the privacy of their bedrooms, when caught by the camera, troubled him. Where Gable, in *Wife vs. Secretary,* is supposed to appear naked from the waist up, Breen writes to Mayer, "Please put an undershirt on him."[12]

The cash register ruled, and placating Breen while trying to also please the public demanded deftness. *Wife vs. Secretary* tames Jean Harlow's persona, not eliminating her sexiness (with Harlow that couldn't be done) but toning it down. Previously cast as a come-and-get-me platinum blonde, she's a more subdued "brownette" here, dressed demurely. As Gable's efficient, businesslike secretary "Whitey," she wears office-appropriate blouses, jackets, and skirts. The original script placed Whitey at home in luxurious digs that, as Breen saw it, made her seem too much like a kept woman. Revisions by the uncredited script doctors Frances Goodrich and Albert

Hackett downgraded her to a modest home shared with her parents, who invite boyfriend Jimmy Stewart over for dinner with the folks. Even toned down, however, Harlow remains a shapely knockout who inspires everyone who sees her alongside boss Gable to suspect hanky-panky. Gable's wife, Linda (Loy), at first a trusting soul who brushes aside suggestions that her handsome husband is having an affair with Whitey, eventually succumbs to jealousy, which nearly wrecks her marriage. Whitey, who's attracted to boss Gable but doesn't want to be a husband-stealer, tells Linda she'd be a fool to leave her marriage, and Linda listens. Husband and wife kiss and make up.

While superficially conforming to the Code, *Wife vs. Secretary* at the same time teases its audience with suggestive situations. Gable at one point climbs into a phone booth with Harlow, and at another goes off with her for a few days of after hours professional collaboration in Havana, while wifey Loy frets at home by the phone. One might argue that all the teasing is dirtier than actual sex would be, but Breen allowed the teasing, while nixing the real thing.

Although she's clearly in anguish, Linda remains a sympathetic character. The *Hollywood Reporter* opined, "Myrna Loy performs the wife as only Myrna Loy can. The wife is obviously wrong in her suspicions, [but] is a grand person and made appealingly human by Miss Loy. Her graciousness, breeding and excellent sense of values are stressed to make impossible a hint of the shrew." Over and over again her equanimity and willingness to shrug off a husband's failings were the qualities that won praise for the wives Loy portrayed. She was Mrs. Congeniality, rarely complaining, attempting to reform her mate, or resorting to outbursts of anger or blame.[13]

The private Loy began to insist on drawing a distinction between her true self and the perfect wives everyone associated with her name. When Gladys Hall asked if she'd really like to join her husband in a drunken round of barhopping, the answer came back a resounding "No." Hall pressed, "You wouldn't be the Good Sport, the Gamest Girl in the world and stay with him?" Myrna instantly shot back, "I would NOT!"[14]

At least one moviegoing wife griped to a reporter that Loy's Perfect Wife set a standard impossible to match. This fan surmised that a husband would compare his for-real wife with Nora Charles on the screen and find his spouse wanting. "Naturally, no husband who sits and watches Miss Loy being so sweet—no matter whether he comes home drunk or makes eyes at the blonde down the street—is going to be satisfied with his own wife," this woman complained.[15]

During the 1930s, Loy-as-wife twice found herself struggling through hard times onscreen, first in *To Mary—with Love* and later in *Lucky Night* (1939), when the characters she played were married to men down on their luck. Both times, short on cash, her character has to scrimp, do her own housework, and take a low-paying job to help make ends meet. Although struggling economically in a way that Depression-era audiences recognized, Mary clearly was not from the working class, nor was the actress portraying her. Loy was no Barbara Stanwyck or Mae West. Her diction was so elegant that for a scene in *Third Finger, Left Hand* where she briefly turned herself into a hip-swinging Brooklyn tart who pronounced *worms* as "woims," she had to work with a dialect coach. In both *To Mary—with Love* and *Lucky Night* Loy's character starts life as a lady, suffers hardship, and ends with at least the promise of better days to come. Usually, though, she played not just a lady but a lady of wealth and privilege.

In *Wife vs. Secretary* she and husband Clark Gable share a posh house decorated by Cedric Gibbons in what he called "Neo Greek" style; the place comes equipped with a grand curved staircase, pseudo-Greek decorative art, and a British manservant in livery. The missus has her pick of furs to wear in town, but in the boudoir it's all about floaty chiffon negligees trimmed in lace. Loy is wearing one of these confections when lovey-dovey husband Gable slips a diamond bracelet into her breakfast trout on her birthday as a surprise gift. No forgetting the wife's birthday in this cozy picture-book ménage.

Wife vs. Secretary, directed by the gifted but sometimes syrupy Clarence Brown, extols marriage, placating censors. Not so the irreverent *Libeled Lady,* where wedlock comes off as a jerry-built, totally arbitrary arrangement. Since the Code adopted the Roman Catholic view that the union of man and wife is a sacred, eternal bond, and since it decreed that Hollywood movies must always handle matrimony with respect, it's a wonder that this comic gem ever managed to get produced and distributed, let alone gross $2.7 million to become one of the year's biggest hits.

When he saw the first-draft script, Breen stormed: "Present treatment of material is, in our opinion, *in violation of the Production Code.* Unless changes are made, as suggested below, it will be our duty to reject a picture made from this script." The head censor lambasted the screenplay's "general tendency to treat the institution of marriage casually and with ridicule."[16]

Breen won some major compromises and deletions. Specific lines of dialogue implying that Jean Harlow's character, Gladys, had long been her boyfriend's mistress were removed, and bits of business (Gladys stuffing a key into her bra) squelched. William Powell would not be permitted to spank Myrna Loy. Even after MGM made what it considered the necessary revisions, two months after he first listed his objections, Breen was still howling that parts of the script "reflect unfavorably upon marriage and the sanctity of the home." But a few weeks later, after Metro made more relatively minor changes, the picture was cleared for release. Its impertinent take on wedded bliss remained intact.[17]

Lawrence Weingarten, the film's producer, also doubted that his film would ever find its way into theaters. "When I sent the script to Myrna Loy, she disappeared, went to Europe," he recalled. He claimed that Harlow, presumably because she now wanted to shake her bad-girl image and to play nicer girls, didn't want the role, a statement disputed by Harlow's biographer, David Stenn, who says she did want to join the four-star cast. Weingarten claimed that "Spencer Tracy had never played comedy before and he wanted to [instead] do *The Plough and the Stars*," a John Ford movie based on a Sean O'Casey play that would have required MGM to allow Tracy to be loaned to RKO; Thalberg had agreed to the loan-out, but after Thalberg's September 1936 death, L. B. Mayer vetoed it, probably because Tracy had suddenly become a hot property. Weingarten claimed further that "Bill Powell played [in *Libeled Lady*] because it was his last picture on the contract [he had] and he wanted to get a new contract." As Weingarten remembered it, when he agreed to produce *Libeled Lady*, he was up against reluctance from three out of four stars.[18]

Somehow *Libeled Lady* got made, and the four lead players harmonized like a crackerjack barbershop quartet. Though Powell received more critical plaudits than the others, and Harlow won top billing, the movie showcases egalitarian ensemble acting at its best. The critic for *Time* magazine raved: "the balancing is done with as much precision as if the roles had been weighed in an apothecary's scales." Jack Conway, an underappreciated "action director" who had once been an actor and assistant director under D. W. Griffith, injected his sense of rapid-fire antic fun into the whole enterprise. All four lead players felt affection for the film and for each other. Harlow relished another chance to work with Powell for the first time since *Reckless*, a 1935 musical that had cynically exploited both Paul Bern's violent death and her romance with Powell.[19]

Harlow was going through another rough patch in her tumultuous personal life. Forlorn after an imposed hospital abortion, when she had the chance, she would drink too much. She had also managed to get so badly sunburned that she became ill; shooting *Libeled Lady* had to be suspended for a few days. Powell, for his part, was flourishing, despite some recent eye trouble. His career kept flying high, and he felt totally at ease working with both Harlow and Loy.

Spencer Tracy, notorious for disappearing during shoots to go on benders, behaved himself while making *Libeled Lady*. His recent work playing a priest in the Jeanette MacDonald megamusical *San Francisco* (directed by Woody Van Dyke) contributed to a hit that was breaking box-office records and making L. B. Mayer glad that he'd managed to lure Tracy to MGM. *Libeled Lady*'s opening tracking shot, showing Harlow, Powell, Loy, and Tracy arm in arm, striding toward the camera and beaming as the credits roll, tells us that at least for the duration of the movie, happy days are here.

The completely improbable plot of *Libeled Lady* turns on a revenge theme. A newspaper, the *New York Evening Star,* has printed a bogus story about an American heiress trying to steal a British lady's husband. The snooty, though in this case blameless, heiress is Connie Allenbury (Myrna Loy), and neither she nor her short-tempered moneybags father (Walter Connolly) likes this scandal-mongering one bit. Before the *Evening Star* editor Warren Haggerty (Spencer Tracy) can stop the presses, pull the first edition from the trucks setting out to distribute it, or apologize to the furious Allenburys, they've read the incendiary news story. The libeled Miss Allenbury sues the *Evening Star* to the tune of $5 million. Haggerty goes apoplectic. He does lots of screaming in this movie. If Connie Allenbury wins her suit, the paper goes under. So Haggerty concocts a scheme. He will engage former *Star* ace reporter Bill Chandler (William Powell) to return to the *Star*. Chandler will marry some woman, any woman willing to say yes, and then entice Connie Allenbury into a tryst. Connie will be discovered fooling around with a married man, and, fearing bad publicity, she'll be forced to drop the suit.

Haggerty, it turns out, has his own problems. On the day the newspaper printed the bogus story, he'd agreed to finally marry his longtime sweetheart, Gladys. Haggerty cancels the wedding, as he's evidently done several times before. Gladys, in her white satin wedding gown and carrying a bouquet of orange blossoms as Mendelssohn's "Wedding March" erupts in the background, storms into Haggerty's pressroom, on a tear. "I won't stand for it!" she screams. "You can't do this to me!" Then comes the plaintive line, which she'll repeat later: "If you don't want to marry me, just say so." For the private Jean Harlow, the words must have carried a sting, since Powell didn't want to make her his offscreen wife.

Breen was entirely correct in his belief that *Libeled Lady* kids marriage. Gladys, stuck on Warren Haggerty even though he's mean to her, goes through with a farcical wedding to Powell's character, the conniving Bill Chandler. Once again Haggerty and his all-consuming newspaper job are jerking her around. But Gladys, though shrill, is a sucker for Haggerty and obliges him one more time by getting hitched to a guy she refers to as "that baboon." Harlow, a terrific comedienne, hits the note just right: love tinged by hurt and outrage. Apparently Gladys isn't legally divorced from her first husband, so the marriage to baboon Chandler won't be binding; it's just a put-up job that will help Haggerty out of a tight spot. But in this zany world all connections between lovers or spouses are tied with a slipknot. Every one of the four leading characters has to have a mate, but it doesn't seem to matter who that mate is. This is a square dance in which you swing your partner and your corner lady too. "She may be his wife," says sputtering Haggerty in one outburst, "but she's engaged to me."

Gladys begins to fall for her make-believe husband, Bill Chandler, while Haggerty sustains his not-so-slow burn, and Chandler gradually succumbs to the charms of the woman he was hired to entrap, haughty Connie Allenbury. As Myrna Loy plays her, Connie changes during the movie. She starts out as an icy snob, so full of herself she can't be bothered to correctly pronounce Chandler's name after he's behaved chivalrously toward her on an ocean liner, but she gradually defrosts as she gets to know him. At her father's suburban New York estate she's even willing to turn temporarily into a homey type and fry up some pancakes for him. She ends up proposing to Chandler, and they immediately rush off to recite their vows, even though Chandler might still be married to pretend-bride Gladys.

If you think about it, which this fast-paced movie doesn't give you one second to do, you wonder why anyone in *Libeled Lady* would *want* to marry. Marriage doesn't come off as a particularly attractive bargain. "You mustn't fight," Haggerty advises Chandler and Gladys once they've gotten temporarily hitched. "Why not?" Bill shoots back. "We're married." Like Nora Charles, Connie Allenbury is wealthy, well spoken, urbane, and capable of great charm, but we're far from the happy-couple territory of *The Thin Man.*

Libeled Lady credits three screenwriters. "In those days we felt that multiple writers are better than one," recalled Weingarten. "Maurine Watkins was the playwright, George Oppenheimer [handled the] comedy, and Howard Emmett Rogers was our plot man." Before she arrived in Hollywood, Watkins, a former *Chicago Tribune* reporter, wrote the

1926 play *Chicago,* a lurid tale of murder laced with gin, jail, and jazz, which after its Broadway run would inspire three widely spaced, highly successful Hollywood movies. Instead of death row, *Libeled Lady* focuses on the smart-alecky world of the newsroom, a favorite of comedy writers since Hecht and MacArthur scored their stage, then screen, triumph with *The Front Page. Libeled Lady* involves conniving, fast-talking reporters and spoiled socialites. It doesn't troll at the bottom of the social cesspool the way *Chicago* does, but it's still an urban tale—tough, snide, and cynical. The scheming Bill Chandler bluffs his way to a big paycheck from the *Evening Star* by pretending he's become a sought-after novelist who just got handed a big advance. The truth is, he's about to be kicked out of his hotel because he's overlooked the little matter of paying his bill. Even his riotous trout-fishing escapade, filmed on location in the Sierra Nevada foothills, is part of an intended scam. He's trying to palm himself off to Connie and her father as a gentleman of means who's an avid sportsman instead of the raffish, unscrupulous reporter/con man he really is.[20]

As hilarious as it is nonsensical, *Libeled Lady* nearly broke the bank, cleaning up both at the box office and in the reviews it generated. Praising its crackling dialogue and situations that "reek with lowdown and slapstick," *Variety* pronounced it "a sockeroo of a comedy" and a "till ringer." Edwin Schallert in the *Los Angeles Times* named it "one of the maddest, merriest and best of the year." Years later, when it was being revived in New York, Vincent Canby held up *Libeled Lady* as one of the great screwball comedies and an example of studio system filmmaking at its best, a collaborative effort showcasing the teamwork of superb professionals. He praised the breakneck pace, the lightness of touch, and the warmth and sheer joyousness of the scenes Powell and Loy share. "There is probably nothing else in movies to equal the élan of their courtship scenes, except those of Astaire and Rogers." Katharine Hepburn, who knew a thing or two about fast-paced screwball comedy, privately called *Libeled Lady* the "funniest damn thing I've ever seen in my life."[21]

Powell's stellar turn in *Libeled Lady* got no nod when Oscar time rolled around in March of 1937. He was competing with himself this banner year, and his brilliant performance as a hobo turned butler in *My Man Godfrey,* a Universal film, stole the nomination. Warner Bros.' Paul Muni would end up receiving the Best Actor Oscar for his portrayal of Louis Pasteur. MGM and Warner Bros. pictures tended to monopolize the Academy Awards, simply because those two studios had the most voting members.

At the Biltmore Hotel's Academy Awards banquet Powell waited and watched, sharing a table with three other Hollywood luminaries. His date was Jean Harlow, but on this glittering night he was double dating with his ex-wife, and recent costar, Carole Lombard. How civilized. She too had been nominated and would be chosen Best Actress for her standout zany turn in *My Man Godfrey.* Lombard's current lover and future husband, Clark Gable, still not divorced from wife Ria, completed the foursome. Although MGM, as usual, walked off with multiple trophies, *Libeled Lady,* nominated for Best Picture, didn't win. Chaplin's *Modern Times* wasn't so much as mentioned, although it was a top-grossing film of 1936.

The movie chosen Best Picture of 1936 was *The Great Ziegfeld,* which to some critics, both when it first made the rounds and later, seemed more remarkable for its "legs and tinsel" extravagance than for its excellence. The choice now stands out as a prime example of Academy fallibility. *Ziegfeld* includes seven go-for-broke production numbers and twenty-three songs. Graham Greene, at the time a reviewer for the British *Spectator,* tagged it "this huge inflated glass-blown object." He likened the interminable film, which clocks in at three hours, to the feat of a flagpole sitter who makes you wonder how he manages to stay aloft.[22]

Greene got it right. *The Great Ziegfeld* provides a case study in the way Metro could confuse quantity with quality. In its ads MGM boasted of the "countless beauties, trained lions, ponies, dogs and other animals" on hand and bragged, "So BIG that only MGM could handle it." One of the top box-office winners of the decade (it brought in $4,673,000 worldwide), and one of MGM's most lavishly mounted musicals, *The Great Ziegfeld* suffers from elephantiasis. A total of 250 tailors and seamstresses spent six months sewing the costumes Adrian designed for it; they used fifty pounds of silver sequins and twelve yards of white ostrich plumes. The revolving stage built for one mammoth production number, "A Pretty Girl Is like a Melody," required multiple tons of steel to support 182 bedecked dancers. *The Great Ziegfeld* was MGM's first "special" to be "road-showed" since 1933's *Dinner at Eight.* A road show involved opening a movie in major cities and prime movie palaces, at boosted ticket prices comparable to those for live theater productions.[23]

Ziegfeld cost more than $2 million to produce and took nearly two years to plan. Universal first owned the rights to the story, and began production, but when costs spiraled beyond what Universal could afford, MGM paid its competitor $300,000 and took over. The blockbuster employed about a thousand people, was in production for more than two months, and expended sixteen reels of film, after cutting. In keeping with the post–*Grand Hotel* MGM tradition of packing several stars into one movie, it put three names on the marquee: William Powell, Myrna Loy, and Luise Rainer. Thanks in part to Powell's generosity, Rainer had made enough of a splash in *Escapade* to now rank as a star. Fannie Brice, Frank Morgan, and Virginia Bruce got second billing. But along with the movie-star names, the additional names of former "Ziegfeld Follies" Broadway revue luminaries joined the credits, with singer and comedienne Fannie Brice heading the list. Eddie Cantor was played by his former understudy, not by Cantor himself (too costly). A stand-in played Will Rogers, too; the real Rogers had been killed in a plane crash in August 1935.

Myrna Loy was chosen to play Ziegfeld's second wife, the actress Billie Burke, fairly late in the day, more than a year after the June 1935 announcement that William Powell would portray Ziegfeld. Powell had been busy costarring with other actresses, for instance Rainer, Rosalind Russell, and Jean Arthur, while Myrna took her unscheduled vacation in Europe, and MGM, now eager to reinstate the Powell-Loy team as preeminent, promoted *The Great Ziegfeld* as another Powell-Loy vehicle. In fact, Loy isn't a full-fledged costar; she doesn't appear at all until the latter portion of *The Great Ziegfeld*. This was the first picture for which MGM signed her, though not the first released, following her return to the studio after going absent without leave from the set of *Escapade*.

According to *Variety,* Ziegfeld's widow, Billie Burke, who partially owned the rights to the Ziegfeld story, and who today is probably best remembered as Glinda the Good Witch in *The Wizard of Oz,* had a hand in picking Myrna to portray her younger self, although Billie Burke's biographer reveals that Miriam Hopkins would have been her first choice. MGM thought Loy should be grateful. Being chosen for this relatively small role in a very expensive, much-hyped A picture was meant to fulfill the "promise on [the] studio's part that Miss Loy would be given better assignments." Presumably Miss Burke preferred not to play her younger self.[24]

Although MGM awarded Loy top billing alongside Powell, Luise Rainer stole most of the distaff thunder and would receive her first Oscar for her performance as Ziegfeld's first wife, Anna Held, the French chanteuse with the hourglass figure. The award came mainly in response to just one of Rainer's scenes, the celebrated "Hello, Flo" telephone call congratulating Ziegfeld on his second marriage. Rainer pulled out all the stops performing this overwrought one-sided conversation, which she later said she based on a production she'd seen of Cocteau's *La voix humaine*. Rainer's emotional tour de force involved tipping off the audience, allowing them to measure the distance between Anna Held's inner torment and the polite, cover-up words she speaks into the receiver to her ex-husband. Over the phone, her voice filled with repressed tears, she insists that she's happy, "never better," but we know she's heartbroken. She throws herself, face down, on a bed and collapses in sobs the moment after she hangs up the phone.[25]

It couldn't have been easy for Myrna, whose rise to stardom came in small, slow steps stretched over a decade, to see the newcomer Rainer ascend to such widely publicized acclaim in just her second Hollywood film, also her second opposite Powell. Myrna was too discreet to reveal in public the envy or frustration she must have felt.

The critics judged Myrna Loy less sparkling than usual in *The Great Ziegfeld*. "Miss Loy is a stately Billie Burke, and somewhat lacking, we fear, in Miss Burke's effervescence and gaiety," Frank Nugent wrote in the *New York Times*. Cecilia Ager, usually a Loy enthusiast, found her Billie Burke pretty, but "stilted, like her rigidly waxed and set blond wig." Harrison Carroll in the *Los Angeles Herald Express* acknowledged the hurdles Loy faced in trying to portray a living woman who was widely known and still active as a Metro actress. He praised Loy for not attempting to imitate Burke's mannerisms.[26]

Myrna's lack of sizzle didn't stem from deficient acting on her part but rather from the mushy script written by William Anthony McGuire, a former assistant to Ziegfeld. (McGuire also was the original producer of *The Great Ziegfeld*, before Universal pulled out and MGM's Hunt Stromberg took the reins.) The screenplay's Billie Burke is sympathetic, yes, but no showstopper. She's a gentle nurturer, not a sassy showbiz headliner. The actual Billie Burke, a redhead, emerged out of a circus family into Broadway stardom. In the movie Burke marries Ziegfeld when he's getting on in years and his career is beginning to slip. She's much younger than he and at her professional peak. Ziegfeld's eventual decline involves a drop in his professional status when the Follies no longer dominates Broadway. He faces financial ruin after the crash of 1929, and a slackening of his masculine zip. As a younger man, the lady-killer Ziegfeld borrowed, spent, and invested money recklessly, constantly teetering on the brink of ruin but always managing to land on his feet, in triumph, with a string of hits lighting up the Broadway sky and a gorgeous woman more than willing to provide arm candy. Famous for "Glorifying the American Girl," he can seduce any ambitious dancer or singer he wants; the

Follies lovelies, and would-be Follies lovelies, vie for his attention and favor.

While married to Anna Held, he dallies with another Ziegfeld star, Audrey Dane, played by Virginia Bruce and modeled on Lillian Lorraine, Ziegfeld's side-dish lover during his marriage to Anna Held. Anna (Luise Rainer) discovers Flo alone with Bruce, stretched out on a chaise longue, and explodes, "Flo! You should at least close the door!" One of the Anna Held songs Rainer sings earlier is "It's Delightful to Be Married," but being married to Flo Ziegfeld turns out to be less than a joy ride. Ziegfeld's philandering prompts an indulgent implied wink from the screenwriter, not a cluck of disapproval. Breen allowed it. But old age will provide a measure of comeuppance for the bounder.

As Powell plays him, the elderly Ziegfeld's belief in himself falters in his twilight days. He sits at home, ailing and passive, looking out at the Broadway skyline emblazoned with his famous name: a reminder of headier days. The actual Ziegfeld wasn't even in New York during his last years. In the movie his devoted valet, Sidney (Ernest Cossart), waits on him and humors him. Flo now survives on memories of past glories, illusions about the future, and the earnings of Billie Burke. Her role, like that of the valet, is to try to prop him up. There's not much room for effervescence here. Burke and Ziegfeld have a daughter, Patricia, but Dad, shorn of his moxie, is Billie's biggest baby. When Flo goes broke, Billie volunteers to sell the diamond tiara he gave her for Christmas, along with the rest of the jewels he's bestowed. She's being generous, but at the same time, such gestures of largesse wrest command. Trying to inject courage, she gently nudges, "Flo, I'm disappointed in you. I didn't think you'd ever lose confidence in yourself." He's lost more than his self-confidence, though. This movie's ending is all about Ziegfeld's loss of potency, directly linked to his lost ability to rake in money.

Billie Burke played Myrna Loy's older, unmarried sister in another extravagant Metro biopic released the following year, this one far less successful at the box office than *The Great Ziegfeld*. *Parnell* starred Clark Gable as the Irish patriot Charles Stewart Parnell and Myrna Loy as the married woman he loved, Katie O'Shea. Based on a Broadway play, *Parnell* purports to tell the story of the late nineteenth-century Irish home rule champion and member of Parliament brought down by the malice of Parnell's one-time political ally, caddish Captain Willie O'Shea, husband of Katie and also a member of Parliament. Katie, though separated

PLATE 1. David T. and Ann Williams, paternal grandparents of Myrna Loy, ca. 1880. Montana Historical Society.

PLATE 2. Aunt Lu Wilder, maternal grandmother Isabella Johnson, and Della Johnson in Helena, ca. 1900. Montana Historical Society.

PLATE 3. Myrna Adele Williams, 1905. Montana Historical Society.

PLATE 4. *Left to right:* Della Johnson Williams; Myrna's brother, David; seven-year-old Myrna; and David F. Williams in a Pasadena park in 1912. Courtesy of the Academy of Motion Picture Arts and Sciences.

PLATE 5. Myrna Williams
at age fifteen, 1920. Montana Historical Society.

PLATE 6. In March 1940 Myrna Loy revisits the Williams ranch in Crow Creek Valley
and poses in front of a log house built by her grandfather. Montana Historical Society.

PLATE 7. "Fountain of Education," Venice High School sculpture by Harry F. Winebrenner, 1922. Myrna modeled for the figure "Inspiration." Los Angeles Herald Examiner Collection, Los Angeles Public Library.

PLATE 8. Myrna Loy and an unidentified dancer in the Grauman's Egyptian Theatre Prologue to *The Ten Commandments*. Photo by Henry Waxman, 1924. Viewed by Rudolph Valentino and Natacha Rambova, this and other Waxman photos led to Myrna's first screen test. Courtesy of the Academy of Motion Picture Arts and Sciences.

PLATE 9. The September 1925 issue of *Motion Picture* magazine introduced Myrna Loy with a question, "Who is she?" She is shown wearing the Adrian-designed costume she wore in *What Price Beauty?* Her first film, it was shot in 1925 but not released by Pathé until 1928. Courtesy of Sunrise Silents.

PLATE 10. Joan Crawford *(second from left)*, still known as Lucille Le Sueur, and Myrna Loy *(second from right)* as dancers in *Pretty Ladies* (MGM, 1925). Photofest.

PLATE 11. Myrna Loy the exotic, in a retouched press photograph. *San Francisco News-Call Bulletin,* Dec. 24, 1926. San Francisco Public Library History Center.

PLATE 12. Cast and crew of *Don Juan* (Warner Bros., 1926), a film with synchronized sound but no audible dialogue. *Standing (left to right):* Myrna Loy, photographer Byron Haskins, Emily Fitzroy, William Koenig, unknown, director Alan Crosland, J. L. Warner, art director Ben Carré, Joseph Swickard, Walter Mayo, Helene Costello, Ern Westmore, assistant director Gordon Hollingshead. Seated: Warner Oland, Estelle Taylor, John Barrymore, Mary Astor, Montagu Love. Courtesy of the Academy of Motion Picture Arts and Sciences.

PLATE 13. A publicity herald for *The Girl from Chicago* (Warner Bros., 1927). Private collection.

PLATE 14. Tom Wilson, Myrna Loy, and Heinie Conklin in blackface in *Ham and Eggs at the Front* (Warner Bros., 1927). Courtesy of the Academy of Motion Picture Arts and Sciences.

PLATE 15. Myrna Loy and Conrad Nagel in *State Street Sadie* (Warner Bros., 1928). Private collection.

PLATE 16. Myrna Loy and Anna May Wong in *The Crimson City* (Warner Bros., 1928). Courtesy of the Academy of Motion Picture Arts and Sciences.

PLATE 17. Myrna Loy and Maurice Chevalier in the musical *Love Me Tonight* (Paramount, 1932). Private collection.

PLATE 18. Myrna Loy *(right)* and
Irene Dunne in *Thirteen Women*
(RKO, 1932). Private collection.

PLATE 19. Myrna Loy in
costume for her last exotic
role, as Fah Lo See in *The
Mask of Fu Manchu* (MGM,
1932). Photo by Clarence Sinclair Bull. Private collection.

PLATE 20. Warner Baxter *(far left)*, Myrna Loy, and Charles Butterworth play cards during a break in shooting *Penthouse* (MGM, 1933) as director Woody Van Dyke *(standing)* looks on. Courtesy of the Academy of Motion Picture Arts and Sciences.

PLATE 21. William Powell *(center)*, Myrna Loy, and Clark Gable in a publicity still for *Manhattan Melodrama* (MGM, 1933), Loy's first picture with Powell. Private collection.

PLATE 22. Ad for *The Thin Man* (MGM, 1934), the movie that made William Powell and Myrna Loy, as Nick and Nora Charles, one of Hollywood's iconic acting teams. Courtesy of the Academy of Motion Picture Arts and Sciences.

PLATE 23. Nora Charles disguised herself as a man to search a warehouse in a scene that was cut from *The Thin Man*. Courtesy of the Academy of Motion Picture Arts and Sciences.

PLATE 24. George Hurrell shot this portrait of Myrna Loy in 1932, soon after she signed with MGM. Private collection.

PLATE 25. Portrait of Myrna Loy by Ted Allan, 1934. Private collection.

PLATE 26. Cary Grant and Myrna Loy confer with Amelia Earhart *(center)* on the set of *Wings in the Dark* (Paramount, 1935). Private collection.

PLATE 27. Spencer Tracy and Myrna Loy, costars in *Whipsaw* (MGM, 1935). Private collection.

PLATE 28. Myrna Loy and William Powell being filmed in *Escapade* (MGM, 1935) shortly before Loy left the movie to go on strike against the studio. Director Robert Z. Leonard is standing, in dark suit. Photographer Ernest Haller is seated, with arms on knees. Private collection.

PLATE 29. Myrna Loy with her stepson, Terry Hornblow, in Beverly Hills, ca. 1937. Myrna Loy Collection, Boston University.

PLATE 30. Jean Harlow, Clark Gable, and Myrna Loy on the set of *Wife vs. Secretary* (MGM, 1936). Director Clarence Brown is seated, and Ray June is behind the camera. Photo by Virgil Apger. Private collection.

PLATE 31. William Powell and Myrna Loy take in a view of the newly completed Bay Bridge from San Francisco's Telegraph Hill during a break from filming *After the Thin Man*, 1936. *San Francisco News-Call Bulletin*, 1936. San Francisco Public Library.

PLATE 32. Mr. and Mrs. Arthur Hornblow Jr. outside their custom-built home
on Hidden Valley Road in Beverly Hills,
ca. 1937. Courtesy of the Academy of
Motion Picture Arts and Sciences.

PLATE 33. Arthur Hornblow Jr. flanked
by his wife, Myrna Loy *(left)*, and Claudette Colbert at Paramount. *San Francisco News-Call Bulletin*, March 24, 1939.
San Francisco Public Library.

PLATE 34. *Left to right:* Della
Williams (Myrna Loy's mother),
Aunt Lu Wilder, David Williams
(Myrna Loy's brother), Myrna Loy,
and Arthur Hornblow Jr. at the
train station as Myrna and Della
depart for Montana on March 12,
1940. Courtesy of the Academy of
Motion Picture Arts and Sciences.

PLATE 35. The cover of *Hollywood* shows Tyrone Power as Major Safti and Myrna Loy as Lady Esketh in *The Rains Came* (20th Century–Fox, 1939). Private collection.

PLATE 36. William Powell in drag and Myrna Loy playing along in *Love Crazy* (MGM, 1941). Courtesy of the Academy of Motion Picture Arts and Sciences.

PLATE 37. Myrna Loy in the Bundles for Bluejackets uniform she wore while working at a Los Angeles–area canteen for enlisted World War II servicemen and women in 1942. MGM Collection. Courtesy of the Academy of Motion Picture Arts and Sciences.

PLATE 38. Myrna Loy and her second husband, John D. Hertz Jr., at the Stork Club in Manhattan, 1942. Private collection.

PLATE 39. Wedding of Myrna Loy and Gene Markey at Terminal Island, San Pedro, California, Jan. 3, 1946. Admiral William Halsey (left) was best man. Private collection.

PLATE 40. Myrna Loy and Fredric March, as Milly and Al Stephenson, stare into mirrors in *The Best Years of Our Lives* (Goldwyn/RKO, 1946). The film won the Academy Award for Best Picture. Courtesy of the Academy of Motion Picture Arts and Sciences.

PLATE 41. Two radio broadcasts called *Hollywood Fights Back* protested the HUAC hearings. Myrna Loy, Fredric March, and Lucille Ball were among the participants. *San Francisco News-Call Bulletin,* Oct. 27, 1947. San Francisco Public Library.

PLATE 42. Myrna Loy and Cary Grant take a break from filming the high school relay race in *The Bachelor and the Bobby-Soxer* (RKO, 1947). *San Francisco News-Call Bulletin,* March 6, 1947. San Francisco Public Library.

PLATE 43. Cary Grant and Myrna Loy, as Jim and Muriel Blandings, contemplate a model of their future home. Promotion for *Mr. Blandings Builds His Dream House* (RKO, 1948). *San Francisco News-Call Bulletin,* April 19, 1948. San Francisco Public Library.

PLATE 44. Myrna Loy campaigns for Democratic presidential candidate Adlai Stevenson. *San Francisco News-Call Bulletin,* Sept. 28, 1956. San Francisco Public Library.

PLATE 45. Montgomery Clift and Myrna Loy became close friends during the filming of *Lonelyhearts* (United Artists, 1958). Private collection.

PLATE 46. Myrna Loy and Paul Newman as mother and son in *From the Terrace* (20th Century–Fox, 1960). Private collection.

PLATE 47. Myrna Loy toured with the national company of Neil Simon's *Barefoot in the Park* for more than two years. *Left to right:* Sandor Szabo, Richard Benjamin, Myrna Loy, Joan Van Ark. Photofest.

PLATE 48. Myrna Loy's last film, made for the Boston affiliate of ABC television in 1981, was *Summer Solstice,* costarring Henry Fonda. Private collection.

from her husband, wasn't yet divorced when she began living with Parnell in the grand home near London that she shared with her wealthy aunt. After Willie O'Shea sued Katie for divorce, naming Parnell as corespondent, Parnell's Irish political career abruptly tanked, and his cause was defeated in Parliament. Blamed for Parnell's fall, the fiery Katie was vilified in Ireland, especially by Irish Catholics. Parnell and Katie finally married, but Parnell, a broken man, had a weak heart and died young. This is a rough outline of the real story, but the movie pretends that Katie O'Shea and Parnell never had to sneak around and never got married after the divorce. It portrays both Katie O'Shea and Parnell as romantics, sentimental softies. It also leaves out their three illegitimate children, one of whom came over from England as an adviser for *Parnell.*

When Joseph Breen first read the Elsie Schauffler play that inspired the film *Parnell,* he fretted about the impact Parnell's story might have on movie audiences in both the United States and Great Britain. He thought that a film about Parnell's struggle for home rule risked alienating both those who sympathized with the Irish Catholics in their struggle against Britain and those, primarily Protestant, who supported British rule over Ireland. (Parnell was actually Anglo-Irish, and Protestant, with an American mother. Katie was English and Protestant. Willie was Irish Catholic.) Breen warned, "No matter how you soft pedal that discussion, you are certain to come in for considerable opposition from *both* Irish and English." And of course Breen, himself a puritanical Irish American Catholic, voiced deep misgivings about a movie focusing on an illicit love affair that prompted a divorce scandal and public charges of adultery and even harlotry. In Ireland Katie was denounced as a whore and called "Kitty," a synonym for *prostitute.* Worries about offending people in the audience doomed *Parnell* from the get-go; it was bowdlerized to death even before the S. N. Behrman–John Van Druten screenplay existed.[27]

Myrna stuck up for *Parnell,* defending her own and Gable's performances, and the romance at the heart of the story, but few who have seen the treacly movie agree with her. The essential dishonesty at the core of *Parnell* did it in. Put simply, nobody believed it. And in the United States in 1937 nobody cared a lot about Charles Stewart Parnell. If people were thinking about Britain and divorce, their attention was riveted on the recent abdication of King Edward VIII and his subsequent marriage to a divorcee. Neither as a political leader nor as a man who broke taboos did Parnell stir the passion in the United States that he still did, forty plus years after his demise, in the United Kingdom, especially in Ireland. To Americans his story seemed remote and dated. The British accents of players such as Alan Marshall didn't help.

Myrna Loy fans responding to her in *Parnell* missed the wry, sophisticated, and modern woman they knew from other films. The historical Katie was known for her high-voltage emotions. In the movie, smothered in bonnets, bows, bustles, and floor-length taffeta gowns, she's downright prim. Frank Nugent of the *New York Times* called Loy's Katie O'Shea "about as fiery as a Wellesley daisy chain. Hers is a portrait in pastels, mostly in pink and blue and white. She is O so brave, O so sweet, O so true, but she is not O'Shea."[28]

Myrna said she read "some twenty books on Parnell and his times" and endured 150 fittings for the 15 Adrian-designed period costumes. "There were sketches drawn for hundreds of hats. I dreamed of hats. I had to practice standing, walking," because Katie O'Shea "didn't stand nor walk as does the girl of today." Her Katie is both overstudied and overdressed.[29]

Joan Crawford, originally slated to play Katie O'Shea, turned down the role at the last minute because she decided after misfiring in *The Gorgeous Hussy* in 1936 that she was done with costume pictures. She also, understandably, didn't like the lifeless *Parnell* script once she had a chance to read it. She and Myrna swapped pictures, Crawford taking on what had been planned as Loy's role opposite Powell, that of a jewel thief posing as a society woman in *The Last of Mrs. Cheyney*. This kind of sudden switching around happened all the time at MGM, but Gable blamed Crawford for the box-office disaster that *Parnell* became, and he didn't talk to her for years.[30]

The Gable fans who rejected his Parnell wanted to see the devil-may-care actor they knew and loved. They didn't recognize this somber, earnest, at times maudlin figure, turned out in dark Victorian frock coats and mutton-chop sideburns but no beard, who asks Katie on the day they meet, "Have you never felt there might be someone, somewhere, who, if you could meet them, was the person that you'd been always meant to meet?"

The tepid adultery depicted in *Parnell* left audiences cold. Misplacing the blame, critics charged that the actors were at fault and that the lead roles had been miscast. "Myrna Loy behaves as though she missed *The Thin Man*, and not even mutton chop whiskers and a turret-top collar can make Clark Gable look, sound or act like the uncrowned King of Ireland," sniffed *Time* magazine's reviewer. Where was the heavy breathing promised in ads that claimed, "Their Romance Rocked the Foundation of an Empire! The Most Powerful Romance Ever Filmed!" It's missing in both the script and in Stahl's weeper-style direction. The actors could only do so much with a production predicated on evasion and fear of offending. For Breen to approve the picture, scenes "showing physical contact between Parnell and Katie" had to be "reduced to an absolute minimum." [31]

Beautifully photographed by Karl Freund and sumptuously mounted on seventy-four Cedric Gibbons sets that take us to London's House of Parliament and New York docks, as well as to Ireland's fields of famine; and with a cast that included such stalwarts as Edna May Oliver, Montagu Love, and Edmund Gwenn, *Parnell* cost more than $1.5 million to make and lost $637,000—hard numbers to swallow for Gable, the much-indulged King of Hollywood. A fan attending a *Parnell* preview in Santa Ana wrote on a postcard in response to the screening, "I prefer Loy and Gable in light comedy." Another commented tellingly that Gable's face was too rakish for the role. "Clark's mug does not fit the character. Not enough idealism manifested in his features." Given the inhibitions dominating Hollywood at the time, *Parnell* should never have been attempted in the first place. [32]

One MGM movie about adultery that, because of the Code, never did see production was called *Infidelity* and was scripted by none other than F. Scott Fitzgerald. In 1934 Fitzgerald had listed Myrna Loy, Katharine Hepburn, Miriam Hopkins, Helen Hayes, and Ann Harding as the five Hollywood actresses he thought had what it took to portray Nicole Diver, the beautiful, rich, and mentally ill wife of the psychiatrist Dick Diver, in a proposed, unrealized screen adaptation of *Tender Is the Night*. A few years later, Fitzgerald imagined a role for Loy in *Infidelity*, a screenplay about a married couple haunted by old loves. Fitzgerald had rejoined Hunt Stromberg's stable of MGM screenwriters in 1937 after an absence of six years. Trying to stop drinking and at an emotional and financial low ebb, he'd returned to MGM, despite previous frustrations as a screenwriter, in a desperate attempt to resuscitate his bank account and get his life together. [33]

While working on the screenplay for *The Women*, he revised *Infidelity*, undertaken as a vehicle for Joan Crawford. Breen immediately ran interference, objecting to the very idea of a film about adultery. Making what he called "a deep bow to the censors," Fitzgerald tried to salvage the project. He rethought the plot, turning it into a story about thievery instead of adultery. He also revised the casting choices he wanted, replacing (in discussions with Hunt Stromberg) steamy Joan Crawford with tamer, classier Myrna Loy, who in his eyes seems to have represented a combination of desirability and gentility. As soon as he imagined the cast change, he wrote to Stromberg, "the whole thing brightened for me." But it didn't brighten for MGM, which lost interest in the project.[34]

Myrna never knew about Fitzgerald's plans for her. The *Infidelity* debacle shows, though, how Hollywood's play-it-safe climate victimized her, as well as Fitzgerald. The power of the Code, combined with the conservatism of MGM, kept stifling potentially strong movies. The original Fitzgerald script might have made a first-rate film, but it didn't stand a chance. "MGM has meant safety, not speculation, for eleven years," an ad in *Variety* proclaimed, touting the studio's forty-nine productions slated for release in a banner year, 1935–36. The formulaic, the corny, the plush, and the safe kept winning out.

Irving Thalberg's death in September of 1936 contributed to a downturn at MGM that prevailed in the later 1930s. Although Myrna never had a lot of direct contact with him after the career-changing moment when he told her, face-to-face, that she must tear off the veil that was separating her from her audience, his shocking but not altogether unexpected death at age thirty-seven brought a shift at the studio that had an impact on everyone who worked there. The name *Thalberg* had spelled quality. He had most recently produced a string of big films based on literary classics: *Camille, Romeo and Juliet, The Good Earth.* Now, as Joan Crawford put it, "Thalberg was dead and the concept of the quality 'big' picture pretty much went out the window." At his funeral, which Myrna attended, along with just about every other Hollywood luminary, the officiating Rabbi Magnin read a message from President Roosevelt, saying, "The world of art is poorer with the passing of Irving Thalberg." One could argue that "art" was never the goal at MGM, but with Thalberg around, it was often a by-product of efforts to entertain and make money. Post-Thalberg MGM would undertake fewer productions based on literary classics or Broadway plays. Good screenwriting would carry less weight. Mayer turned against what he considered the highbrow interests of his onetime protégé. Now child actors, middlebrow fare, and family themes—the Andy Hardy series, for instance—took the lead. The long-established MGM screenwriter Anita Loos said of Thalberg at the time of his passing that "he'd taken the studio to the top of a toboggan run. From now on there's only one direction MGM can go."[35] Box office also declined generally around 1938. In the summer of that year Ruth Waterbury reported in *Photoplay* that Hollywood production had reached an all-time low. "The public is staying home in droves," she wrote, "and why not? We can get every movie star of any importance almost any night on our radios, free." The decline in production was also a response to the diminishing market in Europe as war clouds gathered and Hollywood filled up with refugees fleeing Hitler.[36]

With the golden movie year 1939 (when MGM profits would hit $9.5 million) still to come, I don't want to dig MGM's grave. But William Powell was about to confront a health crisis that would remove him from the screen for close to two years. Myrna Loy could anticipate performing in some potentially quite popular and lucrative movies, sans Powell, in the immediate future. But a season of trouble awaited her, and the course of her life was about to shift.

CHAPTER 12

Trouble

Jean Harlow's death in June 1937 came as a blow, to Myrna and to just about the entire American film community. The sudden demise of any twenty-six-year-old jolts survivors, but Harlow wasn't just anyone. She was Myrna's dear friend and MGM colleague, the screen's embodiment of youthful lusciousness. In life Harlow had a childlike quality, an unaffected niceness that clashed with her dangerous bombshell image. Her mother called her "The Baby," and the words "Our Baby" are inscribed on her tomb. Babies aren't supposed to die.

Jean had been Bill Powell's lover and would-be fiancée for close to three years, and during that time Myrna watched their interplay from a ringside seat. Although they got along splendidly, sharing Kansas City memories and a love of fun, it was becoming more and more clear that they didn't want the same things out of their relationship. They kept butting heads over the issue of marriage. In some ways Harlow's frustrating situation reprised what Myrna had gone through with Arthur: a delectable young Hollywood actress yearning to marry the older (in Powell's case much older) man she adores and looks up to. Drawn to father figures, as was Myrna, Harlow called Powell "Daddy." Ever eager to please Bill, she would sew buttons on his shirts. But she began to realize that she couldn't change Bill's understandable wariness of Hollywood trips to the altar. He wanted no more two-career marriages, no more children, and he didn't like the idea of Jean's dominating mother hovering over her every move.

Powell could be generous and indulgent to Jean. He spent ample time with her and presented her with a huge star-sapphire ring, which the press, and sometimes Harlow herself, mistook for an engagement ring. He often shared his palatial Beverly Hills house with her. But he wasn't going to budge on the marriage issue, and Jean, though still crazy about him, had begun dating someone else. She told Louella Parsons she knew that she and Bill Powell would never wed.[1]

To complicate Myrna's grief, she was tormented by the feeling that she might have prevented this tragedy but failed. She'd spotted evidence of Harlow's deteriorating health and tried to intervene. In San Francisco in the fall of 1936, while Jean was briefly away from her overbearing Christian Scientist mother, Myrna alerted Bill Powell to her alarm, advising him that Jean needed to be examined and evaluated by a first-rate physician, pronto. Powell made no objection, but he didn't share Myrna's sense of urgency and wasn't convinced that Harlow's situation was life-threatening, believing his sweetheart merely had the flu.

Since she didn't succeed in her efforts to get Harlow to see a doctor, Myrna set up a medical appointment for her ailing friend with Dr. Saxton Pope, a San Francisco physician connected with the University of California Hospital. Saxton Pope Jr. was Myrna's own San Francisco physician during her 1935 hospitalization. She avoided getting medical care in fishbowl Los Angeles because she wanted to preserve her privacy. Myrna saw the Popes—Saxton and his wife, Jeanne—socially, too. The social connection allowed Myrna, not usually a meddler, to concoct a scheme that might save Jean. Since Harlow didn't keep the medical appointment Myrna set up, and wouldn't submit to a physician's examination in San Francisco, social encounters between Dr. Pope and Harlow would have to suffice. The doctor could at least take a look at Harlow and appraise her general demeanor.

Dr. Pope agreed, after spending time with Jean, that something was seriously wrong with her health, and her heavy drinking didn't help. Her face was puffy and gray, she complained of exhaustion, and she had little appetite. On the sly he felt her pulse and found it irregular. He had no authority to take any medical steps so long as Jean wasn't his patient, and he did nothing more than talk to Myrna about his concern. Before the advent of kidney dialysis or transplants, there was little he could have done to restore her health, but this is clear only in hindsight. Harlow did get medical attention before she died, contrary to what Myrna believed. Two different Los Angeles physicians attended her during her final days. Only one of them made the correct diagnosis of nephritis. It's a myth—

one that Myrna, along with many others, believed—that the Christian
Science credo of Harlow's mother prevented care that might have saved
Harlow's life. In that era kidney failure spelled doom.[2]

When she succumbed to uremic poisoning brought on by acute
nephritis, Harlow had been suffering from kidney failure for at least a
decade but didn't know it. She'd been sidelined by several recent episodes
of illness and had been forced to miss days of work at MGM, but the
underlying cause hadn't been explained. We would say now that her im-
mune system had been compromised, hence the frequent infections and
physical overreactions.

Actor illnesses were inconvenient for movie studios. It was expensive
to halt a picture midproduction. "I just don't dare to have a cold in the
head," Myrna once complained in an interview. "It would cost the studio thousands of dollars. I have to act like a piece of breakable porce-
lain, which Heaven only knows I'm not." Jean Harlow's box-office value
was such that her sick days really hurt MGM in the wallet. Her star
wattage had recently won her an invitation to meet President and Mrs.
Roosevelt in Washington and a coveted spot on the cover of *Life*. At
MGM her status soared (as did Myrna's), partly because after Thalberg's
death the ranks had continued to thin among the studio's top actresses:
grieving Norma Shearer withdrew for a time, and Joan Crawford's recent screen outings hadn't matched her earlier box-office triumphs. Even
the luminous Garbo, who could command a salary of $275,000 for just
one picture, had seen a dip in popularity. Her 1937 costume movie *Conquest* lost more than a million dollars, and she soon would be branded
"box office poison." Harlow's salary that last year of her life was listed
as $146,120, compared to Myrna Loy's $123,916, William Powell's
$164,533, and Gable's $235,338. She hadn't yet completed her final film,
Saratoga, a racetrack comedy romance costarring Clark Gable, when she
collapsed on the set near the end of May 1937.[3]

Saratoga was Harlow's sixth film opposite Gable; their fifth had been
the previous year's *Wife vs. Secretary,* in which all the characters suspect
that Harlow and her boss, Gable, are carrying on an affair, but the audience knows that they actually aren't. You could say that Harlow and
Gable had grown up together as movie stars. At the time of their first
joint screen outing, in a 1931 gangster drama called *The Secret Six,* Harlow was just twenty and new to Metro, which had borrowed her from
Howard Hughes. Neither Harlow nor Gable played prominent roles in
The Secret Six, but in their next film together the following year, *Red
Dust,* they costarred, and their torrid love scenes ignited a bonfire. By

this time Harlow's contract with Hughes had been bought by MGM; she was being groomed for major stardom. Gable, too, was a comer. Each had that special something it takes to trigger the fantasies of millions. In the words of the MGM still photographer Clarence Sinclair Bull, "Hell, they were everybody's lovers."[4]

Gable was shaken by Harlow's sudden death in the midst of shooting *Saratoga* and was outraged, as was his sweetheart Carole Lombard, when Jack Conway, the director of *Saratoga,* and L. B. Mayer jointly called Lombard the same day Harlow died to ask Carole to take over the part that Harlow had left incomplete. Lombard had been considered for the role of the story's horse-breeding heiress Carol Clayton early on, before Harlow got the assignment. Since she started going with Gable, Lombard had been trying to angle a way to work with him again, but subbing for Harlow on the heels of her shocking death wasn't exactly what she'd had in mind. Harlow's movie double took the assignment, instead, and fans, eager for a last glimpse of the actress now enshrined as one of Hollywood's immortals, flocked to see *Saratoga,* when it was quickly completed and rushed into release. It became a top box-office winner of 1937, proving that the publicity generated by a young star's unexpected and shocking demise can readily be spun into box-office gold.[5]

During Harlow's final illness, Powell and Loy were filming *Double Wedding,* directed by Richard Thorpe. Harlow had stopped by the *Double Wedding* set on her last day at MGM, and Thorpe heard her tell Powell, "Daddy, I don't feel good. I'm going home." She survived less than a week after that, but, of course, work on *Double Wedding* had to resume after a one-day pause for the funeral. Loy and Powell had trouble continuing to clown around on cue after that, but they completed the film. No wonder neither Powell nor Loy could muster any fondness for that picture, with its antic wedding ceremony at the conclusion.[6]

Myrna complained in her autobiography about the way Harlow was distorted beyond recognition and maligned in the press, as well as in sensationalized biographies and biopics. Just as she would jump to Joan Crawford's defense after Christina Crawford's tattle-tale book *Mommie Dearest* (and the 1981 movie based on it) came out, she stood up for Harlow, who was indeed subjected to tabloid-style smears too many times. But Myrna's defense went overboard. She sanitized Harlow, overlooking the frank sexuality that had catapulted her to stardom and the questions that Paul Bern's probable suicide raised. She characterized her friend as the good-girl victim of exploiters and gossipmongers bent on tarnishing an idol. Myrna's cleansed Harlow is intelligent, well-mannered, joyful and easy to be with, "a sensitive woman with a great deal of self-respect" (*BB*, 143), not the cheap sexpot she'd often been taken for. But in her zeal to protect her friend, Myrna denied Harlow's zesty essence. What happened to the free spirit notorious for going without underwear, the secret drinker, or the promiscuous blonde who'd dallied with the married Max Baer and (the also married) Howard Hawks? Harlow grew up a lot during her last few years and evolved into a brilliant screwball comedienne, but she was never prim.

Dr. Saxton Pope and his wife, Jeanne, kept in touch with Myrna through the decades. Myrna would see them on visits to the Bay Area. The doctor wrote in anguish to Myrna the moment he read the headlines about Harlow's passing. Addressing Myrna by the nickname Victor McLaglen had conferred, "Minnie," he broke out, "How horrible about Jeansie. Thoughts come thronging back to me. Her fatigue. Your insistence that she be examined (and we let her talk us out of it)." He sympathized with Powell, he said, "But most of all I am inexpressibly sorry for Jeansie. How she must hate being dead. How she must hate being away from Bill. No lap to sit on, nobody to shower with that mad, complete, childlike love." The letter confirms what others have said about Harlow and her feelings for Powell.[7]

If Myrna found Harlow's death hard to bear, Bill Powell found it totally devastating. Behind dark glasses, and leaning on his mother's arm, he sobbed without stint at her Forest Lawn funeral, an MGM production at which Jeanette MacDonald broke down while trying to perform "Indian Love Call" and Nelson Eddy sang "Ah, Sweet Mystery of Life." Clark Gable, Eddie Mannix, the photographer Ray June, and directors Jack Conway and Woody Van Dyke served as solemn pallbearers. Myrna took her place among the 250 invited attendees, most of them tear-drenched. Just nine months back she and many of the same mourners had gathered at the funeral of Irving Thalberg, who with Paul Bern had launched Harlow's MGM career. In honor of Harlow, Anita Loos recalled, "L. B. Mayer sent a heart of red roses five feet tall pierced by a golden arrow. Bill Powell strode up to the coffin to place a single [gardenia] on her breast." Carole Lombard muttered inside the flower-decked Wee Kirk o' the Heather that she hoped there would be no such superproduction when her turn came.[8]

Guilt infused Powell's despair: not only had he dashed Harlow's hopes to marry him, but he had also failed to recognize how sick she was, refusing until near the last moment to fully credit the alarm that others who saw her, including Myrna, had expressed months earlier. He spent

$25,000 on Harlow's "mortuary chamber" at Forest Lawn, lined in marble and fitted with a stained glass window. Soon after *Double Wedding* wrapped up, with his last picture on his current MGM contract behind him, Powell took off on an extended trip to Europe.

When he returned to California, he had to brace for another blow: at age forty-five he had been given a diagnosis of cancer of the rectum, a fact he chose not to advertise. A man of inherent formality and reticence about private matters, Powell was the sort who doesn't even admit to having a rectum. Not until the 1960s would he talk for the record about his ordeal, which involved a "temporary colostomy" followed by the implanting of platinum needles containing radium. At the time he underwent his first surgery, in March 1938, the nature of his malady was left undefined, but it was characterized as serious. He had to undergo a total of three surgeries. Myrna visited him in the hospital and was amazed to be greeted by a salt-and-pepper-haired Powell; he'd managed to conceal his true hair color from her and everyone else, and he turned out to be touchy on the subject of his age. He joked, "There's a factory down here that gives off silver dust," blown in through an open window (*BB*, 162). Some weeks later, Harrison Carroll reported in the *Los Angeles Evening Herald Express*, "Bill Powell was well enough to pay a surprise call the other day on Myrna Loy. The maid sneaked him into the house and Myrna found him sitting in the living room with a bouquet of flowers in each hand, picked from her own garden."[9]

Powell would visit no soundstage for close to two years, another costly absence for MGM, ever eager for another Powell-Loy bonanza. At the beginning of 1938, according to *Variety*, the team of Powell and Loy ranked as the fourth biggest box-office champs, worldwide, among American stars, beating out Fred Astaire and Ginger Rogers. Only Gary Cooper, Garbo, and Clark Gable surpassed them. For a time, no one knew when, or if, Powell and Loy could be redeployed as Nick and Nora Charles. Other actors—Reginald Gardiner and Melvyn Douglas—were considered to play Nick, in case of Powell's continued absence. Myrna declared that she chose not to be Nora to a new Nick. She thought "a complete change of faces would be better than a partial switch." Virginia Bruce was named as a possible substitute Nora.[10]

As it turned out, no substitutes needed to be chosen. Powell had recovered enough to begin filming *Another Thin Man* in July of 1939, but he still tired easily. Woody Van Dyke accommodated his special needs by reducing the number of hours of shooting to six each day, working with four soundstages, each already equipped with a setup, so that he could go forward speedily. He also increased the size of the crew and hired doubles for the key actors, to ensure rapid-fire shooting. *Another Thin Man* emerged as a confused film that attests to Hammett's dysfunction at the time he worked on the story. The presence of the Charleses' new family member, baby Nick Jr. (William A. Poulsen), doesn't add much. Nora rushes around, checking to be sure that the baby's bottle has been warmed and interviewing nannies while trying to talk on the phone. The tyke serves as an excuse for a birthday party staged by thugs and as a reason for Nick to find himself seated on a couch while holding an incongruously huge stuffed panda. The shifty-eyed baby nurse looks like a suspect, but there's not much else to justify this cute baby's existence. The plot is a labyrinth of dead bodies, lively nightclub scenes, and sleazy criminals with names like "Creeps" and "Dum-Dum"—so many that they're hard to sort out. The flaws didn't matter that much. What counted was that the Nick and Nora team was back. Fans turned out to see them on-screen, and the film made more than $2 million in worldwide rentals.

On the first day of shooting Myrna honored Bill Powell's wish to play it light, bypassing a big emotional "welcome back" scene. She made every effort to treat his return to work matter-of-factly. All that she and Woody Van Dyke did was to kid him about showing up a bit late. But the crew greeted his MGM homecoming with a standing ovation.

During Powell's recuperation Myrna worked with Robert Taylor on *Lucky Night* (she found him stuffy) and shared the screen with Rosalind Russell, Walter Pidgeon, and Franchot Tone in the forgettable love quadrille *Man-Proof*, whose principal claim to fame is Myrna Loy's extremely funny drunk scene. MGM seems to have forgotten its vow to improve the quality of her pictures after she returned from being on strike. She next made two popular but formulaic films with Clark Gable, both about pilots, their planes, and their romances.

The airborne heroics of Charles Lindbergh and Amelia Earhart, the endeavors of aviator-filmmaker Howard Hughes, the growth of commercial aviation, the popularity of stunt pilots, and advances in aerial photography all fueled what seemed an insatiable appetite for movies about flying. Beginning well before *Wings*, the 1927 Best Picture choice, filmmakers and moviegoers carried on a love affair with aeronautic feats and the skilled and daring pilots accomplishing them. Several directors, William Wellman, Victor Fleming, and Howard Hawks among them, had piloting skills and loved to make movies about flying. Myrna's embarrassing *Wings in the Dark* made its own "contribution" to the genre, and

Night Flight drew on the piloting expertise of director Clarence Brown, a onetime World War I flying instructor.

Test Pilot, Loy's first of two 1938 aviation films, boasted three popular stars: Loy and Gable, cashing in as Hollywood's newly anointed king and queen, joined by the recent Academy Award winner Spencer Tracy. As daredevil test pilot Jim Lane, Gable restored his he-man image after the *Parnell* debacle. In our first glimpse of him he's joshing with two floozies after a tipsy night on the town. Carousing is obviously his way of decompressing from a job that demands that he risk his life racing and testing planes. Loy plays his appealing wife, Ann, the woman who tries to tame him, and Tracy is cast as Gunner Morris, Gable's mechanic, best friend, and sidekick at Drake Aviation. Box-office-savvy Metro guessed rightly that pairing Gable and Tracy again after their huge success in *San Francisco,* in which bad-boy Tracy scored by playing against type as a priest, would pay off. Once he attained the status of a top star with acting talent to match, Tracy sustained his reputation as the actor's actor.

Tracy and Loy both tended to underplay. He kept seeking reassurance, as they worked out a scene, that he hadn't hammed it up too much. Perfectionists, each abhorred the scenery-chewing school of acting and strove above all for an ease that seemed spontaneous but was anything but. The scene in which Tracy loudly cracks and eats walnuts while Gable, looking abashed, faces Loy after coming home from a weeklong bender had been prepared in detail the previous night, according to Joseph Mankiewicz. At the time of *Test Pilot's* shooting, Tracy was staying at Mankiewicz's Santa Monica house. "Christ, he used up five pounds of nuts, and then he pretended on the set it had just occurred to him. It was perfectly timed so he would never crack a nut on Clark's line. But you would always have to cut to him." Myrna must have worked out her casual knitting in one scene, or her boisterous shouts at baseball players during a Kansas game, in a similar way.[11]

In *Test Pilot* all three top-billed stars, along with such supporting players as Lionel Barrymore and Marjorie Main, lined up under Gable's favorite director and chum, Victor Fleming, who cultivated a reputation as a ladies' man, race car driver, aviator, and tough guy. Fleming had guided Tracy's winning turn in *Captains Courageous,* in which the actor's Kipling-derived character, a curly haired Portuguese fisherman, dies at sea. As *Motion Picture Herald* commented, Metro's big men "might have figured out that killing [Tracy] in *Captains Courageous* had something to do with making the public love him in that picture and, therefore, that to kill him again in this one *[Test Pilot]* might be equally effective." His *Test Pilot* character, Gunner, a laconic, gum-chewing charmer who tails Gable's Jim like a loyal puppy, dies heroically trying to protect his friend when Gable's plane crashes and burns.[12]

Fleming, who had previously directed Loy in *Renegades* and *The Wet Parade,* did well by her in this film. She got a chance to shine in a sympathetic dramatic role that called for shows of deep emotion—quite a change from nonchalant Nora Charles. She'd played ruthless schemers, the first one European, the second a spoiled-brat American, in her two earlier Fleming-directed films.

Myrna's personal favorite among all her films, *Test Pilot* is action-packed, brisk, and entertaining, though sometimes sappy. Gable's flowery outbursts about the "girl in the blue dress" in the sky, and Loy's about him being in love with her truest rival, "a lady with wings," are cringe-worthy. *Test Pilot* nonetheless won a Best Picture nomination, and its worldwide grosses of close to $4 million made it one of the big box-office winners of the year, but it is no masterpiece. "Judicious cutting and less banal dialogue would have lent it the distinction it lacks," wrote the spot-on critic for the *New York Daily Mirror.*[13]

The film garnered enough notice on its first run to inspire an E. B. White poem that was published in the *New Yorker,* called "An Earthbound Boy" (with the subtitle "After seeing the movie 'Test Pilot' "), all about the land-locked poet's secret yearning for honeysuckle-sweet Myrna Loy, who's smitten by enviable sky prince Gable.[14]

One reason Myrna so enjoyed making *Test Pilot* was that she simply found it a kick to be offset by two dynamite, top-tier leading men, one on each arm. Another cause for celebration was that she got to portray a character with a background very like her own. Myrna had always yearned to play a woman with western ranching roots. MGM bought the rights to *Sea of Grass,* Conrad Richter's 1936 novel of love, desertion, and illegitimacy in pioneer days, planning it as a vehicle for her and Spencer Tracy, but kept postponing production (*BB,* 192). It would eventually appear in 1947, after Myrna had left Metro; it costarred Tracy and Hepburn and was directed by Elia Kazan.

As *Test Pilot*'s Ann Barton, Loy is a warmhearted, initially cheerful, college grad from a Kansas farm who's smart and romantic, as well as pretty. She falls hard for reckless Jim Lane when he drops out of the sky during a cross-country race and lands his damaged plane with its broken oil pump in her parents' wheat field. She promptly dumps her decent but humdrum farmer fiancé and takes to the skies with handsome bruiser Lane, the "prince" she says she's always been waiting for, and she hurriedly weds him before they land at Drake Aviation's flight field in New York. Jim proves fearless when racing a plane, or diving and looping a B-17 bomber, but he's problematic as a husband. He's hooked on booze and can suddenly disappear on a bender, with the money he's recently won sure to disappear along with him. Ann spends her married life biting her nails when her husband's aloft and crying her eyes out after he lands. She threatens to leave Jim but can't bring herself to do it. Instead of rapping her errant husband on the head with a frying pan, as columnist Ed Sullivan suggested a real wife would have done under these circumstances, she forgives all and quietly goes into the kitchen to make sandwiches. "Miss Loy as the perfect wife," Sullivan concluded, "is a species of wish fulfillment." Myrna agreed. "Even in *Test Pilot*," she told Gladys Hall, "I was the brave, good-sport Little Woman who stands by, a gallant grin on her face, her heart in irons."[15]

As it does in so many other films of the day, booze looms large in the script credited to Vincent Lawrence and Waldemar Young, which is based on a story by a former pilot, Frank Wead. Whether it was also based, without credit, on a book called *Test Pilot* by the martyred test pilot Jimmy Collins is a matter for debate. Collins's widow sued MGM, charging her late husband's opus had been plagiarized, but she didn't prevail in court.[16]

Jim Lane's irresponsible binges exact a toll on his marriage and on his friendship with Gunner, who keeps trying to bail out his buddy. Joseph Breen's notes from the Production Code office harped on the film's "unnecessary drinking and drunkenness" and insisted on cutting a montage showing champagne bottles and spilling glasses.[17]

Gunner initially resents Ann; she's horning in on his turf. He makes no secret of his profound attachment to Jim, blowing him a kiss and affixing a wad of gum to his plane every time Jim takes off on a flight. He accepts a room in the newlyweds' apartment and at one point tells Jim, "I love you." He develops feelings for Ann, too, especially after they go through a shared hell watching Jim almost crash when he loses control of a spinning, fully loaded bomber as he attempts to reach an altitude of thirty thousand feet; Jim will spin out of control again later, in the bars. Ann and Gunner become allies, two planets circling Jim's sun. When Jim takes off on a drinking spree, Gunner acts as a kind of babysitter to his pal, following him from bar to bar to make sure he gets home, eventually, in one piece. Gunner displays much more awareness of Ann's suffering than does Jim, whose devil-may-care bravado is a cover for caddish selfishness. Until the formulaic happy ending, Jim remains blithely unconcerned about the impact his behavior has on others. But neither Ann nor Gunner can bear to break with him. This is a love triangle plot, but here the third wheel just might be the wife, not the best friend.

Since Tracy was an alcoholic, booze figures in the offscreen story of *Test Pilot*'s filming too. When Fleming and Gable took off in a B-17 from March Field for an alcohol-fueled lark on Catalina Island, Tracy faced a lot of ribbing because he refused to join the party. He was convinced it would only lead to one of his notorious benders, and he wanted to stay sober—at least for a while. Myrna defended his decision, angrily taking on Fleming and Gable for their poor judgment in trying to get Tracy to join them. Didn't they know about Tracy's drinking problem? (*BB*, 152). Yes, Myrna could lose her cool, on occasion. And Spencer Tracy seems to have had a genius not just for screen acting but also for finding women to mother him.

From all reports, Tracy and Gable grudgingly admired one another, and they kidded a lot. Gable would call Tracy a Wisconsin ham, and Tracy would ride his costar about his box-office bomb in *Parnell*. The columnist Sidney Skolsky reported that on the first day of shooting *Test Pilot* Tracy gathered up the electricians and other crewmembers, organizing a chorus to greet Gable by half shouting, half jeering, "Comes now the bee-youtiful King. All hail, all hail!" Their bonhomie concealed more than a little mutual envy. As Howard Strickling saw it, "Spencer Tracy would have given his right arm to have been the guy Clark Gable was—to be worshipped. Clark would have given his right arm to have been recognized as the actor's actor."[18]

Test Pilot was Myrna Loy's first picture under her new $4,000-a-week contract. In addition to the raise MGM presented her with a spiffier dressing room on the second floor of a new building, next to Garbo's and Joan Crawford's dressing rooms, and allowed her to work at a less punishing pace than before. In 1938 and 1939 she'd make only three films yearly, compared to the six she'd made in the single year 1936. Back in her Warner Bros. days she'd sometimes appeared in as many as ten films a year. She'd fought for and won better working conditions at MGM, but she failed to fight for (and wouldn't necessarily have won, even if she had) the superior scripts and first-rate directors that she needed to keep her name and career on the A list.

MGM didn't cut its directors much creative slack; producers ran the show in Culver City. Joan Crawford sniped that an MGM director, caught in the system's wheels, "had all the authority of a hamster." She maintained that a Metro cameraman carried more weight than a director. Myrna didn't have great luck with her MGM directors. She worked with Capra, as Powell worked with Gregory La Cava, while on loan to another studio, and although Cukor, brought to MGM by David Selznick, directed Jean Harlow, Jeanette MacDonald, Joan Crawford, Norma Shearer, Katharine Hepburn, and Garbo—all the other top-ranked actresses at MGM during Myrna's heyday—he missed out on directing her. The Sam Woods, the Richard Thorpes, the Robert Z. Leonards who presided over so many Loy films at MGM were competent journeymen, contract pros, nothing more. Jack Conroy, director of *Libeled Lady* and *Too Hot to Handle,* had brio, but his forte was ensemble work. He wasn't *her* director, nor was Victor Fleming or Clarence Brown, each capable of distinguished work. Brown, who was Garbo's favorite director, helmed mediocre Loy films at MGM, *Emma* and *Wife vs. Secretary,* in addition to *Night Flight.* Her best work for him came when both were loaned to 20th Century–Fox for *The Rains Came,* where Brown exulted in an A-film assignment and a chance to do things his way. Only Woody Van Dyke, among all of Loy's MGM directors, took up cudgels for her cause. Van Dyke, however, spread thin, overworked, and never associated with any single star, was no *auteur.*[19]

Ray June, behind the camera along with eighteen assistant cameramen employed for *Test Pilot,* lingers on Myrna's sometimes smiling, sometimes tear-stained face for close-ups that manage to be both crisp and romantic. But June had been a cameraman in the Signal Corps in World War I; this was an aviation film, and the aerial shots of military aircraft diving, looping, ascending, and sometimes crashing to earth were what pushed moviegoers to the edges of their seats. The *Hollywood Reporter* claimed that 838 planes were used and half a million miles flown in the course of filming at such locations as Lindbergh Field in San Diego, March Field in Riverside, and the Cleveland Air Races. Paul Mantz, once Amelia Earhart's navigator, provided technical advice, and Slavko Vorkapich, renowned for his montage sequences, worked on special effects. Myrna marveled at the technological mastery that made this film fly.[20]

Since *Test Pilot* made money during an otherwise drab season for MGM, Metro immediately got busy with another Gable-Loy aviation picture, *Too Hot to Handle,* this one with Gable playing a waggish and thoroughly unscrupulous newsreel photographer. Walter Pidgeon portrayed a rival cameraman, and Jack Conway directed most but not all of the shoot. He caught the flu and had to step down during the last weeks of filming, when Victor Fleming replaced him.[21]

Because of Conway's zany sense of humor, there are some absurdist moments in *Too Hot to Handle,* notably when Gable dons what is supposed to be a native chief's feathered mask for a voodoo sequence meant to invoke the Amazon jungle. Mainly this movie serves as just another excuse for more spine-tingling aviation thrills and more sigh-worthy shots of swaggering Gable in goggles and leather, his (false) white teeth gleaming, his dimple dimpling.

Instead of another weepy wife, in *Too Hot to Handle* Myrna Loy plays an intrepid aviatrix, as she had in *Wings in the Dark,* out to demonstrate that "a woman's place is in the cockpit." This time *Variety* saw the casting as part of a Hollywood trend toward movies about women with professions: "Studios Turn to Femmes in Profesh, after Overboard on He-Man Fare," proclaimed one headline. The claim was that "femmes" in the audience were clamoring for movies about career women because they were fed up with male-oriented thrillers and that "because women seem to have turned thumbs down on both drawing-room dramas and comedies, it was necessary to dig for a new brand of bait." Other roles cited as part of the new trend were Kay Francis as a doctor in *Unlawful,* Gloria Stuart in *Lady Lawyer,* and Barbara Stanwyck playing a lady sleuth in *The Mad Miss Manton.* The trade press was declaring screwball comedy a thing of the past, but as we will see, the burial turned out to be premature.[22]

In *Too Hot to Handle* the battle of the sexes spurs verbal skirmishes between Gable's Chris Hunter and Loy's Alma Harding. Soon after they meet, Hunter tells Harding exactly what he thinks of her in particular and of women pilots in general: not much. "[You're a] comic little dame who thinks she's a man, flying around the world with grease on her face and her hands in her pockets." Alma Harding doesn't cower when baited, however; instead, she puts up her dukes, showing her mettle as a pilot by flying Hunter through night fog to film a burning munitions ship and accusing him, before falling in love with him, of having a camera where he ought to have a heart. Alma, headed for the altar by the end, gets to have the last word. Spoofing Chris Hunter's past suggestion that she needs lessons in how to be a woman, she delivers the parting shot in the last frame: "Maybe I can show him how it feels to be a man."

Chris Hunter redeems himself in the hokey denouement by rescuing Alma's brother, a pilot lost after a plane crash in Brazil and held captive by hostile natives. Earlier, Chris showed he could be heroic when he pulled Alma from a burning plane. That stunt may or may not have inspired a for-real rescue of Myrna by Gable; Myrna wasn't sure years later whether she'd actually been in peril because the "controlled" fire flamed out of control or whether the reported and photographed brush with life-threatening danger was just another MGM bid for publicity (*BB*, 155).

Myrna believed she did best in feisty parts opposite Gable. She'd played his "little woman" in *Night Flight* and *Test Pilot,* but Alma Harding fit the two-fisted mold. At times Myrna behaved like assertive Alma off camera and had to stand her ground, when, for instance, she chewed out Gable and Fleming for trying to get Tracy to drink with them. During the *Too Hot to Handle* shoot, Myrna recalled, "Clark was always trying to put me on the spot between scenes, there was constant one-upmanship. He liked tough women," and he would soon be marrying one, ex-tomboy Carole Lombard. Myrna saw a lot of Carole, who, when not working, hung around Clark's MGM sets to keep an eye on her relentless Romeo, who didn't try too hard to be a one-woman man. Myrna remembered Carole as "very beautiful and very feminine, but she could swear like a stevedore, and she could really take off! And he [Gable] loved it; he would just sit back and grin." At a barbecue for the *Too Hot to Handle* cast at the actor Leo Carillo's San Diego ranch, Carole, dressed in jeans, a cowboy shirt, and western riding boots, practiced her lasso skills. Very different from Gable's considerably older, somewhat matronly previous wives, she knew how to box and learned to shoot a shotgun so that she could join Clark on hunting trips.[23]

After the picture wrapped, Gable and Myrna celebrated by sharing a bottle of champagne, a rite that had become a tradition whenever they made a picture together. By now they fit like a well-worn pair of shoes and were looking forward to teaming up again, after he completed his loan-out to Selznick for *Gone with the Wind.* The movie they expected to make together would be a Joseph Mankiewicz production based on a Robert Sherwood play about Hannibal called *The Road to Rome.* Sherwood wrote the screen adaptation. As it turned out, because of its pacifist theme, *The Road to Rome,* a brilliantly written comedy that had played on Broadway in the late 1920s and had starred Jane Cowl, was never made into a movie, to Myrna's enduring regret. As late as 1974 she still fretted about the zinger lines from *The Road to Rome* that she never got the chance to deliver on camera. Because the Sherwood script was shelved, *Too Hot to Handle* turned out to be the last of seven Loy-Gable collaborations.[24]

"World events dwarfed the rigors of picture-making in 1938," Myrna recalled (*BB*, 155). Her two aviation movies made that year each had a military subtext reflecting a preoccupation with preparing for war. *Test*

Pilot, which begins with an onscreen note of thanks to the U.S. Army Air Corps for its assistance, also assures the public via a slide that American military secrets have been protected and that no foreign power could glean secure information about current bomber plane technology by watching the movie.

A newsreel cameraman's filming of the December 1937 Japanese Navy attack on the USS *Panay* while it was anchored in the Yangtze River probably inspired the Sino-Japanese war sequence (about faked newsreels) in *Too Hot to Handle.* The man who cowrote the screenplay, the former Fox Movietone newsreel photographer and editor Laurence Stallings, had covered the Italian invasion of Ethiopia in 1936. He'd served in France as a marine, decades back, and lost a leg as a result of an injury during World War I. An autobiographical novel he wrote was adapted for the screen as the famous war film *The Big Parade.* His colleague Len Hammond, who wrote the story for *Too Hot to Handle,* had also worked for Fox Movietone News. The movie broached farce, but it grew out of the experiences of men who had actually carried newsreel cameras into war zones and maybe even staged a few events filmed as news, the way Gable's character does. References to the Italian invasion that were part of the original script had to be cut, for fear of offending Italy.[25]

As so often happens when Hollywood tries to copy a previous hit, *Too Hot to Handle* fared less well than *Test Pilot* at the box office during its first run. This isn't the movie's fault. Because of the crisis in Europe, foreign markets for American films were drying up, and the overseas receipts for *Too Hot to Handle* came in at only half what *Test Pilot* had pulled in. Hitler warned that he planned to confiscate the earnings of Jews, or of companies owned by Jews, that were deposited in German banks, prompting retrenchment among American film companies doing business there; MGM numbered among them. Despite all of these developments *Too Hot to Handle* still made it to third place on the list of MGM box-office winners for 1938.[26]

At the same time that these movies were courting an audience, the threat of war in Europe kept Americans pinned to their radios. A deep-voiced CBS reporter named Edward R. Murrow, posted in London for live coverage of the worsening European situation as Germany continued to annex neighboring territories, drew huge numbers of American listeners. In *Variety* the gagman Joe Laurie Jr. commented in his column, "That near-war [over Hitler's carving up of Czechoslovakia] sure ruined my business. Everybody and his brother stayed home to listen to the radio. Nearly everybody's opinion was, 'Let's keep out of it,' but I don't know if they meant the war or my theater."[27]

Soon after the notorious Munich appeasement agreement between Britain and Germany, the Nazis broke the accord by occupying the Sudetenland, previously part of the small democracy of Czechoslovakia. These events took place in the fall of 1938, just as *Too Hot to Handle* was arriving in theaters. The question of the day was: if German expansionism violates international law, what should be the stance of the United States? Hollywood gave the matter its own spin. American studios with German offices were advised that their cash in Berlin banks might be confiscated. The trade press conjectured that "if the crisis comes to a head, the studios could see a loss of 30–40% of world revenues."[28]

Until the Japanese invasion of Pearl Harbor, neutrality was the official U.S. policy under President Roosevelt, but some citizens, businesses, and organized groups in Hollywood and elsewhere took stands that were far from neutral. The political and moral divisions that would fracture the movie colony after the war were already taking shape, and at Hollywood dinner parties, not previously noted for serious conversation about international matters, world politics became the topic of the day. In earlier times, Dorothy Parker cracked, "the only 'ism' in which Hollywood believed was plagiarism." Not anymore.[29]

"The town has become cause-conscious," ran an article in *Photoplay* called "Hollywood Wakes Up." Gary Cooper, part of the right-wing, ultrapatriotic Hollywood Hussars, practiced marching and drilling in uniform, and Victor McLaglen joined a similar ultraconservative paramilitary group. Ginger Rogers and Adolph Menjou, according to Myrna, sided with the isolationists. But the right-wingers were a minority. Liberals dominated the movie colony, with a sprinkling of communists, most of those screenwriters. There was a sizable group of anti–New Dealers, prominent among them Louis B. Mayer and the Metro screenwriter John Lee Mahin, coauthor of the *Too Hot to Handle* screenplay.[30]

Jewish moguls and other Jewish employees pulled weight in the American film industry, and Hitler's anti-Semitic attacks gripped Los Angeles, which was rapidly filling up with Jewish refugees from Europe. Because she had many Jewish friends, dating back to her enduring childhood bond with Betty Berger Black, Myrna identified with Jews. "I have very few WASP friends; most of my friends are Jewish," she told a biographer of half-Jewish Melvyn Douglas, "or half-Jewish, anyway. So, to me, it's my second language."[31]

When Germany invaded Czechoslovakia, destroying its democracy and turning it into a puppet state, Jan Masaryk, who had been the Czech ambassador to Great Britain, had to give up his diplomatic post, but he stayed in London as foreign minister of the Czech government in exile and made broadcasts for the BBC that were carried in the United States. In California Myrna heard Masaryk say over the radio, after the Munich accord sold out the Czechs, that the German takeover signaled the beginning of a terrible war. Upset and deeply moved, she immediately cabled her support to Masaryk, who answered with a return cable, addressed simply to "Myrna Loy, Hollywood, California." His telegram consisted of just two words: "Bless You" (*BB*, 156). Myrna treasured this acknowledgment that her words mattered to him. She would become good friends with Masaryk, a son of the former Czech president Tomas Masaryk. Jan had an American mother, spoke fluent English, and had spent time in the States.

Because Myrna Loy was an internationally famous American movie actress, the London press got wind of the exchange of telegrams with Masaryk, which infuriated the Third Reich. On a trip to Europe with Arthur in the summer of 1939, just months before Britain and France declared war on Germany, Myrna learned that as payback for her support of Masaryk and her implied criticism of Hitler's policies, her films had been banned in Germany. She considered this ban a badge of honor. As she put it, "Why should I be entertaining the Third Reich?" (*BB*, 160).

MGM saw things differently. Arthur Loew, one of the twin sons of one-time Metro Pictures owner Marcus Loew, chaired overseas operations of MGM's parent company, Loew's, Inc. He wrote a letter to Myrna, warning her to stop mixing her career with politics. Myrna couldn't believe her eyes. Loew was Jewish. She had spoken out against Hitler, the persecutor of the Jews, and her Jewish bosses were trying to muzzle her. Louis B. Mayer himself admonished her not to make public statements against Hitler because the studio had receipts in Germany that it wanted to claim. Germany would ban American films entirely by August of 1940. By the time Myrna broke from Metro in 1945, she had a long list of grievances against the studio; this attempt at silencing her may have topped the list.

When she and Arthur returned from Europe, Arthur took great pains overseeing the safe handling of the bottles of rare French wine he had acquired in France. Myrna had graver matters on her mind. She told a reporter that sailing back to the United States on the *Normandie* had given her the creeps, because two French warships convoyed the luxurious French ocean liner.[32]

Her support for Masaryk, and the response to it, changed Myrna. Though she grew up at ease with spirited conversation about politics, during her twenties and early thirties she had focused so totally on her career that she had room for little else but Arthur and their life together. Now she had taken her first steps on a worldwide stage. She knew that henceforth, what she said and did about national and international events might have an impact on others. She would never go back to a life of political disengagement.

In Hollywood, as a person with a moral compass during the buildup to World War II, she found she had lots of company. Aghast at Germany's government-sanctioned anti-Semitism, Warner Bros.' studio chief, Jack Warner, a son of Polish Jews, was the one Hollywood mogul who took a vigorous stand against the Nazis. He folded the Warner Bros. office in Berlin way back in 1934, after Hitler had been in power just a year. Jack Warner also bucked Hays Office policy and German objections by encouraging production of *Confessions of a Nazi Spy,* which depicted Nazi spies as a threat to the United States. *Confessions of a Nazi Spy,* directed by the émigré Anatole Litvak, costarred Edward G. Robinson, an outspoken critic of the Nazis. Joseph Breen considered the film an unfair representation of Hitler and a violation of good business practice, since it would alienate Germany and its supporters.[33]

At MGM Louis B. Mayer put profit above principle and kept doing business in Nazi Germany for as long as he could, until 1940. Backed by the Hays Office, which did its best to block or defang anti-Nazi films, Paramount and Fox took the same business-first position.

Outside the studios, the movie colony had raised more than $35,000 for the Spanish Loyalist cause, much of it when Ernest Hemingway came to town in 1937 to show *The Spanish Earth,* a documentary about the Spanish Civil War that he helped write and narrate. During Hemingway's fund-raising visit to filmland, he turned up on the set of *Double Wedding* but according to Myrna was more enthused that day about sharing a bottle of hooch with William Powell than he was about beating the drum for his cause (*BB,* 149). Hemingway, fresh from his stay in civil war–torn Spain, worked harder against Franco on other occasions. At a private dinner at Robert Montgomery's house he raised $1,000 from each of the ten guests for ambulances for the Loyalists.[34]

The Hollywood pro-Loyalists, led by Dashiell Hammett, formed a Motion Picture Artists Committee to Aid Republican Spain, which arranged several screenings of *The Spanish Earth,* one of them at the home of

Fredric March and Florence Eldridge. Anna May Wong, Luise Rainer, Melvyn Douglas, Dorothy Parker, and Lewis Milestone all lent their names to the Spanish Loyalist cause. They were all people Myrna Loy knew and in several cases had worked with. Myrna didn't make her own views on the Spanish Civil War public, but it's evident that she steered clear of alliances with the far left.[35]

Another group, the Hollywood Anti-Nazi League, formed under the leadership of the MGM screenwriter Donald Ogden Stewart. Myrna eventually told the Justice Department that she didn't belong to it. In an affidavit she signed in 1955, she told the FBI that when she was solicited to become a member, she stated that she'd only join if the name of the group were changed to "Hollywood Anti-Nazi and Anti-Communist League," a position she shared with the writer Rupert Hughes. During the various Red scares that focused a magnifying lens on Hollywood, the Anti-Nazi League and the Motion Picture Artists Committee came under fire for being infiltrated by communists. Donald Ogden Stewart, the Yale-educated author of smart comedies about rich blue bloods (such as *Rebound*), had indeed taken a sharp turn to the left and proudly proclaimed himself a communist. But in 1937 the Hollywood Anti-Nazi League had broad support, even if it wasn't broad enough for Myrna. Studio executives Jack Warner and Carl Laemmle sat on the board, along with the communist writer John Howard Lawson. Fritz Lang, the émigré director, and Myrna's fellow actors Melvyn Douglas, Paul Muni, Gloria Stuart, and Fredric March were among those active in the organization. According to Gloria Stuart, who participated in the group's founding, its backers also included Ernst Lubitsch and Oscar Hammerstein II.[36]

The Anti-Nazi League organized a huge rally at the Shrine Auditorium early in 1937, the fifth anniversary of Hitler's rise to power. Eddie Cantor, John Ford, and Dorothy Parker spoke; an estimated ten thousand people attended, and many would-be attendees were turned away because the auditorium could seat no more people. But support for the Anti-Nazi League was by no means unanimous. As early as August 1938, the Texas Democrat Martin Dies, a senator who then chaired the House Committee on Un-American Activities, would brand the members of the Anti-Nazi League as dupes of the communists.

Myrna did join fifty-five other celebrities in signing a petition, circulated by her ardently pro–New Deal and anti–Third Reich friend Melvyn Douglas, urging President Roosevelt to embargo all German-made goods. Henry Fonda, Joan Crawford, and George Brent were among the other signers. Because the petition had been drawn up in Washington in 1939 at the Fifth Congress for Peace and Democracy, later considered a subversive and communist group, Myrna's signature and the petition would be duly noted by the Department of Justice and used against her during the 1940s Red scare.[37]

Myrna and Arthur, Roosevelt Democrats who opposed communism and dictatorship in any form, worried especially about Britain's vulnerability to German attack. Arthur, part Polish-Jewish (on his mother's side) and part British Protestant, felt a "there but for the grace of God go I" sense of identification. He realized that Hitler regarded Britain as an enemy power and that England happened to be located within easy bombing distance of Germany. He knew that Britain was doubly vulnerable because it was allied with Poland in a mutual aid treaty. The Nazi invasion of Poland finally triggered the official start of World War II in September 1939.

Arthur's London-based father and his Scottish second wife, Nora, had a son, Herbert Hornblow, now a flight lieutenant in the Royal Flying Corps. Herbert was about to depart for America for a visit with Myrna and Arthur when his leave was suddenly cancelled because of the British mobilization for war. Arthur senior managed to escape London's bombing during the Blitz. He and his wife moved to New Jersey, where he would die of a stroke in 1942.[38]

Films sympathetic to England had come into fashion in the United States. *Goodbye, Mr. Chips* (produced at MGM's Denham Studio, near London) and the Bette Davis–Errol Flynn vehicle *The Private Lives of Elizabeth and Essex* are just two examples, both from the benchmark year the war began in Europe, 1939. Myrna had been considered for the role of Mrs. Chips, but her temporary jump over to 20th Century–Fox prevented it. She went to Fox to appear in another pro-British movie, *The Rains Came,* based on a best-selling novel set in India and written by the Pulitzer Prize–winner Louis Bromfield, a friend of Myrna and Arthur. Its coadapter, Philip Dunne, was one of Hollywood's liberal stalwarts and a leader of the embattled Screen Writers' Guild, which Thalberg and Mayer had vehemently opposed.

In the hands of Dunne, his cowriter Julien Josephson, the dynamo 20th Century–Fox producer Darryl F. Zanuck, and the director Clarence Brown, *The Rains Came* became a kind of homage to the fading traditions of the British Empire. A statue of Queen Victoria, prominently placed in the town square of the mythical provincial Indian city of Ranchipur, stands as an enduring, but endangered, symbol of the Britain of bygone days. In the devastating, epic-scale flood of the title, the biggest onslaught of water in a movie since *Noah's Ark* (for which Zanuck wrote the screenplay back in 1929), the reprobate character Tom Ransome (George Brent) clings to Victoria's bronze likeness. A holdover from an outworn, decadent, and aristocratic British lifestyle, Ransome clings to the drowning but still erect statue when his boat tips over during the flood; the waterlogged bronze Queen saves his life. The use of symbols in this film is effective but not what one would call subtle.

In the movie's opening sequence we meet Ransome, an attractive, high-born drinking man and philanderer who can't manage to finish the portrait he's been painting. Ransome tells his visitor, Major Rama Safti (Tyrone Power), a handsome, well-educated, high-caste Indian physician, that for him Queen Victoria seems like an old friend. The immobile queen constantly reminds him of the golden days "before the world went to seed," when people still sang in Vienna and citizens had yet to become preoccupied with war, dictators, and appeasement. The movie is supposed to take place between the two world wars, but it is a decidedly 1939 voice that says, via Ransome, that the current world is "trying to commit suicide."

Filmed between April and July, *The Rains Came* premiered in September, just two weeks after the official start of World War II in Europe. Fox considered postponing the glittering premiere because of the war but decided to go ahead with it as planned. Seats were at a premium, and gaping fans jostled for glimpses of the gowns worn by Claudette Colbert, Irene Dunne, Joan Bennett, Dorothy Lamour, Lana Turner, and Linda Darnell. Miss Loy wore a white lace Balenciaga gown and carried a white ermine wrap. This was not a night for austerity or self-denial among Hollywood's elect.[39]

The Rains Came is set in Ranchipur, but Zanuck made it clear from day one that he wanted to make a film about the British in India rather than one focused primarily on India itself. At a story conference Zanuck said that an epic about India would seem dated and would surely flop. The producer sought, and received, the approval of the British consul in Los Angeles, as well as that of the Indian Office in London.[40]

None of the key *Rains Came* roles is played by an Indian or even by an actor from anywhere close to India; the racial situation in Hollywood hadn't evolved much since the days when Myrna Loy played Azuri covered in brown skin dye. The actors cast as Indians are all Caucasians in brown makeup: Tyrone Power, born in Ohio, came from a theatrical family of Irish extraction. His Major Safti, the "pale copper Apollo," wears a turban and shimmering Indian robes or medical whites that offset his darkened complexion. The wonderful, diminutive Russian-born actress Maria Ouspenskaya, a veteran of the Moscow Art Theater, portrays the Maharani. Myrna's onetime costar and pursuer Joseph Schildkraut, born in Vienna, is the prayerful Mr. Bannerjee.

Myrna Loy is Lady Edwina Esketh, the coldly beautiful, amoral wife of a boorish British peer she loathes, a man she married merely for money and status. Lady Esketh simply does as she pleases in her sex life, shrugging off the Seventh Commandment. She seeks excitement and relief from boredom, not true love. Myrna strenuously defended her right to portray an imperfect wife, and to vary the kinds of roles she took on, pointing out to the press that variety should be part of any actor's portfolio. Spencer Tracy, she reminded people, had started out typed as a gangster and had recently been convincing as a priest, just as Gable, once considered a heavy, sometimes played heroes. "I want to be wicked for a change," said Myrna after casting decisions were announced.[41]

Because of the Code, Lady Esketh couldn't be quite the tramp onscreen that Bromfield depicted in the novel, but she is allowed to be casual about going upstairs for a quick tryst with Ransome, her former lover back in England, when she encounters him at a lavish party at the Maharajah's palace. Her roll in the hay accomplished, she nonchalantly dons her wrap and goes home with her scowling husband. "I'm pretty much the ruthless, shameful woman that Bromfield made her," Myrna said of her Lady Esketh.[42]

Joseph Breen had warned Selznick in 1937 that the Bromfield novel would be an unacceptable basis for a movie because of the prominence of adultery in it. For some not readily apparent reason he allowed Zanuck to go forward with it two years later. Perhaps his reasoning was based on economics: 1938 had been a rough year, and Hollywood badly needed hits.[43]

Zanuck had by now established himself as one of the savviest and most powerful studio heads in Hollywood. He had formed 20th Century Pictures in 1933, and when that company merged with Fox the following year, he became head of production at 20th Century–Fox. Zanuck seems to have handpicked Myrna to play Lady Esketh, a much-coveted role. Marlene Dietrich was named early on as Zanuck's choice; Constance Bennett and Kay Francis were also in the running. Greer Garson, the redhaired beauty at MGM newly imported from Britain, dearly wanted the role as well, but Mayer refused to lend her to Fox. The competition for leading lady in *The Rains Came* wasn't publicized as widely as the race for the role of Scarlett O'Hara in *Gone with the Wind* had been, but it was still much discussed by fans and in the Hollywood press.

Once Myrna was chosen, discussion focused on the startling contrast between Lady Esketh and the roles Myrna Loy had recently played. A number of fans, forgetting that Myrna Loy had cut her teeth as a screen she-devil, wondered if she would be up to the task. "No picture in years has created so much interest in the inner film circles," Louella Parsons wrote after the premiere at Grauman's Chinese Theatre. Even before releasing *The Rains Came*, 20th Century–Fox was deluged with mail on the subject of casting the female lead. "Fox reported that out of 939 letters received from fans, 822 approved [of] the change of character for Myrna Loy."[44]

Maybe Zanuck chose Myrna Loy at least in part because of a 1937 interstudio agreement to swap a few Fox stars with a few of MGM's. Mayer wanted Tyrone Power for the male lead in *Marie Antoinette*, and he was willing to trade some Metro stars in return. Myrna Loy owed Fox a picture. But that couldn't be the only reason she got this plum role. Zanuck could, and did, call his own shots. He saw something in Myrna that made him believe she could take on Lady Esketh, a woman combining fire and ice, who may have been modeled on Lady Edwina Mountbatten, rumored to have fallen in love with Nehru in India. Once the cameras started rolling, however, Zanuck goaded Loy nonstop. Myrna, who occasionally socialized with the Zanucks, felt constantly undermined by him; she could never win the boss's approval on the set and wasn't sure why. She speculated that Zanuck might have harbored resentment because she did so well after he fired her from Warner Bros. He had made a bad call, and perhaps he was punishing Myrna for it (*BB*, 157). He may also have thought that as an actress in *The Rains Came* she didn't come across as toxic enough in the beginning of the picture. Zanuck upbraided the screenwriters for making Lady Esketh too sympathetic at the start, too much of a lady. "She should be a bitch and remain so up to the point of the disaster."[45]

Making sure Edwina Esketh impressed the audience in the first part of the picture as the unfeeling creature Bromfield created was essential to the story. The change that comes over her after she falls in love with Major Safti had to supply dramatic contrast; there had to be a clear before and after for her transformation to take on meaning. This is the tale of a spoiled, shallow woman deepened by experience, an adventuress who takes an emotional journey toward spirituality, love, and redemption. Her oaf of a husband, who secretly kept a list of as many of her lovers as he could identify, dies in the earthquake, so Edwina no longer can be considered unfaithful to him. More than that, Major Safti's unselfish caring, for her and for the sick patients he tends, sets an example. She intended merely to ensnare Safti in an affair, but she falls in love with him, the first real love she has known. After plague lays siege to Ranchipur following the earthquake and flood, Lady Esketh volunteers as a nurse in Major Safti's hospital. She sheds her glamorous gowns, dons a uniform and a mask that covers the lower portion of her face, and empties slop pails. And she does the very thing Louis B. Mayer insisted Myrna Loy must never do in an MGM picture: scrub the floor.

Of course, Lady Esketh must fall victim to the plague and die for her sins, beautifully, with her eyes open. She must leave Major Safti free to take on his future role as the new maharajah, the incarnation of hope for India. Clarence Brown, who had learned as a director of silent films how to help actors convey emotion without words, deftly guided the hospital scenes that rely on exchanged glances between the masked Loy and Tyrone Power. Brown counseled Myrna to ignore Zanuck's negative comments on her interpretation of Lady Esketh. Myrna had won her director's respect, and the feeling was mutual. Louis Bromfield, with whom the Hornblows were spending weekends at the beach, also bolstered her self-confidence, assuring Myrna that her Lady Esketh was the best performance of her career (BB, 157).

During filming, Hollywood-watchers were advised, "Miss Loy has the Lady Esketh role, eventually mastering it after a protracted bad start in which she is at a painful disadvantage in the sepia camera portraiture." The sepia is nowhere evident in the 2005 black-and-white Fox Home Entertainment DVD. But Myrna, whose bout with strep throat had delayed production, looks smashing throughout. For much of the picture she wears a Gwen Wakeling–designed backless, halter-neck gown that shows off her beautiful back and shoulders. Her trademark erect, queenly carriage serves her well as Lady Esketh strides with haughty but sensual grace. Her skin is powdered very white to highlight the contrast between her and the movie's *homme fatal*, Major Safti.[46]

Tyrone Power, who had recently married a French actress known simply as Annabella, completely captivated Myrna. She and Arthur had hit some rocky shoals in their marriage. Myrna never told her friends exactly what the trouble was, but it is clear that she was no longer confident of her husband's enduring or exclusive affection. "I felt my world falling to pieces around me." Myrna did not discuss her marital problems with Power, but he sensed her fragility and treated her with gentleness and sensitivity. "I'm sorry to report that we weren't lovers," Myrna said in her autobiography, acknowledging her attraction to him, "but he was married to that damn Frenchwoman" (*BB, 159*). She saw Tyrone Power as a magnetic and spiritual person who once told her that if he could be anything, he'd be the wind, so he could be light and free, and go anywhere. She didn't mention his devastating good looks, but she didn't have to. Anyone who had seen Tyrone Power in a movie, or seen just a still photo of him, knew.[47]

The Rains Came was a big-budget, full-tilt production with special effects by Fred Sersen that copped the very first Academy Award for Special Effects, competing against *Gone with the Wind* and *The Wizard of Oz* (among other contenders). It also won nominations in Art Direction, Cinematography, Musical Score, Film Editing, and Sound Effects. It delivered all the spectacular disasters a dedicated movie-lover could ask for, not just a deluge of rain but a flood triggered by an earthquake that breaks a dam, as well as a fire and a plague. (The earthquake in *San Francisco* had been a big winner, and the disaster in Samuel Goldwyn's *The Hurricane* had also scored in 1938.) Fox paid $52,500 just for the rights to the novel, $500,000 for sets, and the cost of production came in slightly under budget at about $2 million. The film made $1.5 million in rentals and garnered mixed reviews. Howard Barnes, in the *New York Herald Tribune,* found it too long and "only sporadically diverting." But *Daily Variety* praised the brooding atmosphere and named it one of the important films of the season. *The Hollywood Reporter* singled out Myrna Loy's performance as "one of her finest, and a distinct achievement." The movie deserves more attention than it gets today.[48]

Myrna had consulted Arthur, as she tended to do before making a big career decision, about the wisdom of playing Lady Esketh. He initially advised her against taking on the role but changed his mind. He came to see her point, that she needed to stretch. As the world plunged into war, Arthur was coming to a decision about his own need for expanded horizons on the home front.

CHAPTER 13

Things Fall Apart

Myrna never stopped thinking of Arthur as the love of her life. "Of all the men I've known, he was the one," she confessed in the autobiography she published in her eighty-second year (*BB, 165*). During her later years in New York, decades removed from the break with him, her eyes would fill with tears if she heard a song she associated with Arthur. But Arthur's feelings for her were another story. His emotional skittishness, need to control every detail, and tendency to hold back had dogged their relationship. Getting married had been Myrna's dream, not his. As the 1930s drew to a tumultuous close, after three years as man and wife and several more of unwed coupledom before that, Arthur's conjugal devotion faltered. Even splitting up proved tortuous; that took three years.

People around them began noticing signs of discord in the spring of 1939, when Myrna took off for six weeks in the desert to recuperate from a strep throat before reporting to the set of *The Rains Came*. She seemed emotionally spent, as well as physically ill. The usually sure-footed Myrna was losing her bearings.

Eager to squelch rumors of a pending split and to advertise his role as a still loving and dutiful husband, Arthur showed up at the Los Angeles Union Pacific station to be photographed kissing Myrna good-bye when she and her mother embarked in February 1940 on a nostalgic trip back to Montana, Myrna's first since she left Helena at age fourteen. There was significance in the fact, reported in the press, that Myrna had taken over the red barn behind the Hornblow manse in Beverly Hills and would furnish it with items her Scots grandmother had brought with her to Montana when she'd traveled west by ox cart in the 1860s. At the dawn of the new decade Myrna cast a backward glance, reclaiming her forebears' pioneer past. The family heirlooms, including cut-glass stemware and fine china that she held on to through numerous changes of address, belonged to *her*.

Larry Barbier, an MGM publicist who accompanied Myrna and Della to Montana, made sure that the press covered every step of the actress's sojourn in Big Sky country. Newspapers nationwide featured photos of Myrna Loy visiting a deserted gold mine, Myrna Loy at a country schoolhouse, and Myrna Loy posed in front of a split-rail fence near the broken-down barn at the Williams ranch, the onetime family homestead north of Helena. The press also reported her triumphant return to Helena's vintage Marlow Theater, where she'd once danced. At a reception in her honor the mayor presented Helena's favorite daughter a bouquet of wildflowers.[1]

While on Montana turf, Myrna helped her mother purchase part of the defunct Williams ranch. Now that she didn't have to live there all the time, and could skip the frigid winters, Della doted on the ranch's craggy old trees, its tumble-down wooden structures, the expansive fields, and the surrounding snowcapped mountains she knew so well from her Radersburg girlhood and the years she spent at the ranch as a young wife and mother. Estate documents refer to it as the Home Place, and that name says it all. Herds of grazing horses and lowing cattle no longer populated the fields, and the staff of ranch hands had long since departed, but the landscape, at once dramatic and serene, exerted a powerful pull.[2]

By turning over a portion of the ranch to Della, Myrna helped to right a wrong. Myrna's father, David, had neglected to will his share of the property to Della, preferring to leave it instead to his two children. Still partly owned by Myrna's surviving Williams aunt and uncle, the ranch land had been leased to tenants in recent years and had fallen into disrepair. It was a simple matter for Myrna and David Jr. to deed their share of the property to Della and for Myrna to pay the small amount of cash needed to buy additional acreage near the neglected ranch and begin restoring it. Della, who still had Johnson family in the Helena area, would henceforth, so long as her health permitted, spend summers at the ranch. Although Myrna didn't often see her relatives back in Montana, she stayed in touch with some of them over the years. In reconnecting with

Williams, Qualls, and Johnson kin and the land itself, Myrna further defined an identity completely independent of Arthur.

In Los Angeles concerned friends and professional gossips alike speculated about the future of the Perfect Wife's marriage. When that tired epithet was hurled Myrna's way by an insistent Hearst newspaper reporter, she grew snappish:

> "I'm not the perfect wife. I don't even like to discuss it. Let's just forget it, shall we?"
>
> "Certainly [the questioner promises], we'll forget it. You mean that you're not a perfect wife on screen, don't you?"
>
> "No, not necessarily. I'm not one in real life. Or in pictures, for that matter. [Nora Charles is] jealous. And now [with the release of *Another Thin Man*] she wakes Nick up in the middle of the night to play with the baby. And she always insists on tagging along. She's too dumb at times, too smart at times. It bewilders Nick. Perfect wives shouldn't bewilder their husbands."[3]

Arthur had grown restless. As his producing career gathered steam (recent or in-the-works Hornblow productions included the Mitchell Leisen screwball comedy *Midnight,* with Claudette Colbert, and *I Wanted Wings,* an air force picture featuring the newcomer Veronica Lake), rumors of his attentions to "still another actress" crept into the pages of *Photoplay.*[4]

The plain truth is that Myrna no longer fascinated Arthur. He would tell his third wife, the former Leonora Schinasi Morris, with whom he eventually settled into an enduring and loving marriage, that without screenwriters to supply her witty lines, Myrna's conversation fell short. Twenty-two years younger than Arthur, Leonora, a glamorous, highly verbal, socially prominent New York heiress once known as "Bubbles," at age eighteen came to Hollywood to marry the Warner Bros. actor Wayne Morris. She soon divorced Morris and after an interval of several years married Arthur in 1945, at the home of her dear friends Bennett and Phyllis Cerf. (Phyllis, a cousin of Ginger Rogers, had been an actress [billed as Phyllis Fraser] in Hollywood.) Leonora later became a writer who collaborated with Arthur on several books for young people that were edited by the publisher and Random House cofounder Bennett Cerf. She also published a book on Cleopatra for young people and two adult novels about Hollywood, but at the time of her marriage to Arthur she had penned only a few fashion columns and book reviews and could not be called a career woman. She had been, however, a stylish, popular, and vivacious beauty who traveled in elite circles. Gloria

Vanderbilt was a good friend, and later Babe Paley and Pamela Harriman would be as well. Much later, she'd make a splash at Truman Capote's trend-setting Black and White ball. During her three decades with Arthur, Leonora's life revolved around him, their homes, and their glittering social circle. That suited Arthur.[5]

"*I* was the love of his life, not Myrna," the still elegant octogenarian widow of Arthur Hornblow Jr. proclaimed in an interview. She fondled, and then held up for display, a heavy, jangling gold-link bracelet that Arthur had presented to her as a special gift. From a gold disk, one of three that dangled from the precious bauble, she brandished Arthur's engraved inscription: "The beloved bearer is the true and only Mrs. Arthur Hornblow Jr."[6]

Arthur's constant faultfinding and apparent rejection caused Myrna untold anguish. When he criticized Terry, something he did readily, Myrna sided with her stepson. Arthur could be patronizing. He looked down on Myrna's Montana-bred mother, beloved Aunt Lu, and brother, David, who all remained financially dependent on Myrna until the mid-1940s, when David finally settled into a job as a mechanical designer at Hughes Aircraft and became self-supporting. To a lesser extent Arthur looked down on Myrna, too. He used to joke that when he met her, she was just a barefoot country girl. She continued to feel that she didn't and couldn't measure up. It was hard not to internalize his disdain.

While the Hornblows' marital boat rocked, Myrna remained reticent, as usual. Even in her autobiography, out of consideration for Arthur's family, friends they shared, and Myrna's own preference for privacy, she didn't discuss Arthur's infidelity. He had affairs, including a brief fling with Kay Francis. She chose to keep mum even to close friends, but as she retained her dignity and integrity, Myrna's health and self-confidence took a dive. She would tell the judge who granted her 1942 Reno divorce that her husband's conduct "caused her great unhappiness and injured her general health."[7]

At home in the big, custom-built Hornblow home on Hidden Valley Road, her shortcomings and foibles seemed to grate on Arthur. He'd become impossible to please and fussed about minute details. He put sticky stuff on the bottoms of mantelpiece objects to make sure the housekeeping staff wouldn't move them from an exact spot. When Terry visited during summer vacations, Arthur frightened the boy with his austere bearing, his list of Thou Shalt Nots and his harsh punishments. When they entertained guests, he obsessed about the wine he served. The MGM writer Bob Hopkins, who got to know Arthur when he jumped from Paramount to MGM in the early 1940s, joked that Arthur "can't read a script unless it's room temperature."[8]

Arthur had invested quantities of money, care, and thought on their Coldwater Canyon home's design and décor, which Myrna enjoyed and helped plan and finance but didn't care as much about. When the marriage finally ended, she relinquished her claim on the lavish wedding gifts and other furnishings of their home; Arthur took everything, including heaps of fine silver, and that was okay with Myrna. She liked the feeling of walking away unimpeded by truckloads of possessions and would repeat the pattern. Even before her first trip to the altar, Myrna made it clear that with the exception of some family heirlooms and a few pieces of jewelry, she wasn't attached much to material things. She once left behind a valuable painting and some Wedgwood china in a Westwood house she rented from Dorothy Manners.[9]

The traveling-light, I'll-go-my-way-and-you-go-yours policy applied to income, too. Myrna paid her own way and was probably far too casual (for her own future security) about money. She did have a few small investments, and she owned the mountain retreat at Lake Arrowhead, but for her, estate planning didn't rank high on the list of priorities. At the opposite extreme from Hollywood penny-pinchers such as Cary Grant and Clark Gable, she enjoyed spending her large income freely. Like her less-affluent father she splurged on gifts, bought what she wanted for herself, and squirreled away little. Unlike her father she always looked after her family.

One month after moving into their just-completed dream house in 1937, she and Arthur had signed a postnuptial agreement stating that they would share equally in household expenses and that each of them would keep earnings separate. Before the divorce Arthur handed her a bill for close to $6,000, claiming that Myrna owed it for shared expenses that he had fronted. Arthur never behaved irresponsibly when it came to money, but he kept close tabs.[10]

The Hornblows' unforgiving work schedules got in the way of wedded bliss, too. After a day of shooting on a set, Myrna might come home "too tired to know if I'm Myrna Loy, Mrs. Arthur Hornblow or Kitty O'Shea. I just stumble into bed, if I don't have to memorize lines." If Arthur found himself free for a few days, and wanted to take off somewhere, Myrna would sometimes be able to join him, but she often couldn't, because of her obligations at the studio. Being married to a movie actress, especially a star, required a maturity, forbearance, and un-selfishness that few husbands can muster. Arthur Hornblow Jr. didn't make the cut.[11]

Even though Myrna's commitment to the marriage remained huge, she had few hours to devote to being a caregiver. She needed care herself. "The men who *work* with us see us at our best, exciting, glamorous, meticulous," Carole Lombard once tellingly observed. "The men we *marry* see us at our worst, dead tired, at the day's end, with makeup off and the curlers on." Still, Myrna had participated in planning the house and running it. She had become close to her young stepson, Terry, taking him fishing and on boat trips, providing him with pets and other kids to play with when he came to stay. She had hosted Arthur's aging father when he visited from London, as she had his former nanny. She planned many a menu with Sergei the Russian chef, tried to wear clothes that Arthur liked, and cohosted innumerable parties on Hidden Valley Road. She'd joined Arthur doing the things they both relished: traveling, attending plays and movie premiers, dining at French restaurants. She'd involved herself with Arthur's productions, offering her suggestions on casting decisions, and relied, in turn, on his astute counsel about her career. "Her friends knew how her interest in Arthur's productions quite outweighed her interest in her own," wrote Elizabeth Owens. "They knew how she carelessly let herself be maneuvered out of the leading feminine role in *Boom Town* [a 1940 MGM film, the top moneymaker of its year, in which Claudette Colbert ended up playing the role originally intended for Myrna Loy] and into the very much less important *Third Finger, Left Hand*."[12]

Looking back, Myrna faulted herself, deciding she had been too compliant and too eager to accommodate Arthur. "Perhaps I should have kicked him in the teeth a couple of times, instead of trying to be the perfect wife he wanted" (*BB*, 170). Although she'd once walked out on MGM, confrontation didn't come naturally to her. Cary Grant, her admirer and costar in three movies, said he saw her lose her cool only once, when she got mad at herself for flubbing a line.[13]

Myrna's inability to bear children also continued to grieve her. She bought a complete layette for the baby of her personal maid Theresa Penn, sent ice cream and cake to the hospital when the baby was born, and befriended a boy who sold newspapers around the MGM lot. Myrna had an instinctive rapport with young people and would serve as a surrogate aunt to any number of them. According to the intrusive, and not always reliable, Hedda Hopper, Myrna and Arthur briefly considered adopting.

Hopper published an item saying that the couple wanted to adopt two children, neither one a baby. The couple, she said, "would prefer to have a little boy and girl out of an orphanage, about the age of five or six." If they ever entertained such an intention, they didn't act on it. Undertaking joint parenthood made no sense at the moment, given that the prospective parents might be splitting up. Arthur's failure to share Myrna's yearning for children increased her unhappiness and sense of isolation. She gained several pounds, which prompted catty whispers. She battled the flu and departed for another desert retreat.[14]

Arthur's feelings about Myrna are encapsulated in a remark from Irene Mayer Selznick. When she read Myrna's revelations about her deep and enduring affection for Arthur in *Being and Becoming*, Irene talked about this with Arthur's current wife, Leonora, Irene's close friend. "I saw a lot of Arthur and Myrna," Irene told Leonora. "Poor thing! Her adoration was not returned." But though Irene Selznick spoke with the authority of an eyewitness, she harbored no particular fondness for Myrna, and her comment makes things too simple. Arthur did treat Myrna with harshness and cruelty, at times, but what made their breakup such a heartbreak was that he couldn't make up his mind. He would cold-shoulder her one day and then begin to court her again the next. Each time she left him, down to the last, he kept signaling that he desperately wanted her back. Who wouldn't find such behavior crazy-making?[15]

The first Arthur-Myrna separation came in November 1940. "Myrna Loy Admits Rift; Plans Suit for Divorce; Actress Declares Marriage Has Proved Failure," read the headline for the *Los Angeles Times* story. Louella Parsons had interrupted her weekly radio broadcast to announce the separation as breaking news, a "scoop." Arthur soon issued a most gracious and affectionate statement: "We have tried for a long time to adjust the inescapable complications of our careers. That has not been possible. That still leaves her one of the loveliest women in the world." A clean, permanent break would have caused far less pain, but that wasn't in the cards—yet.[16]

Myrna won plaudits in the press for keeping her own counsel. "Myrna Loy has won the respect and admiration of everyone in Hollywood following the breakup of her marriage," blabbered Louella Parsons, who was herself a cause of Myrna's elusiveness. "Not once, since her dignified explanation that she and Arthur Hornblow were parting, has Myrna appeared in a nightclub. Instead she has taken a very small house and only her most intimate friends are invited to visit or dine with her. Occasionally she accepts party invitations. But she always arrives early and leaves early. There is not the slightest doubt that the breakup caused her great sorrow. But Myrna is not the type to wear her heart on her sleeve."[17]

The movie community, and those tracking it, could get cynical about Hollywood vows of eternal devotion, but the marriage of Myrna Loy and Arthur Hornblow had been widely exalted as an exception to the rule. "The marriages of Lana Turner, Hedy Lamarr, Carole Landis—this year's crop of swift unions and swift dissolves—were all obviously madcap from start to fierce finish," Elizabeth Owens wrote in a *Photoplay* article called "Why the Perfect Wife's Marriage Failed." Owens got specific: "Hollywood positively hoped that the Norma Shearer–George Raft romance would not last—and it didn't. Everybody knew almost from the moment of the wedding that [Joan] Crawford and [Franchot] Tone would eventually part. But Myrna Loy and Arthur Hornblow Jr.! That was really a marriage, not just a flaming romance that had been solemnized with a ceremony." To boost her claim that theirs had been a real love story, and elicit a heart-tugging sigh, Owens reminded readers that Arthur had hand-picked Myrna's wedding bouquet in Mexico back in June of 1936.[18]

A few months after their announced breakup, Arthur and Myrna, explaining that they'd separated too hastily, jointly proclaimed reconciliation. They'd been spotted together at a sneak preview of Arthur's air force picture, *I Wanted Wings*. Then they turned up dancing cheek to cheek at the Mocambo, a new nightclub on the Sunset Strip, Myrna radiant in a green gown and Arthur beaming. "When they were not dancing they were casually holding hands under the table." Myrna moved back in with Arthur, who had already sold the big house on Hidden Valley Road and was living more modestly on Cherokee Lane in Beverly Hills. "She says no more big houses for them." They called off the divorce and went on several vacation trips together, one to Mexico City, where they stayed near the home of Diego Rivera; one to the Canadian Rockies, where they celebrated Myrna's thirty-sixth birthday; and a third to New York.[19]

Bill Powell and his new bride, Diana Lewis, joined them in New York, and the foursome went to the theater and out on the town together. The new Mrs. Powell, nicknamed "Mousie" because she was petite, was twenty-one and Powell forty-seven when they'd wed the previous year. On their first date, according to Mousie, they'd attended a dinner party at Arthur and Myrna's home, where Ronald Colman and Reginald Gardiner were also guests. Mousie laughingly remembered the occasion: "Mr. Poo [Powell] knocked my hand and the glass of wine I'm holding spills all over me. The next thing, he drops his roll in his soup and it dunks me.

The next thing, he squirts a lime and it get[s] me in the eye." These two were clearly in synch. Diana Lewis gave up her own embryonic MGM movie-acting career soon after the wedding. The Powells stayed together until the end of Bill's life in 1984. An adoring, attractive, much younger wife not committed to a big career of her own—that seems to have been the winning ticket.[20]

The temporary, very public reconciliation of Arthur and Myrna was as much discussed and freighted with significance as their initial separation announcement had been. Because the wife in question was Myrna Loy, Hollywood's paragon of wifedom, her domestic situation carried symbolic value, or at least it seemed to. "When lovely Myrna Loy—she of the sweet smile and the tip-tilted nose—blew back to the arms of husband Arthur Hornblow Jr. recently with the announcement that she was abandoning 'hasty' divorce plans, it was by no means another Hollywood interlude," wrote Fred Dickenson in one American newspaper. "It was the sort of triumph for domesticity designed to rekindle the light of love in the newly betrothed and bolster the faith of the Hays office in life's noble sentiments. It was, in short, the perfect thing for the Perfect Wife to do." The public wanted to preserve its idealized image of Myrna and her dream marriage, founded (they'd been told) on love, mutual respect, parallel career success, and good taste. But the public's hopes, along with Myrna's, would be dashed.[21]

As if to prove that art can imitate life, the theme of divorce crept into Myrna's cinematic life in the early 1940s. Always a popular and timely topic in marriage-mad Hollywood, divorce took front-and-center position in the plots of the two Powell-Loy screwball comedies that MGM released while Myrna went through her private marital unraveling.

The reconciliation of an estranged couple is a built-in component of what Stanley Cavell called "the Hollywood comedy of remarriage," but for the Loy-Powell comedy team it marked a departure. True, they'd played an estranged couple in *Evelyn Prentice,* but that was no comedy. In these two Loy-Powell comic vehicles they portray spouses on the brink of divorce, not an already divorced pair like Hepburn and Cary Grant in *The Philadelphia Story* or Rosalind Russell and Cary Grant in *His Girl Friday.* Both times it's the wife, Myrna Loy, who wants out of the marriage, and each time Powell is the panicky husband who'll do anything, however off the wall, to win back the affection of his smart, beautiful, in-control, at times lofty, and dismissive wife.[22]

Both these comedies are subversive in that they make a husband's sane, play-by-the-rules conventionality ridiculous and unpardonably dull. He's only attractive when he's nutty, bumbling, morally sleazy, or otherwise out of bounds. Powell, as husband, is more than willing to make a slapstick fool of himself, and Loy, as wife, loves him *for* his antic disposition, not in spite of it. Showing that he can charm Myrna Loy and make her frown dissolve into a smile does double duty, quashing plans for divorce as it sells the movie.

In *I Love You Again,* based on a novel by Octavus Roy Cohen, Powell has a split personality. He plays two versions of the same man, one virtuous, sober, and yawn-inspiring, the other an appealing cad. Before he's whacked on the head with an oar, he's a paragon of middle-American small-town respectability. As stuffed shirt Larry Wilson of Habersville, Pennsylvania, he's shown himself to be a tightwad stalwart of the Rotary Club and the Hoot Owl Association, an upstanding citizen who manages a pottery plant and never drinks anything stronger than ginger ale mixed with grape juice. His idea of a good time is to stuff a dead skunk and turn the result into living room decor. But the anti–Larry Wilson, the man he used to be and reverts to when amnesia strikes, is con man George Carey, a smooth-talking, sharp dresser and lowlife spendthrift who'll bend any rule to scam a dollar or steal a laugh. Comedy-writing veterans George Oppenheimer, Charles Lederer, and Harry Kurnitz shared credit for the witty script. Lederer, also a contributor to the script of *Love Crazy,* co-wrote, with Ben Hecht, the script for *His Girl Friday,* also released in 1940, and had been one of the screenwriters on *Topaze.*

Powell's personality number one, the boring Larry Wilson, was away on a cruise excursion when the bop on the bean induced amnesia. His wife, Kay (Myrna Loy), comes to greet the boat at the pier—and to tell Larry that she's decided she wants a divorce. Ditching her uptight husband will give her a shot at a new life, with more fun in it. She has a promising future husband already lined up. But of course Larry isn't Larry any more; post bop on the bean, he's transformed into personality number two, George Carey. George has no clue who this lovely woman named Kay might be, but he certainly finds her attractive and would like to keep her around. Kay soon discovers what an entertaining fellow her husband has become. Suddenly, he's a great kisser. The former tightwad even takes her to a high-end department store to buy her an expensive negligee, the same winning strategy that erring husband Clark Gable employed for fretting wife Myrna Loy in *Test Pilot.* The movie doesn't try to explain how Kay managed to fall for and marry no-fun Larry in the first place, but excesses of logic aren't called for here.

Although her role in *I Love You Again* offered Myrna Loy little to do that she hadn't done before onscreen, she excelled at playing a gorgeous, even-tempered, clever but caustic straight woman to Powell's quick-change artist who can drool like a backward four-year-old or coo like a dove. She did get to crown Larry/George with a plate of scrambled eggs and to tell him, "I've often wished I could turn your head—on a spit over a slow fire."

Myrna found joy in playing a forceful wife who holds the power card in her marriage. Her Kay is the decision maker, the one who has her head on straight and who can sink or save the marriage. "Heretofore I've always had to do the chasing after Bill," Myrna told the *New York Post.* "This time he has to chase me, and believe me the chase is a merry one." Being pursued by Bill Powell onscreen while in private life Arthur sent mixed messages, some of them signaling rejection, held obvious appeal.[23]

In *Love Crazy* Powell is again a shape-changer, Loy again cool, alluring, and steady in her determination to get a divorce, this time from a husband she thinks cheated on her on the night of their fourth wedding anniversary. Directed by Jack Conway, of *Libeled Lady* fame, and produced by the estimable Pandro Berman, who was new to MGM but had supervised many Fred Astaire–Ginger Rogers hits at RKO, *Love Crazy* begins with an in-joke: Powell, in a cab with a box of red roses to present to his wife on their special day, sings along with a recording of a song from *The Great Ziegfeld,* which Luise Rainer had performed in that movie, "It's Delightful to Be Married." (Anna Held wrote the lyrics.) In *The Great Ziegfeld* Powell portrayed the philanderer Flo Ziegfeld, but this time he's the devoted husband, Steve Ireland, a man convinced that "there's nothing wrong with anyone's life that a good marriage can't cure." He's all lovey-dovey with Susan, his wife (Loy), as they set about celebrating this romantic occasion in a madcap way. They dance together in their chic, upscale apartment and plan to honor a tradition they've established of repeating on their anniversary the rituals they'd followed on their wedding day: going for a long hike, rowing on a lake, and ending up, before bed, with an intimate and festive dinner. Today though, instead of repeating the anniversary ritual in the order in which the events originally occurred, they're going to do everything backwards. Before Susan's intrusive mother (Florence Bates) interferes with their planned celebration, they'd intended to have the maid serve dinner with courses presented in reverse order, dessert served first. Zaniness has clearly been Steve Ireland's signature, and Susan loves him for that—until she decides that he's done her wrong, and it would be delightful to be *un*married.

In the elevator of their chic Manhattan apartment building, Steve runs into an aggressive old flame, Isobel (Gail Patrick), and the slapstick mania begins when the elevator gets stuck between floors and Steve gets his head locked between the closing doors when he tries to climb out. Seductive Isobel lures him into her apartment, trying to put the make on Steve, but he resists. He's anxious to get back to Susan and their anniversary festivities. His meddling mother-in-law, however, gets wind of Steve's stop at the old flame's apartment and plants seeds of distrust in Susan, who makes up her mind to divorce Steve right away. Steve won't agree; he doesn't want to lose his wife. When a lawyer advises him that Susan wouldn't be able to divorce him for five years if he can demonstrate to psychiatrists on "the lunacy board" that he's gone insane, the high jinks follow apace. One minute he's at a party in top hat and tails, masquerading as Abraham Lincoln. He "frees" a black butler and liberates a bunch of top hats. The next minute he's an inmate in the loony bin, caught in the branches of a tree when chasing after a bird. He finally reverts to drag, just as Cary Grant does in the celebrated cross-dressing scene in *Bringing Up Baby*. The cops are looking for Steve after he escapes from the insane asylum, so to elude them Steve reinvents himself as Steve's matronly older sister. Looking Victorian in a wig, granny glasses, a long dark skirt, a lace jabot and a prim jacket stuffed with skeins of yarn to fill out the bosom, Steve even sounds like an old biddy. His very proper baritone speaking voice has shot up an octave or two, into the soprano register. Susan is his ally in the farce. By the time Steve is outed by the unspooling of the yarn that served as his fake bosom, she's ready to forgive all and take him back into the bedroom.

These two comedies scored well both with critics and at the box office. The *Hollywood Reporter* pronounced *I Love You Again* "one of the best laugh pictures of the year." Writing about *Love Crazy*, Bosley Crowther of the *New York Times* applauded "the steady progression toward insanity" as a respite from the tired domesticity that the most recent *Thin Man* caper had served up. He concluded, "Everyone who worked on this picture must have trained rigidly on a routine of old slapstick comedies and a diet of loco-weed," and that was fine with him. On MGM's list of its top ten moneymakers of 1940–41, *Love Crazy* occupied the ninth spot, with *Gone with the Wind* in top position and *The Philadelphia Story* at number two.[24]

Myrna savored the manic humor in these two films and delighted in Powell's brilliant daffiness, but her downcast frame of mind clashed with the fare MGM was offering her. As she put it, between her marital problems and the Nazis, "I wasn't in the mood for froth" (*BB*, 170).

The war in Europe escalated during the unspooling of Myrna's private world. Nazi tanks rolled into Paris and took the city in June of 1940, during one of the intervals she and Arthur were together, not separated. They'd rented a Malibu beach house from Madeleine Carroll for the summer. After learning of the siege, Jerome Kern, who had worked with Arthur on the musical *High, Wide and Handsome,* came by with friends for a beach house get-together. Kern sat down at the rickety upright piano and began to play a song he'd newly created with Oscar Hammerstein II (their only collaboration not written to order), "The Last Time I Saw Paris." The song also marked the only time that the Hammerstein words preceded the Kern music. The next year, "The Last Time I Saw Paris," by then recorded by Kate Smith and Noel Coward, turned up in the movie *Lady Be Good;* Ann Sothern sang it, and it won the Academy Award for Best Song. That June day in Malibu, everyone present wept as Kern played the soon-to-be-famous melody in the presence of Arthur and Myrna, softly intoning the elegiac words that for many summed up welling emotions for the stricken city of light (*BB*, 165). Myrna and Arthur had visited Paris together during that 1935 premarital honeymoon and again just a year back, in the summer of 1939.[25]

With the notable exception of Maurice Chevalier, who returned to his homeland and performed in occupied Paris, Hollywood talent promptly united in various efforts to support the besieged British and the French. At a benefit for the latter, Lotte Lehmann sang, accompanied by Bruno Walter. Tyrone Power and Fredric March served as masters of ceremony, and Myrna, grandly gowned, sold cigarettes along with Bette Davis, Merle Oberon, Norma Shearer, Irene Dunne, and Olivia de Havilland. With Cary Grant (who would soon costar with Myrna in a Lux Radio Theater version of *I Love You Again*), Rosalind Russell, and Charles Boyer, Myrna sold peanuts at a Buy-a-Bomber benefit. She joined Merle Oberon, Claudette Colbert, Annabella, and Maureen O'Sullivan as cigarette girls at a Cocoanut Grove fund-raiser for Franco-British War Relief. At the same event Bill Powell, Charles Laughton, Herbert Marshall, Ronald Colman, and Laurence Olivier joined a jocular chorus line to belt out "The Man on the Flying Trapeze" (*BB*, 164–65).[26]

On December 7, 1941, Japan invaded Pearl Harbor, and FDR subsequently declared war. Myrna happened to be in New York with her close friend Natalie Visart. They were both taking breathers, Myrna from the tumult of life with (and without) Arthur, and Natalie from her labors as costume designer for DeMille's *Reap the Wild Wind*. Still involved with the director Mitchell Leisen, Arthur's frequent collaborator at Paramount, Natalie had an office near Arthur's on the Paramount lot. Arthur would pump her for news about Myrna during the intervals when he and Myrna were separated. Altogether, Myrna left Arthur five different times, and each time took a piece out of her hide.

The pre-Christmas escape to the elegant Manhattan St. Regis Hotel allowed Myrna to test her wings. She had neither Arthur nor an MGM publicist to shepherd her, plan her every move, or shield her from autograph hounds and crowds of fans. On her own in Manhattan, or with Natalie, she found herself mobbed wherever she went and tried to avoid places like Fifth Avenue during daylight hours. Myrna had mixed emotions about this venture into relative independence, finding it at once liberating and scary. MGM stars were notoriously coddled and usually kept on a short leash. Myrna had yet to experience riding in a Manhattan subway or a municipal bus. She had rarely even hailed a cab on her own.

She learned about the Japanese invasion via a phone conversation with Arthur's first wife, Juliette, who called the hotel while nine-year-old Terry Hornblow was visiting Myrna there. Juliette, who was living on the East Coast, told Myrna, "We've been attacked!" (*BB,* 168).

Arthur had been thinking about flying to New York to join Myrna, but when the United States declared war on Japan, he decided this was no time to travel. He wanted to stay in California, where the fear of a further Japanese attack ran high, and where he might be of service. Myrna immediately got on a plane to return to Arthur's side, and to try to calm Della, whose anxiety about an imminent Japanese invasion of California had made her hysterical.

Myrna learned on her arrival in Los Angeles that the city had been transformed. Fear, anger, and patriotic defiance had taken hold. People wore stricken expressions, and a rush to enlist in the armed forces had begun. The Burbank airport was cloaked in camouflage. The wail of testing air raid sirens periodically punctured the silence. There was talk of camouflaging the major movie studios to make them look less like airplane hangars and more like innocent orchards. The Hornblow station wagon had been commandeered for use during blackouts as an air raid precaution, and Arthur himself had signed up as an air raid warden. "Yachts and pleasure craft of film stars are being eyed by the Navy for takeover," *Variety* reported. Soldiers with antiaircraft artillery had been posted up the hill from the Hornblows' Coldwater Canyon house. Myrna sent a portable stove to keep them warm.[27]

During the tumultuous interval before Myrna and Arthur decisively terminated their marriage, Myrna remained busy both as an actress and as a volunteer for the war effort. The fourth *Thin Man* movie, *Shadow of the Thin Man* hit theaters a few weeks before Pearl Harbor. Major W. S. Van Dyke of the U.S. Marine Corps Reserve directed, in what would be his last venture as Myrna's boss. Because he was ill with lung cancer, he'd been turned away from active service in the marines, to his chagrin. With a so-so script by Irving Brecher and Harry Kurnitz, this was the first *Thin Man* movie without direct input from Hammett, who was currently working on an adaptation of Lillian Hellman's *The Watch on the Rhine.*

Shadow of the Thin Man serves up a smooth-edged, predictable version of Nick and Nora. They now have a son (Dickie Hall) in military school and a maid (Louise Beavers) to pour their martinis. Although they tool around in an open-top convertible and spend plenty of time at the racetrack, where the shooting of a jockey triggers the mystery plot, it's not their raciness but their cutesy home life that defines them. They live in a spacious San Francisco apartment with art deco mirrors, and Nora, clad in a filmy peignoir, can go to a wrought-iron balcony and peer through binoculars to spot Nick reading to their uniformed young son on a park bench. She doesn't realize that he's reading the horse racing form, not a book of fairy tales for kids. This joke, like the one mocking Nick as he's forced to drink milk to oblige his son, shows signs of strain. The deft, sardonic touches of the Hackett-Goodrich scripts are glaringly absent. "The Charleses, we're afraid, are settling down," opined the *New York Times.* "Some of their former reckless *joie de vivre* is gone." The formula might be getting stale, but audiences nonetheless flocked to see *Shadow of the Thin Man,* which grossed $2.3 million.[28]

When it came to leaving an imprint, *Shadow of the Thin Man* couldn't touch another Hammett spin-off, *The Maltese Falcon,* the noir version (there had been two prior films based on the story) directed by John Huston that was released a few weeks before *Shadow of the Thin Man.* Featuring Humphrey Bogart as a tense, cynical, tough-guy Sam Spade, *The Maltese Falcon* made Bogart a star and turned his dark-haired Spade into a touchstone. Bogart's Sam Spade became the private eye antihero of the decade, as Powell's Nick Charles had been for the 1930s. Nick and Nora's romp at the racetrack seemed nostalgic and slightly quaint by comparison.

Melvyn Douglas, Myrna's costar in 1940's *Third Finger, Left Hand,* and more famously Garbo's in the previous year's *Ninotchka,* had become so visible as a leader in anti-Nazi and pro-Roosevelt circles that his schedule of political speeches and meetings ran neck and neck with his acting career. He was considering a run for Congress. Stirred to activism after a trip to Nazi Germany with his wife, Helen Gahagan Douglas, Douglas became a spokesman for the Motion Picture Democratic Committee, a group dedicated to promoting the New Deal in California. He campaigned hard for Culbert Olson, the first Democrat to be elected governor of California in forty years, and was a delegate to the Democratic National Convention in 1940. That same year, his wife became a member of the Democratic National Committee. Horrified by Melvyn Douglas's well-publicized political outspokenness, Louis B. Mayer reprimanded him privately, telling the MGM actor that he could think whatever he pleased, "but you don't do yourself any good at the studio when you take part in activities which are bound to offend a lot of people." Melvyn offered to cancel his contract, but Mayer didn't warm to that idea—since Douglas had shown he had plenty of box-office appeal as a sophisticated leading man in comedies. The conference in Mayer's office ended in a stand-off, but Douglas believed that afterward the studio brass cold-shouldered him. He began working more often at Columbia Pictures and would soon enlist in the army.[29]

Although Melvyn Douglas, like Myrna, was a liberal anticommunist, he incurred the wrath of Red baiters because he'd worked in cooperation with known reds, such as Donald Ogden Stewart, and because he'd spoken out, along with leftists, against isolationism and Hitler. The 1939 Nazi-Soviet Pact fractured the left and destroyed the alliances between liberals and radicals that had made the now defunct Hollywood Anti-Nazi League possible. In the early 1940s a new wave of "fellow traveler" accusations against movie stars swept Washington. Rep. Martin Dies fingered Jimmy Cagney, Fredric March, and Humphrey Bogart for their possibly "un-American activities," and in the California State Assembly Melvyn Douglas again found himself accused of being a communist. Some of the slurs against Douglas were tinged with anti-Semitism, harping on his Jewish original surname, Hesselberg. The *Los Angeles Times* tepidly defended him as merely a "parlor pink."[30]

Three months before Pearl Harbor, a Senate subcommittee set about investigating "war mongering" propaganda in Hollywood, attacking American-made motion pictures for delivering a covert anti-Nazi and pro-British message. Two of the movies singled out were the box-office sensation *Sergeant York,* starring Gary Cooper as the World War I hero Alvin York, and Chaplin's highly popular spoof of Hitler, *The Great Dictator.* North Dakota Republican Gerald Nye accused Hollywood's producers, "all born abroad and animated by the persecutions and hatreds of the Old World," of injecting prowar propaganda into American films. Harry Warner, head of the studio that made *Sergeant York,* argued in a hearing on Moving Picture Propaganda, "You may correctly charge me with being anti-Nazi. But no one can charge me with being anti-American."[31]

The U.S. engagement in the war put Red Scare tactics on a back burner for a while—but they'd be back, and Myrna would put in her rounds battling them.

Myrna's activism in the early years of the war mainly involved lending her presence and her name to raise money for overseas relief and to support American troops. She joined other Hollywood luminaries—Carole Lombard, Clark Gable, Charles Laughton, Tyrone Power, Spencer Tracy, and Ronald Colman—on an international radio broadcast, "America Calling," to raise money for Greek War Relief. Bob Hope and Jack Benny were cohosts, Melvyn Douglas narrated, and Myrna and Mary Martin appeared in a sketch with Hope and Benny.[32]

She traveled to New York to appear with John Garfield and Janet Gaynor at a Navy Relief Show in Madison Square Garden. She persuaded Victor Fleming, Spencer Tracy, John Garfield, and Frank Morgan to pledge ten dollars a month for a group called Bundles for Bluejackets, which supported the U.S. Navy. She donned a blue uniform, and, along with Virginia (Mrs. Darryl) Zanuck and Kay Francis, worked the night shift at a Bundles for Bluejackets canteen that served coffee and doughnuts to men and women from a nearby training base in San Pedro Harbor, Long Beach. Myrna said she enjoyed the company of Kay Francis, someone Arthur had known since the days of his first marriage. "She was a little ahead of her time, using four letter words that shocked me terribly, but I liked her" (*BB,* 168). Myrna probably didn't know that Kay and Arthur had gone beyond a platonic relationship; if she did know, she didn't make an issue of it when working at the canteen.[33]

Many photos were taken of Myrna in uniform during the war years. Putting on a uniform tagged her as someone in service, and that was how she wanted to be known. Even her daywear took on a military cast, as a penchant for clothes with no frills and clean lines took hold among designers. Her favorite movie costumer, Dolly Tree, designed a fitted topcoat for her with the same tailoring and collar found in officers' overcoats.[34]

Just days after Pearl Harbor, a group of Hollywood actors got together to form the Hollywood Victory Committee, an organization whose mission was to funnel talent into hospital tours, shows at training camps for the military, and bond rallies (*BB*, 168). "We had our first meeting on Beverly Drive, over a delicatessen, with everybody screaming and interrupting everybody else," recalled Rosalind Russell, whose Danish wedding, to Frederick Brisson, Myrna had recently attended with Arthur. Gary Cooper turned out to be the champion seller of war bonds. Clark Gable chaired the Screen Actors division of the Victory Committee, and he in turn enlisted Myrna, who remembered Mrs. Gable, that human firecracker professionally known as Carole Lombard, as the most gung-ho patriot in the bunch, the first to pledge all-out support.[35]

A more politically engaged person than Clark Gable usually was, Carole Lombard, one of the highest paid actresses in Hollywood and much beloved in the movie community, had visited FDR in the White House shortly after his election to his third term and had been an ardent New Deal Democrat from day one of the Roosevelt presidency. A passionate advocate for the United States and the Allies after Pearl Harbor, she'd sold more than $2 million worth of bonds and was returning from a bond rally in her home state of Indiana when she and her mother (and others) were killed early in 1942, in a Nevada plane crash. She and Gable had been married just under three years, and Lombard was only thirty-three when her plane crashed into the side of a mountain. Myrna referred to Carole as Hollywood's first war casualty (*BB*, 169). FDR awarded her a posthumous Medal of Freedom.

Myrna, Bill Powell, Spencer Tracy, and Gable himself were the only Metro actors present at the grim private funeral. A few other luminaries, Jack Benny and Lombard's frequent costar Fred MacMurray among them, joined the select group of stunned mourners. Ernst Lubitsch, who'd just finished directing Lombard in the yet-to-be-released anti-Nazi comedy *To Be or Not to Be,* also paid his respects. Inconsolable, Gable refused to speak with any of them. Lombard, who had overruled her mother's wish to take the train back to California instead of flying, had specified in her will that she wished her funeral to be a simple, dignified occasion. She wanted none of the mawkish, overproduced spectacle she'd witnessed at Jean Harlow's Forest Lawn funerary extravaganza.[36]

Grief-stricken, Gable enlisted in the air corps eight months after Lombard died, in part because Lombard had urged him to sign up. Explaining that with the country at war, acting had lost its luster, he became a tail-gunner on a B-17 bomber. A tiny diamond shard found in the plane wreckage where Lombard died—part of an earring he'd given to Carole—found its way into a piece of jewelry he now wore around his neck, along with his dog-tag, at all times. In uniform Gable looked very much like the pilots he'd portrayed in *Night Flight, Test Pilot,* and *Too Hot to Handle,* except that he'd shaved off his mustache after enlisting and had lost sparkle; he now wore a somber expression. He'd enlisted in the air force as a private but soon became a second lieutenant and when aloft in his B-17 bomber refused to wear a parachute, insisting that if his plane went down, he wanted to go with it. Hitler enjoyed Gable onscreen, and Goering, his air minister, offered a $5,000 reward for Gable's capture.[37]

L. B. Mayer made it clear that studio profits still mattered more to him than defeating Hitler or winning the war. He discouraged Jimmy Stewart from enlisting in the air force, which Stewart went ahead and did early on, before Pearl Harbor. Mayer pulled strings to keep Mickey Rooney on the back lot instead of in the military. Rooney enlisted anyhow in 1944. Robert Montgomery also listened to his conscience, instead of Mayer, and drove an American Field Service ambulance in France after the German invasions of Holland and Belgium. He later joined the U.S. Navy. FDR's 1942 birthday celebration in Washington, a high-profile event that raised money for the March of Dimes, was attended by four movie actors in uniform, two of them from MGM: Lieutenant James Stewart, U.S. Army; Lt. Commander Robert Montgomery and Lt. Commander Douglas Fairbanks Jr. of the Navy; and Ensign Wayne Morris, also of the Navy.[38]

With so many Metro leading men overseas, the women stars held sway, but Myrna's acting career didn't benefit from this era of female dominance, any more than it benefited from the wartime economic boom. Although she remained on the *Motion Picture Herald* list of top stars for 1940, her name disappeared from the lineup the following year, never to reappear. In *Variety*'s reckoning Bette Davis was the top actress in both 1941 and 1942, with Dorothy Lamour giving her a run for her money and Judy Garland taking front position among actresses at MGM.[39]

Myrna faced more direct competition at her home studio in the person of an actress newly signed by MGM, Katharine Hepburn, whose film career rebounded wildly after hitting a low point in 1938, when she was tagged "box-office poison." Hepburn had redeemed herself onstage with her Broadway triumph in Philip Barry's *The Philadelphia Story*. She then shrewdly bought the film rights to the play, with financial help from Howard Hughes. Studios competed to acquire the movie rights, which, naturally, Hepburn controlled. She not only starred; she also picked her director (Cukor) and costars. MGM won screen rights to the Barry play, and Hepburn's vibrant performance as Tracy Lord copped an Oscar nomination, one of six for *The Philadelphia Story*. Hepburn soon signed a multipicture MGM contract and became the top-ranked comedy actress at MGM, with Roz Russell, originally hired to replace absent Myrna Loy in 1935, also a contender. Hepburn's series of nine movies opposite Spencer Tracy would follow. Apart from her brilliance as a performer, Katharine Hepburn displayed an aggressive me-first business savvy that Myrna Loy simply didn't possess.

There are other explanations for Myrna's slide in star standing, one being that she'd already had a long run by Hollywood standards and had passed her thirty-fifth birthday. She needed a role that would break the mold, and that role didn't materialize. Another was that Hollywood at the time was experiencing what Joan Crawford called "the British invasion," when a number of U.K. actors came to work in Hollywood and flourished. Irish-born Greer Garson enjoyed the favor of both Louis B. Mayer, who brought her over from London, and the moviegoing public. Garson had been cast in her debut MGM role in *Goodbye, Mr. Chips* after Myrna took herself out of the running by going over to Fox to play Lady Esketh in *The Rains Came*. Garson became the upper-class movie wife of choice after she took the title role in 1942's *Mrs. Miniver* opposite Walter Pidgeon. Directed by William Wyler, *Mrs. Miniver* earned the highest grosses since *Ben-Hur* and dominated the 1942 Academy Awards, winning six statues, including Best Picture, Best Actress, and Best Director. Celebrating British courage and grit in the face of the German bombardment, the picture captured the emotional and patriotic fervor that many Americans, in solidarity with England, were feeling. The movie was released just six months after Pearl Harbor. The Minivers, giving everything they had, including their enlisted son, to defeat the Luftwaffe, became the poster couple of the war era.

After the extended prologue, Myrna's divorce from Arthur finally occurred early in June of 1942, with more whimper than bang. A friend,

Gladys Belknap Rowley, met Myrna's train when she arrived in Reno to establish residence, as required by law. Myrna welcomed having an occasional local companion, but these were sad and lonely days. She'd rented a five-room house at Washoe Pines Ranch, south of Reno, which she and Theresa Penn occupied. At the divorce hearing, which lasted all of three minutes, Arthur, not present, was represented by his attorney. Arthur was in the process of jumping from Paramount to MGM and was completing his last Paramount film on his expiring contract. The prospect of running into him on the MGM lot in the future did not fill Myrna's heart with glee. She pleaded mental cruelty, and the divorce went uncontested. Wearing "a gray tweed suit, and a large tailored hat which accentuated her gray eyes," Myrna promptly departed alone for New York by plane.[40]

To the shock of everyone who knew her, she was renouncing Hollywood and her career. A new suitor awaited her in New York, along with an altogether different kind of life.

CHAPTER 14

Rebound

There it was for all to see, in every daily newspaper in the States, even the sober *New York Times:* "Myrna Loy Bride of John Hertz Jr."[1]

Myrna had known John Daniel Hertz Jr. for only a short time when they wed. They met on Hidden Valley Road at a dinner party hosted by Arthur and Myrna in their waning days as a married couple. John's father, John Hertz Sr., founder of Hertz Car Rental and Yellow Cab, was a hard-driving, rags-to-riches Chicagoan born in Austro-Hungary. A partner at Lehman Brothers and owner of prize racehorses, he had extensive ties to the financial wing of Paramount Pictures. Always overshadowed by his father, John Jr., at thirty-four years old, was three years younger than Myrna. The junior John held an executive position at New York's Buchanan advertising agency, which had an account with Paramount and did publicity for Greek War Relief, one of Myrna's causes. John Hertz Sr. controlled the Buchanan agency, so the son owed his job, as well as most of his wealth, to his tycoon dad, with whom he wasn't even on speaking terms when he and Myrna recited their vows.

John Jr. had attended a military academy and Cornell, and as a young man he had distinguished himself as a yachtsman and polo player; but compared to Myrna, he hadn't done much living. He'd led a protected, rich-kid life, dating debutantes, sailing his yacht, and shuttling between New York and points west. Conveniently, his father held a major interest in Trans World Airlines.[2]

Myrna didn't know when she married John that he had a history of profound mental instability or that he abused alcohol (and possibly opiates as well) or that he had logged many hours with psychiatrists. She wasn't remembering her own insight into herself, divulged years earlier in an unusually candid interview: "I am one of those perverse creatures," she'd confessed, "who has a positive talent for falling in love with the wrong man. I mean someone whom I should have sense enough to know would be temperamentally unsuited to me." "Falling in love" may not even accurately describe Myrna's headlong romance with John. She turned to him out of extreme need while in a fragile emotional state.[3]

Not especially attractive physically, John appeared to be offering Myrna pure devotion during and immediately following her meltdown with Arthur, when she sorely needed just that. "You're the beloved of millions," he'd told her on the night they first met, after he'd impulsively taken her hands in his, "but your hands are cold and sweaty" (*BB*, 172). He seemed to be supplying a shoulder to lean on and lots of coddling, all in a locale, New York City, that promised glamour and stimulation three thousand miles away from the place she wanted to escape, Los Angeles. What better place for starting over than Manhattan? Myrna had thought of it as her ideal refuge from the day she first saw it, back in 1935.

Arthur happened to be in New York when news of Myrna's remarriage hit the papers. He would read about his former wife becoming Mrs. John Hertz Jr. and understand that she had irrevocably moved on.

Eleven-year-old Terry Hornblow attended school nearby. Distraught when he learned that Myrna had divorced his father, he feared he would lose contact with his stepmother, with whom he'd formed an abiding attachment. His mother, Juliette, assured him that he could continue to spend time with Myrna, and to Myrna's enduring gratitude she allowed that to happen.

When, separated from Arthur, Myrna had stopped in New York in March of 1942 to do fund-raising for war relief, John had aggressively pursued her, sending her bouquet after bouquet of gorgeous flowers, inundating her with invitations, squiring her around Manhattan's chic café society nightclubs, and phoning her at all hours, day and night, at Park Avenue's Drake Hotel, where she was staying. John's midnight calls were a trademark. While in Nevada to get her divorce, between crying jags Myrna spent considerable time on the phone talking to him (*BB*, 176). When she boarded the plane for New York, Reno divorce papers in hand, she hadn't yet made up her mind to remarry. Six days later, yielding to John's tireless entreaties, she did just that.

The spur-of-the-moment wedding, at which Myrna wore a Little Bo

Peep bonnet that made her look girlish, took place at the East Side Manhattan home of John's sister Helen (at the time Mrs. Robert Leylan and later the wife of Paul Hexter), with whom Myrna would become fast friends. Looking back on this disastrous second marriage, Myrna cited the friendship with Helen as one of its ancillary benefits. Helen's affection and generosity continued after they ceased to be sisters-in-law. She telephoned Myrna in the 1980s, following one of Myrna's many operations, offering to lend her funds, if she needed them; Helen pleaded that she had far more money than she needed, implying that Myrna would be doing her a favor by relieving her of some of it. Myrna declined but was touched (*BB,* 184). No member of Myrna's family attended this second wedding.

The newlyweds honeymooned in Miami, where a reporter who tracked them down inquired about Myrna's plans for future films. "Mrs. Hertz thought her next picture would be another of the Thin Man series," the article reported, "but her husband interposed, 'She may have other plans—not dramatic.' " John didn't want Myrna to work. Not thinking through her decisions very thoroughly, Myrna knew with certainty that after close to twenty years of laboring in Hollywood with few downtimes, she needed an extended rest.[4]

The *Thin Man* movie that Myrna mentioned, the one that in 1945 became *The Thin Man Goes Home,* was slated for production in June of 1942, although the script had not yet been written. Harry Kurnitz was working on the story (which he would complete with Robert Riskin) just as Myrna prepared for Reno and the divorce from Arthur. She had told MGM she could not report for work then, being in no condition to do so. Metro put the picture on hold and, because she was leaving her contract unfulfilled, put Myrna under "technical suspension." Her contract still had four years to go before it expired or would need to be renegotiated. Loew's chief, Nick Schenck, based in New York, took Myrna's newest unauthorized work furlough as a personal affront. According to Myrna, he considered her irresponsible and was furious with her.[5]

Myrna and John settled into luxurious quarters in a rented eight-room terraced duplex at 322 East Fifty-seventh Street, a building renowned for its double-height living rooms in every unit. As Myrna threw herself into decorating the apartment, John tried to help by bringing Myrna's brother, David, and his new wife, Lynn, to New York and setting David up with a job. Myrna's lifelong friend Betty Black considered David a ball and chain to his older sister. He aspired to be an artist, but because his mother and sister had spoiled him, he kept wanting to work from the top down, not from the bottom up. David and Lynn Williams would return to California as soon as Myrna's marriage to John collapsed.[6]

Bill Powell and Mousie came to New York to say hello, and Bill was photographed at the fashionable Stork Club with John and Myrna. In one newspaper the photo caption read, "The Perfect Wife and Two Perfect Husbands." On the surface everything looked posh and festive. But John's dark side manifested itself in his paranoid response to Powell. He resented Myrna's deep affection for her favorite costar and convinced himself that Myrna and Bill had been having an affair. He also harbored jealousy of her fame and the attention she generated wherever she went.[7]

Even before she left California, Myrna had allowed her business affairs to come undone. She hadn't been paying attention. Her agent Myron Selznick's office, together with Myrna's Los Angeles attorney, Martin Gang, tried to make sense of her chaotic finances. In June of 1942 she had earned $80,000 so far for the year (more than $1 million in current dollars) but owed $50,907 in federal income taxes. She owed Arthur $5,771 for that share of household expenses he insisted she owed, and she was paying Bundles for Bluejackets more than $600 to outfit a submarine crew. Unless she returned to work, her earnings from MGM would be sharply reduced. In an economy move, Della's allowance was cut to fifty dollars weekly, Aunt Lu's to twenty-five dollars. Della, alarmed by her reduced circumstances, insisted in a letter to the Selznick office secretary that she cared only for Myrna's happiness and wouldn't dream of asking John Hertz Jr. for money. Myrna, with sadness, terminated the services of her maid and friend, Theresa Penn, who remained in Los Angeles, but Myrna stipulated that the child actor Dickie Hall (Nick Charles Jr. in *Shadow of the Thin Man*) was to continue to receive fifteen dollars a week from Myrna's bank account for piano lessons.[8]

Because John had plenty of money and didn't want a working wife any more than Myrna wanted to report to MGM, Myrna felt free to put off the studio, but she didn't go so far as to slam the door and bolt it. She still had a viable contract, a famous name, and a loyal following. Mayer wanted her to continue to make pictures, even as she violated the terms of her contract by moving to New York and going into near-retirement.

She visited Los Angeles and Della in the fall following her new marriage, and it was reported that she was being considered for a role in *A Guy Named Joe* opposite Spencer Tracy and Van Johnson. Irene Dunne instead took that part. Newly signed to an MGM contract, Dunne had briefly been mentioned as a possible pinch-hitter for Myrna Loy in the next *Thin Man* picture, but neither Metro nor the public seemed to warm to the idea of anyone but Myrna Loy taking on the role opposite Powell.[9]

Although Myrna's private life took up plenty of space, the war and world politics remained major concerns for her. Via her new sister-in-law, Helen, Myrna had met Jan Masaryk, and the two had formed a bond that solidified her identification with him and with Hitler's European victims as a group. Masaryk visited New York often, spending time with Myrna whenever he could. A spirited, warmhearted, and fascinating guest, he loved to cook, to play the piano, and to tell stories about his past life as the son of the first Czech president. Casual and lighthearted among friends, he was at the same time a man of depth and compassion, someone who along with his countrymen had sustained political body blows, which he countered with shows of defiance and courage. He confided his dream of one day returning to a democratic Czechoslovakia.

As a celebrity Myrna realized that her participation in public war relief campaigns could help immeasurably. In Madison Square Garden, on the last day of September 1942, she joined a throng of stellar performers—Charles Laughton, Ethel Merman, Al Jolson, Kate Smith, and the Ink Spots—at a gala Army Emergency Relief show that lasted four and a half hours. Twenty thousand people attended, making the event a standing-room-only success. Mayor La Guardia took baton in hand to conduct a band playing a Sousa march. Danny Kaye and Lily Pons spoofed *A Night at the Opera*. Lieutenant Burgess Meredith recited a poem and Lillian Gish a prayer. Myrna executed a mock striptease, auctioning off articles of her shed clothing to the highest bidder. Her hat fetched $30,000 in bond sales, her long crimson evening gloves, $25,000. By the end of the marathon event, the assistant secretary of the treasury announced that the department's goal of $775 million in bond sales had been reached (*BB,* 181). The newspapers reported that at the Madison Square Garden gala Myrna Loy sold more bonds than any other actress.[10]

John's work for Greek War Relief brought him into the sphere of Eleanor Roosevelt, a booster in the campaign to generate humanitarian aid to the German-occupied nation. Myrna accompanied John to Washington, and there she made her first of several visits to the Roosevelt White House. She'd hoped to meet FDR in the flesh. Myrna idolized the president and had reason to believe that he in turn counted himself among her ardent fans. According to FDR's private secretary, Grace Tully, "the President's favorite actress was Myrna Loy. He plied Hollywood visitors with questions about her, wanted very much to meet her." Myrna Loy films had been screened at the first floor White House movie theater that

FDR installed and even, she'd been told, aboard ship during the 1941 Atlantic Charter Conference between Roosevelt and Churchill (*BB*, 179). In the first week of his presidency, FDR viewed *When Ladies Meet*. According to *Variety*, President Roosevelt, a confirmed moviegoer, saw five times as many films as Coolidge did when president, four times as many as Hoover.[11]

To Myrna's disappointment, she never did enjoy the much-anticipated face-to-face encounter with FDR. For one reason or another the overburdened president had to be elsewhere each time she visited the White House. The last time, a few months before his death, he was away at Yalta. On that occasion, in January of 1945, Mrs. Roosevelt took Myrna, Gene Kelly, Joe E. Brown, Jane Wyman, Danny Kaye, Alan Ladd, and Veronica Lake, all in Washington to attend the annual Birthday Ball Benefit events for the March of Dimes, on a tour of the Oval Office and FDR's private study. Not realizing that the president would be absent, Myrna had dressed with special care in a knockout black dress and a white organdy John Frederic hat. When Mrs. Roosevelt saw her, she said, "Oh my dear, my husband is going to be so distressed [that he missed meeting you]" (*BB*, 188). She knew FDR's soft spot for Myrna Loy and conveyed to Myrna the message that it didn't threaten her.

Myrna got to know Eleanor Roosevelt quite well over time and admired her more than any other woman in public life. One of the things she most esteemed about the first lady was her willingness to work without stint. She ran herself ragged, along with all those she enlisted as helpers, explaining, "I am my husband's legs." Essentially a shy person, Mrs. Roosevelt learned to get beyond that shyness and draw others in. An autographed portrait of her, inscribed "To Myrna Loy, with my warmest good wishes," held a place of honor in Myrna's last New York apartment. Mrs. Roosevelt would often call on Myrna to help out on behalf of causes they espoused in common, from fund-raising and troop support during the war to bolstering the United Nations in the postwar years and aiding the senatorial campaign of Helen Gahagan Douglas in 1950. After a day of being led around by the energetic Mrs. Roosevelt, Myrna would tell Betty Black (who was living in Washington), "That old gal has just worn me to pieces."[12]

During that first White House visit, Mrs. Roosevelt graciously made Myrna feel that she, not the first lady, deserved the spotlight. She briefly left John and Myrna in the Blue Room and promptly returned with Secretary of Labor Frances Perkins, who wanted to be introduced to Myrna Loy.

The president and Mrs. Roosevelt invited Myrna to their Hyde Park home to help them entertain a distinguished visitor, Queen Wilhelmina of the Netherlands. Myrna was to appear in a short play, "Button Your Lip," written by Private First Class Irving Gaynor Neiman, about a Brooklyn-born rookie in the army who yearns to meet the woman of his dreams, Myrna Loy. It had recently been staged as part of a program of award-winning one-act plays written and acted by enlisted men that producer John Golden had presented on Broadway under the joint title *The Army Play by Play.* On opening night on Broadway, at a performance attended by Mrs. Roosevelt, Mayor La Guardia, and the Duke and Duchess of Windsor, Myrna had delighted everyone by walking onstage in the closing scene. As presented in Hyde Park for the Dutch Queen and FDR, Myrna was to again play herself in "Button Your Lip." But on the day of the performance she had to cancel her Hyde Park appearance because her husband, in a drunken rage, had assaulted her the previous night and left her with a hideous black eye. Mrs. Roosevelt stood in for Myrna in the sketch, calling out from her seat, "Miss Loy cannot be here. Can't I take her place?" "First Lady Takes Role of Myrna Loy," read the *New York Times* headline.[13]

Later, when she came to know Mrs. Roosevelt better, Myrna confessed to her the true reason she had cancelled her appearance in Hyde Park, and the first lady had expressed shock and sympathy, saying, "Oh, what a terrible thing." She added that if she, the first lady, hadn't volunteered to pinch-hit for Myrna, the imposing, voluminous Queen Wilhelmina might have had to do so. The image of such a possibility prompted gales of shared laughter. "We had the greatest time over that," Myrna recalled, adding that despite her depth and breadth of information about so many topics of the day, Eleanor Roosevelt possessed a certain innocence. Myrna insisted that Mrs. Roosevelt could not possibly have been a lesbian, which a biographer had suggested, and that she wouldn't have even known the meaning of the word (*BB,* 180). Perhaps the innocent one here was Myrna.

John's alcohol-fueled violent rages seemed to come without provocation. They could not be explained rationally. Yes, he resented Myrna's fame and the time she spent away from him, but their true origin resided in John's mental illness.

Since she was taking a leave from films, but still had the high energy and work ethic that had always driven her, Myrna got busy during her Mrs. Hertz period in New York as a volunteer for the American Red Cross. By April of 1943, less than a year into her second marriage, she had taken on an unsalaried full-time job as assistant to the director of the Military and Naval Welfare Service for the North Atlantic area. Her duties involved serving as a liaison between entertainers and military hospitals or rest homes, setting up visits by Broadway and Hollywood performers to wounded or disabled members of the armed forces. Myrna made countless hospital visits herself, sometimes returning home alone by bus or train. In contrast to the pampering she'd enjoyed as a star, she now carried her own luggage and accepted uncomfortable travel conditions without complaint. She squeezed into crowded coaches and resigned herself to the possibility that a train reserved for the troops might sidetrack her scheduled train. "Recently," she told the *Los Angeles Times*, "we had as many as ten companies entertaining servicemen in forty-two East Coast centers." The Red Cross work got into her blood. "Once you have seen these men and talked with them, watched their faces light up and heard them call you by your first name (to them you are something of home), you can't stay away too long."[14]

In a later interview she acknowledged how much her experiences visiting wounded or disabled sailors, marines, and soldiers had moved her and helped prepare her for her postwar role in *The Best Years of Our Lives*. "Those incredible youngsters," she said, referring to the convalescents she visited. "It's when they joke about their crippling injuries that you want to cry. But you mustn't pity them. Nor must you pretend to ignore their injuries. You are supposed to be natural with them—and sometimes I don't quite know how." Myrna at times privately succumbed to tears. "The blind soldiers would run their hands over my face and say, 'Yes, that's Myrna Loy.' I'd go into the ladies room and cry."[15]

On her hospital visits she sometimes signed a soldier's plaster cast or bestowed a kiss on request. A 1945 Hearst newsreel showed her in a hospital ward autographing a soldier's leg cast as Gene Kelly, outfitted as the real-life sailor he was, dances in front of men in wheelchairs.[16]

During the war years Myrna fielded numerous marriage proposals. "I received more than fifty thousand letters from lonely soldiers overseas asking me to marry them. Each one declared he knew I'd make him a perfect wife. It nearly drove me crazy."[17]

Frank Sinatra, with a draft classification of 4-F, agreed to make some hospital visits. He was welcomed, along with Bob Hope and Jack Benny, with wild enthusiasm, but the star who scored highest with the male patients was Betty Grable, the singing, dancing blonde with the upswept hair, the dazzling smile, and the legs that had been insured for $1 million. Myrna went with her to visit Halloran Hospital, on Staten Island,

and the wounded men went bananas. Grable, the top box-office attraction of 1943 and *the* pinup girl of the World War II era, gamely handed out autographs and planted her lipstick imprint on plaster casts as she made her way among the injured, some in wheelchairs, bandaged, on crutches, or with only a single arm (*BB*, 183).

The gratification Myrna found in her Red Cross work helped her cope with an increasingly miserable, indeed terrifying, domestic life with John Hertz. Erratic, often drunk and prone to violence—he once hurled a Rodin sculpture at Myrna and tried to shoot his nurse through a door—he drove Myrna to consult a psychiatrist. Once again, John's sister, Helen, played a key role; she introduced Myrna to her own therapist, Ruth Mack Brunswick. Dr. Brunswick, an American-born analyst with an office on Washington Square, had gone to Vienna after completing medical school to study with and be analyzed by Freud. She remained in Vienna for many years—until the Anschluss of 1938—and became one of Freud's close associates. She taught at the Psychoanalytic Institutes in Vienna and, after her flight from Vienna, in New York. Dr. Brunswick was well known for her writings about the Wolf Man and later as the analyst of Karl Menninger. After she died at age forty-seven in 1946, it became known that she had become addicted to pain killers. Myrna probably never learned this.[18]

Dr. Brunswick had the good sense to advise against psychoanalysis for John, who obviously needed intervention, on the grounds that his mental illness was of a type and severity that made him unlikely to benefit from such talk-based treatment. From what she'd heard from both Helen and Myrna, the doctor judged him to be insane (*BB*, 184). Leonora Hornblow, who in her youth knew John socially, reported that he ended his days in a mental institution.

Myrna valued her psychiatrist and believed that her ten-month analysis (surely a record for brevity), during which she trekked twice a week to Dr. Brunswick's office on Washington Square, helped her to understand herself and restored a sense of wholeness. Dr. Brunswick told her within a year that, in effect, she was cured; she need not prolong the therapy (*BB*, 191). The details of Myrna's analysis remain unknown, but apparently Myrna's anger became the focus of the psychiatric sessions. Dr. Brunswick unlocked vaults of what had been mostly repressed rage directed against several important men in her life: her father, for burdening her with more family responsibility than a child should be asked to shoulder; L. B. Mayer, for boxing her in and undervaluing her as an actress; and Arthur, for being hypercritical and failing to love her enough.

Myrna believed that she worked through a portion of this rage, but her anger at John also bubbled over, and during the course of the analysis she left him.

After she determined to end her second marriage, Myrna simply packed her luggage and exited the household that she and her husband had shared, taking nothing with her but her elegant clothes and jewelry. Feeling lucky simply to be escaping alive, considering John's vengeful nature, access to weapons, and total lack of self-control, she hurriedly moved into an apartment in the Waldorf Towers in March of 1944, a few months shy of what would have been her second wedding anniversary.[19]

When she knew she would soon be single again, Myrna eagerly agreed to return to California and report for duty as Nora Charles in *The Thin Man Goes Home*. Her salary for the $1.4 million picture would be $100,000. Her joint agents, Myron Selznick in Hollywood and Leland Hayward in New York, would share ten percent of her earnings.[20]

After announcing her impending second divorce, Myrna agreed to an interview with Louella Parsons, who reported, "Myrna Loy has never seemed so carefree. Living in New York has given her a chic she didn't have when she spent all her time in Hollywood." Asked why her marriage to Hertz had failed, Myrna diplomatically explained, "There is no happiness possible when two people have divergent interests. You do not think alike and you cannot find real congeniality or mutual enjoyment." Myrna faulted herself for marrying Hertz before she had a chance to get to know him. Parsons advised, "Next time be sure. Don't marry in a hurry." "There will be no next time," Myrna assured her. "Twice is enough."[21]

Myrna's return to California happened to coincide with the death of Myron Selznick, her high-powered agent, whose wealth and star-studded list of clients couldn't prevent him from drinking himself to death at age forty-five. At his funeral William Powell read a eulogy written by Gene Fowler. Just about every luminary in Hollywood came to pay last respects: Hal Wallis, L. B. Mayer, Darryl Zanuck, Sam Goldwyn, Jack Warner, Alfred Hitchcock, Ernst Lubitsch, Eddie Mannix, Hunt Stromberg, Walter Wanger, Ingrid Bergman, Loretta Young—they were all there, though Selznick's ex-wife Marjorie Daw and their fourteen-year-old daughter, who lived on the East Coast, were not. The writer of his *Los Angeles Times* obituary didn't try to mask the combination of awe and ire Myron Selznick had aroused. "He was constantly at loggerheads with producers and was credited with raising to their present level the high salaries of screen artists." L. B. Mayer had banished him from meeting his clients on the MGM lot.[22]

For about a year after the death of Myron Selznick, Leland Hayward alone represented Myrna Loy as her MGM contract termed out. MCA would absorb Hayward's clients in 1945, and Lew Wasserman became Myrna Loy's agent from then until the early 1960s, to be replaced by the independent agent Robert Lantz.

When she returned to MGM to make *The Thin Man Goes Home* after an absence from the screen of nearly three years, the studio made Myrna feel cherished. Bill Powell, accompanied by the latest incarnation of Asta, had greeted her train in Pasadena, and the press covered the homecoming. On the first day of shooting *The Thin Man Goes Home,* everyone on the set, from the prop man to the makeup crew, wanted to give her a hug, and some members of the crew carried signs reading, "Don't Leave Us Again, Myrna" (*BB,* 185). A genuine red carpet strewn with crepe-paper roses had been laid out to welcome her, and she found that MGM had readied a new dressing room, decorated in "her favorite shades of periwinkle blue, violet and rose, with fresh flowers to match."[23]

But Myrna couldn't deny her awareness that things had changed. This was a different MGM, where Joan Crawford no longer worked, having bought out her contract to sign with Warner Bros. Elizabeth Taylor, twelve years old, was filming *National Velvet.* Seven-year-old Margaret O'Brien was also a rising star, and Norma Shearer had retired. Van Johnson, typed as a boy next door, was the leading man of the moment. MGM was making fewer pictures than in the past but spending more money on those it did make. Woody Van Dyke had died, and Richard Thorpe, who possessed Van Dyke's knack for speed without sharing any special rapport with Myrna, was replacing him at the helm. Myrna had worked with Thorpe on the sets of *Double Wedding* and *Man-Proof,* and he'd demonstrated his professionalism. But she keenly felt Van Dyke's absence. Hunt Stromberg, producer of all previous *Thin Man* pictures, and one of the mainstays of Loy's career, had also left MGM, released from his contract after eighteen years there. F. Scott Fitzgerald once referred to Stromberg as "a sort of one-finger Thalberg, without Thalberg's scope, but with his intense power of work and his absorption in his job."[24]

This time Everett Riskin served as producer, in collaboration with his writer brother, Robert, coauthor with Dwight Taylor of the screenplay for *The Thin Man Goes Home.* Between them, the Riskin brothers had assembled a formidable list of comedy credits: Everett produced *The Awful Truth* and the 1938 *Holiday,* while Robert had written scripts for several Frank Capra pictures. But neither Riskin was at the top of his game for this production. Robert was employed as chief of the Overseas Motion Picture Bureau of the Office of War Information, producing documentaries, when he took time out to work on *The Thin Man Goes Home* screenplay. He considered this Culver City job, taken on to please his brother, a distraction from weightier pursuits. He wrote to his wife, Fay Wray, that he found his *Thin Man* assignment "dreadfully dull," and his lack of enthusiasm is evident in the script.[25]

Everett Riskin decreed that because of wartime liquor rationing, Nick and Nora's constant tippling, one of the givens of the *Thin Man* franchise, would be banished in *The Thin Man Goes Home*. Drinking on the screen, he feared, would have a negative effect on a "thirsty audience." So, in the opening scenes on the crowded train, where Nick and Nora are passengers traveling with Asta (but without Nick Jr.) to visit Nick's parents in small-town Sycamore Springs, we find Nick sipping from a flask of apple cider. Nora explains that Nick has gone on the wagon to please his disapproving father (Harry Davenport), a conservative and respected physician, who dismisses his son as a no-account. By the last frame in the picture, Nick has won the admiration of his father, who pops a button with pride, but he has also, by giving up booze and trying so hard to please his parents, gelded the character Dashiell Hammett created. "In real life," writes the film historian Ed Sikov, "the transformation of a drunken malcontent to a self-possessed man of the world is cause for celebration; in a series of dark detective comedies, it's deadening."[26]

Nora, too, has been altered almost beyond recognition. The script turns her into an airhead who can jitterbug but who natters on to her father-in-law about his son Nick's accomplishments and can't figure out how to assemble a deck chair. After she jabbers to a reporter about Nick's detective work when she should have remained mum, Nick turns her on his knee and delivers a spanking (an act Powell was prohibited from performing in *Libeled Lady*), as his dad approvingly clucks, "You know, I've always wanted to do that to your mother." She's been demoted from competitive partner to pesky brat in need of punishment.

Situating Nick and Nora in a small town filled with eccentric characters like Anne Revere's Crazy Mary and Gloria DeHaven's self-dramatizing Laura provided novelty, but that novelty came at a dear price. Every one of the three writers for *The Thin Man Goes Home*—Riskin, Dwight Taylor, and Harry Kurnitz, who cowrote the story—was a native New Yorker who might have provided sassier and more authentic dialogue in an urban setting. As *Variety* put it, the "production as a whole lacks much of the sophistication and smartness which characterized the early Thin Man films." Even Myrna's outfits, designed by Irene, tip towards the dowdy.[27]

Myrna sensed that by now the cynicism that powered the earlier *Thin Man* movies no longer fit the national mood, that during the war marriage and murder didn't seem like laughing matters, and that "the noble, self-sacrificing Minivers and Curies" had replaced the flippant Charleses, who epitomized the spirit of the 1930s (*BB*, 192). Still, she found that *The Thin Man Goes Home* came through with some hilarious scenes. She recalled one particular line with fondness, the one, possibly ad-libbed, where she tells Nick not to move out of his hammock: "You might get all sweaty and die." The throngs of moviegoers who bought enough tickets to make it a minor hit concurred. The film made just over $500,000 in profits.

Myrna returned to New York to resume her Red Cross work as the Allies invaded Normandy. In early August 1944, just as she turned thirty-nine, she flew to Mexico to divorce Hertz in Cuernavaca on grounds of "Incompatibility of Character." Footloose for a spell, she zoomed from one perch to the next, settling for a few months in Bel Air in a rented house that MGM found for her, facing a golf course. Feeling spunky, she hosted many weekend parties at which Bing Crosby might drop by after a round of golf and sing a tune, accompanied by Hoagy Carmichael at the piano.[28]

Dwight Taylor, the screenwriter son of famed stage actress Laurette Taylor, turned up at one of the parties, and Myrna found him fiercely attractive. But her dear friend Natalie Visart claimed him for her own, sensing the moment she laid eyes on him that he would become her husband. Visart and Taylor, breezy author of the screenplay for *Top Hat* and the book for Cole Porter's *Gay Divorcée,* soon married and began a family, though Natalie's involvement with Mitchell Leisen didn't end when she became Mrs. Taylor. Myrna remained close to the Taylors and their daughter.

During the brief interlude when she was unattached, Myrna was seen out and about in Los Angeles with the Viennese-born actor Helmut Dantine, who played the German pilot in *Mrs. Miniver.* Twelve years younger than Myrna, intelligent and darkly handsome, he provided a short-term diversion, and fodder for the gossip columns, but Myrna wasn't really interested in him. She had already embarked on a serious relationship with Gene Markey.

The screenwriter, novelist, and 20th Century–Fox producer Gene Markey is most often mentioned today in connection with the many beautiful women he bedded and wedded, but it wasn't just women who found him hard to resist. Trained as a cartoonist, he could charm a child with an improvised drawing or story. A popular companion, he was a sailing, drinking, and Naval Intelligence buddy of John Ford and a pal of Douglas Fairbanks Jr. The entertaining, quicksilver, and debonair Markey was a perennial favorite at parties. His stepdaughter, Diana Anderson (Joan Bennett's daughter by her first marriage), speaks adoringly of him. Markey also continued to be one of the best friends of Arthur Hornblow Jr. They tried to have lunch together once a week when both were in Los Angeles.

In becoming involved with Gene Markey, Myrna remained at least a peripheral part of Arthur's world. Arthur's romance with his soon-to-be second wife, Leonora "Bubbles" Schinasi Morris, was in full bloom, though for now they lived on opposite coasts. Leonora wrote to him from Park Avenue about running into Captain Markey, at the time the head of a Naval Intelligence unit, one night in New York, at the nightclub "21":

> I heard the unmistakable tones of Captain Markey, screaming out for all to hear, "Bubbles, my pie, are you going to pass Daddy by?" Needless to report, I fell into his manly arms with a cry of glee, and after much hugging realized he was with a lady, Miss Loy. We greeted each other cheerfully, heartily told the other how beautiful she was looking and were little ladies. I stopped at the table to say goodnight and Gene made me stay with them for a minute. We had much merry talk. Gene, never a man to mince words, asked for you immediately, told me how much you missed me and what a noble fellow you were. Myrna smiled sweetly and said she agreed and we all grinned at each other in high good humor and suddenly burst out laughing. Gene went on to say that Myrna liked me so much. "I like her," I said, "I always have." [Arthur and Myrna had visited teenaged Leonora and her mother at their New York home in 1935.] "I don't approve of it," said Gene, "it doesn't go well with my plot and plans for you two to get on so well, you can't have Myrna and Arthur," said he, "you'll have to choose between them." "I will," I said, "just the way you have, Captain darling." We talked away blithely and contentedly. Myrna didn't talk much, mainly because the poor girl didn't have a chance to open her mouth, as neither Gene nor I are the silent types. And besides, Myrna listens so well. I promised her that I would phone her before I left. They both said to send you love, individually and together, when I wrote. . . . So you can imagine the cozy family scene. Both Gene and I agreed that if all concerned, and all the people they had been married to, married just once more, we could have a complete colony.[29]

Leonora kept her competitive feelings about Myrna under wraps when she found herself sitting next to her at a dinner that included Marc Connelly and the Ira Gershwins. In her letters to Arthur, however, the gloves came off. At dinner, she told him, "Myrna said five sentences, I counted." She scrutinized every detail of Myrna's clothing and accessories, commenting to Arthur that Myrna carried "a wonderful cigarette case of woven gold" and looked "very thin and beautiful in black with a black hat" but with a tacky bunch of fake flowers pinned to the pocket of her dress. "I thought to myself, 'your once husband Mr. A. Hornblow would have removed that in short order.' " She further reported, "My mink compared most favorably with hers in colour, texture, style and so forth."[30]

Collier Young, an intimate of both Gene and Arthur, told Leonora that he had seen Myrna the previous night and that "she was dewy-eyed over the gallant captain." Collier further reported that "poor Gene wonders aloud if his current romance will affect his profound friendship for you [Arthur]." Leonora assured Arthur that she felt secure about his devotion, "that I cheerfully presumed that you were harboring no candle of regret and undying love for Miss Loy, that I would take on anyone my weight who said that you were, that neither Myrna nor Gene need worry!"[31]

At the conclusion of the war Gene, who would attain the rank of commodore in the U.S. Navy, was stationed in Washington, D.C., where Myrna made frequent stops to visit patients at Walter Reed and nearby Bethesda Naval Hospital. As Myrna got to know and be known in the capital, her name started appearing in the Washington society pages, which noted, for example, that at a party to benefit convalescent soldiers, "Myrna Loy shared the spotlight with Mrs. James Doolittle, wife of the Tokyo-raiding Doolittle." The gossip columnists also speculated about a possible forthcoming third marriage for Miss Loy. Borrowing the lingo of a popular song of the day, one wrote, " 'Is you is or is you ain't?' That's what Washington wants to know from Myrna Loy and Gene Markey. Is the lovely Myrna married to the Naval Captain? Or are those luncheons at the Mayflower, dinners at the Statler, or Army and Navy Club just friendly?"[32]

Washington's Hotel Carlton became another of Myrna's perches. It was there that she learned, by overhearing a man in a suit who had just emerged from a car, that "Germany has surrendered" (BB, 189). The horrendous war in Europe was at last coming to an end. Roosevelt had died in April 1945, just the previous month, so for Myrna the jubilation was somewhat muted. Harry Truman now occupied the White House.

When Truman was still vice president, Myrna had met him during one of her visits to the Roosevelt White House. She met him again at a charity show soon after he became commander in chief, and she liked his gutsy, forthright, and unpretentious style. But he didn't come close to inspiring the hero worship she reserved for FDR.

With the war in Europe concluded, a new political era under way in the United States, an enamored Gene Markey at her side, and dramatic plans for restarting her film career after having lived on the East Coast for three years, Myrna Loy headed back to the City of Angels.

CHAPTER 15

Postwar

After an association of thirteen years, Myrna Loy and MGM parted company without ceremony soon after she returned to the Los Angeles area in 1945. Already nursing a bundle of grievances from the past, she protested loudly when Louis B. Mayer refused to let her go to England on loan to Noel Coward to appear as Elvira in a David Lean–directed screen version of *Blithe Spirit.* Myrna believed she had been born to play Elvira, the ghost wife who haunts her husband's second marriage. She charged that Mayer was holding her back, chaining her to MGM when he had no other good role in mind for her. "Do you want me to wait around until I'm dead?" she asked him. She still had one year to go on her contract but sensed she must establish her independence right away, before her career lost any more momentum.

When Leland Hayward first requested her release, Mayer said no. Myrna decided to speak to her boss on her own. The manipulative mogul, near to tears, accused her of ingratitude for all the studio had done for her and assured her, "I couldn't care more about you if you were my own horse" (*BB,* 192–93). Mayer loved his thoroughbreds, so this was intended as a high compliment. When Myrna agreed to return to MGM now and then to make an occasional *Thin Man* picture, he relented and let her go. As it turned out, she would come back only once, to make *Song of the Thin Man,* the swan song to the series.

The *Los Angeles Times'* Philip K. Scheuer rightly saw her rupture with MGM as indicative of a major transition in Hollywood. "[It] was more than the amicable dissolution of just another star-producer contract. It marked the end of an era which, beginning in the Thirsty Thirties, had drenched the screen with slick stories of marital infidelity (and, much less frequently, fidelity)." Screen wives, both faithful and straying, "had broken away one by one. Norma Shearer, to virtual retirement, Joan Crawford to another studio and a hoped-for fresh start, Greta Garbo to be alone. Miss Loy was the last of the old guard to seek release."[1]

Not only had MGM wives been breaking ranks, but Hollywood actors in general were also asserting their independence, preferring to freelance rather than be bound by long-term studio contracts. The star system itself had lost sheen. Cary Grant jumped ship, refusing to allow any single studio to control his professional destiny and shunning further multiyear contracts after his Paramount obligation termed out in 1936. Irene Dunne had abandoned RKO in 1935, and the California Court of Appeals had backed Olivia de Havilland's recent suit against Warner Bros., affirming an actor's right to refuse bondage of indefinite duration or unwanted assigned roles. A studio could no longer require a player to work beyond the seven-year term of a contract.

Asked by Scheuer what kind of roles she would look for now that she had her freedom, Myrna replied that she didn't seek glamour parts. "I've got to trip over a rug every so often. My sense of humor won't let me wear a long face—and neither will my freckles."[2]

She soon announced that her first picture as a freelancer would be a period piece for Universal, *So Goes My Love,* a charming but less than earth-shattering venture that few remember. It cast her as the pretty, nurturing wife of a madcap inventor (played by Don Ameche) in Brooklyn at the threshold of the twentieth century. The Travis Banton costumes steal the show.

Although she wanted to avoid any professional commitment that would bind her as tightly as her contract with MGM had, she did sign an agreement with RKO tying her to that studio for three years, making one picture a year. Soon after, she accepted Sam Goldwyn's invitation to appear in *The Best Years of Our Lives,* which would be distributed by RKO.[3]

A landmark film that became the biggest commercial success of the decade, *The Best Years of Our Lives* still defines the postwar era, and it gave Myrna Loy the chance to shine in what she considered her best piece of work. *Best Years* came into being because of a *Time* magazine article about marines home on furlough after years overseas who worry aloud about how they will be received. Frances Goldwyn, moved by the plight of the anxious returning servicemen, told her husband, Sam, he should make a picture on the subject. After mulling it over, Goldwyn agreed that at a time when millions of Americans who had served in the military were being demobilized, such a film would strike a chord. He commissioned the journalist and novelist MacKinlay Kantor to write a novel based on the homecoming-soldiers theme. The resulting book, an extended narrative poem written in free verse and weighing in at four hundred–plus pages, was published in 1945 as *Glory for Me*. Robert Sherwood, the Pulitzer Prize–winning playwright who had served in the Roosevelt administration as a speechwriter and director of the overseas Office of War Information, agreed to adapt Kantor's book for the screen.[4]

Because of Arthur Hornblow's long association with Goldwyn productions, Myrna knew Sam Goldwyn quite well, though she hadn't appeared in a Goldwyn picture since *Arrowsmith* in 1931. To her the Goldwyn name spelled quality, taste, and independence, but she was well aware that Sam could be extremely difficult and often clashed with his directors. He and William Wyler, slated to direct *The Best Years of Our Lives*, respected one another but constantly collided, unable to agree about whose judgment should prevail or who deserved plaudits for a collaborative success. They began working together in 1936 and had already locked horns during five previous productions.

At a dinner party that included Robert Sherwood, Gene Markey, and Frances Goldwyn, Goldwyn offered Myrna the role of Milly Stephenson, explaining that the part would not be large or glamorous. Instead of designer clothes, she would wear dresses bought off a department store rack and worn for weeks before shooting, so that they wouldn't look too new. She would be playing a woman old enough to have an adult daughter, Teresa Wright, who was actually in her late twenties but was meant to appear about nineteen. (Olivia de Havilland, who turned down the role of Milly, at age thirty would have been far too young.) Goldwyn emphasized that this movie would not be a star vehicle but an ensemble piece with a distinguished cast and a prestigious director, Wyler, who very much wanted her to play Milly, wife of banker Al Stephenson, a returning infantry sergeant who would be portrayed by Fredric March. Loy's long association with wife roles, her age (forty-one), and her natural, understated acting style, recommended her as the ideal Milly.

Wyler's painstaking directing style stood at the opposite pole from that of "One Take" Woody Van Dyke. A perfectionist who took his time, Wyler would shoot forty takes if he felt them necessary to achieve exactly what he wanted. Striving for unadorned realism, he relied heavily on the honesty of Gregg Toland's crisp black-and-white photography and on Toland's mastery of deep focus, which allowed the viewer to see three planes of action—foreground, background, and middle—going on simultaneously. Wyler also depended on an actor's intuition, shooting long scenes for maximum continuity and refraining from offering line readings of his own. He described his directing approach for this film as similar to a theater director's. Prior to shooting a major scene, "we would spend the morning sitting around a table, reading the script, much as it is done in the early stages of theater rehearsal." Before she experienced Wyler's methods for herself, Myrna was apprehensive. She told Goldwyn she'd heard (from Bette Davis, for one) that Wyler was a sadist. "That isn't true," Goldwyn insisted. "He's just a very mean fellow" (*BB*, 197).[5]

In return for accepting a small part, Goldwyn offered to pay Myrna $100,000 for her appearance as Milly Stephenson and to give her top billing. Her contract with Goldwyn specifies, "The name of no other member of the cast may precede the Artist's name, nor be displayed in type larger than that used to display Artist's name."[6]

The Best Years of Our Lives tells the parallel stories of three veterans who have met for the first time inside the cabin of a cramped B-17 plane flying them home to Boone City, a stand-in for Cincinnati. As they peer through the Plexiglas nose cone to view the farmland below, each vet admits to a case of the jitters. Fred Derry (Dana Andrews), a decorated bombardier, was a soda jerk before the war and will be looking for work. He hardly knew his cover-girl-pretty wife Marie (Virginia Mayo) before they got married in a hurry during his basic training, and he doesn't know what to expect from her. Homer Parrish, a sailor portrayed by double amputee Harold Russell, a nonprofessional who had served in the army, uses prosthetic metal hooks as substitutes for his burned hands. Despite his deft manipulation of the hooks, he dreads his first encounter with his family and high school sweetheart, Wilma (Cathy O'Donnell), who live on a leafy street of modest middle-class homes. Al Stephenson isn't particularly eager to return to his old banker job and worries that after four years of separation, his son, daughter, and wife will consider him a stranger. He's older and wealthier than his two new buddies but just as scared. By placing the action in the "average" Midwest and offering a cross-section of social classes, the script strove to tell the story of the American Everyman.

Each of the protagonists has to figure out who he is. Fred doesn't know whether he's a war hero or a nobody. When he shows up in civilian clothes instead of his showy air force officer's uniform, decorated with medals, his wife, Marie, greets him with taunts. Reminders of past selves keep surfacing. Fred suffers flashbacks of himself piloting a bomber under fire. Homer studies photographs in his bedroom, showing him as a high school athlete with two good arms and hands. Al contemplates a framed portrait of himself and examines his own face in a bedroom mirror, uncertain about exactly whom he's looking at.

Milly Stephenson resembles Nora Charles in some ways. Both are upbeat and game, and both have husbands who drink too much. But where Nora epitomized breezy, aristocratic, and elegant Manhattan wifehood freed from domestic drudgery, Milly is entrenched in a small city's respectable and homey upper-middle-class routines. She's emotionally direct, not flippant. On her own she has been running a household in an upscale apartment building and has held together her diminished family of three. She feels comfortable in the apron she wears when we first see her.

In the famous homecoming scene Milly is in the background, setting out three supper plates on a small terrace. She and Al have been married for twenty years, but she still "looks young and alluring and very much alive," as Sherwood presents her. From someplace out of the frame, she calls out, "Who's that at the door?" when she hears the doorbell ring. We see Al (in uniform) from the back, framed by the doorway, as he makes his way down a long corridor to be greeted by Milly's outstretched arms. Al has hushed his two children by covering their mouths with his hands, not wanting them to announce his arrival and spoil the surprise. But Milly has guessed that he's back. After tongue-tied moments and their first ardent embrace, she registers both joy and uncertainty. "I look terrible," she finally says, her voice breaking. "Who says so?" Al answers. His choppy movements and darting eyes convey his own edginess and self-doubt. Seated, he takes out a cigarette and offers one to Milly. He's forgotten that she doesn't smoke.[7]

Ill at ease in an apartment where he feels more like a guest than a member of the household, Al suggests a night on the town with Milly and their daughter, Peggy. At a local bar owned by Homer's uncle Butch (Hoagy Carmichael), he bumps into the two veterans he met earlier in the day. Both Al and Fred proceed to get so drunk they can't walk on their own steam. Milly and Peggy have to practically carry them into the car, which Peggy drives. Back in the Stephenson apartment, where Fred is spending the night, the men have to be put to bed like young children. Peggy removes Fred's shoes and loosens his belt before settling him into her bed with its incongruous frilly canopy. She will sleep on the living-room couch. In the course of the night she will come in to comfort him when a nightmare flashback to a burning B-17 torments his sleep. Milly, in the master bedroom (furnished, over Joseph Breen's objections, with a double bed), has to coax Al into his pajamas and turn him onto his stomach to prevent his snoring. Milly and Peggy are the competent, take-charge maternal figures. The men they tend, Al and Fred, are passive and dependent, as is Homer when, in his own bedroom scene, he shows Wilma how helpless he is without the harness that attaches his hooks to his arms.

Each of the three returning soldiers will see his manhood restored to some degree in the course of the movie. After losing a drugstore soda fountain job because he punched a belligerent customer who questioned America's justification for fighting World War II, Fred Derry will at last find work salvaging parts of junked airplanes. Divorced from his shallow and unfaithful wife, he is free to start over with Peggy Stephenson, with whom he's fallen in love. Al, recovered from his hangover, reclaims the passion in his marriage, seizing Milly in his arms when she enters their bedroom with a breakfast tray, which he puts aside. The dissolve clues us that they are making love. He later asserts himself at work, persuading the bank president to take risks on loans to veterans who lack collateral. And Homer accepts Wilma's love and ability to see beyond his disability. Their wedding at Wilma's home concludes the movie. As Homer and Wilma recite their vows, Milly stands at the center of the background, flanked by Al and Peggy.

Although central, the marital relationship between Al and Milly shows signs of strain and resists being idealized. They fall into step on the dance floor in an improvised scene at Butch's bar, but Al is so drunk he thinks she's someone else. "You remind me of my wife," he says. Al's drinking puts Milly on edge. She counts the number of drinks he's downed at the bank dinner, where Al just misses making a fool of himself, delivering a rambling after-dinner speech. In a late-night confrontation with their overwrought daughter, who has announced she's determined to break up Fred's failed marriage to Marie, Peggy reveals how little she knows about her parents' story. She insists that Al and Milly can't possibly understand her heartbreak over being in love with the married Fred, because according to her they have no experience of struggle; they've always had things perfect: "You loved each other, and you got married in a big church" and honeymooned in the South of France. Milly assures her that she's mistaken. Looking directly at Al, she says, "How many times have I told you that I hated you—and believed it, in my heart? How many times have you said that you're sick and tired of me—that we're all washed up? How many times have we had to fall in love all over again?"

This is Myrna Loy's moment to shine. Her intimate, unguarded tone cuts to the core and is deeply moving. We feel the "powerful yet quiet femininity" Teresa Wright discerned in her. "It's so inner" and sensual (*BB*, 199). For Wright, Al and Milly became, via March and Loy, the gold standard for depictions of married love on the screen.[8]

The rapport that developed between Wyler and Myrna Loy astonished Myrna and made for one of the peaks of her professional career. Fredric March told her, "I can't believe the radar you two have going. You don't even need to talk." When she substituted a gesture for a line, or in one instance sensed that a bit of dialogue didn't work and should be cut, Wyler allowed her instincts to prevail and thanked her for helping him. He said that because Myrna Loy played it, the role of Milly Stephenson became bigger than it seemed in the script (*BB*, 198). The two retained the warmest feelings for each other. The *Los Angeles Times* film critic Kevin Thomas remembers seeing them meet unexpectedly at a big party and fall into a spontaneous embrace.[9]

Wyler put a great deal of himself into this movie. As an air force officer who took a handheld camera onto B-17 and B-25 flights in order to film documentaries during the war, he had suffered hearing loss so profound that he questioned whether he would ever be able to resume directing. On the set of *Best Years* he discovered that he could hear the actors by attaching a headset and amplifiers to the sound equipment. He identified with Russell's disability, likening his enhanced headset to Russell's hooks.[10]

The homecoming scene also had autobiographical resonance for Wyler. On leave from the air force, he'd reunited with his wife, Talli, at the Plaza Hotel in New York. She remembered standing in the doorway at the end of a long hall, "and he came down the hall toward me. That's how the scene in the picture came about."[11]

The pared-down documentary style Wyler used in his air force films *Memphis Belle* and *Thunderbolt* infuses *The Best Years of Our Lives*, his first postwar feature. Teresa Wright recalled, "Willy Wyler and Toland wanted it *[Best Years]* to have the look of an American newsreel. They wanted it to have the feel of a live newspaper article." Working with Toland in their sixth collaboration, Wyler cut down the number of shots in the movie to a minimum, using fewer than two hundred, compared to three to four hundred shots per hour in the average film. His goal was to both clarify and simplify. In a celebrated essay first published in 1948, André Bazin called this "stripping away." He hailed *The Best Years of Our Lives* as the proving ground for Wyler's "invisible" and democratic style, which allows the viewer to decide which of several actions that occur simultaneously to follow. "Thanks to depth of field, . . . the viewer is given the opportunity to edit the scene himself."[12]

Although Bosley Crowther of the *New York Times* endorsed it "not only as superlative entertainment but as food for quiet and humanizing thought," not every critic applauded *Best Years*. Writing in the *New Republic,* Manny Farber called it "a horse-drawn truckload of liberal schmaltz." Farber thought the movie pulled its punches and "never has sufficient nerve to hit hard-headed business, or toadying clerks as well as it would like." But he commended it as "an extremely sensitive and poignant study of life like your own."[13]

James Agee devoted two long essays in *The Nation* to *Best Years*. Like Farber he found the picture too timid in its social criticism, and he remained unconvinced that three veterans from such different backgrounds would ever mingle with social ease once they returned to civilian life. Despite these reservations, however, he praised the "force, beauty and simplicity" of many scenes and likened Toland's cinematography, in its honesty and feeling for people, to the photographs of Walker Evans. Wyler simply bowled him over. Always a good director, in Agee's eyes "he now seems one of the few great ones. He has come back from the war with a style of great purity, directness, and warmth."[14]

The Best Years of Our Lives, which cost $2.1 million to make, earned $11 million in the United States and Canada within a few years, out grossing *Gone with the Wind*. It swept the Academy Awards, taking home Oscars for Best Picture (other contenders were *Henry V, It's a Wonderful Life, The Razor's Edge,* and *The Yearling*), Actor, Supporting Actor, Director, Screenplay, Music Score, and Film Editing, plus an honorary award to Harold Russell. The outstanding performances of Myrna Loy and Dana Andrews went unrecognized by the Academy, as did, shamefully, the cinematography of Gregg Toland. At the Brussels World Film Festival in June 1947, however, Myrna Loy was chosen Best Actress of the year; at the same time Gérard Philippe was picked as Best Actor for his work in *Diable au corps*. Myrna went to Brussels to personally accept her award from the prince regent of Belgium.

True to their tradition of conflict, Wyler and Goldwyn, who would never again work together, finished off their years of partnership with a long legal battle. According to his contract, Wyler was supposed to receive 20 percent of the profits for *The Best Years of Our Lives*. He claimed in a 1958 lawsuit that Goldwyn had underreported profits for the first four years after the picture's release, by $2 million, and that Goldwyn owed him $408,356. They settled out of court when Wyler agreed to accept a payment of $80,000.[15]

In private life Myrna rejoined the ranks of the married when she became Mrs. Gene Markey early in 1946. The ceremony in the chapel of Roosevelt Navy Base, at Terminal Island, San Pedro, might have been titled "Here Comes the Groom." It was all about Gene Markey, who on his wedding day sported navy dress blues with the wide gold commodore's band on his sleeve, and on his chest displayed the Bronze Star he'd won for leading a reconnaissance mission in the Solomon Islands. He had served in the Pacific on the staff of Admiral William F. "Bull" Halsey's Third Fleet, and because Gene wanted Admiral Halsey as his best man, the date of the wedding was chosen to accommodate Halsey's schedule. Halsey would be in the Los Angeles area to lead the Tournament of Roses parade, so an early January date was chosen. Gene also wanted his old sailing and drinking buddy, John Ford, who became a navy captain during the war and had reconnected with Markey during service in New Delhi, to participate in the wedding party. Ford, who had directed Myrna in *The Black Watch* and *Arrowsmith* but had seen little of her since, gave the bride away. Myrna didn't even know he would escort her down the aisle until the day of the wedding. Natalie Visart Taylor designed her blue suit and matching hat with violet veiling to match the bouquet of violets she carried.

Myrna arrived twenty minutes late to her own wedding. Her car, driven by Lieutenant Commander Collier Young, had encountered a roadblock in Long Beach. Young, whose then-wife Valerie served as matron of honor, was close to Gene, and the two couples had made a frequent foursome in Washington. The Youngs would soon divorce, and in 1948 Collier would marry Ida Lupino.

With twenty guests on hand, including former navy men Douglas Fairbanks Jr. and Robert Montgomery, a navy chaplain performed the brief ceremony, after which the newlyweds, each marrying for the third time, promised, "This time it will stick."[16]

Gene had arranged a celebratory lunch at Mike Romanoff's, in Beverly Hills. When the last toast had been toasted, he delivered Admiral Halsey to his next appointment, while Collie Young took Myrna home. That night friends joined the newlyweds for a big party at Mocambo, which Myrna called "a typical Markey extravaganza, but hardly a wedding celebration" (*BB*, 196). What she meant was that it was a party for Gene Markey and his navy buddies more than for the bride and groom.

Gene had been ill and was winding down his duties as a producer at 20th Century–Fox, so Myrna, newly signed for her role in *The Best Years of Our Lives,* was going to be paying most of the bills. Gene had a pattern of marrying beautiful women who made more money than he did and who maintained him royally. As a wedding gift Myrna bought him a fine wine cellar. She also kept him outfitted in tailor-made British clothes. According to Betty Black, he traveled to Europe with twenty steamer trunks packed with suits, coats, sports jackets, evening wear, shoes, shirts, and ties. Betty viewed the balance of power in the new marriage as a replay of the situation with Arthur, in that Myrna indulged and deferred to her husband. Everything was for Gene. He contributed his Irish charm, elegance, and immense social grace, and he certainly knew how to flatter a woman. Although ten years older than Myrna, he remained boyish in her eyes. She said many times that she could never resist him.[17]

Gene had a twelve-year-old daughter by Joan Bennett, Melinda, whom Myrna considered a decided plus. The feeling was mutual; Melinda much preferred Myrna to her previous stepmother, Hedy Lamarr. Melinda, who aspired to become an actress, lived with her mother but would come regularly to visit her father and stepmother, sometimes accompanied by her older half-sister, Diana. Melinda found Myrna welcoming and genuine, "a delightful lady, smart and kind." She and Myrna grew very fond of one another.[18]

The Markeys made their home in a clapboard house off Sunset Boulevard in Pacific Palisades that Myrna had bought, a replica of a Connecticut saltbox that was painted dark red. Overlooking Rivas Canyon, it included a lime-tree orchard, a perfect lawn, and an English garden that reminded Myrna of the one her Johnson grandmother used to keep in Helena. The house had belonged to a skilled craftsman named Avery Rennick, who hand-built the furnishings and copied the paneled walls in the sitting room from a display in the American Wing of the Metropolitan Museum of Art.

As she did during her first years with Arthur, Myrna became quite social. Gene seemed to know everybody. As a couple they attended dances hosted by the Darryl Zanucks and small dinners at the home of Cole Porter in Brentwood. Since a devastating riding accident, Porter relied on the world to come to him. He pumped Myrna for gossip but found her a reluctant and disappointing source. What she adored was to listen to him play the piano and sing his songs. He would send Myrna yellow roses following a visit (*BB,* 210).

At the nearby home of Douglas Fairbanks Jr. and his wife, Mary, she would exchange blank stares with Garbo, who never once acknowledged Myrna; or she'd converse with Evelyn Waugh, who these days was spending his time at Forest Lawn, doing field work for *The Loved One*. She was introduced to Somerset Maugham, but he had little use for her because she refused to play cards. Members of the British aristocracy would often be included on the Fairbanks guest list, to Gene Markey's delight. Titles impressed him, and Myrna called him a Bourbon by temperament. He and Myrna had very different ideas about who and what mattered. He once chastised her for chatting at a party with the African American actress Louise Beavers, who'd played the maid in two of Loy's films. Markey told Myrna, "You don't care who you talk to," and Beavers privately referred to him as a skunk. But for the present, at least, harmony prevailed in the Markey-Loy household.[19]

Myrna got help in practical and money matters from her new secretary, Leone Rosson, an attractive, single (divorced) Texas native with a good grasp of finance, on whom Myrna would come to depend. Five years older than Myrna, Leone became her business manager, bookkeeper, and functional right hand, through many decades. She often accompanied Myrna on trips, and when Myrna lived in New York, she used Leone's Los Angeles address on South Orange Drive as her own official address. Myrna's bills would be sent directly to Leone, who wrote the checks, managed bank accounts, and filled out the Screen Actors Guild health insurance forms.

Gene shied from politics, but Myrna took sides in a Hollywood increasingly polarized by the cold war. "You could feel this cold wind blowing into Hollywood from the East, chopping the city into factions," she recalled (*BB*, 205). As the new Red Scare took hold, conservatives demonized liberals, left-wingers called conservatives fascists, and schisms displaced the solidarity of the war years.

From the moment of its founding, in the spring of 1945, Myrna took up the mission of the United Nations as her own crusade. In the nuclear age, she believed, world war would mean human annihilation; nations must find a way to negotiate their differences. She had visited Lake Success, attended a meeting of the United Nations Human Rights Commission chaired by Eleanor Roosevelt, and been moved by the sights of the circle of flags in front of the building and the delegates inside sitting around a circular table. "The symbol of the U.N. seems to be the circle: no beginning, no end, and no one nation below or behind another," she said.

But there were many Americans who regarded internationalism as a threat to U.S. patriotism and branded it and its advocates un-American.[20]

Myrna's political troubles began when she read the preamble of the U.N. charter at a Carnegie Hall meeting of the American Slav Congress, unaware that the Department of Justice had listed the organization as subversive and communist. This single action was enough to get her smeared as a fellow traveler, six weeks before the premiere of *The Best Years of Our Lives.*

The smear ran obscurely at first, as an editorial in *American Photo-Engraver,* a small-circulation trade union publication of the American Federation of Labor. Its author was Matthew Woll, a vice president of the American Federation of Labor. Myrna became a far more visible target after Woll's attack ran for a second time in *The Hollywood Reporter,* and it became the talk of the movie community. Woll's reprinted editorial called for the creation of a league for political decency that would spur movie boycotts just as the Legion of Decency had when it declared war on screen immorality back in 1934. This time the protests would be directed against "many high-salaried stars and script writers who are part of the Communist fifth column in America." Arguing that "glamour must not be allowed to serve a possible treasonable purpose," Woll named Edward G. Robinson, Orson Welles, Burgess Meredith, Myrna Loy, James Cagney, and Lionel Stander, along with other high-profile film colony offenders he alleged had "sponsored Communist or Communist-dominated organizations."[21]

Woll's blast continued:

> It is difficult to understand how American movie stars, whose wealth and fame is made possible by money paid into box offices by millions of hard-working and patriotic Americans, can lend their names to support regimes which are killing and maiming members of our country's armed forces, yet that is precisely what Myrna Loy did recently when she announced herself a sponsor of the American Slav Congress, a Communist front organization designed to beat the propaganda drums for Tito in the U.S. Somehow we do not recall hearing of a protest from Miss Loy when Tito's fliers shot down an unarmed American plane which resulted in the deaths of five U.S. airmen.

He ended his broadside with a call to movie industry leaders to "root out the fifth columnists and fellow travelers from the movie capital of America."

Myrna was in the middle of filming *The Bachelor and the Bobby-Soxer* when Woll's attack appeared in the press. Although her costars, Cary Grant and Shirley Temple, kept their thoughts to themselves, RKO's production chief, Dore Schary, jumped to Myrna's defense, promising to back her up with all the support she needed. Schary was a bookish writer of plays and screenplays who became a producer and in the early 1940s had headed the B-picture unit at MGM. After clashing with Mayer about an anti-Hitler movie Schary wanted to make, he left MGM and partnered with David O. Selznick at Vanguard Pictures. Still allied with Selznick, he came to RKO in 1945 and stayed until Howard Hughes bought the company three years later. A liberal Democrat who believed movies should comment on world issues, he left a complicated professional legacy. Joan Crawford hated his message pictures and labeled him a "cornball." Esther Williams, who worked under him in the late 1940s and early 1950s at MGM, found him condescending and treacherous. But in Myrna's eyes he could do no wrong. She claimed him as a cherished friend and political ally from that point on.[22]

Surprisingly, the conservative Louella Parsons also spoke out in her Hearst-papers column on Myrna's behalf. "I happen to know that Myrna worked herself to skin and bones during the war, going to hospitals every day and in Red Cross work," she wrote. "How [Woll] could accuse Myrna of being un-American is something those of us who know her well aren't able to understand. I do believe there are Communists in our town who should be exposed, but you can never make me believe that Myrna is one of them."[23]

Myrna dispatched an angry letter of protest to the *Hollywood Reporter*, which published it along with one from Orson Welles. She demanded a retraction, itemizing and denying Woll's charges, one by one. "I am not part of a Communist fifth column. I am not serving a possible treasonable purpose. I have not sponsored Communist or Communist-dominated organizations. I am not a person guilty of treason. I have not lent my name to support regimes which are killing and maiming members of our armed forces. I did not announce myself a sponsor of the American Slav Congress. . . . I am not engaged in misguided and dangerous activities. I am not a Communist. I do not belong to the Communist party. I do not flout American patriotism. I am not disloyal."[24]

Myrna's lawyer, Martin Gang, filed a $1 million libel suit against the *Hollywood Reporter* and its editor, W. R. (Billy) Wilkerson, claiming that the *Reporter* had reprinted a "false and malicious" story designed to "discredit and defame Loy and to expose her to hatred, contempt and the ridicule of the public." Wilkerson soon caved in and published a front-page retraction. He knew he could not substantiate any of Woll's allegations and that he would lose in court. Matthew Woll also backed off, admitting he had misjudged Miss Loy. He conceded that, since publishing his initial attack, he'd studied the record and found "that she has not supported any activity harmful or inconsistent with the American way of life." Citing her war work, he now pronounced her "a patriotic American citizen." Satisfied that a wrong had been righted, Myrna withdrew her lawsuit.[25]

But cold winds continued to blow. In Hollywood "it suddenly became risky, even dangerous, to be a Democrat," Lauren Bacall remembers. "Fear was rampant—the ruling emotion." An inquisition was under way.[26]

Stalwarts of the right-wing Motion Picture Alliance for the Preservation of American Ideals, among them the director Sam Wood and actors Robert Taylor, Adolphe Menjou, and Gary Cooper, convinced that communists enjoyed undue influence in the film industry and were disseminating anti-American beliefs, cozied up to cold warriors in Washington, inviting them to expose and root out the lurking Hollywood reds and pinks. A group of congressmen eagerly joined the battle.

Bacall and Humphrey Bogart were among the civil libertarians from the movie world who flew to Washington to protest the House Un-American Activities Committee (HUAC) hearings devoted to investigating communist infiltration of the motion picture industry. The HUAC sessions began in October 1947, chaired by J. Parnell Thomas, a New Jersey Republican who would later go to jail for accepting kickbacks. The actors, writers, and directors on the flight would, they hoped, counterbalance the "friendly" witnesses, such as Menjou and Sam Wood, slated to testify. Myrna did not join the Bogarts, Danny Kaye, Marsha Hunt, June Havoc, Larry Adler, Sterling Hayden, Shepperd Strudwick, Evelyn Keyes, Joseph Cotten, John Huston, Philip Dunne, and Ira Gershwin on the chartered flight to Washington because she was in the middle of filming *Mr. Blandings Builds His Dream House,* another Dore Schary film. But she became a charter member of the Committee for the First Amendment, the group that sponsored the flight, and she contributed $1,000 to it. She was one of 140 in the film industry who signed a petition published in the trade papers expressing outrage at HUAC's attack on freedom of expression. Other signers included Katharine Hepburn, Henry Fonda, Ava Gardner, and Gregory Peck. The FBI tagged Myrna Loy "one of the most vociferous" protesters of the HUAC hearings.[27]

William Wyler and John Huston had approached her on the *Mr. Blandings* set, asking her to help in establishing the anti-HUAC Committee for the First Amendment. Myrna attended the crowded founders' meeting in the living room of Ira Gershwin, along with her *Mr. Blandings* coplayer, Melvyn Douglas. Dore Schary, whose company, RKO, was producing *Mr. Blandings,* had testified at the Washington hearings, explaining to the committee that he would not knowingly employ a subversive but that when he hired someone to work on a movie, what he looked for was "the person best fitted to do the job." He argued that the communist threat to the movie industry was being blown out of proportion. When Schary came back on the *Mr. Blandings* set, he said about the hearings, "A person could get killed out there." According to Melvyn Douglas, Cary Grant responded by excusing himself to get a glass of water. "Whenever a serious subject would come up, Cary would pull back." He simply didn't want to get involved.[28]

In addition to funding the Hollywood protesters' flight to Washington, the Committee for the First Amendment also financed two ABC radio broadcasts jointly titled *Hollywood Fights Back.* Myrna participated in the second one, taking her place among the stellar cast of Hollywood players and directors. Several Democratic senators and prominent members of the arts community (Thomas Mann among them) participated, and all of them read statements over the air denouncing the congressional hearings as a threat to fundamental American freedoms guaranteed by the Constitution. "It's one thing to say we're not good actors," listeners heard from an earnest Judy Garland. "It's another to say we're not good Americans. We resent that." Burt Lancaster proclaimed, "You can't dump a bucket of red paint on Hollywood." The bandleader Artie Shaw warned, "Better get off the bandstand, Mr. Thomas, nobody's dancing!" Reading words that were probably scripted by Norman Corwin, Myrna Loy said, "We question the right of Congress to ask any man what he thinks on political issues. We think a lot of our freedom."[29]

Both William Wyler and Gene Kelly made specific mention of *The Best Years of Our Lives* during the *Hollywood Fights Back* broadcasts. Prior to the hearings, congressional members of HUAC were mentioning *The Best Years* as one of several films guilty of covertly dispensing communist, or at least anti-American, propaganda. During the actual hearings no one on the committee supplied a list of tainted movies; perhaps they feared lawsuits. But *Variety* reported there was a secret list, and *Best Years* was on it. One friendly witness characterized as "a Communist device" the depiction onscreen of a banker unsympathetic to giving loans to GIs; he didn't name his target, but anyone who had seen *The Best Years of Our Lives* would recognize the reference.[30]

Over the airwaves on *Hollywood Fights Back* Wyler protested that in today's Hollywood, "I wouldn't be allowed to make *The Best Years of Our Lives* as it was made a year ago. They [HUAC investigators] are making decent people afraid to express their opinions." Gene Kelly asked the radio audience, "Did you happen to see *The Best Years of Our Lives?* Did you like it? Were you subverted by it? Did it make you un-American? Did you come out of the movie with the desire to overthrow the government?" The questions were designed to make the Red baiters appear absurd.

In a letter to Myrna, Wyler wrote, "It is unfortunate that just six months after it took our industry's most distinguished honors, *The Best Years of Our Lives* is being degraded by the Thomas Committee to the point that it may be considered a disgrace . . . to our entire country."[31]

J. Parnell Thomas abruptly adjourned the hearings at the end of October, but by that time the blacklist had become inevitable. Congress cited for contempt the ten unfriendly witnesses—one producer, two directors, and the rest writers—who had declined to state whether they were communists. Terrified that the negative publicity would destroy the film industry at a time when movie attendance was already declining, a secret meeting of producers convened in New York at the Waldorf-Astoria. In what would become known as the Waldorf Statement, the producers turned against the Hollywood Ten, declaring that the studios in Hollywood would henceforth refuse to hire known communists and would fire those now employed. "Film Industry Rules 'No Jobs' for Reds; Will Fire or Suspend the Cited Ten." Dore Schary went along with the producers' majority decision, even though he had privately opposed it and had announced at the hearings his policy of disregarding politics and hiring the person best qualified for a job. RKO promptly fired two of the Hollywood Ten, Edward Dmytryk and Adrian Scott, the director and producer who had worked under Schary on *Crossfire,* a film noir about anti-Semitism. Myrna bought into Schary's argument that he'd had no choice.[32]

Myrna didn't believe she would face blacklisting, although her name continued to show up from time to time on lists of "Red appeasers" in Hollywood. And it's possible some producers put her out of the running for parts in their films because they didn't like her outspoken views. The retraction she won from the *Hollywood Reporter* gave her reason to trust in her ability to fight back. During the HUAC hearings she wrote to Wyler, "I dare them to ask me to testify!"[33]

CHAPTER 16

Breaking Away

Even though she received no Oscar or nomination for her work in *The Best Years of Our Lives,* Myrna's participation in the much-honored, widely distributed picture garnished her prestige, jacked up her salary, and boosted demand for her presence onscreen.

But she could still take a role that did nothing for her status. For the fun of it, rather than as a career move, she made a cameo appearance in *The Senator Was Indiscreet,* a farcical political satire directed by George S. Kaufman and featuring white-haired William Powell playing a dim-witted, philandering, blowhard U.S. senator who runs for president but winds up exiled to Hawaii. Clad in a Hawaiian-print dress, with flowers in her hair, as the senator's previously unseen wife she utters a single line and flashes the familiar upturned nose and crinkly smile in the last frame. So ended the fourteenth and final screen mating of Myrna Loy and William Powell. For this lark of a performance her payment was a new Cadillac.

The satire in *The Senator Was Indiscreet* now seems so broad that it couldn't offend anyone, but Joseph Breen tried to get the film scrapped, and Senator Joseph McCarthy branded it "traitorous and un-American."[1]

Cary Grant became Loy's leading man in two films owed under her three-picture contract with RKO. Since they last worked together in 1935 in *Wings in the Dark,* which awarded top billing to Myrna Loy, Grant had become a huge star, outranked only by Bing Crosby among Hollywood leading men, according to *Variety.* He commanded at least $150,000 per picture and could pick his own vehicles. For *The Bachelor and the Bobby-Soxer* he was paid $12,500 a week, compared to Myrna's $5,000. A shrewd businessman with a reputation for watching every penny, he began functioning as his own agent after Frank Vincent died during the filming of *The Bachelor and the Bobby-Soxer.*[2]

That movie got off to a rocky start. Myrna, cast as an unmarried and austere lady judge, had twice asked if she could redo her first scene, and the young director, Irving Reis, readily agreed. The persnickety Grant saw this as evidence of favoritism, blew his top, and walked off the set. He objected that Reis lacked the requisite credentials, being too green in the ways of comedy, and he further complained to Schary that Myrna was "getting away with murder" (*BB,* 204). Now it was Irving Reis's turn to show temperament, by walking out. When he returned after a few days, he and Schary agreed to split directing duties. Schary would work closely with the actors, while Reis limited himself to scene blocking and camera setups.[3]

Shirley Temple, who at age eighteen had been improbably cast as Myrna Loy's younger sister and ward, also acted up. Grant threatened to have her fired after he caught her entertaining cast and crew with her Cary Grant imitation. She apologized. Reluctant to share the limelight with another actress, Temple sneaked old, spent flashbulbs into their cameras when photographers tried to take publicity pictures of Myrna. Myrna consulted Gene Markey on what to do about her costar's bratty behavior, since Gene had produced several Shirley Temple movies at 20th Century–Fox and knew the former child star well. He advised Myrna to send Shirley flowers, which Myrna promptly did (*BB,* 205). That seems to have cleared the way to civility.[4]

Up against a director and two costars who couldn't seem to settle down, Myrna displayed what Cary Grant described as "the calmness of a Buddha." Tolerant of his "moods, fretting and fussing," she lost her cool only on the rare occasion when she flubbed a line, which prompted her to retire to the side of the set and pace up and down at a rapid clip while muttering, " 'Oh, shucks!' That is wild, wicked language for Myrna."[5]

In creating his Academy Award–winning script for *Bachelor,* Sidney Sheldon stinted on the role of the lady judge, handing all the choice comedy morsels to Cary Grant's character, Dick Nugent, a dashing artist in his forties saddled with the task of dating an aggressively ardent high school girl (Temple) who sees him as her knight in shining armor. As a would-be teenager, Grant drives a jalopy, rolls up his trouser cuffs, spouts jive-talk, and competes for trophies at a high school picnic, trying to sprint while balancing a potato on a spoon. His acrobatic deftness and exuberance carry the film. Loy's Judge Margaret Turner, on the other hand, never gets a chance to charm us. She morphs from a forbidding cold fish into an alluring, seductively gowned love object for Grant, but that's about it. "For the most part she is merely a backdrop," wrote the savvy critic for the *New York Herald Tribune*.[6]

Since *The Bachelor and the Bobby Soxer* earned $5,550,000, RKO and its partner, Selznick Releasing Organization, immediately rushed Cary Grant and Myrna Loy into another picture, *Mr. Blandings Builds His Dream House*. Shot in just fifty days, compared to the seventy-three required to complete *The Bachelor and the Bobby-Soxer*, the *Mr. Blandings* production ran smoothly, without major dust-ups among cast or crew members, although there were plenty of challenges for the crew. Duplicate outdoor sets had to be built, one showing the excavation site of the rickety old house in Connecticut that Jim and Muriel Blandings hurriedly buy and then have to tear down, the other the construction of the new house that replaces it. The landscape of rural Connecticut had to be recreated, complete with make-believe majestic oaks, at the Hunter Ranch (now Malibu Creek State Park) in the Santa Monica Mountains.[7]

Based on a best-selling novel by Eric Hodgins, an executive at Time, Inc., and a consultant on the movie, *Mr. Blandings* depended on rapport with an audience all too familiar with the postwar housing crunch. Jim Blandings (Cary Grant), a writer of advertising copy, makes $15,000 a year, we're told, ten thousand less than the amount his character earned in the novel. Screenwriters Norman Panama and Melvin Frank guessed that the average American would resent rather than sympathize with the problems of a family trying to make do with $25,000 a year. Since the average American household lived on less than $4,000 a year in 1948, it's hard to believe that the cutback to a salary of $15,000 a year made much of a difference in audience appeal. RKO under Schary was drowning in red ink and *Mr. Blandings* made a disappointing showing at the box office, losing $225,000.[8]

The film opens with wordless scenes of rush hour chaos in Manhattan, narrated by the Blandingses' best friend and lawyer, Bill Cole (a sardonic Melvyn Douglas). We move to the workday morning rush in the Blandings household, where a family of four "modern cliff dwellers" is trying to function in a Manhattan apartment that's far too small for them. "Cary was terribly funny when he was frustrated," Myrna would comment (*BB*, 214), and these city apartment scenes supply him symphonies of frustration. Jim Blandings's socks have been moved from a dresser drawer to a basket high up in an overcrowded closet. He has to compete for his turn in the shower and to fight for a piece of the bathroom mirror when he attempts to shave. Pillboxes rain on him when he opens the door of a medicine chest. Everyone's grumpy at breakfast (served by Louise Beavers as the maid, Gussie), and the two daughters, totally joyless schoolgirls, attack their father by spouting platitudes against the advertising business that they've learned at their progressive private school. Jim vetoes Muriel's proposal that they spend $7,000 redecorating their cramped apartment; why spend money fixing up a place you don't own? When a brochure proclaiming the joys of country life in Connecticut falls into Jim's hands, he jumps at the bait.

In Connecticut Jim and Muriel prove equally clueless about the nuts and bolts of home building and equally unrealistic about how much money their dream house will cost. They supply their architect (Reginald Denny) with a lengthy wish list. They want a sewing room, a room for plants, a built-in bar, a playroom, multiple closets, and bathrooms. "I refuse to endanger the health of my children in a house with less than four bathrooms," says the rather passive and dim, but appealing, Muriel, whose big scene finds her trying to describe to baffled house painters exactly which subtle shade of color she wants for each room. Only their friend Bill Cole has a grasp of market values, and only he keeps an eye on what the Blandingses can and can't afford. But Jim, whose job is threatened because he can't come up with the right slogan to promote Wham Ham, becomes jealous of Bill, suspecting that his friend and his wife are deceiving him by conducting a secret affair. The jealousy theme isn't in the novel, and *Variety* complained that it neither added laughs nor advanced the story.[9]

Nothing goes right, or according to plan, but the Blandingses end up with a home they love, something warm and welcoming that the practical-minded Bill envies. The moral seems to be that you can spend your way to happiness. James Agee called the movie "a bull's eye for middle-class middle-brows."[10]

Mr. Blandings is a hymn to consumerism. Jim's giddiest moment comes when Gussie unwittingly utters a line that he can use in ads as a slogan to sell Wham Ham. His future in advertising immediately brightens. *Mr. Blandings* itself became a pitch to promote new homes just like the one the Blandingses built. More than seventy "Blandings Dream Houses," based on the architectural plans used for the original house, were constructed across the United States and raffled off. The Selznick Releasing Organization also arranged advertising tie-ins with several companies that sold building supplies or home furnishings, among them General Electric, Sherwin Williams, Bigelow Carpets, and International Silver. A shopper could go out and buy the same shade of apple red paint that Muriel Blandings chose for one of her home's many bathrooms.[11]

Cary Grant published a (probably ghostwritten) tribute to Myrna Loy in *Photoplay* called "She's My Dream Wife." In it he called her "one of two expert comediennes in Hollywood," the other being Jean Arthur. (Where were his other brilliantly comic former costars Katharine Hepburn, Irene Dunne, and Rosalind Russell?) He praised Loy as a quick study when it came to learning lines, a good listener who "lets you talk about you," and an accomplished, underappreciated actress who "knows instinctively when a scene is wrong for her or the picture." William Wyler had also spotted, and trusted, that same instinct. Grant didn't have to say, but did, "I love her even as I respect her."[12]

Loy and Grant never made another movie together, although they hoped to costar in a film version of the Terence Rattigan play *O Mistress Mine,* which didn't materialize. They never took off as a romantic screen team, perhaps because, as Pauline Kael suggested, "they're too much alike—both lightly self-deprecating, both faintly reserved and aloof." They were also too close to the same age. Hollywood has often preferred the older-man-with-much-younger-woman formula.[13]

Myrna accepted a role in *The Red Pony* because, with a script by John Steinbeck, a score by Aaron Copland, and a director, Lewis Milestone, who'd won two Academy Awards, it promised to be a quality picture and also because she had long wanted to return on film to her western pioneer and ranching roots. She'd dreamed of portraying a woman like her Montana grandmothers. Filmed in Technicolor in the Salinas Valley before production of *Mr. Blandings* got under way, *The Red Pony* was held from release for nearly two years, until March 1949.

Myrna Loy plays Alice Tiflin, the ranch wife of a discontented former schoolteacher (Shepperd Strudwick) and the mother of a daydreaming son, Tom (Peter Miles), who would rather train his beloved pony than go to school. Looking trim and lovely in waist-hugging, high-collared, apron-covered long dresses, her hair upswept, her lipstick very red, she moves and speaks with a dignified restraint. Her own son calls her "Ma'am." Dutiful and strong, Alice seems isolated from Fred, her depressed, irritable spouse, a city-bred man who feels estranged from ranch life and toys with the possibility of returning to San Jose. Fred resents his son's closeness to the brawny hired man, Billy Buck (Robert Mitchum), whose nonchalant competence makes Fred question his own usefulness at the ranch, and he has no patience with his father-in-law (Louis Calhern, made up to look like Buffalo Bill), whose tall tales about the Old West he has heard too many times. Something dark and menacing hovers in the air. The half-light of the dawn that opens the movie and an ominous close-up of a buzzard set the tone.

An atmospheric coming-of-age tale of young Tommy's grief at the death of his pony, and his reckoning with the broken promises of his idol, Billy Buck, *The Red Pony* falls victim to a contrived happy ending that makes it appear that the menace and sorrow inherent in the story will magically vanish now that Nellie, the mare, has given birth. Without explanation Fred has announced that he doesn't feel like a stranger anymore, and we're asked to believe that all problems are now demolished by hope. The insights of Steinbeck the fiction writer succumb to the facile expediency of Steinbeck the Hollywood screenwriter.

Robert Mitchum is compelling as Billy Buck. Broad-shouldered, laconic, and unsmiling, he is at ease with the horses he grooms, sharing their elemental grace. Myrna remembered him as a "devil" who teased her relentlessly off camera, trying to crack her cool, ladylike façade. He told Hedda Hopper when she visited the set that Myrna as Alice Tiflin had to perform a dance of the seven veils. On a hot day he tried to persuade Myrna to undo the top buttons on her high collar, prompting her to ask, "Would you have me be unattractive?" (*BB*, 213). When the cameras rolled, though, he never faltered.

Myrna had been directed by Milestone before, back in 1926 at Warner Bros., where she played a coquettish French maid in *The Caveman*. She called him Milly and admired him as one of Hollywood's most talented directors, a straightforward, no-gimmicks craftsman who knew how to get the job done.

Milestone's coproducer, Charles K. Feldman, pushed to cast Myrna as Alice Tiflin, over the objections of Milestone, who balked at the high price tag her professional services commanded. Moreover, he argued, if you put Myrna Loy, "a big star with sex appeal," together with Mitchum, the audience will misconstrue the picture as a romance between them.[14]

Loy's salary for *The Red Pony* was $200,000, and Mitchum's, $130,000. Peter Miles, the child actor who played Tommy, got all of five dollars a day. The production was the costliest to date for Republic Pictures, usually characterized as a Poverty Row studio, and far more ambitious than its usual fare.[15]

Despite Milestone's misgivings, Myrna heard directly from John Steinbeck that she fulfilled his visualization of Mrs. Tiflin and that he was glad she had been cast in *The Red Pony*. Too timid to speak to her directly, Steinbeck left a note for her with a waiter at a New York restaurant where they were both having lunch (*BB*, 213).

Although she had battled shyness her entire life, Myrna began in the late 1940s to make public appearances and give talks on behalf of the United Nations, at first mainly addressing groups of women on the West Coast. The death of her dear friend Jan Masaryk in March of 1948 nudged her toward increased activism in the internationalist cause, since Masaryk had served as the Czech U.N. delegate and headed the World Federation of United Nations Associations. Although some believe that Masaryk committed suicide by jumping out of his Prague apartment window soon after the communist takeover of his country, Myrna was convinced he had been murdered because of his prodemocracy and pro-Western stance. She had visited him in his New York hotel a few months prior to his death and found him furtive, somber. A bomb in a package addressed to him had arrived, and although it failed to detonate, he knew his days were numbered.

Myrna's U.N. debut came when Douglas Fairbanks Jr. invited her to be his guest at a dinner for Trygve Lie, the U.N. secretary general, held at the Waldorf-Astoria in New York, and she sat on the dais between Nelson Rockefeller and Benjamin V. Cohen, the undersecretary of state. On that occasion she met Estelle Linzer, a New York associate of Eleanor Roosevelt who worked as program director at the American Association for the United Nations (AAUN). She would become Myrna's close friend, eventually the executrix of her estate. Estelle enlisted Myrna's active participation in the AAUN, soon drafting her as a board member. Myrna created a stir on the banquet dais, which made her realize anew that her fame as an actress could help her draw others in. As an advocate for the United Nations, she could educate Americans about its importance at a time when it was often under attack. She also made a bid to be taken seriously as a participant in world affairs. Estelle Linzer said that Myrna was very anxious to prove herself a person of some depth and knowledge.[16]

The United Nations Educational, Scientific, and Cultural Organization (UNESCO) soon sent her as a delegate to a regional conference in San Francisco that was attended by three thousand diplomats, educators, and civic leaders. Myrna spoke on the radio and gave a speech at a high school, advancing her argument that "many of the tensions between nations can be eased by exchanges of art objects and films." The State Department's George V. Allen and the National Commission for UNESCO urged her to head a Hollywood Film Committee that would promote better understanding among nations via film. Although fewer "message pictures" were being made, Myrna campaigned for more films like *Gentleman's Agreement* and *Pinky,* which she thought promoted tolerance and understanding. Her former producer Kenneth MacGowan, Celeste Holm, and Margaret Herrick, executive secretary of the Academy of Motion Picture Arts and Sciences, were among those who served on the Hollywood Film Committee, but it didn't survive long. McCarthyism and the climate of fear doomed it. "The concept of world peace seemed as threatening, somehow, as the horror of total war" (*BB,* 226). The Film Committee disbanded, but Myrna believed that the ideals of UNESCO nonetheless found their way into films such as Frank Capra's *Here Comes the Groom.* She continued as an adviser to UNESCO on film and eventually served a three-year term on the United States Commission for UNESCO. Myrna told friends that she got more emotional satisfaction from her work for the United Nations than she did from all her decades as a screen actress.[17]

It didn't take a lot of arm-twisting to induce Myrna to say good-bye to Hollywood for more than a year and take up residence in Europe. Gene had a British production in the offing, and the Russian-born Hollywood director Gregory Ratoff wanted Myrna Loy to star in a movie set in Capri that Gene would write. Sir Alexander Korda, who long ago directed Myrna when she played the wild gypsy Nubi in the early talkie *The Squall,* would oversee the Capri production, which would be filmed on location there and in London. The result, *If This Be Sin,* released in Britain with the title *That Dangerous Age,* turned out to be an embarrassment, a complete waste of time, money, and talent. Myrna plays Lady Cathy Brooke, the adulterous but self-sacrificing wife of a neglectful London barrister who will lose his eyesight and perhaps his life without her solicitous care. Oblivious to his wife's needs, he goes around through half the movie wearing a black blindfold. Lady Cathy is in love with a dashing younger man (Roger Livesey), her husband's law partner, but she nobly surrenders her lover to her pretty young stepdaughter. The Capri villa and rocky, seasplashed scenery provided a picturesque background for the cinematographers Anchise Brizzi and Georges Périnal but couldn't make up for a surplus of melodrama, stilted dialogue, and trite characters. Myrna faulted

Gene Markey, a hypochondriac who, instead of doctoring the script, retired to their villa and "collapsed under his mosquito netting" (*BB*, 230). Her husband's self-absorption had clearly begun to grate.

While in England for some location shooting Myrna was introduced to Queen Elizabeth, the consort of George VI now remembered as the Queen Mother, at the Royal Command Film Performance. Her Royal Highness thanked Miss Loy for her charitable service to Britain during the war. Because of Gene's social cachet, Myrna also met and socialized with Marina, Duchess of Kent, widow of the youngest son of George V. Myrna found her warm, cultured, and unstuffy. She and Gene spent Christmas at Warwick Castle as guests of Guy Fulke Greville, the seventh Earl of Warwick, who had once tried his luck as a Hollywood actor under the name Michael Brooke.

While they stayed at Claridge's in London, Myrna became aware that Gene's taste for aristocratic companionship extended to the bedroom. He had been carrying on affairs with several titled women: "nothing less for Gene than a duchess or a countess." When Myrna returned to the hotel after a day of filming at Shepperton Studios, the reception staff at the desk would try to stall her while making furtive calls to warn Gene that his wife was about to arrive. Myrna doesn't, in her autobiography, specify exactly what further evidence of his philandering she discovered; she says merely that she caught him with "lipstick on his face, so to speak" (*BB*, 235). Although humiliated to discover herself a reluctant player in a bedroom farce, she didn't suffer emotional devastation, because what she felt for Gene belonged more in the category of affection than the kind of deep love she had felt for Arthur. But she put Gene on notice that the future of their marriage hung in the balance. He promised to reform and assured her of his abiding devotion to her and no other.

During the marital showdown Myrna developed appendicitis and required surgery followed by a two-week stay at a London clinic. Informed by her doctor that a full recovery from the appendectomy would take a year of rest, she rebelled, rising from her sickbed long enough to attend a memorial service for Jan Masaryk that marked the first anniversary of his death. She then left England with Gene for some months of convalescence—and hoped-for marital regeneration—on the Italian Riviera, and in Rome, Venice, and Florence. As usual, Gene's wide range of privileged friendships opened many doors and treated Myrna to some select hospitality. With Gene she visited Alan Moorehead—one of her favorite writers—in Portofino, and the couple were welcomed for tea with Max Beerbohm in Rapallo. Surrounded by the framed caricatures that had made him famous, Sir Max, subdued, gentle, and close to eighty, failed to dazzle with his wit. At I Tatti, near Florence, the aged art historian Bernard Berenson startled Myrna by attempting to fondle her knee when she sat beside him on a sofa. She withdrew her knee but responded with amusement rather than anger.

George V. Allen, assistant secretary of state for public affairs, whom Myrna had met at the UNESCO meeting in San Francisco, invited her to attend and advise the American delegation at an upcoming UNESCO conference in Paris. She agreed but stopped in the Austrian Tyrol en route to visit Gene during production of a British film, *The Wonder Kid,* being written by Markey as a vehicle for the child actor Bobby Henrey. Bobby's mother, a travel writer, found Myrna "simple and gracious," and described the less modest Gene as something of a dandy, tricked out in a braid-decorated Austrian hunting jacket and "the most beautiful of Tyrolean hats." Myrna told Mrs. Henrey she could not linger in the Tyrol; she had an obligation in Paris. As it turned out, her days in Austria would be the last she and Gene Markey would spend together under one roof as man and wife.[18]

At the UNESCO conference in Paris Myrna once again battled a lack of self-confidence. George V. Allen put her to the test by asking her to deliver a speech to the American UNESCO delegation, which included Milton Eisenhower, the youngest brother of Dwight D. Eisenhower and at that time president of Kansas State University, and the theologian Reinhold Niebuhr, intimidating presences. Myrna stayed up half the night preparing a talk that championed artists as ambassadors of peace. It was greeted with an ovation that she read as a ratification of her legitimacy. Democratic Representative Mike Mansfield of Montana, a participant in the conference, helped her to further UNESCO's visibility when he praised her contribution to the conference on the floor of Congress. "It did my heart good to see how Miss Loy came to every meeting for two weeks, took part in all discussions and even made a speech or two," he said, going on to suggest that she was helping UNESCO gain wider acceptance among ordinary Americans. "It is unfortunate that UNESCO's principles have been hard for the miner, the working man and the housewife to grasp." For Myrna, a Montana-born woman whose formal education had ended in high school, being praised in the Congress of the United States by a Montana congressman had to stir pride.[19]

Instead of rejoining Gene on the continent, Myrna returned to California to answer a call from 20th Century–Fox: Darryl F. Zanuck wanted her to costar opposite Clifton Webb in a film version of the best-selling memoir *Cheaper by the Dozen*. Once again she would serve as poster Mom for the all-American family, this time as Lillian Gilbreth, the competent and level-headed mother of twelve and during the 1920s the wife of despotic efficiency expert Frank Gilbreth. Several of Myrna's actress friends who were also in their mid-forties let her know that they felt that she was committing career suicide by agreeing to play a middle-aged wife with a dozen children; she would never again be considered to portray a younger woman or romantic leading lady. Myrna didn't care. She liked the role of Lillian Gilbreth and was realistic about the way an actress's age influenced casting decisions in Hollywood.

She's appealing in this film but definitely overshadowed by Clifton Webb until the final sequence, after the overbearing Frank Gilbreth's sudden fatal heart attack. At that point Lillian Gilbreth takes command, telling the children that she will keep the Gilbreth industrial engineering firm afloat and deliver her late husband's speeches at professional conferences in Europe. Before this we're barely aware that she has any professional credentials.

Working with Webb, who had recently triumphed as the acerbic babysitter Lynn Belvedere in *Sitting Pretty*, proved to be no lark. Though Myrna attended many parties he hosted with his mother and lifelong companion, Maybelle, and she considered him a friend, on the set she found him dictatorial and a scene-stealer. A soloist by temperament, he tried to dominate every frame.

Cheaper by the Dozen scored at the box office, earning $4.4 million in North American receipts, but Myrna took a pay cut to play in it. She was paid only $80,000, compared to the $200,000 she had earned for *The Red Pony*.[20]

After spending more than a year in Europe, Myrna returned to a Hollywood racked by change and uncertainty. A 1948 Supreme Court ruling had forced the studios to divest themselves of their ownership of theaters. As the Hollywood Ten began to serve their prison sentences, fear of the blacklist continued to cast long shadows in the film community. Television kept gaining ground, at the expense of movie attendance, which plummeted to sixty million per week from its one hundred million peak in 1946. MGM had been supplanted as the dominant studio and 20th Century–Fox now led the field. Zanuck sat in the throne that Louis B. Mayer had long occupied.

Myrna knew that the ground was shifting in her private world as well.

Emotional distance and clashing values, as well as an ocean and a continent, now separated her from Gene Markey. Their planned collaboration on an independent film and TV company went nowhere, although they had formed a corporation, bought some stories, and hired a publicist. Myrna rarely heard from Gene. When he did write to her from England, he assured her that he loved her and asked for news from Pacific Palisades: "How are the poplars and all the other friendly trees? What is the general pattern of life around the little red house?" he inquired. "All of it means a great deal to me. I would like to know how your room looks, and mine. I would like just to be able to look in the window for a little moment."[21]

When Myrna learned from a friend in Europe that Gene had been pursuing an Irish countess, she decided she'd had it. Over the telephone she informed him that she would seek a divorce. "We were away from each other too much," Gene told a reporter for the *London Daily Mirror.* In the United States Louella Parsons broke the story: "Myrna Loy Admits Marriage to Gene Markey Is on Rocks."[22]

A distraught Gene dispatched a few melancholy letters to Myrna from Claridge's, London. In these his occasional use of the lowercase *i* for first person *I* may signify how diminished he felt:

> i shan't go into a post-mortem; it would only be sad. I believe you know how happy i was with you—when you (at least so I thought) were happy with me. I tried very hard—as I think you realize—to make it go: particularly when I took you away to the Continent. From the time you went to Paris I could only judge from your behavior that the bell rung. [That was] the deepest hell i have ever been in.
>
> After I got to Vienna I wanted to write you, asking for a divorce, but I held back for one reason: that I feared it would be a comment on your Fox "mother" film *[Cheaper by the Dozen].* The American Public is an old monster, half daemon, half puritan. "Moral" defects in film stars, it regards with a prurient eye, but divorce—a third divorce—is not good. So I say— in all friendship—I think it best to wait . . . until your picture has been out and is no longer news.
>
> i tried to take care of you—but apparently it went awry somewhere.
> Good luck, always,
>
> G[23]

When he heard from her lawyers in Hollywood that a Mexican divorce was in the offing, Gene reiterated to them his argument that the divorce should be postponed. Myrna would suffer public lambasting if it took place now, just before the release of *Cheaper by the Dozen.* She'd be grouped with such other divorcing stars currently in the news as Ingrid

Bergman, John Huston, and Betty Hutton and would be subjected to "another storm of sneers and jeers at 'loose Hollywood marriages' from women's clubs and the writers of newspaper editorials."[24]

The Mexican divorce did go forward in August when Myrna filed an uncontested petition charging mental cruelty. She'd ended her marriage to John Hertz in the same dingy Cuernavaca courtroom. Her friend and assistant Leone Rosson, who during the four-year marriage had always managed to resist Gene's charm and because she kept the books and knew how expensive he was, accompanied Myrna on the brief, sad journey to Mexico. Myrna told the reporters who greeted their returning plane, "It's too painful to talk about," and quickly dispatched them.[25]

Gene's final letter about clearing his belongings out of the house they'd shared sounded a plaintive note: "There are a few old clothes," he wrote, "but I shan't take anything except my silver (which was my family's), my books—and a few plates for the small apartment that I shall need when I go 'home.' "[26]

Myrna never succumbed to rancor when she thought back on her years with Gene and the many good times they'd shared. She called him "a born courtier, witty companion, [and] skilled lover," who "simply found it impossible to concentrate on one woman" (*BB*, 256). Markey would later marry the wealthy widow Lucille Parker Wright, who owned Calumet Farm in Kentucky, where thoroughbred horses were bred.

Right before the impending divorce was announced, Myrna spent a week in Washington, D.C., meeting and socializing with State Department and United Nations officials. Washington made her feel welcome, important. She thought of moving there. She, too, was looking for a home.

CHAPTER 17

Mrs. Howland Sargeant

As the pace of her film career slackened, Myrna took tentative steps into the burgeoning world of television, hoping for a lead role in a series. She never landed one, although she starred in a few pilots made with the hope that a series would ensue. Instead, she appeared several times in filmed *General Electric Theater* productions and on live variety shows hosted by Perry Como and George Gobel. She was Walter Pidgeon's wife and the mother of Jane Powell, Jeanne Crain, and Patty Duke in a live, made-for-TV remake of the MGM musical *Meet Me in St. Louis*. Since her movies from the 1930s and 1940s were making the rounds on late-night television, Myrna would sometimes find herself face-to-face with her previous self on the small screen, at times startled by the experience. But her acting career, past or present, didn't totally engage her these days. World affairs and her private life occupied the front burners.

During the 1950 California senatorial campaign, Eleanor Roosevelt telephoned to enlist her help on behalf of three-term Democratic congresswoman Helen Gahagan Douglas, Melvyn's wife, who was being smeared as "the Pink Lady," a communist sympathizer, by her rival candidate, Richard Nixon. Mrs. Roosevelt told Myrna, "I want you to help me. Helen is in trouble. She is up against a man who is unscrupulous." Myrna hosted several fund-raisers for Mrs. Douglas, who would be trounced by Nixon in the November election. A reporter asked Myrna during the campaign if she would consider running for Congress if Helen Gahagan Douglas had to vacate her seat to become a senator. Myrna answered that she had been away from California for a while and didn't feel qualified to represent its citizens. "I don't know enough to be in Congress. I'm learning to be a diplomat but I'm no politician. I'm too busy with UNESCO."[1]

Soon after Secretary of State Dean Acheson appointed Myrna Loy to an unsalaried three-year position as a member of the National Commission for UNESCO, she rented her Pacific Palisades saltbox to the actor George Sanders, said another good-bye to California, and bought a house on N Street in Georgetown, a "smart little grey house whose front porch is two steps below street level." A newspaper columnist wrote, "There's a new face in the national capital. It's pretty and freckled and familiar to millions of American moviegoers." Although she maintained an office near the State Department, she was able to work from her desk in the little gray frame house a few days a week.[2]

In addition to her UNESCO work she resumed the military hospital visits to wounded servicemen that had engaged her during World War II, this time calling on veterans of the Korean War.

She had already become close to the man who would become her fourth husband, Howland Sargeant, who was divorced, just shy of his fortieth birthday when they wed, and eight years her junior. A former Rhodes Scholar at Oxford and a graduate (like both Arthur Hornblow Jr. and Gene Markey) of Dartmouth, Howland Sargeant was a career diplomat whose title was deputy secretary of state for public affairs. The Loy-Sargeant romance began a few months after she broke with Gene Markey, at a UNESCO conference in Florence at which Howland headed the U.S. delegation. Taking tea with him at a monastery in Fiesole, or strolling beside him along the Arno, Myrna felt renewed and romantic, full of hope for a future life in which being a movie star would no longer define her.

A New Englander whose mother still lived in the old whaling town of New Bedford, Massachusetts, Howland had an earnest, buttoned-down demeanor. Lacking the dash of Myrna's three previous husbands, he showed scant interest in the clothes he wore or his physical surroundings. Terry Hornblow characterized him as a nice guy, but not a single one of Myrna's close women friends had a good word for him. Estelle Linzer considered him cold and repressed. Natalie Visart Taylor found him pompous. Elsie Jensen Brock, who headed the AAUN West Coast branch, faulted him for being condescending toward people less well educated than he and for failing to recognize Myrna's intelligence. She thought he regarded Myrna as little more than a pinup girl, although Myrna reported that their courtship included stimulating conversations about politics and the United Nations. Howland was exceedingly bright. From the start, though, he resented the flurries of attention that Myrna's celebrity generated. He wanted a conventional, subservient wife, a "little woman" who would yield the spotlight to him.[3]

Attended only by her old friends Betty and Bob Black, Howland and Myrna's wedding was a hurried ceremony, presided over by a military chaplain in Fort Myer, Virginia. Howland had wanted a Presbyterian minister to officiate, but because Myrna had been divorced from Gene Markey for less than a year, the minister they had chosen refused. Bob Black, a colonel in the Pentagon Medical Corps, found the chaplain who rescued them. After the improvised wedding the couple headed almost immediately for Europe on the *Queen Elizabeth*. They would combine their honeymoon with a UNESCO meeting in Paris.

A Republican congressman from Indiana seized the opportunity to lambaste UNESCO as "a mismanaged socialite travel club" and to charge that the Sargeants' Paris honeymoon had been undertaken at the expense of American taxpayers. Another congressman, this one a Democrat from Georgia, set the record straight, insisting that Myrna Loy's new husband had paid for the honeymoon.[4]

Although she kept active on the speaker circuit in and around Washington, delivering talks to groups like the American Newspaper Women's Club, Myrna's most reported role was as hostess or guest at D.C. social events. She and Howland hosted elegant parties with guest lists that often included big names like Secretary of State Dean Acheson and his wife, Alice (a painter, who became a good friend); India Edwards, who headed the women's division of the Democratic National Committee; or Vice President Alben Barkley. The society columns of the *Washington Post* might announce that at a benefit for Georgetown Neighborhood House the tea pourers included Mrs. Dean Acheson, Mrs. David Bruce (wife of the undersecretary of state), and Mrs. Howland Sargeant; or they might tell the world that at a fall cocktail party "Myrna Loy, known as Mrs. Howland Sargeant, wore a straight-cut black wool suit and a white satin cloche covered with jet bugle beads." At Rose Garden teas and Blair House receptions Myrna got to know the first lady, Bess Truman, delighting in her genuineness and lack of pretension. Could there be anyone further removed from Nora Charles than homespun, midwestern Bess Truman?[5]

Myrna soon discovered that as a State Department wife she wore a gag.

Howland was forbidden to talk to her openly about his work, and she was not allowed to voice her own political opinions in public. Since the District of Columbia wasn't a state and the 23rd Amendment had not yet been passed, she couldn't even vote in national elections. When Adlai Stevenson ran for president against Dwight Eisenhower in 1952, she wanted nothing more than to campaign for the eloquent and witty Democratic candidate who bore a striking physical resemblance to Arthur Hornblow, but she had to accept being sidelined. The next time Stevenson sought the presidency, in 1956, Myrna took an active part in the campaign because by that time Eisenhower occupied the White House, and Howland no longer worked for the State Department.

The night Dean Acheson wrestled with his decision to recommend removing General Douglas MacArthur from his command of United Nations forces in Korea, she and Howland were together at the Acheson home. The men sequestered themselves to work on the Acheson brief, while their wives conversed in another room. On the drive home Howland told Myrna nothing at all about what had transpired behind closed doors. Myrna learned about President Truman's dismissal of MacArthur when she read the headlines in the next morning's newspapers (*BB*, 264).

The respect shown her by both the plainspoken president and the patrician secretary of state offered some solace. According to Myrna, Truman sometimes solicited her comments and advice. Dean Acheson, increasingly under fire for his refusal to distance himself from Alger Hiss at a time when Senator Joseph McCarthy kept charging that the State Department employed communist sympathizers, held her in high esteem. When Howland Sargeant was sworn in as the State Department's chief of propaganda, Acheson said, "It strikes me that we're getting two Assistant Secretaries for the price of one." Myrna guessed that the nod in her direction caused her husband to blanch.[6]

Howland, like John Hertz Jr. before him, had misgivings about having a wife in the public eye, and he didn't encourage Myrna to accept acting roles. She did so, nevertheless, when an offer to costar in *Belles on Their Toes*, a sequel to *Cheaper by the Dozen*, came her way. She left Georgetown and Howland for six weeks and moved into a Beverly Hills apartment provided by 20th Century–Fox. Once again she would portray Lillian Gilbreth, the widowed psychologist, industrial engineer, and mother of twelve who must now take over what had been her husband's role of financial provider, company president, and household manager. Myrna, who had been a working woman since her late teens, identified with this role and saw it as a boost to the feminist cause. As Lillian Gilbreth she battled male chauvinist executives who wouldn't consider hiring women engineers and seethed at a men's club that barred her from a speaking engagement when it discovered she was female.

She also relished the chance to share the screen a second time with Jeanne Crain, who would again appear as the oldest Gilbreth daughter, Anne. Nominated for an Academy Award in 1949 for her performance as Ethel Waters's daughter in *Pinky,* Crain had earned the right to share top billing with Myrna for *Belles on Their Toes.* In fact Crain's name appears first in the credits. Myrna also agreed to a pay cut of $30,000 less than her takings for *Cheaper by the Dozen,* another indication that her star had dimmed; she received $50,000.[7]

Jeanne Crain worshipped Myrna Loy. She considered her an enormously subtle actress, whose minimalism belied her mysterious powerhouse capabilities. "The slightest thing she does has a force," she said. She compared her to a deep pool, with a deceptively smooth surface (*BB,* 243). She also admired Myrna's awareness of others and her engagement with global issues.

With Hoagy Carmichael cast as the slightly scandalous housekeeper who brews bootleg beer in the basement, and Debra Paget as a singing and dancing daughter, *Belles on Their Toes* was an agreeable bit of fluff with a soft-pedaled blue-stocking agenda that went down easy. The script by Phoebe and Henry Ephron, full of tuneful nostalgia for the 1920s, concentrated on the romances of the older daughters. *Time* magazine called it a "marshmallow mélange of Technicolor, tunes, slapstick and sentiment."[8]

Rumors kept circulating that Myrna Loy and William Powell would reunite in a television series, but it never happened. He also backed out of a television role opposite her in "Love Came Late" for *General Electric Theater.* Melvyn Douglas replaced him. Begging off, Powell sent her dozens of red roses and invited her down to Palm Springs for dinner, which made her suspect something momentous and difficult was in the offing. When Powell told her in the spring of 1956 that he was retiring, that he was sixty-five and worn out, Myrna felt devastated. It was like losing a limb. She'd clung to the hope that they would find a way to work together again.

When she returned to Washington, Howland continued to keep his emotional distance, shutting Myrna out. The companionship, affection, and emotional closeness Myrna craved, which had flourished before their marriage, began to deteriorate once they became man and wife. His State

Department job encouraged his inherent tendency to keep his own counsel. Instead of conversing with her in the evening, sharing stories and ideas, he would play squash after work, eat a hurried dinner, disappear into his newspaper, watch the news on TV, and go to bed early. On the night Eisenhower defeated Adlai Stevenson in the presidential election, Myrna sat alone watching the election returns on television and weeping. Howland had retired to bed (*BB*, 267).

The installation of a Republican administration in Washington forced Howland into the job market, and the anxiety didn't help the marriage. After a period of uncertainty, during which he toyed with several offers, he accepted a post in New York as head of Radio Liberation, a government-financed network that broadcasted to countries behind the Iron Curtain. Myrna and Howland rented an apartment overlooking the East River in Manhattan but held on for the present to the house in Georgetown. Myrna was overseeing its remodeling. They both hoped they would be returning to live there in a new Democratic administration down the road.

Howland's status as a propaganda officer on the front lines of the cold war didn't protect Myrna from suspicions about her loyalty to the United States. When her application for a renewal of her passport met with delay after delay, she protested with a letter to the Passport Office. Arguing that further postponement would be "professionally and personally embarrassing and detrimental," she included an affidavit stating, "I am not, nor have I ever been a Communist. To the contrary, I have always regarded with complete disapproval the activities of this dangerous faction." She supported, she wrote, "a code of national pride, personal freedom and human nobility." To bolster her credibility she enclosed copies of 1946 letters she'd written to the Hollywood Independent Citizens Committee of Arts, Sciences, and Professions (originally the Hollywood Democratic Committee), tendering her resignation because she considered it too radical.[9]

She got her passport and put it to immediate use when she embarked in the fall of 1955 for a three-month stay in Paris to film *The Ambassador's Daughter*. Olivia de Havilland starred, and for the first time Myrna Loy accepted an "also starring" role, reasoning that if she didn't make her peace with character roles and second billing, she might not work in films at all. Myrna liked the light touch of writer-director-producer Norman Krasna, who had cowritten the script for *Wife vs. Secretary* back in 1936. She also looked forward to playing the wry and sympathetic wife of a U.S. senator, to be portrayed by Melvyn Douglas, but he pulled out at the last minute and was replaced by Adolphe Menjou. Menjou had testified as a friendly witness at the HUAC hearings and was a dedicated right-winger who spotted communists lurking under every bed. He once told Gene Markey that if Myrna Loy did not qualify as an actual communist, she'd do until a real one came along. Myrna had great apprehension about working with him but was buoyed by the friendliness of John Forsythe, de Havilland's love interest in the movie, who told her that he sided with her, politically. Menjou turned out to be congenial both on and off the set, to Myrna's surprise and pleasure. De Havilland, who discovered she was pregnant during filming and didn't have an easy time in the freezing Joinville studios, remembers Myrna as "a fine actress and someone who always impressed me as an equally fine person."[10]

Howland joined Myrna in Paris for a festive New Year's Eve. They traveled after that to Spain and Portugal but subsequently found themselves sharing less and less time together. There had been no major rupture, just a gradual drifting apart. When Della underwent major surgery and had to spend many weeks in a Los Angeles hospital, Myrna took an apartment there and settled in for a long stay. Her beloved Aunt Lu had died in 1953; she and Della had lived together for decades. Although Leone Rosson, Myrna's Los Angeles–based assistant, did her best to stand in for Myrna, calling on Della often and even buying Mother's Day gifts for her, Myrna wanted to be on the scene. She seemed glad to have an excuse to linger in Los Angeles. A few years back she'd turned down a role opposite Charlton Heston in *The Private War of Major Benson* because it would entail too long a separation from Howland, but now she actively sought work on the West Coast. Offered a part in a screen adaptation of the novel *Miss Lonelyhearts,* to be filmed at Goldwyn Studios, she accepted it eagerly.

Dore Schary, long since displaced at RKO and deposed in 1956 as head man at MGM, had recently triumphed on Broadway with his production of his own play, *Sunrise at Campobello,* about FDR. Now, wanting to try his hand back in Hollywood as an independent producer, he acquired the screen rights to the dark and surreal Nathanael West novel *Miss Lonelyhearts* and wrote his own screenplay for a film to be titled *Lonelyhearts.* He assembled a cast of exceptionally talented actors, including Maureen Stapleton, in her first movie role, and Montgomery Clift, the inward-looking and vulnerable leading man whose success signaled a new Hollywood take on masculinity and who had already been nominated for three Academy Awards in the ten years since his screen debut.

Clift had been working for Schary at MGM at the time of the actor's devastating 1956 car accident, which disfigured his face, cost him several teeth, and left him chronically afflicted with back pain. "He would shake with pain." Already a heavy drinker and pill popper when he crashed his car into a telephone pole, he subsequently became so dependent on alcohol, speed, and painkillers that he could only work in the morning.[11]

In addition to the raft of problems that Montgomery Clift brought to the set, Schary faced budget constraints. United Artists agreed to finance the project but only if costs could be kept under $750,000. Clift agreed to take on the role of newspaper lonely hearts columnist Adam White for a nominal salary of only $25,000, plus 10 percent of the grosses. He admired Nathanael West's novel and had high hopes for this adaptation. Robert Ryan, who would deliver a volcanic performance as the sadistic newspaper editor William Shrike, also got a percentage of the grosses. His salary was the highest, at $75,000. Myrna Loy, cast as Shrike's emotionally brutalized wife, Florence, worked for only $22,500. Maureen Stapleton, who would be nominated for an Academy Award for her role as the sex-starved wife of a disabled man, received $10,000. And Dolores Hart, asked to play a completely incongruous role as a wholesome girl next door in love with Clift's Adam White, was paid $7,000. According to Clift's close friend, the actor-writer Jack Larson, Clift and Hart didn't hit it off. Hart would retire from films in 1963 to become a nun.[12]

There was tension between Clift and the director, Vincent Donehue, which Schary tried to mediate. Schary had imported Donehue, a noted stage director from New York, because he'd been impressed by the way Donehue had staged *Sunrise at Campobello* on Broadway, but he was taking a chance with a director new to film. Schary and Donehue rehearsed the actors for two weeks before filming began and shot the script in chronological sequence, just like a theatrical production.

In adapting Nathanael West's novel for the screen, Schary gave some of the characters new names and took many other liberties. He underplayed the Christlike aspect of Miss Lonelyhearts, turning Adam White's suffering into something personal to him rather than symbolic. He removed the sexual relationship between Mrs. Shrike and Adam. Most dissonant with the bleak tone of the book was what he did to the ending. In the novel the bleeding-heart newspaper columnist who takes on the sufferings of those who write letters to him is shot and killed by the "cripple" he has cuckolded via Fay Doyle, the character played by Maureen Stapleton. Schary substituted hearts and flowers. The cuckolded husband tries to shoot Adam but drops the gun. Adam's girlfriend forgives his infidelity, and they are going off together to get married. The blisteringly sarcastic and relentlessly cruel editor Shrike suddenly turns mushy and plucks a flower to give his tormented wife. The feel-good ending contradicts everything we've learned about Shrike's character, prompting disbelief in the audience, but that is the way Schary wanted it. Schary's daughter Jill wrote of him, "Daddy loves all stories about disastrous problems that are overcome. One of the main characters must be a Decent Human Being. His problems must have happy endings."[13]

Clift mocked the happy ending as a travesty, telling Robert Ryan he could find no trace of Nathanael West in it. "Where's the corruption? The misery? Hysteria has been replaced by blandness. Miss Lonelyhearts, meet Andy Hardy." Bosley Crowther of the *New York Times* chided, "With due respect for Mr. Schary's idealism and optimism in this sad world, his wrap-up is naively and incredibly pat."[14]

Montgomery Clift, who was bisexual, had a gift for friendship with women. A good listener, he could be wonderfully caring and supportive. Elizabeth Taylor, with whom he costarred in two more movies after their memorable teaming in *A Place in the Sun*, headed the list. He had been returning from a dinner party at her house when he crashed his car. Intimate friends, and perhaps once lovers too, Taylor and Clift even looked alike. Clift called Elizabeth his true twin, his other half. Most of his other close female friends were older women who mothered him. Salka Viertel, the blacklisted former writer of screenplays for Garbo, was one. The tobacco heiress, fellow drinker, druggie, and onetime torch singer Libby Holman was another, and the comic actress Nancy Walker, who was visiting Clift in California while *Lonelyhearts* was in production, was a third. Myrna Loy would join this select circle.

Clift's astute biographer, Patricia Bosworth, doesn't name her informant, but she quotes someone on the set of *Lonelyhearts* who describes Myrna's electric response to Monty when they first met: "There were sparks. He had this kind of cosmic thing." They began to spend lots of time together. Leone Rosson reported in her terse, telegraphic diary entries: "August 23, 1958: M. L. first dinner date with Monty. August 25: Miss L left with Monty from studio for dinner. August 27: M. L.–Monty. End of Picture. August 28: M. L. lunch Monty. I went to rushes with M. L. and Monty. August 29: M. L.–Monty Bel Air [Hotel]." In early September Clift's driver drove them to La Jolla, where they spent a few days. Leone went with them but stayed in another hotel. Her September 7 diary entry reads, "Picked M. L. and Monty up at 7:30 and we left for L.A." It isn't clear if they were sharing a room.[15]

It's impossible to know if they became lovers. Certainly alcohol impairs sexual performance, and Monty couldn't stop drinking. Jack Larson said he didn't know whether the relationship was sexual but that Monty's confidante Salka Viertel thought it was. Larson also said that Montgomery Clift was a very physical, affectionate man who liked to touch those he loved. He adored Myrna, and she in turn was "wonderful to Monty, very loving."[16]

In her autobiography Myrna dismisses any such notion and denies the rumors, reported in newspapers of the day and repeated in Patricia Bosworth's biography of Clift, that she was deeply in love with him and wanted to marry him. According to Myrna, Monty's sexual ambivalence tormented him. "He could never quite settle for homosexuality. He wanted men but loved women" (*BB,* 289). She implies he was too troubled to take on any committed relationship, but there's no question that she cared deeply for him and may have been sexually attracted to him as well. Myrna depicts herself not as a captive of desire but as a would-be rescuer of a gifted drowning man.

Intelligent, well-read, and perceptive, Clift had been a professional actor since his boyhood and possessed a director's sense of what would work in a scene. He coached Myrna and helped edit down a scene in which she and Robert Ryan go at each other. Myrna offered one of her most concentrated and affecting performances on the screen and won the enduring affection and admiration of Robert Ryan.

Monty wanted to work with Myrna again, perhaps in the theater. He spoke of a production of *Hamlet* in which he would play the tormented Dane, Peter Finch would be Claudius, and Myrna would be cast as Hamlet's mother, Gertrude. He envisioned a dramatization of Colette's *Chéri* featuring Myrna Loy as the aging courtesan. He was too bent on self-destruction to realize either project. Ten years after the accident and six years after *Lonelyhearts* he would die in his Manhattan brownstone at age forty-five.

During the filming of *Lonelyhearts,* Clift drank so much at night and took so many pills that he would pass out. "You'd have to put him to bed," Jack Larson remembers. Myrna tried to get him to stop drinking. In his presence she always drank a Coke. He darkened the windows of his room so he wouldn't have to look at himself. On sedatives and painkillers he would hallucinate, talking to chimeras. Larson would run lines with him and find Clift's copy of the script "a jumble of pages, not consecutive."

When they were both back in New York, Clift and Myrna continued to see each other for a while, attending the theater together, afterward going out to eat and, in his case, drink. Often Clift would have to be literally carried out of a restaurant or bar. Or they'd meet at parties hosted by Clift or by the actor-photographer Roddy McDowall, an important new friend Myrna had met through Clift. When Clift summoned her, she would drop everything else to be with him. Leone Rosson's diary records a night that she and Myrna had scheduled jointly to go over Myrna's financial records. "Monty called so our work night was cancelled" (Feb. 2, 1959). But toward the end of his life, Myrna stopped seeing him. She had come to the forlorn conclusion that he was beyond help and that watching him destroy himself was more than she could bear.

As soon as she returned to Manhattan after the completion of *Lonelyhearts,* Myrna had to face the dissolution of her marriage to Howland Sargeant. Once again she moved out of the home—this time a Beekman Place apartment—which she and her husband had shared. A draft of the letter of farewell that she left for Howland survives, offering a rare unmediated glimpse into Myrna's intimate life. "Dear Howland," it begins:

> This is the most difficult task that I have ever performed. After a long period of searching analysis into our relationship I have come to the conclusion that we should separate. I am sure you will agree that the struggle to adjust our different interests has resulted in too little for either of us. With deep regret I have chosen to leave to avoid the unnecessary cruelty of unfair recriminations. . . . I hope you will always have a warm feeling for the things we have learned together as I most certainly will have. It is my wish to see you again someday. . . . I hope you know how much faith I have in the contribution you have made and will in future make to this sorry old world of ours.
> With love and in friendship always,
>
> $$M^{17}$$

Avoiding direct confrontation, as was her habit, she asked him to contact her attorney.

Although Myrna had realized for some time that her fourth marriage was played out, she found the process of initiating and following through on the divorce shattering. In her bones she knew that this was it: there would be no fifth attempt. Howland represented her last chance, said Estelle Linzer, to create a life similar to the one she had known with Arthur, combining love, marriage, and a home. Myrna found it deeply hurtful that Howland didn't seem to care about losing her. She became with-drawn and depressed, refusing invitations to go out to the theater or movies.[18]

During the months of transition she leaned heavily on the steady, practical support of Leone Rosson, who answered Myrna's call for her to depart Los Angeles and come to New York to help, and of Estelle, a generous, nurturing friend who lived on Manhattan's East Side.

Since leaving Howland, Myrna had been living in Manhattan at the Plaza Hotel. Leone helped her settle into the less costly Volney on East 74th Street, an apartment building offering room and restaurant service for meals. Many "women of a certain age" lived there, mostly widows and divorcees. Dorothy Parker was a resident; she wrote about the Volney in her 1953 play *Ladies of the Corridor*. Lillian Hellman would some-times join Myrna and Dorothy for a meal, before she left the city to take care of Dashiell Hammett in his last days. Hellman never became a steady friend. Myrna found her too thorny and competitive (*BB*, 288).

Myrna counted on Leone to perform all kinds of services for her. Leone met with attorneys and served as an intermediary between Myrna and Howland. She spent time in Georgetown, making an inventory of items in the house on N Street that would be used in the property settlement, since Myrna did not simply walk away this time. The house would be sold and the furnishings divided. Leone had gone to Washington to help select the same pieces of furniture that she now had to catalogue for the divorce. She helped Myrna find permanent quarters and move from the Volney into a modest rented apartment with a terrace at the Royal York at 425 East 63rd Street. Some of the pieces from Georgetown found their way there.

Myrna didn't consider living anywhere else but in New York City, home of the United Nations and of many dear friends. Her current agent at MCA, Mimi Weber, lived right across the street from the Royal York. She felt fully alive in Manhattan, whereas Los Angeles made her con-scious of her has-been status in the movie industry. She had long ago ad-justed to living on the opposite coast from Della and David, and she pre-ferred it.

Leone found Myrna difficult to be with, not at all the cheerful, even-tempered, and thoughtful woman she had known for more than a decade. Leone wrote things like this in her diary: "Went to Volney. M. L. was in bad humor" (Nov. 26, 1958). "M. L. called. She didn't sleep and was very grumpy. We had words" (Nov. 29, 1958). "Miss Loy refused to talk. I blew my top but good" (Dec. 31, 1958). "Dinner at Volney. No Monty.

Big discussion & fight" (Jan. 16, 1959). Leone behaved admirably, realizing that Myrna truly needed her and that after a blowup she must stay steady. She knew that Myrna was distraught and needed time to heal.

The actual divorce took place by mutual consent in Juarez, Mexico, at the end of May 1960. Newspapers reported, "The 54 year old actress charged 'incompatibility of character.'" Once again Myrna Loy found herself seated forlornly at a table for one.[19]

CHAPTER 18

New York Ending

Over a period of months, work, activism, and friends pulled Myrna out of her depression. It dawned on her, after some extended wallowing, that she needed to get out of her own skin, to get busy and to be around other people.

Before her fourth divorce was final, she returned to 20th Century–Fox at the end of 1959 to play Paul Newman's alcoholic and adulterous mother in *From the Terrace*. The role was similar to her battered wife in *Lonelyhearts,* except that this film is in CinemaScope and color, with posh sets providing background for hard-driving East Coast business tycoons and their expensively dressed neglected wives. Based on a sprawling John O'Hara novel, and shot on both coasts, *From the Terrace* opens with Loy's Mrs. Martha Eaton passed out drunk in an empty train. The sequence follows her home to a poignant, stumbling reunion with her just-back-from-the-war son, Alfred. But after that affecting opening, the script abandons the mother-son relationship to focus on Alfred's attempts to reconcile vaunting ambition with true love, which his marriage to a cheating snow queen wife, played by Newman's real wife, Joanne Woodward, fails to provide. We aren't told what becomes of Mrs. Eaton after the script drops her, but we can guess it isn't pretty.

If Myrna had any doubts about her diminished status in Hollywood, the ho-hum response to her presence on the Fox set when she came west put them to rest. Paul Newman's dressing room was piled high with floral tributes, but no one bothered to send flowers to Myrna Loy. Some members of the crew who remembered her from the old days gave her an ovation on the first day of West Coast shooting, but she realized that "I was yesterday and he [Paul Newman] was today" (*BB,* 293). Myrna thought the world of Paul Newman, and they shared similar political views. They would campaign together for Eugene McCarthy's nomination as the Democratic contender in 1968, but these days she didn't play in Newman's professional league.

Loy's next role as Doris Day's gallivanting, Auntie Mame–like Aunt Bea in the thriller *Midnight Lace* offered better outfits (designed by Irene) and a chance to speak some sparkling lines onscreen, rare for Myrna in the 1960s, when she only appeared in three films all told. The producer Ross Hunter revered Hollywood's Golden Age and its leading ladies. His lush Technicolor production gave Myrna a chance to be photographed wearing green taffeta, with real diamonds and emeralds around her neck, and perfectly coifed red hair. Beautifully showcased, she and Doris Day both look elegant throughout the London chill, although Doris Day found her role as a stalked wife emotionally draining. Myrna liked Doris Day and appreciated the collegiality and respect Day showed her. Rex Harrison, on the other hand, who portrayed the villainous husband, behaved as if Myrna were a piece of furniture inconveniently placed in his path.

Myrna had aged out of romantic roles, although in her last film from the 1960s, *The April Fools,* she got to play the privileged, appealing, and mystical American wife of an aristocratic and affectionate former Parisian, Charles Boyer. She made no complaint. The Production Code had finally given way to the Motion Picture Association of America's film rating system, and after 1968 it became possible to show (in an R- or PG-rated film) a couple falling in love while married to others, as Jack Lemmon and Catherine Deneuve do in *The April Fools.* But Myrna didn't really benefit from the increased permissiveness; for her it came too late. Nor was she a particular fan of the new fashion for film nudity or of dialogue that incorporated four-letter words. She lamented the fact that a double standard for men and women still prevailed.

While male actors of her generation—Cary Grant, Gary Cooper, or Clark Gable—still could play romantic leads opposite much younger actresses, women over fifty, when they worked at all, were cast as sexless mothers or grotesque monsters. Only Katharine Hepburn, who triumphed as the addicted mother in *Long Day's Journey into Night* in 1962 and, with fierce command, portrayed Eleanor of Aquitaine opposite Peter O'Toole's King Henry in *A Lion in Winter* six years later, seemed to defy time.

The movie roles Myrna was offered made her angry. "Hollywood seems to have unearthed this cannibal mother, and that's the kind of part available to someone my age," Myrna told a reporter. To such indignities she said no thanks. She'd already served her term playing dragon ladies during her earliest years on the screen. Not for her the ghoulish makeup worn by Bette Davis and Joan Crawford in 1962's *Whatever Happened to Baby Jane?* Those two wanted their names above the title no matter what. Remaining a star mattered less to Myrna than maintaining her dignity. She pointed to England and France as countries that allowed aging actresses to keep working while maintaining both their standards for high quality and their integrity. Not so in U.S. movies. "There are *no* sane older women in films these days," she complained, "simply a lot of psychotic, disintegrated old bags."[1]

She turned down many parts, including one offered by Hitchcock, probably in *Marnie.* A September 1963 entry in Leone Rosson's diary says only that Myrna was sent a Hitchcock script but that she didn't like the part—perhaps as Marnie's mother—and rejected the offer. She also declined to play Lana Turner's evil mother-in-law in a 1966 remake of *Madame X,* a Ross Hunter production. Following *Midnight Lace,* Myrna Loy would be absent from the screen for eight years.

She yearned for a witty role in a good comedy, but film comedy as she had known it had gone missing, along with the satiric sense that nurtured it. "One problem," according to Myrna, was that "you can't write comedy unless you want to poke fun at things and yourself. There has been a long period of outrageous conformity in this country." Prewar comedy, she remarked to an interviewer, had style, but now "people don't dress up any more, and writers are writing about the kitchen and the bedroom and not the parlor." She apparently didn't think much of films like the Doris Day–Rock Hudson romantic comedy *Pillow Talk,* which Ross Hunter acknowledged had been inspired by the Powell-Loy style in their 1930s and early 1940s comedies.[2]

Claudette Colbert had turned down the part of Aunt Bea in *Midnight Lace* because she wanted to maintain the fiction that she was too young to be Doris Day's aunt, but Myrna had no problem playing older women. She knew that her face proclaimed her age, but she never considered having a facelift. The only other kind of cosmetic surgery she'd contemplated was having her ears pinned, as David Selznick had requested, but she didn't follow through even on that. In her view, pretending to be young when you weren't amounted to folly. "I don't know why anybody thinks it's important to keep their youth," she once said. "What's much more important is learning not to depend on youth or beauty. The true secret of survival is to be curious about life, to be interested in lots of things." When she saw her younger self in an old movie on television, she said, "I don't feel any pangs. I feel surprise—was that me? But I can't yearn for yesterday. There's too much to do today." Joan Crawford once confessed in an interview that she envied Myrna Loy "like mad because she latched on to the secret of growing old gracefully—and usefully." Myrna Loy had a gift for living in the present.[3]

Back in Manhattan, after completing *Midnight Lace,* Myrna threw herself into John F. Kennedy's campaign for the presidency against the Republican Richard Nixon. Many Democratic activists in the New York theater and film communities had a hard time letting go of their loyalty to Adlai Stevenson after he lost his bid to be nominated for a third time as the Democratic presidential candidate. Alice Lee "Boaty" Boatwright, a publicist for Universal (later an agent for ICM) who met Myrna while doing publicity for *Midnight Lace* and became a dear friend, had been active in a group called "Broadway for Stevenson." The core members of that group, which included Lauren Bacall, Betty Comden, and Phyllis Newman, were reluctant to get behind JFK. Myrna, who sat on the New York State Democratic Committee, succeeded in persuading Boaty and other Stevenson loyalists that Nixon had to be defeated, that he was a menace and that they must rally behind Kennedy. At a special performance of Gore Vidal's *The Best Man,* organized by and for the Stevenson faction, Adlai Stevenson himself urged his devotees to throw their support to Kennedy.

Myrna stumped for Kennedy all over New York State and New Jersey, making speeches and attending rallies, luncheons, and dinners. She'd proven her ability to draw crowds. She joined Eleanor Roosevelt at a spontaneous campaign rally in Spanish Harlem, her last public outing with Mrs. Roosevelt, who died in 1962. Although she spent a fair amount of time in his presence, sometimes even riding in his private helicopter, Jack Kennedy barely acknowledged her existence. There was no small talk exchanged, no expression of thanks from him, although Jackie Kennedy never failed to be gracious and friendly (*BB,* 298). Myrna felt invisible to JFK, which would surely not have been the case if she had been younger and a potential bedmate. She never allowed his personal coldness to stand in the way of her political commitment. She rejoiced in Kennedy's victory.

Myrna attended the Kennedy inaugural ball, where Hubert Humphrey spilled champagne on her green taffeta gown. She was later invited to a White House reception commemorating the centennial of the Emancipation Proclamation and was then asked to serve in the Kennedy administration on the National Committee against Discrimination in Housing. After Lyndon Johnson signed the Civil Rights Act in 1968, he sent Myrna one of his signing pens.

The overlap between New York activist Democrats and the East Coast performing arts community eased Myrna into her next professional venture as a stage actress. She had been thinking about breaking into theater since her first days with Arthur Hornblow but had never managed to bring it off. By now, in her fifties, she had developed monumental insecurities about her ability to cross over to the stage.

Noel Coward reinforced those doubts when she auditioned in the late 1950s for one of his plays, *The South Sea Bubble*. Coward had always been friendly to Myrna and had often visited her movie sets in Hollywood. He'd tried to borrow her from MGM to play Elvira in the film version of *Blithe Spirit*. He'd incorporated her name into the lyrics of one of his songs, "Mad about the Boy"; rhyming *boy* with *Loy* had proven irresistible. They'd sat side by side at many a dinner and post–opening night celebration in New York. Coward once paid her a treasured compliment, telling her that onscreen she'd "never played a false note" (*BB*, 309). They had some good friends in common, including Cary Grant and Roddy McDowall. Roddy and Myrna had been wowed by a singer named Tammy Grimes when they heard her at a club called Upstairs at the Downstairs, and they were responsible for bringing Noel to hear her; that led to her being cast by Coward in *Look After Lulu* (*BB*, 291). Roddy, by now very close to Myrna, also had a part in the Broadway production of *Look After Lulu*. He accompanied Myrna to her 1959 tryout for the man she referred to as the Master. During her reading for *The South Sea Bubble*, however, Coward kept interrupting to remind Myrna that her voice could not be clearly heard and that this was "theatah" and she must learn to project (*BB*, 306). She became so humiliated that she crawled away, convinced she should give up all thoughts of ever performing on the stage.

But she needed to work, both to generate income and to preserve her sense of self. "Work is important to me to fill my life," she told Dorothy Manners. "I must be occupied or I feel I'll rust." Movie roles no longer sufficed; they neither paid the bills nor fulfilled her. Television offered occasional jobs and opportunities to work with such talents as Helen Hayes, Peter Falk, John Cassavetes, and Tony Randall, but she found it a frustrating medium because there was never enough time to polish a performance. After her appearance in an episode of *The Virginian,* she said, "I wish I'd had more time to do it better. I was raised . . . when they made movies fast. . . . I don't need a dozen retakes, but TV is just too terribly fast for me. It's frightening. I'm not sure I'll watch the show. I know I won't be satisfied with myself." In television work, you might get hired on a Tuesday, receive the script on Wednesday, fly out to California on Thursday, report to the set on Friday. The whole hurried process seemed much more haphazard than shooting a film.[4]

Her new but already devoted friend Boaty Boatwright urged her to find a summer stock role that could serve as her theatrical debut. Boaty took the proposition one step further by volunteering to produce this first venture on the strawhat circuit. The play they chose for the debut was *The Marriage Go Round,* an American comedy by Leslie Stevens that had been a hit on Broadway with a cast headed by Claudette Colbert and Charles Boyer. It had quickly been turned into a movie featuring Susan Hayward and James Mason. The plot concerned a married couple, both professors at a university, and the mayhem created by the intrusion into their household of a seductive young guest from Sweden. Once again, Myrna Loy would be cast in the familiar role of wife, although this wife had a Ph.D. and a job.

Through Barbara Handman, a leader in liberal causes in New York who had been one of those convinced to switch her allegiance from Stevenson to Kennedy, Myrna met Bobbie Handman's husband, Wynn Handman, a noted stage acting coach who had helped other performers, among them Red Buttons, Jan Murray, and Dan Dailey, prepare for speaking roles in the theater. Before body mikes became the norm, stage actors had to learn (as Noel Coward had hurtfully reminded Myrna) to project their voices so that they could be heard and understood in the back rows of a large house. Projecting felt artificial to Myrna. Once she graduated out of exotic vamp roles, she had always striven for a relaxed, natural acting style. "Myrna was an exceptionally honest person," Wynn Handman recalled, "and that carried into her acting. There was much *reacting* in her acting." Wynn Handman had to persuade her that on the stage, projecting is honest. He also had to teach her how it is accomplished.[5]

Prior to the July 1961 opening of *The Marriage Go Round* in New Hampshire, Myrna Loy and Wynn Handman met several times a week at her East Side Royal York apartment for coaching sessions. To help open up Myrna's voice, Handman rehearsed her in roles from classic Greek drama. He told her, "You have a big voice, but you don't like noise. So you don't like the sound of loud voices."[6]

When casting for *The Marriage Go Round* was completed, rehearsals with the other actors began in the barnlike Lakes Region Playhouse in Laconia, New Hampshire. Handman assumed directorial duties, Claude Dauphin was leading man, and a Swedish actress known as Siri took the bombshell part. Myrna had to figure out how to retain for ensuing performances the things she'd learned; in movies you shot a scene, sometimes multiple times, but then it was over, and you moved on. She wanted the security of knowing that the props would always be placed in the same place and that her movements would always follow an established pattern. She practiced how to hold for a laugh. Also new and welcome to her was the comparative fixity of the script. "In films, you don't know what you're doing from one day to the next."[7]

In box-office terms the summer stock production of *The Marriage Go Round* at various New England and upstate New York regional theaters was a smash hit. Every performance sold out, and extra shows were added to make a grueling total of nine each week. Producer Boaty Boatwright made more money than she'd ever made before. The *New York Times* reported that the show set a new house record at the Westport Country Playhouse. "Myrna Loy was everyone's darling," said Handman. "Audiences swarmed to see her." In 1961 her fan base from the movies was still solid and seeing her "live" was a novelty.[8]

The few critics who weighed in offered qualified praise. *Variety* opined, "Myrna Loy is a deft comedienne in this first attempt at legit." The trade weekly applauded her "winning personality on stage" but also found fault, adding, "She'd be considerably better if she'd had adequate direction or if, like [Claude] Dauphin, she were experienced enough on stage to know how to . . . retain the serious undertone of a scene without abandoning the surface comedy." In subsequent years the jury came in divided on the subject of the effectiveness of Loy's theatrical voice. Some judged it an expressive instrument. Others found it wanting. "Her voice is too weak, and her stage manner is at times both lackluster and nervous," a Newark critic carped. Responding to her turn as Dona Ana opposite Ricardo Montalban in Shaw's *Don Juan in Hell,* the *Los Angeles Times* judged her reading "perfectly lucid" but "lacking in volume and self-assurance."[9]

The goal of appearing on the Broadway stage proved elusive. Alan Pakula's 1962 production of James Kirkwood's autobiographical *There Must Be a Pony* was scheduled to open at the Cort Theater in Manhattan but never did. *Dear Love,* a two-character play by James Kilty that set out to do for the letters of Robert and Elizabeth Barrett Browning what Kilty's *Dear Liar* had done for George Bernard Shaw's correspondence with Mrs. Patrick Campbell, toured all over the country but closed in New Haven, never negotiating the leap into the big time. A planned production of Alan Ayckbourn's *Relatively Speaking*, retooled for Broadway and costarring Ray Milland, failed to get off the ground, although Myrna did appear in a touring production of the play in 1978, her final year on the stage.

Myrna Loy's most enduring and wide-reaching stage success began in 1964 when she took the role of Mrs. Banks, a suburban widow, in the national tour of Mike Nichols's production of Neil Simon's *Barefoot in the Park*. Mildred Natwick played Mrs. Banks in the Broadway version and would again in the 1967 movie. The play focuses on a couple of newlyweds adjusting to life in a bare-bones walk-up apartment in New York City. Mrs. Banks is the unworldly mother of the kooky bride, Corie. With a cast that initially featured Richard Benjamin as the young husband, Paul; Joan Van Ark as Corie; and Sandor Szabo as an oddball neighbor, the *Barefoot* tour lasted more than two years and included bookings in Central City, Colorado; San Francisco; Boston; Toronto; Honolulu; and Washington. It played four sold-out weeks at the Huntington Hartford Theater in Hollywood and seven months at the Blackstone in Chicago.

The demanding tour kept a breathless pace and sometimes necessitated stopovers of only a few days. Leone Rosson met the company at many venues, helping with driving, publicity, and all kinds of personal services for her boss. A congenial woman with an intuitive feel for Myrna's needs, she would replenish supplies of hose and cosmetics, for example, knowing everything about the sizes Myrna wore and her favorite brands and colors. She freed Myrna to immerse herself in theater while at the same time getting acquainted with regions that were new to her. "I never really got a chance to see the U.S. before," she told Bob Thomas. "During all those years at MGM I was working so hard I never got a chance to travel. Now I'm making up for it."[10]

Richard Benjamin recalls that wherever they were playing, one scenario kept repeating itself. The tightly knit company would go out for dinner after a performance. Inevitably, a distinguished-looking gentleman—a different one in every town, but always with gray hair—would approach Myrna politely. He would apologize for intruding, and then tell her, "I had to tell you that I have always loved you."[11]

The *Barefoot* tour allowed Myrna to reconnect with many strands of her past. Although he never came to see the show, perhaps because he had grown quite deaf, William Powell sent her American Beauty roses wherever she had an opening. Teresa Wright came to a performance in Chicago and Rosalind Russell to one in Hollywood. Judy Garland, who never worked in a movie with Myrna but who befriended her at MGM and used to phone her at strange hours of the morning, turned up at the Huntington Hartford. Adlai Stevenson visited backstage at Chicago's Blackstone Theater. Terry Hornblow, now a practicing neurologist with a wife and a young family, attended a show, as did some of Myrna's cousins from Montana. Jeanette MacDonald turned up at a matinee. In San Francisco Myrna saw old friends who decades earlier had tried to help Jean Harlow, the Saxton Popes. Roddy McDowall sent her funny, affectionate postcards along the way. He teasingly called her "Fu" because of her part in *The Mask of Fu Manchu,* a film he once screened for friends at his home. Political allies welcomed her. In Kansas City she received a message from Harry Truman, inviting her to visit him and the Truman Library in Independence. She did, and found him frail and somewhat forlorn. While playing in Washington, she was invited to have tea at the White House with Lady Bird Johnson and lunch at the Senate with Mike Mansfield.

Myrna considered Mike Nichols a genius. She recalled that at first, during *Barefoot* rehearsals, Nora Charles "got a little in the way [of Mrs. Banks]. I felt that audiences would not accept me as a suburban matron who had not been anywhere." Having a hard time making Myrna Loy appear frumpy, Nichols agreed to let her develop the part as she wished. "We discussed it and although I was reluctant and fearful at first, I soon found that by stressing her [Mrs. Banks's] neuroses, her fear of being unloved, the woman became a very real character."[12]

The only major snag came with cast changes in Chicago, which to Myrna felt like the breakup of a family. Richard Benjamin left to undertake directing a production of *Barefoot* in London. And Christina Crawford, Joan Crawford's adopted daughter, replaced Joan Van Ark. Initially, Myrna was delighted to find herself in the same cast with the daughter of her ally from the days of *Pretty Ladies.* She hoped Joan Crawford, still a friend, would come to see the show. That never happened because Joan and Christina were not on good terms, and Myrna found Christina anything but a team player. "Christina wouldn't stand where she was supposed to, she said her line any way she wanted to, she upset everyone in the cast, especially me."[13] To complicate matters, Christina became romantically involved with the stage manager, Harvey Medlinski, whom she would marry. Medlinski allowed Christina to do as she

wished onstage. Myrna asked Richard Benjamin to come back briefly from London, hoping he could intervene. He came but to no avail.

Myrna summoned her new agent, Robert Lantz, to Chicago. After the 1962 breakup of MCA she had briefly worked with the William Morris agency but soon signed with the cultured, Berlin-born, New York–based Lantz, a highly regarded independent agent who also represented, among many others, Elizabeth Taylor, Roddy McDowall, and Mike Nichols. Lantz arrived at the Blackstone, with Neil Simon in tow. After both saw Christina Crawford perform, she was fired. Christina blamed Myrna, and the breach between them only worsened after the 1978 publication of *Mommie Dearest,* her tattletale memoir. Myrna always defended Joan Crawford and would never put her down. Despite Crawford's drinking problem, she and Joan continued to see one another for an occasional lunch in New York and to speak regularly on the phone. Following Crawford's death in 1977, Myrna attended two memorials for her, one in New York and a second, requiring a special trip to Los Angeles, that was organized by George Cukor and the Academy of Motion Picture Arts and Sciences. After the one on the West Coast Myrna wrote to Cukor, "Sorry to hear we were so rude to Christina at the Memorial—isn't it shocking!" She had refused to talk to Christina or even to be present in the same room with her just prior to the Los Angeles tribute, at which Myrna Loy spoke as Joan Crawford's oldest friend.[14]

Despite the turbulence of the Chicago run, the Blackstone Theater production of *Barefoot in the Park* enjoyed immense popularity and yielded Myrna a prize, the Sarah Siddons Award, presented annually for an outstanding performance in a Chicago theatrical production. Carol Channing and Dorothy Lamour were among those who came to cheer at the awards banquet at the Ambassador West Hotel, and the ever-devoted William Powell sent a telegram of congratulations.[15]

After the Mike Nichols production had run its course, Myrna toured a new version of *Barefoot in the Park* directed by a New England woman who would direct Myrna in future tours of other plays, Burry Fredrik. Altogether, Myrna Loy would portray Mrs. Banks close to a thousand times. The role became a mainstay, a kind of financial security blanket.

Between touring productions of *Barefoot in the Park,* Myrna's mother, Della Williams, died of pneumonia at age eighty-six, after a fall. For the last years of her life she had been living in a nursing home in the San Fernando Valley, close to the home of her problematic son, David. Chronically at the brink of financial ruin after losing his Hughes Aircraft job, David remained a thorn in his sister's side. He caused her no end of worry and grief, angering her by signing checks on Della's bank account when Della was seriously ill. On the day of Della's death Leone Rosson wrote in her diary, "Myrna called at 1:15. Had a row with David about Della. David called 10:15 [to say] that Della had passed away" (Oct. 6, 1966).

Della was cremated in North Hollywood, and Myrna carried her ashes to Helena, where a funeral took place, and Della's remains were laid to rest in Forestvale Cemetery, beside the grave of her long-dead husband. Myrna loved the site, "full of worn crosses and moss-covered stones" (*BB*, 211). She felt that the reality of death was acknowledged there, not denied as it is in a place like Forest Lawn. Her brother, David, did not go to Helena with Myrna; her lifelong friend Betty Black did. After the graveside rites Betty returned to Southern California, but Myrna lingered a while in Montana, visiting relatives in Great Falls and old haunts, including Della's portion of the Williams ranch.

At home in New York Myrna fashioned her own family. During warm weather months she visited the Handmans in Nantucket and the Robert Lantzes on Fire Island. She went every year to Farmington, Connecticut, to spend the Christmas holiday season with Terry Hornblow; his wife, Doris; and their three children. Doris would drive into Manhattan to pick her up. Like her father, and like Nora Charles, Myrna loved gift giving and always arrived piled high with packages. She was a relaxed, low-maintenance guest who would pitch in with meal preparation, read to the kids, and lounge around in her silky, quilted robe, her hair in curlers, with a turban covering them. Once some neighbors gave a party in her honor, and she put on makeup, heels, and what she called "lady clothes" and transformed herself into the glamorous Myrna Loy, working the room and charming everyone in it. In private Terry called her "Minnie," which had also been Arthur's name for her, and the children called her "Aunt Myrna."[16]

According to Terry Hornblow, Myrna continued to keep different parts of her life compartmentalized, completely separate. He didn't get to know the Handmans, Boaty Boatwright, or Estelle Linzer, all members of Myrna's Manhattan inner circle. He never met Roddy McDowall, who in her later years served as another of Myrna's surrogate sons. Roddy phoned her frequently, squired Myrna around, invited her over, checked up on her when she was ill. He wrote to her when she went on tour, telling her how much he loved her, sending her a kiss. A generous friend to many, the gay, British-born Roddy had been a child actor and, in addition to

becoming a skilled photographer, was a serious, knowledgeable film buff
with a deep appreciation for Hollywood's Golden Age. He and Myrna
worked together, on both the movie *Midnight Lace* and a 1974 telefilm,
The Elevator. He collected films and used to invite friends to screenings
at his New York home on Central Park West. He valued Myrna Loy's
achievements as a movie actress more than all of her four husbands put
together.

Through Roddy, Myrna met Sybil Burton and her then-husband
Richard, who because of Myrna's Welsh heritage liked to claim her as
one of their own. After Richard Burton married Elizabeth Taylor, Sybil
remarried and became a business partner to Roddy McDowall. Sybil
opened the trendy New York disco called Arthur, where she and Roddy
once, according to Leone Rosson's diary, hosted a party for Myrna. When
Sybil had a daughter, Amy, by second husband Jordan Christopher, Myrna
became that child's godmother. She was also godmother to Boaty Boatwright's daughter Kara Baker, born in England. Myrna went to London
for her christening.

Myrna had long enjoyed a special rapport with young people. She considered Terry and Doris Hornblow's three kids her grandchildren. She
identified with the college students who supported Eugene McCarthy's
bid for the Democratic nomination in 1968, who joined what was called
"the children's crusade." She shared their antipathy to the war in Vietnam and said that if she'd followed through on her plans to attend the
Democratic convention in Chicago, she surely would have been arrested
during the violent antiwar demonstrations. But she had to cancel her Chicago plans because at the time of the convention she was filming *The
April Fools* in Studio City. She told the TV interviewer James Day that
she was becoming more radical as she aged.[17]

Natalie Visart and Dwight Taylor's daughter Laurel, a high school student during the late 1960s, considered Myrna family and, like so many
others, called her "Aunt Myrna." Laurel recalled being "completely intoxicated by the air of female independence [Myrna] exuded" when visiting the Taylors. Myrna stood out as "the only woman of my parents'
social circle who seemed utterly complete and sufficient without a man.
I remember she had this wonderful posture that was elegant and Princess
Grace–like, but she was also like a tree rooted in the earth, nothing was
going to blow her over. To me, she was very much part of the times, ab-
sorbed by politics and the efforts to stop the Vietnam War." Laurel had
volunteered for the Eugene McCarthy campaign and had also joined a
youth group at Ethical Culture. Myrna, she recalls, "liked to talk to me

about issues as though I were an equal, encouraging my first ventures into liberal politics." When Laurel later had a baby out of wedlock, Myrna backed her decision to keep the baby and confided that she had been unable to have children. Laurel, a new mother, dropped out of college for a while and moved close to her parents. Myrna "enjoyed my beautiful baby and my Mom's delight in being a grandmother, [but] she took me aside and told me I had to get back to my studies." After Laurel returned to school and won a traveling fellowship after graduation, "Myrna was very proud of me and invited [baby] Chloe and me to stay with her in New York after we disembarked."[18]

Myrna continued to find men attractive and had a few beaus—in her autobiography she mentions George Kozel, a builder who escorted her to the Kennedy inaugural ball—but felt certain that another marriage didn't make sense. Estelle Linzer claimed that Clark Eichelberger, a diplomat who had helped in the formation of the United Nations and became the executive director of the AAUN, was in love with Myrna, but he had a wife. The marital phase of Myrna's life was over. "I'll go to bed alone with my hair in curlers and plugs in my ears." According to the writer Pope Brock, whose informant was an actor, she once at lunch advised much-married Elizabeth Taylor and Ava Gardner to consider the merits of the single life.[19]

Myrna fulfilled her dream of appearing on Broadway by playing Kim Hunter's mother in the 1973 revival of Clare Boothe Luce's *The Women,* which originally ran on Broadway nearly forty years prior, became a popular George Cukor–directed movie in 1939, and this time around showed its age. "Now it is not so new and not so naughty," Clive Barnes wrote in the *New York Times.* All about the catfights and backstabbings of a passel of upper-crust women defined by their men, *The Women* had little to say to New York audiences in the era of Gloria Steinem and closed after sixty-three performances. The all-star cast, which included Alexis Smith, Dorothy Loudon, and Rhonda Fleming, as well as Kim Hunter, received an award for ensemble acting and functioned as a working cooperative. All of the name players received the same salary and equal billing. Myrna took on the offstage role of company mother hen, clucking over the well-being of her brood. Safety was a worry, since the cast had to negotiate a production mounted on moving platforms.[20]

Backstage drama brewed during tryouts in Philadelphia. Lainie Kazan, a voluptuous brunette whose career as a singer and actress was just getting started, had been cast in a nonsinging role as the husband-stealing shopgirl Crystal, the role played by Joan Crawford in the Cukor movie. As written and conceived by Clare Boothe Luce, Crystal is a blonde. Lainie Kazan had agreed to wear a blonde wig but found that the masquerade made her feel ridiculous. With her olive complexion, "I looked like a Puerto Rican hooker." Convinced that the wig was sabotaging the authenticity of her performance, she begged for permission to remove it. Luce said no, refusing to revise her vision of Crystal. Lainie Kazan was abruptly fired and replaced. Myrna did everything in her power to support the devastated, cast-off actress. "She took me aside and told me I was talented and beautiful and that my being fired had nothing to do with me." In the eyes of Lainie Kazan, Myrna Loy remains "one of the kindest, most generous people I've ever known."[21]

Shortly before she appeared in *The Women,* Myrna agreed to submit to a public interview conducted by her friend and publicist John Springer in Manhattan's Town Hall as part of his Legendary Ladies of the Movies series. Myrna had attended Springer's interview with Bette Davis, who took questions called out spontaneously from members of the audience. She wanted none of that, insisting that she would only answer questions that had been submitted in writing and screened in advance. She needed to feel in control, so that was the protocol Springer followed, although he couldn't keep Lillian Gish from calling out, "Myrna Loy, what a joy!" Inevitably, during the question-and-answer period someone in the audience asked about her relationship with William Powell. Myrna told the crowd that she had visited him in Palm Springs the previous summer (their last encounter, as it turned out) and that they had reminisced together and "cried a lot." Springer, who qualified as a film historian and writer, preceded his interview with clips from fifteen Loy films, ranging from *The Squall* to *From the Terrace.* He knew Myrna well and would later write insightfully about her in his book about actresses of the 1930s, *They Had Faces Then.* In it he hailed Myrna Loy as the only actress who played leading roles in movies in every decade from the 1920s through the 1970s. She proved, he wrote, that it is possible to be "warm and cool all at once."[22]

Although she never established herself as a major Broadway player, Myrna became part of the vibrant New York theater scene through her involvement with the American Place Theatre, which she helped Wynn Handman to found and for which she served as board member and trustee. At board meetings Handman relied on Myrna's sound judgment and total commitment. Handman's mission was to create a nonprofit theater devoted to producing plays by living American playwrights who

worked outside the commercial mainstream. The American Place Theatre's original home was a Gothic church, St. Clement's, in Hell's Kitchen,
which one of the founders, Sidney Lanier, an Episcopalian minister, helped
to secure.

At the Founder's Reception in 1963 at the home of Mr. and Mrs.
Ronald Tree, Robert Lowell, whose play *The Old Glory* would be the
debut production for the new venture, read three of his poems. Robert
Penn Warren also read some of his poetry, and Myrna read an excerpt
from Gertrude Stein's piece about Alfred Stieglitz, "If Anything Is Done,"
which included the words "an American place."[23]

Kennedy's assassination occurred the day after the Founder's Recep-
tion. It shocked and horrified everyone. The very first event staged by the
American Place Theatre turned out to be a memorial service at which
Robert Lowell and a shivering Tennessee Williams, who belonged to the
American Place board, read poetry. Myrna recited Emily Dickinson's "Af-
ter great pain a formal feeling comes" (*BB*, 316).

Over the years the American Place helped launch some distinguished
actors, including Dustin Hoffman, Frank Langella, and Faye Dunaway.
It introduced plays written by Sam Shepard, Ed Bullins, Anne Sexton,
and Joyce Carol Oates, among many others. Its most celebrated production was probably William Alfred's *Hogan's Goat,* which resulted in
awards for William Alfred and featured Faye Dunaway. It led to Dunaway's first Hollywood contract. Eventually the American Place moved
to its own theater in an upscale building, which proved costly and un-
sustainable. It found more humble quarters and as of this writing remains
a going concern, now mainly devoted to performances in schools.

Myrna Loy took on her last screen roles because they promised her a
chance to perform surrounded by talent she admired. She accepted the
part of another tippling old lady in *Airport 1975,* for instance, because
Bill Frye, a friend who had produced her TV movie *The Elevator,* promised she would have a scene with the brilliantly manic Sid Caesar. Caesar's shyness in her presence surprised her; improvising with him proved
to be hard work (*BB,* 346). In some ways *Airport 1975* is a descendant
of Myrna's earlier aviation films like *Night Flight* and *Too Hot to Handle.*
Stunt flying and near-disaster still promised excellent box office. *Airport
1975,* which today plays like an inadvertent comedy, grossed more than
$47 million. It was the inspiration for the 1980 spoof *Airplane.*

Although Myrna Loy appeared in only one scene of the 1978 black
comedy *The End,* she performed it opposite Pat O'Brien, with whom

she'd last worked in 1931 in *Consolation Marriage*. They played the dotty, aged parents of the star and director, Burt Reynolds, who took the role of Sonny, a handsome loser who's been told by doctors that he has a rare blood disease and has only a few months left to live. In their absurdist scene the geriatric parents remain cheerfully indifferent to their distraught son, who plans to rob their medicine cabinet of sleeping pills to help him commit suicide. The mother (Loy) would rather watch television, the father (O'Brien) paint by numbers, than respond to Sonny or, indeed, show any sign of life at all other than as human robots. When Reynolds plants an affectionate kiss on his mother's cheek, she looks genuinely startled. Myrna couldn't get enough of Burt Reynolds's affection and teasing banter. The attention of a young hunk with a good sense of humor delighted her. He would take her out for dinner when he came to New York and call her Mom.

Seventy-five-year-old Myrna jumped at a substantial role in *Just Tell Me What You Want*, a comedy directed by the respected New York–based Sidney Lumet, who started out as a child actor in the Yiddish theater and went on to distinguish himself at the helm of such films as *12 Angry Men*, *Dog Day Afternoon*, and *Network*. Myrna found him an interesting and accomplished workaholic who meticulously planned every camera angle and never stopped going. As William Wyler had done prior to shooting *The Best Years of Our Lives*, Lumet rehearsed the actors as if they were preparing a play. Lumet considered Myrna Loy one of the greats, an actress whose power derived from what she held back. In her performances, he said, "you can feel ten things she's not showing for the one detail you can see" (*BB*, ix).

Just Tell Me What You Want tells the story of a brash, hard-charging New York tycoon, Max Herschel (Alan King), who doesn't care how he gets what he wants so long as he gets it. His young, glamorous mistress and colleague, TV producer Bones Burton (Ali MacGraw), matches him in nervy ambition. She turns him into a blubbering crybaby when she marries a playwright (Peter Weller) who is younger and prettier than Max. Myrna Loy as Max's tart-tongued, all-knowing, ever-reliable executive secretary, Stella Liberti, sees through her boss and sasses him but panders to him nevertheless. She has all the phone numbers and addresses at her command, and Max can't make a move without her.

Alan King, funny and totally convincing as in-your-face Max, endeared himself to Myrna by telling her his dream as a kid had been to play Nick to her Nora. He took to calling her "Nora." According to Myrna, Ali MacGraw needed a lot of reassurance about her acting, which Myrna willingly provided. Warner Bros. disappointed one and all by pulling the movie from distribution after just two weeks.

Myrna's last major role was in a made-for-television film in which she starred opposite Henry Fonda. *Summer Solstice* was TV's answer to the successful feature film *On Golden Pond,* which Fonda had just completed opposite Katharine Hepburn. Myrna liked, admired, and politically saw eye to eye with Fonda, but they had never worked together. In *Summer Solstice* they are poignant and tender as a timeworn couple looking back on fifty years of a marriage that has been anything but tranquil. Husband and wife each took lovers, and their son drowned in childhood. Now they are wistfully gentle as they recall scenes from the past. Stephen Collins and Lindsay Crouse portrayed their younger selves. "You're more beautiful than ever," Fonda tells white-wigged Loy as he caresses her lined face. "Wrinkles," she answers, truthfully. "I worked hard to put those there," he says.

"Mr. Fonda and Miss Loy turn the older couple into a truly memorable portrait," wrote the TV critic John O'Connor in the *New York Times.* "He is craggy, seemingly distant, but clearly passionate. She is serene, seemingly passive, but totally devoted. Acting together for the first time in their careers, Mr. Fonda and Miss Loy demonstrate splendidly why they remain stars."[24]

On her eightieth birthday Myrna learned that after twenty-eight years of marriage Terry Hornblow was divorcing his wife, Doris, who with their children had provided Myrna with a loving extended family and a feeling of bedrock stability. Leone Rosson wrote in her diary, "Myrna was upset about Terry and Doris divorcing and about being eighty. She had an awful day" (Aug. 2, 1985).

One of the activities that helped sustain Myrna through the difficult 1980s was working on her autobiography with friend and writer James Kotsilibas-Davis, a former New Englander whom she first met when he interviewed her for an article in *Life* magazine in 1968. The original book contract was signed with Coward McCann in 1980, but Myrna didn't want to collaborate on the kind of kiss-and-tell memoir her first editor and publisher had in mind. She and Kotsilibas-Davis moved to Knopf, which supported the substantial book she did want to create. Jim Kotsilibas-Davis did all the writing. What Myrna did was talk and talk, allowing her memory to be prodded by the many interviews Kotsilibas-Davis conducted with Myrna's friends and colleagues. Kotsilibas-Davis also incorporated quotes from interviews Myrna had given to previous interviewers, culled from clippings. He traveled with Myrna to Los Angeles in May of 1981, revisiting her remaining friends there and past haunts. They had lunch together at the MGM commissary, along with Myrna's manager, Mimi Weber (who now lived in Los Angeles), George Cukor, David Chasman (MGM's vice president in charge of production), and Sam Marx, the man who had purchased screen rights for *The Thin Man*. This was a nostalgic, emotion-drenched visit. Myrna had not set foot on the MGM lot since 1947's *Song of the Thin Man*. William Powell, who rarely left Palm Springs these days, was much in Myrna's thoughts. He would die at age ninety-one in 1984, beloved by Myrna till the last.

At MGM Cary Grant emerged from a board meeting to greet them. Her next and final encounter with Grant would come the following year when she attended a Friars Club roast of him, hosted by Frank Sinatra at the Waldorf-Astoria. She sent him one of her rare surviving letters, addressing him as "Dear, dear Cary." She wrote, "I enjoyed every accolade for you and didn't blame you for weeping a bit. I was trying to get word to you to say blow your nose, and your voice will clear a bit. Of course you would have been *horrified* at the idea. I was proudest of all. Thank you dear—you look divine and I wish your mother could have been there."[25]

Myrna and Jim Kotsilibas-Davis flew together from Los Angeles to Montana and spent a week there, in Radersburg and Helena. Kotsilibas-Davis said, "That trip gave me more of a sense of Myrna than anything. We saw the whole world she came from, that feeling of vastness and cleanliness and integrity."[26]

Helena would later honor her with a performing arts center named the Myrna Loy Center, housed in what used to be the Lewis and Clark County Jail, an imposing granite structure. As a girl, Myrna had been afraid to walk anywhere near that building, and she was amused but pleased when the planners, led by Arnie Malina, asked for permission to use her name. Open since 1997, the center thrives today as a venue for movie screenings, theater, concerts, and dance performances, with prison bars still affixed to the windows and vintage Myrna Loy photos adorning the walls of the inside lobby. The sidewalk in front of the center, inscribed with the names of donors, includes the names Paul Newman and Joanne Woodward.

Myrna and Jim Kotsilibas-Davis spent countless hours together during the six years it took to complete *Being and Becoming*. The sessions of reminiscing at times became wrenching for Myrna. "There were many days when Myrna would break down and cry," Kotsilibas-Davis recalled. Myrna said, "Going through my past was like intense psychotherapy."[27]

The American Place Theatre celebrated the publication of *Being and Becoming* with a benefit gala that also marked the theater group's fifteenth anniversary. The humorist Cynthia Heimel put together a program of Myrna Loy film clips titled "When in Doubt, Act like Myrna Loy," a celebration of her style and savoir faire. "Who else could play poker with the boys in the baggage car and never remove her hat?" The gala's guest list included Harry Belafonte, Betty Comden, Jules Feiffer, Carrie Fisher, Adolph Green, Helen Hayes, Anne Jackson, Penny Marshall, Roddy McDowall, Phyllis Newman, Maureen O'Sullivan, Tony Randall, Calvin Trillin, and Joanne Woodward. They all watched the scene in *After the Thin Man* where Nora cajoles a groggy Nick into dragging himself out of bed to cook her some scrambled eggs. They all heard Wynn Handman say, "Myrna Loy's legacy is her total honesty, her irresistible charm, her great sense of humor, a delicate touch, her dignity as a woman."[28]

A long overdue tribute from the Academy of Motion Picture Arts and Sciences arrived with a gala at Carnegie Hall in January of 1985. Although several films she appeared in had been honored with awards or nominations, no Myrna Loy performance had ever been singled out by the Academy, and that hurt. Robert Osborne conjectures that "the reason she never won a competitive Oscar or nomination is because she was *never* bad. She didn't do the bad work that makes good work look better." Until 1970, when she presented the Academy Award for Best Director to Jon Voight, who accepted for John Schlesinger for *Midnight Cowboy*, she had never even been chosen to participate as an Oscar presenter. Robert Osborne suggests that her exclusion was due to Arthur Freed's antipathy to her politics. Only after Freed stopped producing the telecasts was she asked to participate.[29]

As she approached her eightieth birthday, the Academy president, Gene Allen, and the program coordinator, Douglas Edwards, began planning the tribute to be held at Carnegie Hall, with a prior reception at the Russian Tea Room and a party afterward at the Waldorf-Astoria. The Academy spokesmen explained, "We thought Myrna Loy deserved this kind of event, given her time in the industry and the consistency of her talent." Betty Comden and Adolph Green wrote the script for the tribute, which Lauren Bacall hosted. Bacall told the crowd that she admired Myrna Loy "as a person, an actress and a face, but also as a woman aware of what went on in the country and world. She is not a frivolous human being. And she's a great wit, which I'm a sucker for."[30]

To select the clips that would be shown, Douglas Edwards screened fifty-five Loy films and chose excerpts from twenty-two of them. The evening's coup would be a screening of *The Animal Kingdom*, all of it, featuring Myrna Loy as the stunning but soulless wife of Leslie Howard. It had not been shown in New York since 1932, had been missing for decades, and had been tagged a lost film. The film historian Ronald Haver rediscovered it, and the UCLA Film Archive restored it.

From the stage, before the screening, Maureen Stapleton told about the time she asked to borrow Myrna Loy's lipstick and then realized that the lipstick had touched lips that had kissed Clark Gable, Spencer Tracy, Fredric March, and William Powell. Lena Horne came forward to hail the guest of honor for living "a useful, purposeful life," for being "aware of the problems of others and ready to do something about them. To look like that and be like that—that's a great woman. I salute you, Madam." Miss Loy herself, fragile but resplendent in a sequined gown, cradled long-stemmed red roses and stood up from her dress circle seat to acknowledge tumultuous applause. Among those who joined the ovation were Lillian Gish, Joseph L. Mankiewicz, Sidney Lumet, Robert Mitchum, Maureen O'Sullivan, Tony Randall, Burt Reynolds, Sylvia Sidney, Harold Russell (the double amputee who portrayed Homer in *The Best Years of Our Lives*), and Teresa Wright (*BB*, ix–x).

It took another five years for the Academy to finally, during the 63rd Annual Academy Awards for 1990, bestow an honorary Oscar for Lifetime Achievement. Anjelica Huston, whose father, John, had worked with Myrna on the Committee for the First Amendment and whose grandfather Walter had appeared with her in *The Prizefighter and the Lady,* presented it, praising Loy's "sweet way with a sharp line." No longer strong enough to travel, Myrna was shown by satellite from her New York apartment, saying simply, "You've made me very happy. Thank you very much."[31]

Earlier, in 1988, Anjelica Huston and Senator Ted Kennedy had sat at Myrna's table at the dinner that followed the Kennedy Center Honors, when Loy was one of five honorees. Robby Lantz, who years back had been Nancy Davis's agent, escorted Myrna; Walter Cronkite served as master of ceremonies for the awards presentation; and Kathleen Turner introduced Myrna Loy's segment. At the White House reception, Ronald Reagan, whose presidency Myrna Loy vociferously opposed, called her "lovely and mysterious," extolling her "great ease and comfort, as though she were possessed of answers to questions you hadn't even thought of asking in the first place." When the Kennedy Center Awards were broadcast on CBS television two weeks later, Myrna watched them from her Lenox Hill hospital bed, with Wynn and Bobbie Handman beside her.[32]

Myrna never liked talking about her illnesses. Hers pursued and tormented her far too long. In the 1970s she survived two mastectomies and underwent chemotherapy. In subsequent years she was admitted to Lenox Hill Hospital repeatedly, enduring treatment for two other forms of cancer (bowel cancer and squamous cell carcinoma of the nose), fractures, neurological problems that affected her balance, and heart disease. Her acting days were over by the time she turned eighty, but she carried on, supported by a full-time helper, Cynthia Hill; by devoted and attentive friends; and by a physician, Dr. Naham Winer, who with his entire family had adopted her as one of their own.

She clung to life beyond her capacity to enjoy, or even to remember, it. Her memory began to fail around the time her autobiography appeared. After a party celebrating that event, coming home in a taxi she shared with Miles Kreuger, a historian of musicals who was a friend of the party host Jim Kotsilibas-Davis, she couldn't recall her own address to give to the cab driver.[33]

She died during surgery at Lenox Hill Hospital on December 14, 1993. "Myrna Loy, Model of Urbanity in 'The Thin Man' Roles, Dies at 88," ran the headline to a lengthy obituary in the *New York Times*.[34]

Fewer than fifty people attended her underpublicized memorial at the Campbell Funeral Chapel in New York. No member of the Hornblow family had been informed of the event, and none attended. Myrna's will, however, bequeathed the contents of her apartment to Terry and made his three children major beneficiaries of her estate.

In his eulogy Roddy McDowall told the mourners—who included Alan King; the Handmans; Lawrence Quirk; Betty Comden; James Kotsilibas-Davis; the family of her physician, Dr. Nahum Winer; John, June, and Gary Springer; the actress Jan Miner; Estelle Linzer; and Alan Pakula—that Myrna Loy had no surviving immediate family. (Her brother, David, had died in 1983.) He acknowledged Myrna's friends Estelle Linzer and Robbie and Sherlee Lantz, as well as her caregivers Cynthia Hill and Lorna David. He recalled Myrna as "one of the least vain people I have ever met," a woman "full of waltzing gentility," a "flirtatious American-Edwardian" who carried off "a wry mix of romance and reserve. There was no tone like her baccarat crystal laugh." He confessed, "Her love provides one of the golden threads in the tapestry of my life."[35]

When Robert Lantz took the podium, he spoke of how bracing he found it that Myrna's "rueful acceptance of human shortcomings was untainted by sanctimony, that her attentive, intelligent curiosity was never intrusive, that her crystalline wit had no wounding edge. She was the screen's most approachable sophisticate, an aristocrat who knew neither snobbery nor disdain." She never became a boring matron, he said, "because there was a touch of the tousled in her immaculately groomed person. She was the Grand Copain of movies and of those who were blessed to know her."[36]

No memorial for her took place in Los Angeles, nor is there any sort of marker for her there, other than the replica of the 1922 statue of her as "Inspiration" at Venice High School. Her ashes are interred near the graves of her parents in Helena's Forestvale Cemetery, under the capacious dome of the Montana sky.

For all her generosity of spirit, Myrna Loy shunned halos. John Ford's "only good girl in Hollywood" remains an embodiment of buoyancy, companionability, engagement with the world, elegant urbanity, cool affection, and wry humor. She once said of herself, "If you want to know the secret of the perfect wife I played, well, she was really a rascal—just like me."[37]

Myrna Loy's Film, Television, and Theater Credits

FEATURE FILMS

1. *Pretty Ladies*

Sept. 6, 1925; six reels, silent, b&w.

Directed by Monta Bell; produced and distributed by MGM.

Cast: ZaSu Pitts (Maggie Keenan), Tom Moore (Al Cassidy), Ann Pennington (Herself), Lilyan Tashman (Selma Larson), Bernard Randall (Aaron Savage), Conrad Nagel (Maggie's dream lover), Norma Shearer (Frances White), Lucille Le Sueur (Bobby), Roy D'Arcy (Paul Thompson), Lew Harvey (Will Rogers), Jimmie Quinn (Eddie Cantor); ML as uncredited chorus girl.

2. *Satan in Sables*

Nov. 14, 1925; eight reels, silent, b&w.

Directed by James Flood; produced and distributed by Warner Bros. Pictures.

Cast: Lowell Sherman (Michael Lyev Yervedoff), John Harron (Paul Yervedoff), Pauline Garon (Colette Breton), Gertrude Astor (Dolores Sierra), Frank Butler (Victor), Francis McDonald (Émile); ML was inserted into a scene with Lowell Sherman.

3. *Sporting Life*

Nov. 29, 1925; seven reels, silent, b&w.

Directed by Maurice Tourneur; produced by Carl Laemmle/Universal Jewel; distributed by Universal Pictures.

Compiled with the assistance of Karie Bible.

Cast: Bert Lytell (Lord Woodstock), Marian Nixon (Norah Cavanaugh), Paulette Duval (Olive Carteret), Cyril Chadwick (Phillips), Charles Delaney (Joe Lee), George Siegmann (Dan Crippen), Oliver Eckhardt (Cavanaugh), Ted "Kid" Lewis (Boxer); ML in uncredited role as chorus girl.

4. *Ben-Hur (abbreviated credits)*

Dec. 30, 1925; twelve reels (128–29 min.), silent, b&w (with Technicolor sequence).

Directed by Fred Niblo; produced by (in arrangement with) Abraham L. Erlanger, Charles B. Dillingham, and Florenz Ziegfeld Jr.; produced and distributed by MGM.

Cast: Ramon Novarro (Judah Ben-Hur, also known as Arrius the Younger), Francis X. Bushman (Messala), May McAvoy (Esther), Betty Bronson (Mary), Claire McDowell (Miriam Princess of Hur), Carmel Myers (Iras); ML plays bacchante as part of the general's harem. Her scene was cut and survives only in a still.

5. *The Wanderer*

Feb. 1, 1926; nine reels, silent, b&w.

Directed by Raoul Walsh; produced by Famous Players-Lasky, Adolph Zukor, and Jesse L. Lasky; distributed by Paramount Pictures.

Cast: Greta Nissen (Tisha), William Collier Jr. (Jether), Ernest Torrence (Tola), Wallace Beery (Pharis), [Frederick] Tyrone Power (Jesse), Kathryn Hill (Naomi), Kathlyn Williams (Huldah), Snitz Edwards (Jeweler); ML has bit as dancer in orgy scene.

6. *The Caveman*

Feb. 6, 1926; seven reels, silent, b&w.

Directed by Lewis Milestone; produced and distributed by Warner Bros. Pictures.

Cast: Matt Moore (Mike Smagg), Marie Prevost (Myra Gaylord), John Patrick (Brewster Bradford), Myrna Loy (Maid), Phyllis Haver (Dolly Van Dream), Hedda Hopper (Mrs. Van Dream).

7. *The Love Toy*

Feb. 13, 1926; six reels, silent, b&w.

Directed by Erle C. Kenton; produced and distributed by Warner Bros. Pictures.

Cast: Lowell Sherman (Peter Remsen), Jane Winton (The Bride), Willard Louis (King Lavoris), Gayne Whitman (Prime Minister), Ethel Grey Terry (Queen Zita), Helene Costello (Princess Patricia), Maude George (Lady in waiting); ML has bit as dancer.

8. *The Gilded Highway*

March 13, 1926; seven reels, silent, b&w.

Directed by J. Stuart Blackton; produced and distributed by Warner Bros. Pictures.

Cast: Dorothy Devore (Primrose Welby), John Harron (Jack Welby), Maclyn Arbuckle (Jonathan Welby), Myrna Loy (Irene Quartz), Florence Turner (Mrs. Welby), Sheldon Lewis (Uncle Nicholas Welby), Andrée Tourneur (Annabel).

9. *Why Girls Go Back Home*

March 27, 1926; six reels, silent, b&w.

Directed by James Flood; produced and distributed by Warner Bros. Pictures.

Cast: Patsy Ruth Miller (Marie Downey), Clive Brook (Clifford Dudley), Jane Winton (A Model), Myrna Loy (Sally Short), George O'Hara (John Ross), Joseph Dowling (Joe Downey).

10. *The Exquisite Sinner*

March 28, 1926; six reels, silent, b&w.

Directed by Phil Rosen, who replaced Josef von Sternberg; produced by MGM. Shelved before distribution.

Cast: Conrad Nagel (Dominique Prad), Renée Adorée (The Gypsy Maid, Silda), Paulette Duval (Yvonne), Frank Currier (Colonel), George K. Arthur (His Orderly), Matthew Betz (The Gypsy Chief, Secchi), Helena D'Algy and Claire Du Brey (Dominique's sisters), Myrna Loy (The Living Statue).

11. *So This Is Paris*

July 31, 1926; seven reels, silent, b&w.

Directed by Ernst Lubitsch; produced and distributed by Warner Bros. Pictures.

Cast: Monte Blue (Dr. Eisenstein), Patsy Ruth Miller (Rosalind Eisenstein), Lilyan Tashman (Adela, a dancer), André Beranger (Alfred, her husband), Myrna Loy (Maid), Sidney D'Albrook (Cop).

12. *Don Juan*

Aug. 6, 1926 (New York premiere); Feb. 19, 1927 (general release); ten reels, first Vitaphone film with synchronized sound effects and musical score, b&w.

Directed by Alan Crosland; produced and distributed by Warner Bros. Pictures.

Cast: John Barrymore (Don Juan/Don José), Mary Astor (Adriana Della Varnese), Willard Louis (Pedrillo), Estelle Taylor (Lucretia Borgia), Helene Costello (Rena, Adriana's maid), Myrna Loy (Maia, Lucretia's maid).

13. *Across the Pacific*

Oct. 2, 1926; seven reels, silent, b&w.

Directed by Roy Del Ruth; produced and distributed by Warner Bros. Pictures.

Cast: Monte Blue (Monte), Jane Winton (Claire Marsh), Myrna Loy (Roma), Charles Stevens (Aguinaldo), Tom Wilson (Tom, Monte's servant), Walter McGrail (Captain Grover).

14. *Millionaires*

Nov. 13, 1926; seven reels, silent, b&w.

Directed by Herman C. Raymaker; produced and distributed by Warner Bros. Pictures.

Cast: George Sidney (Meyer Rubens), Louise Fazenda (Reba), Vera Gordon (Esther Rubens), Nat Carr (Maurice), Helene Costello (Ida), Arthur Lubin (Lew), Jane Winton (Lottie); ML an uncredited bit player.

15. *The Third Degree*

Dec. 25, 1926; eight reels, silent, b&w.

Directed by Michael Curtiz; produced and distributed by Warner Bros. Pictures.

Cast: Dolores Costello (Annie Daly), Louise Dresser (Alicia Daly), Rockliffe Fellowes (Underwood), Jason Robards (Howard Jeffries Jr.), Kate Price (Mrs. Chubb), Tom Santschi ("Daredevil Daly"); ML an uncredited bit player.

16. *Finger Prints*

Jan. 8, 1927; seven reels, silent, b&w.

Directed by Lloyd Bacon; produced and distributed by Warner Bros. Pictures.

Cast: Louise Fazenda (Dora Traynor), John T. Murray (Homer Fairchild), Helene Costello (Jacqueline Norton), Myrna Loy (The Vamp), George Nichols (S. V. Sweeney), Martha Mattox (Mother Malone), Franklin Pangborn (The Bandoline Kid).

17. *When a Man Loves*

Feb. 3, 1927 (New York premiere); Aug. 21, 1927 (general release); ten reels, silent, b&w.

Directed by Alan Crosland; produced and distributed by Warner Bros. Pictures.

Cast: John Barrymore (Chevalier Fabien des Grieux), Dolores Costello (Manon Lescaut), Warner Oland (André Lescaut), Sam De Grasse (Comte Guillot de Morfontaine), Holmes Herbert (Jean Tiberge), Stuart Holmes (Louis XV, King of France), Marcelle Corday (Marie); ML in bit role as prostitute.

18. *Bitter Apples*

April 23, 1927; six reels, silent, b&w. (ML's first star billing)

Directed by Harry O. Hoyt; produced and distributed by Warner Bros. Pictures.

Cast: Monte Blue (John Wyncote), Myrna Loy (Belinda White), Paul Ellis (Stefani Blanco), Charles Hill Mailes (Cyrus Thornden), Sidney De Grey (Joseph Blanco).

19. *The Climbers*

May 14, 1927; seven reels, silent, b&w.

Directed by Paul L. Stein; produced and distributed by Warner Bros. Pictures.

Cast: Irene Rich (Duchess of Arrogan), Clyde Cook (Pancho Mendoza), Forrest Stanley (Duke Córdova/El Blanco), Flobelle Fairbanks (Laska, the Duchess's daughter), Myrna Loy (Countess Veya), Anders Randolf (Martínez).

20. *Simple Sis*

June 11, 1927; seven reels, silent, b&w.

Directed by Herman C. Raymaker; produced and distributed by Warner Bros. Pictures.

Cast: Louise Fazenda (Sis), Clyde Cook (Jerry O'Grady), Myrna Loy (Edith Van), William Demarest (Oscar), Billy Kent Schaeffer (Buddy), Cathleen Calhoun (Mrs. Brown, Buddy's mother).

21. *The Heart of Maryland*

July 23, 1927; six reels, silent, b&w.

Directed by Lloyd Bacon; produced and distributed by Warner Bros. Pictures.

Cast: Dolores Costello (Maryland Calvert), Jason Robards (Maj. Alan Kendrick), Warner Richmond (Capt. Fulton Thorpe), Helene Costello (Nancy), Carroll Nye (Lloyd Calvert), Charles Edward Bull (Abraham Lincoln), Orpha Alba (Mammy), Myrna Loy (Mulatta).

22. *A Sailor's Sweetheart*

Sept. 24, 1927; six reels, silent, b&w.

Directed by Lloyd Bacon; produced and distributed by Warner Bros. Pictures.

Cast: Louise Fazenda (Cynthia Botts), Clyde Cook (Sandy MacTavish), Myrna Loy (Claudette Ralston), William Demarest (Detective), John Miljan (Mark Krisel), Dorothea Wolbert (Lena Svenson), Tom Ricketts (Professor Meekham).

23. *The Jazz Singer*

Oct. 6, 1927 (New York premiere); Feb. 4, 1928 (general release); nine reels (90 min.), silent with sound and talking sequences, musical score and sound effects by Vitaphone, b&w.

Directed by Alan Crosland; produced by the Vitaphone Corporation / Warner Bros. Pictures; distributed by Warner Bros. Pictures.

Cast: Al Jolson (Jakie Rabinowitz, also known as Jack Robin), May McAvoy (Mary Dale), Warner Oland (The Cantor "Papa" Rabinowitz), Eugenie Besserer (Sara "Mama" Rabinowitz), Bobby Gordon (Jakie, at age thirteen), Otto Lederer (Moisha Yudelson [The Kibbitzer]), Richard Tucker (Harry Lee); ML in bit role as chorus girl.

24. *The Girl from Chicago*

Nov. 19, 1927; six reels, silent, b&w.

Directed by Ray Enright; produced and distributed by Warner Bros. Pictures.

Cast: Conrad Nagel (Handsome Joe), Myrna Loy (Mary Carlton), William Russell ("Big Steve" Drummond), Carroll Nye (Bob Carlton), Paul Panzer (Dopey), Erville Alderson (Colonel Carlton).

25. *If I Were Single*

Dec. 17, 1927; seven reels, silent, b&w.

Directed by Roy Del Ruth; produced and distributed by Warner Bros. Pictures.

Cast: May McAvoy (May Howard), Conrad Nagel (Ted Howard), Myrna Loy (Joan), André Beranger (Claude).

26. *Ham and Eggs at the Front*

Dec. 24, 1927; six reels, silent, b&w.

Directed by Roy Del Ruth; produced and distributed by Warner Bros. Pictures.

Cast: Tom Wilson (Ham), Heinie Conklin (Eggs), Myrna Loy (Fifi), William J. Irving (Von Friml), Noah Young (Sergeant), Louise Fazenda (Cally Brown).

27. *Beware of Married Men*

Jan. 14, 1928; six reels, silent with sound sequences and music score by Vitaphone, also a silent version, b&w.

Directed by Archie Mayo; produced and distributed by Warner Bros. Pictures.

Cast: Irene Rich (Myra Martin), Clyde Cook (Botts), Audrey Ferris (Helene Martin), Myrna Loy (Juanita Sheldon), Richard Tucker (Leonard Gilbert), Stuart Holmes (Huntley Sheldon), Hugh Allan (Ralph).

28. *What Price Beauty?*

Jan. 22, 1928 (filmed in 1925); five reels, silent, b&w.

Directed by Thomas Buckingham; produced by Natacha Rambova and S. George Ullman; distributed by Pathé Exchange, Inc.

Cast: Nita Naldi (Rita Rinaldi), Pierre Gendron (John Clay), Virginia Pearson (Mary), Dolores Johnson, Myrna Loy (Vamp), Sally Winters.

29. *A Girl in Every Port*

Feb. 26, 1928; six reels, silent, b&w.

Directed by Howard Hawks; produced by William Fox for Fox Film Corp.; distributed by Fox Film Corp.

Cast: Victor McLaglen (Spike Madden), Maria Casajuana (Chiquita), Natalie Joyce (Girl in Panama), Dorothy Mathews (Girl in Panama), Elena Jurado (Girl in Panama), Louise Brooks (Marie, girl in France), Francis McDonald (Gang leader), Leila Hyams (The sailor's wife), Robert Armstrong (Salami), Sally Rand (Girl in Bombay); ML in uncredited bit as (Girl in the Orient).

30. *Turn Back the Hours*

March 12, 1928; six reels, silent, b&w.

Directed by Howard Bretherton; produced by Sam Sax, Gotham Productions; distributed by Lumas Film Corp.

Cast: Myrna Loy (Tiza Torreon), Walter Pidgeon (Phillip Drake), Sam Hardy ("Ace" Kearney), George Stone ("Limey" Stokes), Sheldon Lewis ("Breed"), Josef Swickard (Colonel Torreon).

31. *The Crimson City*

April 7, 1928; six reels, silent, b&w.

Directed by Archie Mayo; produced and distributed by Warner Bros. Pictures.

Cast: Myrna Loy (Onoto), John Miljan (Gregory Kent), Leila Hyams (Nadine Howells), Matthew Betz ("Dagger" Foo), Anders Randolf (Major Howells), Sojin (Sing Yoy), Anna May Wong (Su), Richard Tucker (Richard Brand).

32. *Pay as You Enter*

May 12, 1928; five reels, silent with sound sequences and music score by Vitaphone, also a silent version, b&w.

Directed by Lloyd Bacon; produced and distributed by Warner Bros. Pictures.

Cast: Louise Fazenda (Mary Smith), Clyde Cook (Clyde Jones), William Demarest ("Terrible Bill" McGovern), Myrna Loy (Yvonne de Russo).

33. *State Street Sadie*

Aug. 25, 1928; seven reels, silent with musical score and talking sequences by Vitaphone, also a silent version (nine reels), b&w.

Directed by Archie Mayo; produced and distributed by Warner Bros.

Cast: Conrad Nagel (Ralph Blake), Myrna Loy (Isobel/State Street Sadie), William Russell ("The Bat"), Georgie Stone (Slinkey), Pat Hartigan ("The Bull").

34. *The Midnight Taxi*

Sept. 1, 1928; six reels, Vitaphone sound, also silent version Oct. 3, 1928, b&w.

Directed by John G. Adolfi; produced and distributed by Warner Bros. Pictures.

Cast: Antonio Moreno (Tony Driscoll), Helene Costello (Nan Parker), Myrna Loy (Gertie Fairfax), William Russell (Joseph Brant), Tommy Dugan (Al Corvini), Bobby Agnew (Jack Madison), Pat Hartigan (Detective Blake).

35. *Fancy Baggage*

Jan. 26, 1929; eight reels, sound with Vitaphone talking sequences, musical score, sound effects, also silent version Feb. 23, 1929, b&w.

Directed by John G. Adolfi; produced and distributed by Warner Bros. Pictures.

Cast: Audrey Ferris (Naomi Iverson), Myrna Loy (Myrna), George Fawcett (Iverson), Hallam Cooley (Dickey), Wallace MacDonald (Ernest Hardin), Edmund Breese (John Hardin), Eddie Gribbon (Steve), Burr McIntosh (Austin).

36. *Hardboiled Rose*

March 30, 1929; six reels, silent with Vitaphone talking sequences, musical score, sound effects, also silent version May 4, 1929, b&w.

Directed by F. Harmon Weight; produced and distributed by Warner Bros. Pictures.

Cast: Myrna Loy (Rose Duhamel), William Collier Jr. (Edward Malo), John Miljan (Steve Wallace), Gladys Brockwell (Julie Malo), Lucy Beaumont (Grandmama Duhamel), Ralph Emerson (John Trask), Edward Martindel (Jefferson Duhamel), Otto Hoffman (Apyton Hale), Floyd Shackelford (Butler).

37. *The Desert Song*

April 8, 1929 (New York premiere); thirteen reels, sound (Vitaphone), b&w, with some sequences in two-strip Technicolor.

Directed by Roy Del Ruth; produced and distributed by Warner Bros. Pictures. (ML's first speaking role)

Cast: John Boles (The Red Shadow/Pierre Birbeau), Carlotta King (Margot), Louise Fazenda (Susan), Johnny Arthur (Bennie Kid, a reporter), Edward Martindel (General Birbeau), Myrna Loy (Azuri).

38. *The Black Watch*

May 8, 1929 (Los Angeles premiere); June 2, 1929 (general release); ten reels, sound (Movietone), b&w.

Directed by John Ford; produced by William Fox; distributed by Fox Film Corp.

Cast: Victor McLaglen (Capt. Donald Gordon King), Myrna Loy (Yasmini), David Rollins (Lieut. Malcolm King), Lumsden Hare (Colonel of the Black Watch), Roy D'Arcy (Rewa Chunga), Mitchell Lewis (Mohammed Khan).

39. *The Squall*

May 9, 1929 (New York premiere); eleven reels, sound (Vitaphone), also silent version June 23, 1929, b&w.

Directed by Alexander Korda; produced by Richard A. Rowland for First National Pictures; distributed by First National Pictures.

Cast: Myrna Loy (Nubi), Richard Tucker (Josef Lajos), Alice Joyce (Maria, his wife) Carroll Nye (Paul), Loretta Young (Irma), Harry Cording (Peter), ZaSu Pitts (Lena).

40. *Noah's Ark*

Nov. 1, 1928 (Hollywood opening); June 15, 1929 (general release); eleven reels, silent with Vitaphone talking sequences and musical score, also silent version July 27, 1929, b&w.

Directed by Michael Curtiz; produced and distributed by Warner Bros. Pictures.

Cast: Dolores Costello (Mary/Miriam), George O'Brien (Travis/Japheth), Noah Beery (Nickoloff/King Nephilim), Louise Fazenda (Hilda/tavern maid), Guinn "Big Boy" Williams (Al/Ham), Myrna Loy (Dancer in Broadway sequence/slave girl in biblical sequence).

41. *The Great Divide*

Sept. 15, 1929; eight reels, sound (Vitaphone), also silent version Oct. 27, 1929, b&w.

Directed by Reginald Barker; produced by Richard A. Rowland and Robert North for First National Pictures; distributed by First National Pictures.

Cast: Dorothy Mackaill (Ruth Jordan), Ian Keith (Stephen Ghent), Myrna Loy (Manuella), Lucien Littlefield (Texas Tommy), Creighton Hale (Edgar Blossom).

42. *Evidence*

Oct. 5, 1929; eight reels, sound (Vitaphone), also silent version, b&w.

Directed by John G. Adolfi; produced and distributed by Warner Bros. Pictures.

Cast: Pauline Frederick (Myra Stanhope), William Courtenay (Cyril Wimborne), Conway Tearle (Harold Courtenay), Lowell Sherman (Norman Pollock), Alec B. Francis (Harbison), Myrna Loy (Native girl).

43. *Show of Shows*

Nov. 20, 1929 (New York premiere); Dec. 28, 1929 (general release); fifteen reels, sound dialogue with songs (Vitaphone), Technicolor.

Directed by John G. Adolfi; production supervised by Darryl Francis Zanuck; produced and distributed by Warner Bros. Pictures.

Cast: Frank Fay (Master of ceremonies), William Courtenay (The Minister), H. B. Warner (The Victim), Hobart Bosworth (The Executioner), Marian Nixon, Sally O'Neil, Myrna Loy (Floradora Sextette and Chinese Fantasy), Alice Day, Patsy Ruth Miller (Floradora Sextette), Ben Turpin (Waiter); additional cast members in this all-star revue include Douglas Fairbanks Jr., John Barrymore, and Loretta Young.

44. *Cameo Kirby*

Jan. 12, 1930; seven reels, sound (Movietone), b&w.

Directed by Irving Cummings; produced by William Fox for Fox Film Corp.; distributed by Fox Film Corp.

Cast: J. Harold Murray (Cameo Kirby), Norma Terris (Adele Randall), Douglas Gilmore (Jack Moreau), Robert Edeson (Colonel Randall), Myrna Loy (Lea), Charles Morton (Anatole), Stepin Fetchit (Croup).

45. *Isle of Escape*

March 1, 1930; six reels, sound (Vitaphone), possibly a silent version as well, b&w.

Directed by Howard Bretherton; produced and distributed by Warner Bros. Pictures.

Cast: Monte Blue (Dave Wade), Myrna Loy (Moira), Betty Compson (Stella), Noah Beery (Shane), Ivan Simpson (Judge).

46. *Under a Texas Moon*

April 1, 1930; eight reels; sound (Vitaphone); color (Technicolor).

Directed by Michael Curtiz; produced and distributed by Warner Bros. Pictures.

Cast: Frank Fay (Don Carlos), Raquel Torres (Raquella), Myrna Loy (Lolita Romero), Armida (Dolores), Noah Beery (Jed Parker).

47. *Cock o' the Walk*

April 11, 1930 (New York premiere); May 15, 1930 (general release); seven reels, sound (Photophone), b&w.

Directed by Roy William Neill and Walter Lang; produced by James Cruze Productions; distributed by Sono Art—World Wide Pictures.

Cast: Joseph Schildkraut (Carlos López), Myrna Loy (Narita), Philip Sleeman (José), Edward Peil (Ortega), John Beck (Cafe manager).

48. *Bride of the Regiment*

May 21, 1930 (New York premiere); June 22, 1930 (general release); twelve reels; sound dialogue with songs (Vitaphone); color (Technicolor).

Directed by John Francis Dillon; produced and distributed by First National Pictures.

Cast: Vivienne Segal (Countess Anna-Marie), Allan Prior (Count Adrian Beltrami), Walter Pidgeon (Colonel Vultow), Louise Fazenda (Teresa, the maid), Myrna Loy (Sophie).

49. *Jazz Cinderella*

Aug. 14 or Sept. 1, 1930; seven reels, sound (Photophone), b&w.

Directed by Scott Pembroke; produced by George R. Batcheller for Chesterfield Motion Picture Corp.; distributed by Chesterfield Motion Picture Corp.

Cast: Myrna Loy (Mildred Vane), Jason Robards (Herbert Carter), Nancy Welford (Patricia Murray), Dorothy Phillips (Mrs. Consuelo Carter), David Durand (Danny Murray).

50. *Last of the Duanes*

Aug. 31, 1930; six reels, sound (Movietone), b&w.

Directed by Alfred Werker; produced by William Fox for Fox Film Corp.; distributed by Fox Film Corp.

Cast: George O'Brien (Buck Duane), Lucille Brown (Ruth Garrett), Myrna Loy (Lola), Walter McGrail (Bland), James Bradbury Jr. (Euchre).

51. *Rogue of the Rio Grande*

Oct. 15, 1930; seven reels, sound, b&w.

Directed by Spencer Gordon Bennett; produced by George W. Weeks for Cliff Broughton Productions; distributed by Sono Art–World Wide Productions.

Cast: José Bohr (El Malo), Raymond Hatton (Pedro), Myrna Loy (Carmita), Carmelita Geraghty (Dolores), Walter Miller (Sheriff Rankin).

52. *The Truth about Youth*

Oct. 19, 1930, or Nov. 3, 1930; seven reels, sound (Vitaphone), b&w.

Directed by William Seiter; produced and distributed by First National Pictures.

Cast: Loretta Young (Phyllis Ericson), David Manners (Richard Dane, The Imp), Conway Tearle (Richard Carewe), Myrna Loy (Kara, The Firefly), Yola d'Avril (Babette).

53. *Renegades*

Oct. 26, 1930; eleven reels, sound (Movietone), b&w.

Directed by Victor Fleming; produced by William Fox for Fox Film Corp.; distributed by Fox Film Corp.

Cast: Warner Baxter (Deucalion), Myrna Loy (Eleanore), Noah Beery (Machwurth), Gregory Gaye (Vologuine), George Cooper (Biloxi), Bela Lugosi (The Marabout).

54. *The Devil to Pay*

Dec. 18, 1930 (New York premiere); Dec. 20, 1930 (general release); eight reels (72 min.), sound, b&w.

Directed by George Fitzmaurice; produced by Samuel Goldwyn; distributed by United Artists.

Cast: Ronald Colman (Willie Hale), Frederic Kerr (Lord Leland), Loretta Young (Dorothy Hope), David Torrence (Mr. Hope), Myrna Loy (Mary Crayle).

55. *The Naughty Flirt*

Jan. 11, 1931; six reels (56–57 or 76 min.), sound, b&w.

Directed by Edward Cline; produced and distributed by First National Pictures.

Cast: Alice White (Kay Elliott), Paul Page (Alan Ward), Myrna Loy (Linda Gregory), Robert Agnew (Wilbur Fairchild), Douglas Gilmore (Jack Gregory), George Irving (John R. Elliott).

56. *Body and Soul*

Feb. 22, 1931; nine reels (82 min.), sound, b&w.

Directed by Alfred Santell; An Alfred Santell / Fox Film Corp. Production; distributed by Fox Film Corp.

Cast: Charles Farrell (Mal Andrews), Elissa Landi (Carla Watson), Myrna Loy (Alice Lester, also known as "Pom Pom"), Humphrey Bogart (Jim Watson), Donald Dillaway (Tap Johnson).

57. *A Connecticut Yankee*

April 5, 1931; eleven reels (95–96 min.), sound, b&w.

Directed by David Butler; a David Butler / Fox Film Corp. Production; distributed by Fox Film Corp.

Cast: Will Rogers (Hank Martin, also known as Sir Boss), William Farnum (King Arthur/Inventor), Maureen O'Sullivan (Alisande/Girl in mansion), Myrna Loy (Queen Morgan le Fay/Seductive woman in mansion), Ward Bond (Queen's knight) (uncredited).

58. *Hush Money*

July 5, 1931; seven reels (68–69 min.), sound, b&w.

Directed by Sidney Lanfield; a Sidney Lanfield/Fox Film Corp. Production; distributed by Fox Film Corp.

Cast: Joan Bennett (Joan Gordon), Hardie Albright (Stuart Elliott), Owen Moore (Steve Pelton), Myrna Loy (Flo Curtis), George Raft (Maxie) (uncredited), C. Henry Gordon (Jack Curtis).

59. *Transatlantic*

Aug. 30, 1931; eight reels (73–74 min.), sound, b&w.

Directed by William K. Howard; a William K. Howard/Fox Film Corp. Production; distributed by Fox Film Corp.

Cast: Edmund Lowe (Monty Greer, The Gambler), Greta Nissen (Sigrid Carlene, The Dancer), John Halliday (Henry D. Graham, The Banker), Myrna Loy (Kay Graham, His wife), Jean Hersholt (Rudolph Kramer, The Lens Grinder), Lois Moran (Judy Kramer, His daughter).

60. *Rebound*

Sept. 18, 1931; ten reels (88 or 91 min.), sound, b&w.

Directed by Edward H. Griffith; a Charles R. Rogers / RKO Pathé Pictures Production; distributed by RKO Pathé Distributing Corp.

Cast: Ina Claire (Sara Jaffrey), Robert Ames (Bill Truesdale), Myrna Loy (Evie Lawrence), Hedda Hopper (Liz Crawford), Robert Williams (Johnnie Coles).

61. *Skyline*

Oct. 11, 1931; seven reels (57 or 70 min.), sound, b&w.

Directed by Sam Taylor; a Sam Taylor / Fox Film Corp. production; distributed by Fox Film Corp.

Cast: Thomas Meighan (Gordon A. McClellan), Hardie Albright (John Breen), Maureen O'Sullivan (Kathleen Kearny), Myrna Loy (Paula Lambert), Stanley Fields (Captain Breen).

62. *Consolation Marriage*

Oct. 15, 1931 (Hollywood premiere); Nov. 21, 1931 (general release); nine reels (82 min.), sound, b&w.

Directed by Paul Sloane; produced by William Le Baron for RKO Radio Pictures, Inc.; distributed by RKO Radio Pictures, Inc.

Cast: Irene Dunne (Mary Brown Porter), Pat O'Brien (Steve Porter), John Halliday (Jeff), Myrna Loy (Elaine Brandon), Lester Vail (Aubrey).

63. *Arrowsmith*

Dec. 26, 1931; eleven reels (108 min.), sound, b&w.

Directed by John Ford; produced by Samuel Goldwyn and Howard Productions; distributed by United Artists Corp.

Cast: Ronald Colman (Dr. Martin Arrowsmith), Helen Hayes (Leora Tozer Arrowsmith), Richard Bennett (Gustav Sondelius), A. E. Anson (Professor Max Gottlieb), Myrna Loy (Joyce Lanyon), DeWitt Jennings (Mr. Tozer), Beulah Bondi (Mrs. Tozer) (uncredited), Claude King (Dr. Tubbs).

64. *Emma*

Jan. 2, 1932; eight reels (70 or 73 min.), sound, b&w. (ML's first MGM role under contract)

Directed by Clarence Brown; a Clarence Brown/MGM Production; distributed by MGM.

Cast: Marie Dressler (Emma Thatcher Smith), Richard Cromwell (Ronnie Smith), Jean Hersholt (Mr. Frederick Smith), Myrna Loy (Isabelle [Countess Marlin]), John Miljan (District Attorney).

65. *The Wet Parade*

March 26, 1932; thirteen reels (118 or 122 min.), sound, b&w.

Directed by Victor Fleming; a Victor Fleming/MGM Production; distributed by MGM.

Cast: Robert Young (Kip Tarleton), Walter Huston (Pow Tarleton), Jimmy Durante (Abe Shilling), Wallace Ford (Jerry Tyler), Myrna Loy (Eileen Pinchon), Joan Marsh (Evelyn Fesseden), Dorothy Jordan (Maggie Chilcote), Lewis Stone (Roger Chilcote), Neil Hamilton (Roger Chilcote Jr.).

66. *Vanity Fair*

March 1932; May 8, 1932 (general release); eight reels (67 or 78 min.), sound, b&w.

Directed by Chester M. Franklin; produced by M. H. Hoffman; a Chester M. Franklin/Allied Pictures Corp. Production; distributed by Allied Pictures Corp.

Cast: Myrna Loy (Becky Sharp), Conway Tearle (Rawdon Crawley), Barbara Kent (Amelia Sedley), Walter Byron (George Osborne), Anthony Bushell (Dobbin), Lionel Belmore (Sir Pitt Crawley).

67. *The Woman in Room 13*

May 15, 1932; seven reels (58, 67, or 69 min.), sound, b&w.

Directed by Henry King; a Henry King/Fox Film Corp. Production; distributed by Fox Film Corp.

Cast: Elissa Landi (Laura Bruce), Ralph Bellamy (Major John Bruce), Neil Hamilton (Paul Ramsey), Myrna Loy (Sari Lodar), Gilbert Roland (Victor LeGrand).

68. *New Morals for Old*

June 4, 1932; eight reels (72 min.), sound, b&w.

Directed by Charles Brabin; produced and distributed by MGM.

Cast: Robert Young (Ralph Thomas), Margaret Perry (Phyl Thomas), Lewis Stone (Mr. Thomas), Laura Hope Crews (Mrs. Thomas), Myrna Loy (Myra), David Newell (Duff Wilson), Jean Hersholt (James Hallett).

69. *Love Me Tonight*

Aug. 26, 1932; ten reels (90 or 104 min.), sound, b&w.

Directed by Rouben Mamoulian; a Rouben Mamoulian/Paramount Publix Corp. Production; distributed by Paramount Publix Corp.

Cast: Maurice Chevalier (Maurice Courtelin), Jeanette MacDonald (Princess Jeanette), Charlie Ruggles (Vicomte Gilbert de Vareze), Charles Butterworth (Count de Savignac), Myrna Loy (Countess Valentine), C. Aubrey Smith (Duke d'Artelines).

70. *Thirteen Women*

Sept. 16, 1932; seven reels (73–74 min.), sound, b&w.

Directed by George Archainbaud; produced and distributed by RKO Radio Pictures, Inc.

Cast: Irene Dunne (Laura Stanhope), Ricardo Cortez (Sergeant Clive), Jill Esmond (Jo), Myrna Loy (Ursula Georgi), Mary Duncan (June Raskob), Kay Johnson (Helen Frye), Florence Eldridge (Grace Coombs), Peg Entwistle (Hazel Cousins), C. Henry Gordon (Swami Yogadachi).

71. *The Mask of Fu Manchu*

Nov. 5, 1932; seven reels (66–67 min.), sound, b&w.

Directed by Charles Brabin; a Cosmopolitan Production; produced and distributed by MGM.

Cast: Boris Karloff (Dr. Fu Manchu), Lewis Stone (Nayland Smith), Karen Morley (Sheila Barton), Charles Starrett (Terrence Granville), Myrna Loy (Fah Lo See), Jean Hersholt (Von Berg).

72. *The Animal Kingdom*
(The film opened the new RKO Roxy Theater in NYC.)

Dec. 28, 1932; nine reels (78, 85, or 90 min.), sound, b&w.

Directed by Edward H. Griffith; produced by David O. Selznick for RKO Radio Pictures, Inc.; distributed by RKO Radio Pictures, Inc.

Cast: Ann Harding (Daisy Sage), Leslie Howard (Tom Collier), Myrna Loy (Cecelia Henry Collier), William Gargan ("Red" Regan), Neil Hamilton (Owen), Ilka Chase (Grace).

73. *Topaze*

Feb. 8, 1933 (New York premiere); Feb. 24, 1933 (general release); eight reels (78 or 80 min.), sound, b&w.

Directed by Harry D'Abbadie D'Arrast; produced by David O. Selznick for RKO Radio Pictures, Inc.; distributed by RKO Radio Pictures, Inc.

Cast: John Barrymore (Dr. Auguste A. Topaze), Myrna Loy (Coco), Reginald Mason (Baron de La Tour-La Tour), Jobyna Howland (Baroness de La Tour-La Tour), Jackie Searle (Charlemagne de La Tour-La Tour).

74. *The Scarlet River*

March 10, 1933; six reels (53 or 57 min.), sound, b&w.

Directed by Otto Brower; produced and distributed by RKO Radio Pictures, Inc.

Cast: Tom Keene (Tom Baxter), Dorothy Wilson (Judy Blake), Creighton Chaney [Lon Chaney Jr.] (Jeff Todd), Betty Furness (Babe Jewel), Rosco Ates (Ulysses Mope), Edgar Kennedy (Sam Gilroy). In one scene Joel McCrea, Myrna Loy, Julie Haydon, Bruce Cabot, and Rochelle Hudson appear as themselves in cameo roles.

75. *The Barbarian*

May 12, 1933; nine reels (82–83 or 88 min.), sound, b&w.

Directed by Sam Wood; a Sam Wood / MGM Production; distributed by MGM.

Cast: Ramon Novarro (Jamil El Shehab), Myrna Loy (Diana Standing), Reginald Denny (Gerald Hume), Louise Closser Hale (Powers), C. Aubrey Smith (Cecil Harwood), Marcelle Corday (Marthe), Hedda Hopper (American tourist).

76. *When Ladies Meet*

June 23, 1933; nine reels, sound, b&w.

Directed by Harry Beaumont; a Cosmopolitan Production; produced by MGM; distributed by Loew's, Inc.

Cast: Ann Harding (Claire Woodruff), Robert Montgomery (Jimmie Lee), Myrna Loy (Mary Howard), Alice Brady (Bridget Drake), Frank Morgan (Rogers Woodruff).

77. *Penthouse*

Sept. 8, 1933; ten reels (88 or 90–91 min.), sound, b&w.

Directed by W. S. Van Dyke; a Cosmopolitan / MGM Production; distributed by MGM.

Cast: Warner Baxter (Jackson Durant), Myrna Loy (Gertie Waxted), Charles Butterworth (Layton), Mae Clarke (Mimi Montagne), Phillips Holmes (Tom Siddall), C. Henry Gordon (Jim Crelliman).

78. *Night Flight*

Oct. 6, 1933; nine reels (89 or 91 min.), sound, b&w.

Directed by Clarence Brown; produced and distributed by MGM.

Cast: John Barrymore (A. Riviére), Helen Hayes (Simone Fabian), Clark Gable (Jules Fabian), Lionel Barrymore (Inspector Robineau), Robert Montgomery (Auguste Pellerin), Myrna Loy (Brazilian pilot's wife), William Gargan (Brazilian pilot).

79. *The Prizefighter and the Lady*

Nov. 10, 1933; eleven reels (90 or 102–3 min.), sound, b&w.

Directed by W. S. Van Dyke; a W. S. Van Dyke / MGM Production; distributed by Loew's, Inc.

Cast: Myrna Loy (Belle Mercer Morgan), Max Baer (Steve Morgan), Primo Carnera (Primo Carnera), Jack Dempsey (Promoter Jack Dempsey), Walter Huston (Professor Edwin J. Bennett), Otto Kruger (Willie Ryan).

80. *Men in White*

April 6, 1934; eight reels (72 or 75 min.), sound, b&w.

Directed by Richard Boleslavsky; produced by Monta Bell; a Cosmopolitan / MGM Production; distributed by Loew's, Inc.

Cast: Clark Gable (Dr. George Ferguson), Myrna Loy (Laura Hudson), Jean Hersholt (Dr. Hochberg), Elizabeth Allan (Barbara Dennin), Otto Kruger (Dr. Levine).

81. *Manhattan Melodrama*

May 4, 1934; nine reels (93 min.), sound, b&w.

Directed by W. S. Van Dyke; produced by David O. Selznick; a Cosmopolitan / MGM Production; distributed by MGM.

Cast: Clark Gable (Blackie Gallagher), William Powell (Jim Wade), Myrna Loy (Eleanor), Leo Carrillo (Father Joe), Nat Pendleton (Spud), Mickey Rooney (Blackie as a boy).

82. *The Thin Man*

May 25, 1934; ten reels (91 min.), sound, b&w.

Directed by W. S. Van Dyke; produced by Hunt Stromberg; a Cosmopolitan / MGM Production; distributed by MGM.

Cast: William Powell (Nick Charles), Myrna Loy (Nora Charles), Maureen O'Sullivan (Dorothy Wynant), Nat Pendleton (Guild), Minna Gombell (Mimi Wynant Jorgenson), Porter Hall (MacCaulay), Henry Wadsworth (Tommy), William Henry (Gilbert Wynant), Harold Huber (Nunheim), Cesar Romero (Chris Jorgenson), Edward Ellis (Clyde Wynant), Edward Brophy (Morelli), Natalie Moorhead (Julia Wolf).

83. *Stamboul Quest*

July 13, 1934; nine reels (85, 87–88, or 90 min.), sound, b&w.

Directed by Sam Wood; produced by Bernard H. Hyman; a Sam Wood / MGM Production; distributed by Loew's, Inc.

Cast: Myrna Loy (Annemarie, also known as Fräulein Doktor and Helena Bohlen), George Brent (Douglas Beall), Lionel Atwill (Von Sturm), C. Henry Gordon (Ali Bey), Rudolph Amendt (Karl), Mischa Auer (Ameel).

84. *Evelyn Prentice*

Nov. 9, 1934; eight reels (70 or 80 min.), sound, b&w.

Directed by William K. Howard; produced by John W. Considine Jr.; a Cosmopolitan / MGM Production; distributed by MGM.

Cast: William Powell (John Prentice), Myrna Loy (Evelyn Prentice), Una Merkel (Amy Drexel), Rosalind Russell (Mrs. Nancy Harrison), Isabel Jewel (Judith Wilson), Henry Wadsworth (Chester White), Cora Sue Collins (Dorothy Prentice).

85. *Broadway Bill*

Dec. 27, 1934; eleven reels (90 or 103 min.), sound, b&w.

Directed by Frank Capra; produced by Harry Cohn for Columbia Pictures Corp.; a Frank Capra Production; distributed by Columbia Pictures Corp.

Cast: Warner Baxter (Dan Brooks), Myrna Loy (The Princess / Alice Higgins), Walter Connolly (J. L. Higgins), Helen Vinson (Margaret Brooks), Douglas Dumbrille (Eddie Morgan), Raymond Walburn (Colonel Pettigrew), Clarence Muse (Whitey), Lucille Ball (Switchboard operator) (uncredited).

86. *Wings in the Dark*

Feb. 1, 1935; eight reels (68 or 70 min.), sound, b&w.

Directed by James Flood; produced by Adolph Zukor and Arthur Hornblow Jr.; distributed by Paramount Productions, Inc.

Cast: Myrna Loy (Sheila Mason), Cary Grant (Ken Gordon), Roscoe Karns (Nick Williams), Hobart Cavanaugh (Mac), Dean Jagger (Tops Harmon), Russell Hopton (Jake Brashear).

87. *Whipsaw*

Dec. 18, 1935; nine reels (78, 80, or 82–84 min.), sound, b&w.

Directed by Sam Wood; produced by Harry Rapf; a Sam Wood / MGM Production; distributed by Loew's, Inc.

Cast: Myrna Loy (Vivian Palmer), Spencer Tracy (Ross McBride), Harvey Stephens (Ed Dexter), William Harrigan ("Doc" Evans), Clay Clement (Harry Ames).

88. *Wife vs. Secretary*

Feb. 28, 1936; nine reels (85 or 88–89 min.), sound, b&w.

Directed by Clarence Brown; produced by Hunt Stromberg; a Clarence Brown / MGM Production; distributed by Loew's, Inc.

Cast: Clark Gable (Van "V. S." Stanhope, also known as Jake), Jean Harlow (Helen "Whitey" Wilson), Myrna Loy (Linda Stanhope), May Robson (Mimi Stanhope), George Barbier (J. D. Underwood), James Stewart (Dave).

89. *Petticoat Fever*

March 20, 1936; eight reels (80–81 min.), sound, b&w.

Directed by George Fitzmaurice; produced by Frank Davis and MGM; distributed by Loew's, Inc.

Cast: Robert Montgomery (Dascom Dinsmore), Myrna Loy (Irene Campion), Reginald Owen (Sir James Felton), Winifred Shotter (Clara Wilson), Otto Yamaoka (Kimo).

90. *To Mary—with Love*

Aug. 1, 1936; ten reels (92 min.), sound, b&w.

Directed by John Cromwell; Darryl F. Zanuck in charge of production; produced and distributed by 20th Century–Fox Film Corp.

Cast: Warner Baxter (John "Jock" Wallace), Myrna Loy (Mary Wallace), Ian Hunter (William C. "Bill" Hallam), Claire Trevor (Kitty Brant), Jean Dixon (Irene Potter).

91. *The Great Ziegfeld*

Sept. 4, 1936; twenty reels (180 or 170 min.), sound, b&w (won Best Picture Academy Award); 2 hrs. 50 min.

Directed by Robert Z. Leonard; produced by Hunt Stromberg; a Robert Z. Leonard / MGM Production; distributed by Loew's, Inc.

Cast: William Powell (Florenz Ziegfeld Jr.), Myrna Loy (Billie Burke Ziegfeld), Luise Rainer (Anna Held Ziegfeld), Frank Morgan (Jack Billings), Fanny Brice (Fanny Brice), Virginia Bruce (Audrey Dane).

92. *Libeled Lady*

Oct. 9, 1936; ten reels (98 min.), sound, b&w.

Directed by Jack Conway; produced by Lawrence Weingarten for MGM; distributed by MGM.

Cast: Jean Harlow (Gladys Benton), William Powell (Bill Chandler), Myrna Loy (Connie Allenbury), Spencer Tracy (Warren Haggerty), Walter Connolly (Mr. J. B. Allenbury), Cora Witherspoon (Mrs. Burns-Norvell), Hattie McDaniel (Maid in hall) (uncredited).

93. *After the Thin Man*

Dec. 25, 1936; twelve reels (107 or 112 min.), sound, b&w.

Directed by W. S. Van Dyke; produced by Hunt Stromberg for MGM; distributed by MGM.

Cast: William Powell (Nick Charles), Myrna Loy (Nora Charles), James Stewart (David Graham), Elissa Landi (Selma Landis), Joseph Calleia ("Dancer"), Jessie Ralph (Aunt Katherine Forrest), Alan Marshal (Robert Landis), Sam Levene (Lieutenant Abrams).

94. *Parnell*

June 4, 1937; twelve reels (115–19 min.), sound, b&w.

Directed and produced by John M. Stahl; a John M. Stahl / MGM Production; distributed by Loew's, Inc.

Cast: Clark Gable (Charles Stewart Parnell), Myrna Loy (Katie O'Shea), Edna May Oliver (Aunt Ben), Edmund Gwenn (Campbell), Alan Marshal (Capt. William "Willie" O'Shea), Donald Crisp (Davitt), Billie Burke (Clara Wood), Montagu Love (Gladstone).

95. *Double Wedding*

Oct. 15, 1937; nine reels (85 or 87 min.), sound, b&w.

Directed by Richard Thorpe; produced by Joseph L. Mankiewicz for MGM; distributed by Loew's, Inc.

Cast: William Powell (Charlie Lodge), Myrna Loy (Margit Agnew), Florence Rice (Irene Agnew), John Beal (Waldo Beaver), Jessie Ralph (Mrs. Kensington-Bly), Edgar Kennedy (Spike).

96. *Man-Proof*

Jan. 7, 1938; eight reels (71 or 74 min.), sound, b&w.

Directed by Richard Thorpe; produced by Louis D. Lighton for MGM; distributed by Loew's, Inc.

Cast: Myrna Loy (Mimi Swift), Franchot Tone (Jimmy Kilmartin), Rosalind Russell (Elizabeth Kent [Wythe]), Walter Pidgeon (Alan Wythe), Rita Johnson (Florence).

97. *Test Pilot*

April 22, 1938; twelve reels (120 min.), sound, b&w.

Directed by Victor Fleming; produced by Louis D. Lighton; a Victor Fleming / MGM Production; distributed by Loew's, Inc.

Cast: Clark Gable (Jim [Lane]), Myrna Loy (Ann ["Thursday"] Barton), Spencer Tracy (Gunner [Morse]), Lionel Barrymore ([Howard B.] Drake), Samuel S. Hinds (General Ross), Marjorie Main (Landlady).

98. *Too Hot to Handle*

Sept. 16, 1938; eleven reels (106 min.), sound, b&w.

Directed by Jack Conway; produced by Lawrence Weingarten for MGM; distributed by Loew's, Inc. Jack Conway became ill during the last month of directing *Too Hot to Handle,* and Victor Fleming took over (see Sragow, *Victor Fleming,* 592).

Cast: Clark Gable (Chris Hunter), Myrna Loy (Alma Harding), Walter Pidgeon (Bill Dennis), Walter Connolly ("Gabby" MacArthur), Leo Carrillo (Joselito), Marjorie Main (Miss Wayne).

99. *Lucky Night*

May 5, 1939; eight reels (90 min.), sound, b&w.

Directed by Norman Taurog; produced by Louis D. Lighton for MGM; distributed by Loew's, Inc.

Cast: Myrna Loy (Cora Jordan), Robert Taylor (Bill Overton), Joseph Allen (Joe Hilton), Henry O'Neill (Calvin Jordan), Douglas Fowley (George), Marjorie Main (Mrs. Briggs).

100. *The Rains Came*

Sept. 15, 1939; 12 reels (100 or 102–4 min.), sound, b&w.

Directed by Clarence Brown; produced by Darryl F. Zanuck for 20th Century–Fox Film Corp.; distributed by 20th Century–Fox Film Corp.

Cast: Myrna Loy (Lady Edwina Esketh), Tyrone Power (Major Rama Safti), George Brent (Tom Ransome), Brenda Joyce (Fern Simon), Nigel Bruce (Lord Albert Esketh), Joseph Schildkraut (Mr. Bannerjee), Maria Ouspenskaya (Maharani), Jane Darwell (Aunt Phoebe), Marjorie Rambeau (Mrs. Simon).

101. *Another Thin Man*

Nov. 17, 1939; ten reels (105 min.), sound, b&w.

Directed by W. S. Van Dyke; produced by Hunt Stromberg for MGM; distributed by Loew's, Inc.

Cast: William Powell (Nick Charles), Myrna Loy (Nora Charles), Virginia Grey (Lois MacFay), Otto Kruger (Van Slack), Nat Pendleton (Lieutenant Guild), Marjorie Main (Mrs. Dolley), C. Aubrey Smith (Colonel MacFay), Ruth Hussey (Dorothy Waters), William A. Poulsen (Nick Jr.).

102. *I Love You Again*

Aug. 9, 1940; ten reels (97 min.), sound, b&w.

Directed by W. S. Van Dyke; produced by Lawrence Weingarten for MGM; distributed by Loew's, Inc.

Cast: William Powell (Larry Wilson / George Carey), Myrna Loy (Kay Wilson), Frank McHugh ("Doc" Ryan), Edmund Lowe (Duke Sheldon), Donald Douglas (Herbert), Nella Walker (Kay's mother), Carl "Alfalfa" Switzer (Harkspur Jr.).

103. *Third Finger, Left Hand*

Oct. 11, 1940; ten reels (96 min.), sound, b&w.

Directed by Robert Z. Leonard; produced by John W. Considine Jr.; a Robert Z. Leonard/MGM Production; distributed by Loew's, Inc.

Cast: Myrna Loy (Margot Sherwood Merrick), Melvyn Douglas (Jeff Thompson), Raymond Walburn (Mr. Sherwood), Lee Bowman (Philip Booth), Bonita Granville (Vicky Sherwood), Felix Bressart (August Winkel).

104. *Love Crazy*

May 23, 1941; ten reels (97 or 99–100 min.), sound, b&w.

Directed by Jack Conway; produced by Pandro S. Berman for MGM; distributed by Loew's, Inc.

Cast: William Powell (Steve Ireland), Myrna Loy (Susan Ireland), Gail Patrick (Isobel [Kimble] Grayson), Jack Carson (Ward Willoughby), Florence Bates (Mrs. Cooper).

105. *Shadow of the Thin Man*

Nov. 1941 (New York opening: week of Nov. 21); nine reels (97 or 99 min.), sound, b&w.

Directed by Major W. S. Van Dyke; produced by Hunt Stromberg for MGM; distributed by Loew's, Inc.

Cast: William Powell (Nick Charles), Myrna Loy (Nora Charles), Barry Nelson (Paul Clarke), Donna Reed (Molly Ford), Sam Levene (Lieutenant Abrams), Louise Beavers (Stella), Dickie Hall (Nick Jr.), Stella Adler (Claire Porter).

106. *The Thin Man Goes Home*

Jan. 25, 1945; (100 min.), sound, b&w.

Directed by Richard Thorpe; produced by Everett Riskin for MGM; distributed by Loew's, Inc.

Cast: William Powell (Nick Charles), Myrna Loy (Nora Charles), Lucile Watson (Mrs. Charles), Gloria De Haven (Laura Ronson), Anne Revere (Crazy Mary), Helen Vinson (Helena Draque), Harry Davenport (Dr. Charles), Leon Ames (Edgar Draque).

107. *So Goes My Love*

April 19, 1946; ten reels (88 or 90–91 min.), sound, b&w.

Directed by Frank Ryan; produced by Jack H. Skirball; a Jack H. Skirball–Bruce Manning Production; distributed by Universal Pictures Company, Inc.

Cast: Myrna Loy (Jane Budden Maxim), Don Ameche (Hiram Stevens Maxim), Rhys Williams (Magel), Bobby Driscoll (Percy Maxim), Richard Gaines (Josephus Ford), Molly Lamont (Garnet Allison).

108. *The Best Years of Our Lives*

Nov. 21, 1946; (165, 170, or 172 min.), sound, b&w.

Directed by William Wyler; produced by Samuel Goldwyn; distributed by RKO Radio Pictures, Inc.

Cast: Myrna Loy (Milly Stephenson), Fredric March (Al Stephenson), Dana Andrews (Fred Derry), Teresa Wright (Peggy Stephenson), Virginia Mayo (Marie Derry), Cathy O'Donnell (Wilma Cameron), Hoagy Carmichael (Butch Engle), Harold Russell (Homer Parrish), Mina Gombell (Mrs. Parrish).

ML Receives Best Actress prize from Brussels World Film Festival.

109. *Song of the Thin Man*

Aug. 28, 1947; (86 min.), sound, b&w.

Directed by Edward Buzzell; produced by Nat Perrin for MGM; distributed by Loew's, Inc.

Cast: William Powell (Nick Charles), Myrna Loy (Nora Charles), Keenan Wynn (Clarence "Clinker" Krause), Dean Stockwell (Nick Charles Jr.), Philip Reed (Tommy Edlon Drake), Patricia Morison (Phyllis Talbin), Leon Ames (Mitchell Talbin), Gloria Grahame (Fran Ledue Page), Jayne Meadows (Janet Thayar), Ralph Morgan (David I. Thayar).

110. *The Bachelor and the Bobby-Soxer*

Sept. 1, 1947; (93 or 95 min.), sound, b&w.

Directed by Irving Reis; a Dore Schary Production; produced and distributed by RKO Radio Pictures, Inc.

Cast: Cary Grant (Dick Nugent), Myrna Loy (Judge Margaret Turner), Shirley Temple (Susan Turner), Rudy Vallee (Tommy Chamberlain), Ray Collins (Dr. Matt Beemish), Harry Davenport (Judge Thaddeus Turner).

111. *The Senator Was Indiscreet*

Dec. 26, 1947; (81–82 or 88 min.), sound, b&w.

Directed by George S. Kaufman; a Nunnally Johnson / Inter-John, Inc. Production; distributed by Universal Pictures, Inc.

Cast: William Powell (Senator Melvin G. Ashton), Ella Raines (Poppy McNaughton), Peter Lind Hayes (Lew Gibson), Arleen Whelan (Valerie Shepherd), Ray Collins (Fred Houlihan), Myrna Loy (Mrs. Melvin G. Ashton) (uncredited).

ML's last appearance with Powell.

112. *Mr. Blandings Builds His Dream House*

March 25, 1948 (New York premiere); June 4, 1948 (general release); (93–95 min.), sound, b&w.

Directed by H. C. Potter; produced by Dore Schary, Norman Panama, and Melvin Frank for RKO Radio Pictures, Inc.; distributed by Selznick Releasing Organization.

Cast: Cary Grant (Jim Blandings), Myrna Loy (Muriel Blandings), Melvyn Douglas (Bill Cole), Reginald Denny (Henry L. Simms), Louise Beavers (Gussie), Jason Robards (John W. Retch).

113. *The Red Pony*

March 28, 1949; (88–89 min.), sound, color (Technicolor).

Directed by Lewis Milestone; produced by Charles K. Feldman and Lewis Milestone; distributed by Republic Pictures Corp.

Cast: Myrna Loy (Alice Tiflin), Robert Mitchum (Billy Buck), Louis Calhern (Grandfather), Shepperd Strudwick (Fred Tiflin), Peter Miles (Tom Tiflin), Margaret Hamilton (Teacher), Beau Bridges (Beau).

114. *Cheaper by the Dozen*

March 31, 1950; nine reels (86 min.), sound, color (Technicolor).

Directed by Walter Lang; written for the screen and produced by Lamar Trotti; produced and distributed by 20th Century–Fox Film Corp.

Cast: Clifton Webb (Frank B. Gilbreth), Jeanne Crain (Ann Gilbreth), Myrna Loy (Lillian Gilbreth), Betty Lynn (Deborah Lancaster), Edgar Buchanan (Dr. Burton), Barbara Bates (Ernestine Gilbreth), Mildred Natwick (Mrs. Mebane).

115. *If This Be Sin,* a.k.a. *That Dangerous Age*

June 30, 1950; (72 min.), sound, b&w.

Directed and produced by Gregory Ratoff; distributed by United Artists.

Cast: Myrna Loy (Lady Cathy Brooke), Roger Livesey (Sir Brian Brooke), Peggy Cummins (Monica Brooke), Richard Greene (Michael Barcleigh), Elizabeth Allan (Lady Sybil), Gerard Heinz (Dr. Thorvald).

116. *Belles on Their Toes*

May 2, 1952; ten reels (89 min.), sound, color (Technicolor).

Directed by Henry Levin; produced by Samuel G. Engel for 20th Century–Fox Film Corp.; distributed by 20th Century–Fox Film Corp.

Cast: Jeanne Crain (Ann Gilbreth), Myrna Loy (Dr. Lillian M. Gilbreth), Debra Paget (Martha Gilbreth), Jeffrey Hunter (Dr. Bob Grayson), Edward Arnold (Sam Harper), Hoagy Carmichael (Tom Bracken), Barbara Bates (Ernestine Gilbreth).

117. *The Ambassador's Daughter*

Aug. 8, 1956 (Los Angeles opening); Aug. 29, 1956 (New York opening); Sept. 1956 (general release); (102 min.), sound, color, CinemaScope.

Directed by Norman Krasna; produced by Norman Krasna; distributed by United Artists Corp.

Cast: Olivia de Havilland (Joan Fiske), John Forsythe (Daniel Sullivan), Myrna Loy (Mrs. Cartwright), Adolphe Menjou (Senator Jonathan Cartwright), Tommy Noonan (Albert O'Connor), Francis Lederer (Prince Nicholas Obelski), Edward Arnold (Ambassador William Fiske).

118. *Lonelyhearts*

Dec. 19, 1958; (101–2 min.), sound, b&w.

Directed by Vincent J. Donehue; written for the screen and produced by Dore Schary, Schary Productions, Inc.; distributed by United Artists Corp.

Cast: Montgomery Clift (Adam White Lassiter), Robert Ryan (William Shrike), Myrna Loy (Florence Shrike), Dolores Hart (Justy Sargeant), Maureen Stapleton (Fay Doyle), Jackie Coogan (Ned Gates).

119. *From the Terrace*

July 15, 1960; (144 min.), sound, color (De Luxe); CinemaScope.

Directed by Mark Robson; produced by Mark Robson for Linebrook Corp.; distributed by 20th Century–Fox Film Corp.

Cast: Paul Newman (Alfred Eaton), Joanne Woodward (Mary St. John Eaton), Myrna Loy (Martha Eaton), Ina Balin (Natalie Benziger), Leon Ames (Samuel Eaton), Elizabeth Allen (Sage Rimmington), Barbara Eden (Clemmie).

120. *Midnight Lace*

Oct. 13, 1960; (107–8 min.), sound, color (Eastmancolor).

Directed by David Miller; produced by Ross Hunter, Martin Melcher, and Universal-International Pictures Co., Inc. / Arwin Productions, Inc.; distributed by Universal Pictures Co., Inc.

Cast: Doris Day (Kit Preston), Rex Harrison (Anthony Preston), John Gavin (Brian Younger), Myrna Loy (Aunt Bea Coleman), Roddy McDowall (Malcolm Stanley), Herbert Marshall (Charles Manning), Natasha Parry (Peggy).

121. *The April Fools*

May 28, 1969; (95 min.), sound, color (Technicolor).

Directed by Stuart Rosenberg; produced by Gordon Carroll and Jalem Productions, Inc. / Cinema Center Films; distributed by National General Pictures Corporation.

Cast: Jack Lemmon (Howard Brubaker), Catherine Deneuve (Catherine Gunther), Peter Lawford (Ted Gunther), Jack Weston (Potter Shrader), Myrna Loy (Grace Greenlaw), Charles Boyer (Andre Greenlaw), Sally Kellerman (Phyllis Brubaker).

122. *Airport 1975*

Oct. 18, 1974; (107 min.), sound, color (Technicolor).

Directed by Jack Smight; produced by William Frye for Universal Pictures; distributed by Universal Pictures.

Cast: Charlton Heston (Alan Murdock), Karen Black (Nancy Pryor), George Kennedy (Joe Patroni), Gloria Swanson (herself), Efrem Zimbalist Jr. (Captain Stacy), Myrna Loy (Mrs. Devaney), Sid Caesar (Barney), Dana Andrews (Scott Freeman).

123. *The End*

May 10, 1978; (94 min.), sound, color.

Directed by Burt Reynolds; produced by Lawrence Gordon, Gordon-Reynolds Productions; distributed by United Artists.

Cast: Burt Reynolds (Wendell Sonny Lawson), Dom DeLuise (Marlon Borunki), Sally Field (Mary Ellen), Joanne Woodward (Jessica Lawson), Myrna Loy (Maureen Lawson), Pat O'Brien (Ben Lawson), David Steinberg (Marty Lieberman).

124. *Just Tell Me What You Want*

Feb. 8, 1980; (112 min.), sound, color (Technicolor).

Directed by Sidney Lumet; produced by Sidney Lumet and Jay Presson Allen; produced and distributed by Warner Bros. Pictures.

Cast: Ali MacGraw (Bones Burton), Alan King (Max Herschel), Myrna Loy (Stella Liberti), Keenan Wynn (Seymour Berger), Tony Roberts (Mike Berger), Peter Weller (Steven Routledge).

Unverified Credits (bit roles)

Naughty but Nice   June 26, 1927; directed by Millard Webb; John McCormick Productions / First National Pictures.

Queen of the Night Clubs   March 16, 1929; directed by Bryan Foy; Warner Bros. Pictures.

The Bad Man   Sept. 13, 1930; directed by Clarence G. Badger; First National Pictures.

TELEVISION

1. *General Electric Theater:* "It Gives Me Great Pleasure," CBS, April 3, 1955.
2. *This Is Your Life,* NBC, May 16, 1956.
3. *General Electric Theater:* "Lady of the House," CBS, Jan. 20, 1957.
4. *The Perry Como Show,* NBC, Feb. 9, 1957.
5. *General Electric Theater:* "Love Came Late," CBS, Nov. 17, 1957.
6. *Schlitz Playhouse of Stars:* "No Second Helping," CBS, Nov. 22, 1957.
7. *George Gobel Show,* NBC, Jan. 13, 1959.

8. *Meet Me in St. Louis* (musical special), CBS, April 26, 1959.
9. *June Allyson Show:* "Surprise Party," CBS, April 18, 1960.
10. *What's My Line?* CBS, July 31, 1960.
11. *I've Got a Secret,* CBS, Nov. 30, 1960.
12. *The U.N. Lives Here,* ABC, Dec. 6, 1960.
13. *Dinah Shore Show,* NBC, April 14, 1963.
14. *Family Affair:* "A Helping Hand," CBS, Feb. 6, 1967.
15. *The Virginian:* "Lady of the House," NBC, April 5, 1967.
16. 42nd Academy Awards (presenter), ABC, April 7, 1970.
17. *Death Takes a Holiday* (telefilm), ABC, Oct. 21, 1971.
18. *Do Not Fold, Spindle or Mutilate* (telefilm), ABC, Nov. 9, 1971.
19. *Columbo:* "Etude in Black," NBC, Sept. 17, 1972.
20. *The Couple Takes a Wife* (telefilm), ABC, Dec. 5, 1972.
21. *Ironside:* "All about Andrea," NBC, Feb. 22, 1973.
22. *Indict and Convict* (telefilm), ABC, Jan. 6, 1974.
23. *Day at Night* (interview), WNET, Jan. 27, 1974.
24. *The Elevator* (telefilm), ABC, Feb. 9, 1974.
25. *It Happened at Lakewood Manor,* ABC, Dec. 2, 1977.
26. *The Dick Cavett Show* (interview), WNET, March 6 and March 12, 1980.
27. *Summer Solstice* (telefilm), ABC, Dec. 30, 1981.
28. *Love, Sidney:* "Sidney and the Actress," NBC, June 16, 1982.
29. Kennedy Center Honors (special), CBS, Dec. 20, 1988.
30. 63rd Academy Awards (honorary Oscar recipient), March 25, 1991.

THEATER

1. *The Marriage-Go-Round,* by Leslie Stevens. Directed by Wynn Handman. Production supervised by Alice Lee Boatwright. With Myrna Loy, Claude Dauphin, Siri. Opened July 3, 1961, Lakes Region Playhouse, Laconia New Hampshire. Performances in Ogunquit, Maine; Nyack, New York; Westport, Connecticut.
2. *There Must Be a Pony,* by James Kirkwood, adapted from his book. Directed by John Stix. Produced by Alan Pakula and Joel Schenker. With Myrna Loy, Donald Woods, Peter Helm, Jan Miner. Opened July 16, 1962, Playhouse Theater, Ogunquit, Maine. Performances in Connamessett, Massachusetts; Westport, Connecticut; Milburn, New Jersey; Mineola, Long Island; Philadelphia, Pennsylvania.
3. *Good Housekeeping,* by William McCleery. Directed by Vernon Schwartz. Produced by Carl Stohn Jr. With Myrna Loy, Maurice Copeland, Sidney Breese. Opened July 30, 1963, Avondale Playhouse, Indianapolis. Performances in Chicago.
4. *Barefoot in the Park,* by Neil Simon. Directed by Mike Nichols. Produced by Saint Subber. With Joan Van Ark, Richard Benjamin, Sandor Szabo, Myrna Loy. Opened July 27, 1964, Opera House, Central City, Colorado. Performances in Boston, Toronto, Cleveland, Honolulu, Hollywood, San Francisco, Chicago, Philadelphia, Washington.

5. *Barefoot in the Park,* by Neil Simon. Directed by Burry Fredrik. Produced by Michael McAloney. With Geraldine Court, Peter White, Sandor Szabo, Myrna Loy. Opened July 10, 1967, Famous Artists Playhouse, Syracuse, New York. Performances in Skowhegan, Maine; Fitchburg, Massachusetts; Mineola, Long Island; Bridgeport, Connecticut.

6. *Janus,* by Carolyn Green. Directed by Burry Fredrik. Produced by Fred Walker and Burry Fredrik. With Myrna Loy, William Roerick, Charles Braswell, Lizabeth Pritchett. Opened June 23, 1969, in Denver, theater unknown. Performances in Lanconia, New Hampshire; Falmouth, Massachusetts; Corning, New York.

7. *Dear Love,* by Jerome Kilty, based on the letters of Robert Browning and Elizabeth Barrett. Directed by Burry Fredrik. Produced by Weston Productions. With Myrna Loy, Jerome Kilty. Opened Sept. 17, 1970, Alley Theater, Houston. Performances in Seattle, San Francisco, Phoenix, Hollywood, Chicago, Toronto, Washington, New Haven.

8. *The Women,* by Clare Booth Luce. Directed by Morton Da Costa. Produced by Jeremy Ritzer. With Myrna Loy, Rhonda Fleming, Kim Hunter, Dorothy Loudon, Alexis Smith. Opened April 25, 1973, 46th Street Theater, NYC.

9. *Don Juan in Hell,* by George Bernard Shaw; from *Man and Superman.* Directed by John Houseman. Produced by Lee Orgel. With Ricardo Montalban, Edward Mulhare, Kurt Kasznar, Myrna Loy. Opened June 21, 1974, in Kalamazoo, Michigan, theater unknown. Performances in 158 cities, including Pasadena, Berkeley, Vancouver, Portland, Denver, Albuquerque, El Paso.

10. *Relatively Speaking,* by Alan Ayckbourn. Directed by Phillip Oesterman. Produced by Don Crute. With Myrna Loy, Peter Pagan, Charles Sweigart, Aileen Bay. Opened May 2, 1978, in Indianapolis, theater unknown. Performances in Dallas, Austin, Tampa, St. Petersburg.

Notes

ABBREVIATIONS

AFI   American Film Institute, Los Angeles

AMPAS   Margaret Herrick Library, Academy of Motion Picture Arts
           and Sciences, Beverly Hills

BB   *Myrna Loy: Being and Becoming,* by Myrna Loy and James
           Kotsilibas-Davis

MHS   Montana Historical Society Research Center, Helena

MLP   Myrna Loy Papers, Howard Gotlieb Archival Research Center,
           Boston University

NYPL   New York Public Library for the Performing Arts, Billy Rose
           Theatre Collection

PCA   Production Code Administration

UCLA   University of California, Los Angeles, Performing Arts Special
           Collections, Charles E. Young Research Library

USC   University of Southern California Cinematic Arts Library, Los
           Angeles

Myrna Loy films were viewed at the British Film Institute, the Library of Congress, the Museum of Modern Art in New York, the UCLA Film and Television Archive, the University of Southern California Cinematic Arts Library, and, in some cases, at home on VHS, DVD, and cable television's Turner Classic Movies.

INTRODUCTION

1. "gotta be a lady": Loy and Kotsilibas-Davis, *Myrna Loy: Being and Becoming*, 116. Subsequent references to Loy's autobiography will be cited parenthetically in the text as *BB*.

1. THE CLIMB

1. "attended by a physician": Myrna Adele Williams Birth Certificate No. 3696, August 2, 1905, Lewis and Clark County Department of Public Health, Helena, Montana.

2. Isabella Johnson . . . used to press: Della Williams, quoted in the script of "This Is Your Life," 8.

3. "I don't like": Myrna Loy (hereafter ML), quoted by Ann Marsters, *Boston Globe*, June 24, 1936.

4. "She has the reserve": Colman, "The Siren from Montana," 63.

5. "practically uninhabited": Howard, *Montana*, 104, quoting the frontier reminiscences of Granville Stuart; railroad station nearest: Holloway and Gaab, *Broadwater Bygones*, 67.

6. population of Radersburg: 1880 U.S. Census; and Holloway and Gaab, *Broadwater Bygones*, 67.

7. "met friendly Indians": Anonymous, "D. T. Williams," n.p.; end of their journey: Cauthorn, "Trip to Montana by Wagon Train," n.p.; family treasures: RKO press release, 1947, Myrna Loy Biography file, Core Collection, 1947, Margaret Herrick Library, Academy of Motion Picture Arts and Sciences (hereafter AMPAS).

8. "unless there came": Moore, "Early Day History of Radersburg," undated ms., n.p.; Wood served: Holloway and Gaab, *Broadwater Bygones*, 67–70.

9. cabinet shop: Moore, "Early Day History of Radersburg," n.p.; taking her along: Della Williams tape recording, Montana Historical Society Research Center, Helena (hereafter MHS).

10. David Thomas Williams: Anonymous, "D. T. Williams," n.p.

11. "traps all the fur": Charles Russell, quoted in Conrad, *Ghost Hunting in Montana*, 77.

12. "She never took": ML, quoted in Hall, "The Truth about the Mysterious Miss Loy," n.p. The 1880 census supplies the information that James Wilder, son of Isabella's first marriage, was born in Iowa.

13. not unusual in Montana: Petrik, "If She Be Content," 287.

14. "but I had to": Della Williams, quoted in Maddox, "My Daughter, Myrna Loy, as Told by Della Williams," 35.

15. sat on bank boards: obituary of David F. Williams, *Helena Independent*, Nov. 8, 1918.

16. Montana legislature: *House Journal of the Eighth Session*, State of Montana, Helena, 1903, n.p.; part owner: Lewis and Clark County Probate Records, Estate of David F. Williams.

17. A photograph exists: Myrna Loy Biography file, Core Collection, AMPAS.

18. military . . . posts: Malone, Roeder, and Lang, *Montana*, 141.

19. The town had: Holloway and Gaab, *Broadwater Bygones,* 66, 11; Brother Van: Della Williams tape, MHS.

20. Group dances: Della Williams tape; Howard, *Montana,* 188.

21. literary society: Della Williams tape.

22. "two suits": Howard, *Montana,* 188; infamous winter: Malone, Roeder, and Lang, *Montana,* 165.

23. Gary Cooper . . . collecting arrowheads: Meyers, *Gary Cooper,* 6.

24. Myrna's earliest memory: Willson, "The Revealing True Story of Myrna Loy," Part 1, 56; "I used to be alone": ML, quoted in Walter Ramsey, *Movie Mirror* clipping, Jan. 1937, Myrna Loy clipping folder, New York Public Library for the Performing Arts, Billy Rose Theatre Collection (hereafter NYPL); "charming wistful": Bachardy, *Stars in My Eyes,* 27; "I liked having friends": ML, quoted in Zeitlin, "Behind the Mystery of Myrna Loy," 70.

25. spanking: ML, quoted in an unattributed clipping, March 1939, NYPL.

26. slate, picture books: Willson, "The Revealing True Story of Myrna Loy," Part 1, 86.

2. NOT YOUR TYPICAL HELENA GIRL

1. Central Park: Schroeder and Graff, *Historic Helena, 1864–1964,* unpaged.

2. the city grew: Petrik, *No Step Backward,* 4.

3. Grandmother Johnson: U.S. Census, 1910; business card: Lewis and Clark County Probate records, estate of David F. Williams.

4. selling insurance: *Polk's Helena City Directory,* 1912–18.

5. refused to even look: MGM bio of ML, 1947, AMPAS; photographs: MHS photograph archives.

6. devoured books: Hall, "The Truth about the Mysterious Miss Loy," n.p.; "I was not": ML, quoted by Karen Heller, *Philadelphia Inquirer,* Nov. 22, 1987.

7. "a nun": Zeitlin, "Behind the Mystery of Myrna Loy," 70.

8. "She was a lace": Hall, "The Truth about the Mysterious Miss Loy," n.p.; "Never once": ML, quoted in Stone, "Somewhat of a Cinderella," 7.

9. living doll show: MHS photo, donated by Helen Nash; "I suffered": ML, quoted in Hall, "The Truth about the Mysterious Miss Loy," n.p.

10. old naturalist: Zeitlin, "Behind the Mystery of Myrna Loy," 70.

11. "in which a small": Della Williams, quoted in Maddox, "My Daughter, Myrna Loy, as Told by Della Williams," 35.

12. "Blue Bird" dance: Willson, "The Revealing True Story of Myrna Loy," Part 1, 87; "Miss Williams": *Helena Record-Herald,* undated clipping, MHS.

13. beloved maternal grandmother: Death Certificate of Isabella Giles Johnson, April 27, 1916, Lewis and Clark County; "he recognized that": Della Williams, quoted in Maddox, "My Daughter, Myrna Loy, as Told by Della Williams," 35.

14. ML, quoted in Hall, "The Truth about the Mysterious Miss Loy," n.p.

15. movies . . . in Helena: Robert M. Clark note, vertical file on Helena theaters, MHS Research Center; favorite actresses: Johnston, "Myrna Loy," 12.

16. voting for Wilson: ML, quoted by Karen Heller, *Philadelphia Inquirer,* Nov. 29, 1987.

17. "disloyal, profane": quoted in the *New York Times*, "Silence Broken, Pardons Granted 88 Years after Crimes of Sedition," May 3, 2006; Infantry paraded: Malone, Roeder, and Lang, *Montana*, 268–69.

18. "by chattel mortgage": Probate records, estate of David F. Williams, Inventory of Debts and Assets, Jan. 21, 1921.

19. Spanish influenza: Mark Sullivan, *Over Here, 1914–1918*, 654.

20. sleepwalking: Zeitlin, "Behind the Mystery of Myrna Loy," 70.

21. Recalling the moment: ML, quoted in *Philadelphia Inquirer*, Nov. 29, 1987.

22. "Funeral services": *Helena Independent*, Nov. 8, 1918; funeral expenses: Estate of David F. Williams, March 10, 1919, Creditor's Claim, Probate records.

3. LIFE WITHOUT FATHER

1. Last Will and Testament of David F. Williams, Los Angeles, Feb. 27, 1918, quoted in full by Nettie Qualls in her Final Report as Executrix, May 13, 1943, Lewis and Clark County Probate records, Estate of David F. Williams.

2. script: "This Is Your Life," May 18, 1956.

3. tried to have her removed: Probate document, Jan. 27, 1919.

4. Helena Business College: *Polk's City Directory*, Helena, 1918; working as a clerk: *Los Angeles City Directory*, 1921.

5. "Her father's family": Della Williams, quoted in Maddox, "My Daughter, Myrna Loy, as Told by Della Williams," 100.

6. Culver City: Pennington and Baxter, *A Past to Remember*, 50.

7. Betty remembered: Betty Berger Black, fragment of interview by Kotsilibas-Davis for *Myrna Loy: Being and Becoming*, Myrna Loy Papers, Howard Gotlieb Archival Research Center, Boston University (hereafter MLP), Box 30, 2155; vacuum cleaner: Lou MacFarlane, fragment of interview by Kotsilibas-Davis for *Myrna Loy: Being and Becoming*, MLP, Box 30, 2155.

8. population of Los Angeles: Henstell, *Sunshine and Wealth*, 13–15; Starr, *Material Dreams*, 28.

9. "I was a wallflower": ML, quoted in Maddox, "The Mystery of Myrna Loy," 77.

10. Denishawn: Paris, *Louise Brooks*, chap. 2; Studlar, "Out-Salomeing Salome," 113; cinema dancers: Kendall, *Where She Danced*, 155.

11. St. Denis . . . and . . . exotic goddesses: Sherman, *Denishawn*, 38; Kendall, *Where She Danced*, 50, 89.

12. female dress reform: Kendall, *Where She Danced*, chap. 3.

13. Delsarte method: McTeague, *Before Stanislavsky*, 18–34; "Dramatic gesture": cited in Kendall, *Where She Danced*, 154; "If dancing is": Shawn, "Dancing Cures the Nerves," 36.

14. *The Exquisite Sinner*: Robert Florey to Kevin Brownlow, Nov. 9, 1968, courtesy Brownlow.

15. "Angels of the Dance" scrapbook: MLP, Box 29.

16. "If her father": Della Williams, quoted in Maddox, "My Daughter, Myrna Loy, as Told by Della Williams," 35; "A talented girl": Ruth St. Denis, quoted in Sherman, *Denishawn*, 16.

17. "I decided that": ML, in United Artists publicity of ML, 1977, Jane Ardmore Papers, AMPAS.

18. "High school boys": Della Williams, quoted in Maddox, "My Daughter, Myrna Loy, as Told by Della Williams," 35; "Your friendship": Howard Buffum to ML, June 23, 1921, MLP, Box 32, folder 1.

19. had broken a string of beads: Lou MacFarlane, quoted in "This Is Your Life" (script), n.p.

20. twenty-five dollars a month: in *BB* ML gives the salary as forty dollars a month (30). The twenty-five-dollar figure, which she gave to Gladys Hall in "The Truth about the Mysterious Miss Loy," is probably more accurate; film splicer: ML, quoted in Harrison Carroll, *LA Evening Herald Examiner,* May 23, 1938.

21. "Southland Produces Venus": *LA Times,* July 16, 1922.

22. "Miss Myrna Williams": *LA Times,* May 27, 1923.

23. "I never wavered": ML, quoted in Hall, "The Truth about the Mysterious Miss Loy," Part 1, n.p.

4. ENTER MYRNA LOY

1. Grauman's Egyptian Theatre: www.americancinematheque.com/egyptian/eghistor.htm; "Finish Grauman Theater," *LA Times,* Oct. 15, 1922.

2. "We approached": Helen Hollywood, *Oakland Tribune,* Nov. 12, 1922.

3. Fanchon and Marco: Arthur Unger, *Variety,* June 29, 1927. Unless otherwise specified all references to *Variety* are to the weekly edition; "The New Picture," *Time,* May 10, 1937.

4. Dancing Favorites: Egyptian Theatre *Ten Commandments* program, MLP, Box 18, folder 3; "Fanchon had us": ML, quoted in Chierichetti, "Myrna Loy Today," 8; "Snap it up": Starr, *Barefoot on Barbed Wire,* 67. I owe this reference to Ned Comstock, senior library assistant at the USC Cinematic Arts Library.

5. "I chanced": ML, quoted in Hall, "The Truth about the Mysterious Miss Loy," Part 1, n.p.; Waxman's studio: Robert Florey to Kevin Brownlow, Nov. 9, 1968, courtesy Brownlow.

6. screen test: Willson, "The Revealing True Story of Myrna Loy," Part 2, 83; "Rudy himself": ML, quoted in Hall, "The Truth about the Mysterious Miss Loy," Part 1, n.p.

7. Valentino . . . "was looking for": ML, quoted in Barthel, "Quartet of Queens," 68.

8. Hazel Schertzinger: Loy, "Reminiscences of Myrna Loy," 1419.

9. "They did not want": ML, quoted in Hall, "The Truth about the Mysterious Miss Loy," Part 2, n.p.

10. only a still: *Ben-Hur* scholar T. Gene Hatcher identifies the still as #154 and confirms that ML's scene was cut. The Hatcher information came to me via Kevin Brownlow in a Sept. 1, 2009, email; "He was poetry": ML, quoted in Hall, "The Truth about the Mysterious Miss Loy," Part 2, n.p.

11. "obviously a curtain": *Variety,* July 5, 1925.

12. "were supposed to look": ML, quoted in Ardmore, "Myrna Loy Brings

Excitement," 10; "I remember how": ML, quoted in Hall, "The Truth about the Mysterious Miss Loy," Part 2, n.p.; "more willpower": ML, quoted in Chandler, *Not the Girl Next Door,* 40.

13. "Joan Crawford used to ask": ML, quoted in Hall, "The Truth about the Mysterious Miss Loy," n.p.

14. "a parasite": Crawford, quoted in Newquist, *Conversations with Joan Crawford,* 32; Crawford's early life: Crawford, *A Portrait of Joan;* Houston, *Jazz Baby.*

15. Rambova's private life: Emily W. Leider, *Dark Lover,* chap. 17.

16. "She told me": ML, quoted in Moak, "The Girl Hollywood Couldn't Beat," 25.

17. "a rather adroit": Mrs. Valentino's New Picture," *LA Times,* June 24, 1925.

18. "She slanted": ML, quoted in Hall, "The Truth about the Mysterious Miss Loy," Part 2, n.p.

19. "There's a great buzzing": review of *What Price Beauty, Motion Picture,* Sept. 1925, 35.

20. "He told me": ML, quoted in Hall, "The Truth about the Mysterious Miss Loy," Part 2, n.p.; sound poet: ML, quoted in Barthel, "Quartet of Queens"; "to float": ML to James Day on WNET-TV's *Day at Night,* Jan. 17, 1974.

21. "the girl who": ML, quoted in Hall, "The Truth about the Mysterious Miss Loy," Part 2, n.p.

5. WARNER BROS.' EXOTIC VIXEN

1. "tall and thin": quoted in Young, "Interview by Robert Gitt and Anthony Slide," 2–3; murdered Flint in court: *LA Times,* July 18, 1930.

2. "Myrna Loy has been signed": "Presenting the Cinema Debutante," *LA Times,* Sept. 27, 1925; Rambova's "entire life": Ed Sullivan, *New York Sunday News,* July 23, 1939.

3. "a kind of halo": ML, quoted in Rubin, "Jay Rubin Interviews Myrna Loy," 4.

4. "Myrna Loy never looks": *LA Times,* April 10, 1927.

5. "Myrna Loy is a revelation": Edwin Schallert, "War Film a Hit Uptown," *LA Times,* Oct. 4, 1926.

6. "where crime": *Crimson City* trailer, Library of Congress—Motion Picture, Broadcasting, and Recorded Sound Division; "Nobody thought of me": ML, quoted by Rex Reed, *New York Times,* April 13, 1969.

7. "the most beautiful figure": "Girls Who Are Good at Figures," *Photoplay,* Nov. 1925, 56–57.

8. It spent roughly half: Glancy, "Warner Bros. Film Grosses, 1921–1951," 56; Warners contracts: ML legal files, 1925–29, Warner Bros. Archive, University of Southern California.

9. drilled holes: Harris, *The Zanucks of Hollywood,* 29.

10. "about cheating": *Variety,* Oct. 31, 1928; "I'm on the other side": ML, quoted in *LA Times,* Sept. 23, 1928; "Myrna Loy, with her exotic": *Variety,* Sept. 5, 1928; "the dual": Mayo, quoted in *Washington Post,* Oct. 13, 1928; "caviar": Delight Evans, quoted in Carr, *More Fabulous Faces,* 62.

11. "one of the best": *Variety*, March 3, 1926.

12. "A Stupendous": ad in *Jamestown Post*, July 25, 1928.

13. Barrymore came to Warners: Kobler, *Damned in Paradise*, 202; Mary Astor: Astor, *A Life on Film*, 45–46.

14. goosed by a buzzer: Stuart and Thompson, *I Just Keep Hoping*, 42.

15. "sets were dark": Astor, *A Life on Film*, 48.

16. "slinking around": Loy, "Reminiscences of Myrna Loy," 1423; *Life*, Aug. 26, 1926, n.p.

17. "Vitaphone Stirs": *New York Times*, Aug. 7, 1926; "Vitaphone Bow": *Variety*, Aug. 11, 1926; *Don Juan* grosses: Glancy, "Warner Bros. Film Grosses, 1921–1951," 56.

18. *Don Juan* premiere in Hollywood: *LA Times*, Aug. 20, 23, 1926.

19. "Who the hell": quoted in Warner and Jennings, *My First Hundred Years in Hollywood*, 168.

20. Jolson had uttered: Custen, *Twentieth Century's Fox*, 93.

21. "I have no fear": Parsons, quoted in Francisco, *Gentleman*, 52.

22. "Articulate films": *Variety*, Jan. 2, 1929; "It was impossible": Mohr, "Reminiscences," 72.

23. "Seated soundstages": Eyman, *The Speed of Sound*, 118–20.

24. Operators: Walker, *The Shattered Silents*, 66.

25. theaters had been wired: Ibid., 209.

26. "the girl with the": *Photoplay*, Oct. 1929, n.p.

27. "all of a sudden": Capra, "Reminiscences," 78.

28. "Jack Warner took me": Loy, "Reminiscences of Myrna Loy," 1425.

29. "little more than": *New York Times*, March 13, 1929; "Mud, Blood": Dolores Costello, speaking in Brownlow and Gill, *Hollywood: The Pioneers*, episode 8.

30. "My contention was": Hal Mohr in an undated Brownlow interview, courtesy Brownlow.

31. "It was a kind of": Loy, "Reminiscences of Myrna Loy," 1429; "Vere ees Pierre?": ML, quoted in Chierichetti, "Myrna Loy Today," 6.

32. "stay away": Loretta Young, quoted in Kotsilibas-Davis interview fragment for *BB*, MLP, Box 30, folder 21, 1089.

33. "really horrible": quoted in McBride, *Searching for John Ford*, 169; "an unwieldy combination": *LA Times*, May 10, 1929.

34. "Hollywood is wasteful": *Photoplay*, Jan. 1928, 24; "has never had": Creighton Peet, quoted in Kay, *Myrna Loy*, 42.

35. "Myrna doesn't": Colman, "The Siren from Montana," 112.

36. "I had airs": ML, quoted in Chandler, *Not the Girl Next Door*, 40.

37. Barry Norton: York, "Doug's Office Boy Makes Good," 96; "first adult love": ML, quoted in Hall, "The Truth about the Mysterious Miss Loy," Part 2, n.p.; Norton later came out: André Soares, telephone conversation with the author.

38. a Chinese man . . . "What depressed me": Steel, "Myrna Loy," 6. I owe this reference to Donna Hill.

39. Zanuck would later: Johnston, "Myrna Loy," 12.

6. BREAKTHROUGH

1. "Los Angeles is": *Variety*, Feb. 12, 1930.
2. "The directors": ML, quoted in a 1939 20th Century–Fox press release, MLP, Box 33.
3. "Myrna Loy makes": *Variety*, April 16, 1930.
4. "Eleanore is": ML, quoted in *LA Evening Herald*, Nov. 15, 1930.
5. "They had to keep": Baxter, quoted in an undated *Screen Mirror* clipping, MLP, Box 33; "Her strange eyes": W. E. Oliver, *LA Evening Herald*, Nov. 14, 1930.
6. "Miss Loy is": Parsons, *LA Examiner*, Dec. 12, 1930; Fox contract: Contract dated Oct. 7, 1930, Fox legal files, UCLA; "This brings": *LA Evening Herald*, Oct. 9, 1930.
7. Fox during . . . turmoil: Gomery, *The Hollywood Studio System*, 43–44; "the worst year": *Variety*, Dec. 19, 1931; Fox profits plummeted: Balio, *Grand Design*, 16.
8. Embassy Club dinner: *Hollywood Daily Citizen*, Oct. 14, 1931.
9. Fox failed to pick up: *LA Evening Herald*, June 11, 1931; Fox dropped its option: May 1 and May 19, 1931, anonymous letters to Harry Reinhardt, Fox legal files, UCLA.
10. Lonsdale to Goldwyn: Berg, *Goldwyn*, 193.
11. "the best and most natural": *LA Examiner*, Feb. 7, 1931.
12. "Jeanne Eagels": ML, quoted in Colman, "The Siren from Montana," 112.
13. "a restraint": *LA Record*, Aug. 12, 1931; "Myrna Loy, who has wrecked": Parsons, *LA Examiner*, Aug. 12, 1931.
14. "I wanted ceilings": James Wong Howe, quoted in Higham, *Hollywood Cameramen*, 88; "one of the most": ML, quoted in *LA Record*, Aug. 8, 1931; "pushes everything back": Howe to John Barber, "Jimmy Wong Howe," undated *World Film News* article, Kevin Brownlow Collection.
15. Howe considered her: Howe to Barber, "Jimmy Wong Howe," undated *World Film News* article, Kevin Brownlow Collection.
16. "Myrna Loy, as I met her": Hal Wiener, *LA Evening Herald*, Oct. 31, 1931.
17. In his autobiography: Stewart, *By a Stroke of Luck*, 176.
18. commanded $30,000 . . . to Myrna's $750: *Rebound* budget, March 1931, RKO Collection, UCLA; "That woman": quoted by ML to Chierichetti, "Myrna Loy Today," 7.
19. "I had a part": Loy, "Reminiscences of Myrna Loy," 130.
20. "I have fallen": Sidney Howard, revised *Arrowsmith* script dated Aug. 19, 1931, Goldwyn Collection, AMPAS.
21. "intelligent and forceful": *New York Times*, Dec. 8, 1931; Sinclair Lewis at premiere: *LA Times*, Dec. 13, 1931.
22. "He got stuck": quoted in McBride, *Searching for John Ford*, 187.
23. in *Transatlantic*: *LA Record*, Oct. 12, 1931.
24. "All the heartbreak": ML, quoted in Moak, "The Girl Hollywood Couldn't Beat," 67.
25. "I'm tired": ML, quoted in Moak, "The Girl Hollywood Couldn't Beat,"

67; "The screen was turning": Manners, "At Last, the Heart-Stirring Love Story of Myrna Loy," 12.

7. CUTTING THE VEIL

1. "as if his words": "Metro-Goldwyn-Mayer," *Fortune*, Dec. 1932; repr. in Balio, *The American Film Industry*, 314; Robert Montgomery considered him: Eyman, *Lion of Hollywood*, 204; "Thalberg was": Mannix quoted in Marx, *Mayer and Thalberg*, vii.

2. "I believe": ML, quoted in Hall, "Should a Girl Forgive?" 5.

3. "His gaiety": *Photoplay*, Nov. 1932, 29.

4. "virgin spring": Jason Joy to Harold Hurley, Aug. 9, 1932, PCA files for *Love Me Tonight*, AMPAS.

5. "easy and graceful": *New York Times*, Aug. 19, 1932.

6. in the original: Nollen, *Boris Karloff*, 86.

7. "The picture is": *LA Record*, Dec. 9, 1932.

8. "final break with": ML, quoted in Hall, "The Truth about the Mysterious Miss Loy," Part 2, n.p.; "adult" pictures: Selznick, quoted in Lasky, *RKO, the Biggest Little Major of Them All*, 77; considered for Broadway: *LA Times*, Oct. 8, 1933.

9. first screen test: Hepburn's "Animal Kingdom" screen test is included in the DVD *Hidden Hollywood: Treasures from the 20th Century Fox Vaults*, Image Entertainment, 2002.

10. "insufferable bossiness": Leslie Howard, quoted in Edwards, *Katharine Hepburn*, 74.

11. Irene Selznick drove: Terry Hornblow to the author, April 21, 2005; "crisp and debonair": Irene Mayer Selznick, *A Private View*, 118.

12. susceptible to his leading ladies: Van Neste, "Leslie Howard," 27, 31.

13. "It takes three": ML, quoted in Henderson, "It Takes 3 to Make a Love Affair," 19.

14. "made a vivid": *Variety*, Jan. 3, 1933; Mordaunt Hall: *New York Times*, Dec. 30, 1932; "Myrna Loy, as I've been": Jerry Hoffman, *LA Examiner*, Jan. 3, 1933.

15. Screen Actors Guild was founded: *Variety*, Oct. 3, 1933; Myrna herself did not join: SAG historian Valerie Yaros, email to the author, Feb. 23, 2007.

16. "an Irishman": Marx, *Mayer and Thalberg*, 72.

17. "It was all": Frances Goodrich letter, quoted in Goodrich, *The Real Nick and Nora*, 63.

18. "Tits and sand": Stromberg, quoted in Marx, *Mayer and Thalberg*, 103; "all shots": James Wingate to E. J. Mannix, PCA files for *The Barbarian*, AMPAS; rerelease denied: Breen to Hay, Feb. 20, 1936, ibid.

19. a musicale: undated clipping, MLP, Box 15, folder 5.

20. "another shining": *Hollywood Reporter*, May 8, 1933.

21. "lovely and distinctive": *New York Herald Tribune*, Sept. 11, 1933; "Myrna Loy reveals": *Variety*, Sept. 12, 1933.

22. He did his editing: David O. Selznick made this observation in an unsent letter to Hitchcock, quoted in Selznick, *Memo from David O. Selznick,* 277; Pauline Kael: in Kael, *5001 Nights at the Movies,* 758.

23. "The reckless pace": Van Dyke, quoted in Sharpe, "W. S. Van Dyke," 107; according to Selznick: Selznick, *Memo from David O. Selznick,* 115; "In his Western": Johnston, "Lord Fauntleroy in Hollywood," 20.

24. "He always knew": Loy, "Reminiscences of Myrna Loy," 1433.

25. "I've had too much": ML, quoted in *Hollywood Citizen News,* April 7, 1933.

26. Howard Hawks left the set: McCarthy, *Howard Hawks,* 182; Hawks had managed: John Lee Mahin, interview by Todd McCarthy and Joseph McBride, in McGilligan, *Backstory,* 248.

27. "national socialist feeling": Quoted in Doherty, *Pre-code Hollywood,* 94.

28. "an unsophisticated": ML, quoted in Lyn, "Unmasking Myrna Loy," 70.

29. "simply delicious": ML, quoted in *LA Times,* Oct. 8, 1933; he feared: Lyn, "Unmasking Myrna Loy," 70; his most recent conquest: Stenn, *Bombshell,* 125–26.

30. Practical jokes: Robert Cannom, *Van Dyke and the Mythical City of Hollywood,* 280.

31. Carnera only agreed: *Variety,* Nov. 14, 1933.

32. "come along": *Variety,* Nov. 14, 1933; "a flyer's": *Variety,* Oct. 10, 1933.

33. "Clark Gable": Will Rogers, quoted in *Variety,* Nov. 14, 1933; "every woman": Irving Thalberg, quoted in Hay, *MGM,* 100; "the affair": Adela Rogers St. John, quoted in Harris, *Clark Gable,* 82; "would have": Gable, quoted in Vieira, *Hollywood Dreams Made Real,* 116.

34. "Phone calls": Marx, *Mayer and Thalberg,* 166.

35. the published caption: *Photoplay,* Nov. 1934, 47; "At the moment": *New York Daily Mirror,* Nov. 27, 1933; "the most voluptuous": Eleanor Barnes, *LA Illustrated Daily News,* Dec. 11, 1933.

36. "My ears": quoted in Tornabene, *Long Live the King,* 177; "He'll never": Hughes, quoted by Lewis Milestone, AFI Oral History, Lewis Milestone Collection, folder 172, p. 139, AMPAS.

37. "He believed": ML, quoted in *Philadelphia Inquirer,* Nov. 29, 1987; "his nearness": Crawford and Ardmore, *A Portrait of Joan,* 88; Joan Blondell reported: Kennedy, *Joan Blondell,* 37; "a caveman": *Photoplay,* Nov. 1931, 67.

38. "a tenderness": *Variety,* June 12, 1934.

39. "presents grave danger": Wingate to Mannix, Dec. 13, 1933, PCA files for *Men in White,* AMPAS.

8. MR. AND MRS. THIN MAN

1. "Myrna Loy and William Powell": *Lion's Roar,* Nov. 1941, n.p.

2. "drinking at the bar": Breen to Mayer, April 6, 1934, PCA files for *The Thin Man,* AMPAS.

3. "It seems to me": Undated letter, Harriet B. Adams to Breen, PCA files for *The Thin Man,* AMPAS; "excessive amount": Breen to Mayer, Sept. 26, 1936, PCA files for *After the Thin Man,* AMPAS.

4. W. S. Van Dyke: Lambert, *Norma Shearer,* 255.

5. The original Nick: Hammett, *The Thin Man,* 27.

6. "got excited": Hammett, *The Thin Man,* 151.

7. "the real": Goodrich, *The Real Nick and Nora;* "it was nice": Hellman, "Dashiell Hammett," n.p.

8. "I hope so": Frances Goodrich, Jan. 1934 letter quoted in Goodrich, *The Real Nick and Nora,* 76; "I don't care": Van Dyke, quoted in Bowers, "Frances Goodrich and Albert Hackett," 464.

9. initial profits: Mannix Ledger, Howard Strickling Collection, AMPAS; "made in Culver City": Harry Haun, "The Queen of Hollywood," *New York Daily News,* Jan. 6, 1985.

10. "We got into the habit": ML, quoted in Loy and Powell, "Why We Are an Ideal Team," 7; "I have never": Powell, quoted in *Lion's Roar,* Nov. 1941, n.p.

11. "Be brave": Powell in unsourced clipping, MLP, Box 33, folder 4; floppy flippers: ML, quoted in Chierichetti, "Myrna Loy Today," 13.

12. "Is your cash register": *Variety,* Nov. 11, 1934.

13. "I wanted it": Howe, quoted in Higham, *Hollywood Cameramen,* 87.

14. "someone like": Powell, quoted in Bryant, *William Powell,* 78; "a bit of a fuss pot": Powell, quoted in Loy and Powell, "Why We Are an Ideal Team," 7.

15. "fancy tail feathers": Powell, quoted in Francisco, *Gentleman,* 99.

16. "write a story": Mayer, quoted in Eyman, *Lion of Hollywood,* 301.

17. "a murder mystery . . . newlyweds": Van Dyke, quoted in Koszarski, *Hollywood Directors,* 312; rights for $22,000: This amount was reported in the *Chicago Tribune,* March 9, 1937, but Sam Marx remembered paying $14,000 (*BB,* 90).

18. sixteen days: Van Dyke, quoted in Koszarski, *Hollywood Directors,* 311.

19. "general tone": Breen to Mayer, Feb. 21, 1934, PCA files for *The Thin Man.*

20. "Don't be so": Hammett, *The Thin Man,* 163.

21. "Santa Claus hasn't": ML, quoted in Hall, "Should a Girl Forgive?" undated typescript, 5.

22. "If women": ML, quoted in Harrison Carroll, *LA Evening Herald Express,* Nov. 22, 1935.

23. Kansas City: Francisco, *Gentleman,* 7–8.

24. Powell at Warner Bros.: Basinger, *The Star Machine,* 401–4.

25. salaries: *New York Times,* Jan. 7, 1937; *Motion Picture Herald,* Feb. 6, 1937.

26. "One could tell": Marx, *Mayer and Thalberg,* 78; "with Stromberg": quoted in Latham, *Crazy Sundays,* 188–89.

27. "We were getting": Hackett, "Reminiscences of Albert Hackett," 31.

28. "Van Dyke certainly": Rudy Behlmer, editor's epilogue, in Van Dyke, *W. S. Van Dyke's Journal,* 114–16.

29. "We couldn't": quoted in Goodrich, *The Real Nick and Nora,* 123.

30. Hammett . . . suffered a breakdown: Johnson, *Dashiell Hammett,* 151–52.

31. suspended Hammett's contract: note in *Selected Letters of Dashiell Hammett, 1921–1960,* 133.

32. rejected Hammett's proposal: Drees, "The Thin Man," 52.

33. "No one ever": Hammett to Hellman, quoted in Drees, "The Thin Man," 53.

9. MYRNA LOY VS. MGM

1. *Motion Picture Herald* survey: reported in *Hollywood Citizen News,* Aug. 14, 1935.

2. Robbin Coons, "Hollywood," *Gettysburg Times,* Nov. 27, 1936.

3. Joseph Breen objected: Breen to Mayer, Sept. 26, 1936, PCA file for *After the Thin Man,* AMPAS.

4. "Miss Loy's costume": Carolyn Anspacher, *San Francisco Chronicle,* Sept. 23, 1936.

5. "We did succeed": Van Dyke, quoted in Koszarski, *Hollywood Directors, 1914–1940,* 315.

6. Otis Ferguson: *New Republic,* Nov. 25, 1936.

7. "Look for": *Variety,* July 17, 1934; Donald Ogden Stewart: Stewart papers, Beinecke Rare Book and Manuscript Library, Yale University.

8. "Not one person": *Motion Picture Herald,* Sept. 22, 1934.

9. "There would be": Russell, *Life Is a Banquet,* 60.

10. "There's all": *Variety,* Nov. 13, 1934.

11. revise the *It Happened One Night* script: Capra, *The Name above the Title,* 164.

12. "He was able": Loy, "Reminiscences of Myrna Loy," 1434.

13. He mounted two cameras: Walker, *The Light on Her Face,* 203.

14. hiring a few rich: *Variety,* July 10, 1934.

15. "our faith": *New York Times,* Nov. 30, 1934.

16. "As a result": Capra, *The Name above the Title,* 404.

17. "Story concerns": *Variety,* July 10, 1935; "a shy little person": Frank Nugent on *Maskerade, New York Times,* Jan. 27, 1937; "so absolutely perfect": ML, quoted in McDonald, "Myrna Knows All the Answers," 74.

18. "I knew": ML, quoted in Chierichetti, "Myrna Loy Today," 13.

19. "artless, unsophisticated": McDonald, "Myrna Knows All the Answers," 74; Gottfried . . . had recommended: Kevin Brownlow, email to the author, June 12, 2008, based on his unpublished interview with Reinhardt; Powell insisted: Rainer interview, quoted in Brenner, "The Last Goddess," 395.

20. "I was just": Rainer, quoted in *People Magazine* interview, April 11, 1988, n.p.; "good looker": Mayer, quoted by Rainer in Brenner, "The Last Goddess," 399; "We've made you": Mayer, quoted by Eyman, *Lion of Hollywood,* 243.

21. "until the whole": ML, quoting Mannix in Chierichetti, "Myrna Loy Today," 13.

22. septic infection: Terry Hornblow to the author, April 21, 2005.

23. "but the nature": *LA Evening Herald,* March 8, 1935; "Chatter": *Variety,* March 19, 1935; "Several weeks ago": Manners, "I Know Myrna Loy—But Not Very Well," 87.

24. Mannix telegram to ML: dated May 10, 1935, MLP, Box 7, folder 5.

25. "with the gay assurance": *New York Times,* May 12, 1935.

26. "we don't die": *New York Herald,* May 19, 1935; "Miss Loy soon": ibid.

27. "descended like a swarm . . . killed": Lyn, "Unmasking Myrna Loy," 71.

28. "there's nothing": ML, quoted in *Picturegoer,* June 15, 1935.

29. "I had to pinch": ML, quoted in *Beverly Hills Shopping News,* Jan. 6, 1936.

30. In the past: *Variety,* May 29, 1935; "The gentle": Samuels, "Loyal to Loy," 55.

31. "Myrna Loy Abrogates": *LA Examiner,* Aug. 14, 1935; "I was given": ML, quoted in *Hollywood Citizen News,* Aug. 14, 1935.

32. "was never a field mouse": Ager, *Variety,* Aug. 14, 1935.

33. *Soak the Rich: Variety,* Aug. 21, 1935.

34. "Some executives": "The Myrna Loy Crisis," *New York Times,* Aug. 25, 1935.

35. "Actress Mends": *New York American,* Sept. 11, 1935; "Myrna Loy Back": *LA Times,* Sept. 4, 1935; new contract: *LA Times,* Nov. 27, 1937.

10. MRS. ARTHUR HORNBLOW JR.

1. "The Arthur Hornblows": Zeitlin, "Happy Ever After," 89.

2. "sleepy, quaint": Lane, "Myrna Talks about Marriage," 42.

3. Fairbanks was an old friend: Jeffrey Vance to the author, July 30, 2007.

4. salary for 1935: U.S. Treasury figures, *New York Times,* Jan. 7, 1937; percentage: *Variety,* Nov. 21, 1933.

5. "High altitudes": *New York Times,* Feb. 1, 1935.

6. "He married a lot": Hackett, quoted in Goodrich, *The Real Nick and Nora,* 55.

7. "genuine disdain": Curtis, *W. C. Fields,* 323–24.

8. Visart would . . . become pregnant: David Chierichetti to the author, March 17, 2008; see also Chierichetti, *Mitchell Leisen,* 12.

9. "perennial Peter Pan": Fontaine, *No Bed of Roses,* 202.

10. "I'm interested": ML, quoted in Harrington, "The Marriage Code of Myrna Loy," 92.

11. "never tells her": Penn, quoted in Zeitlin, "Myrna's Maid Tells on Miss Loy," 84.

12. "we have a few friends": ML, quoted in Hall, "That Other Me," 7.

13. "wines at the right": Owens, "Why the Perfect Wife's Marriage Failed," 62; first big party: *LA Examiner,* Jan. 23, 1938.

14. "the shyest": Manners, "I Know Myrna Loy—But Not Very Well," 30; photo caption: Constance McCormick scrapbook, vol. 1, Constance McCormick Collection, USC.

15. lunch given by Merle Oberon: *LA Examiner,* May 25, 1936.

16. "You certainly know": ML to Cukor, June 27, 1977, Cukor Collection, AMPAS.

17. Trocadero: *LA Examiner,* Feb. 14, 1937.

18. "Venus de Milo": Charles Laughton in an uncredited clipping, British Film Institute, London.

19. testimony of Betty Black: transcript of interview fragment by Kotsilibas-Davis, MLP, Box 30, folder 19, 2176.

20. "Mrs. Popper": *LA Evening Herald Express,* July 2, 1938.

21. "no ballroom": ML, quoted in Zeitlin, "Happy Ever After," 88; "lifted bodily": ML, quoted in Hamilton, "Myrna Loy's Honeymoon House," 87; charm bracelet: unsourced clip, MLP, Box 33, folder 5.

22. "a peasant handkerchief": Willson, "The Revealing True Story of Myrna Loy," Part 3, 81; "I hate clothes": ML, quoted in Hall, "So You Want to Be a Movie Star?" 7.

23. "She never": Theresa Penn, quoted in Zeitlin, "Myrna's Maid Tells on Miss Loy," 30.

24. a bequest: Last Will and Testament of Myrna Loy, a.k.a. Myrna Williams, Oct. 5, 1983, Surrogate Court of the State of New York.

25. six ducklings: Terry Hornblow to the author, April 20, 21, 2005; "i am sorry": Terry Hornblow to ML, 1936 letter, MLP, Box 32, folder 1.

26. Terry found his father: Terry Hornblow to the author, April 20, 21, 2005.

27. stepson Michael: Michael Hornblow to the author, June 10, 2005.

28. "It is curious": *LA Evening Herald Examiner,* Aug. 1, 1936; We Hate Arthur: James Kotsilibas-Davis recollections, transcript fragment, MLP, Box 30, folder 19, 2105.

11. WIFE VS. MISTRESS

1. "When I began": ML, quoted in Dorothy Manners, "Notes on Myrna Loy," 1960 typescript in ML Bio folder, AMPAS.

2. fellow actor Robert Ryan: McDowall, *Double Exposure,* 238; marriage rate: Mintz and Kellogg, *Domestic Revolutions,* 136.

3. "on ribbing terms": ML, quoted in Zeitlin, "Behind the Mystery of Myrna Loy," 70.

4. in *On Golden Pond:* Doris Hornblow to the author, May 13, 2005.

5. "consort": Mordden, *The Hollywood Studios,* 146.

6. "I am presenting": Ed Sullivan, quoted in *New York Daily News,* Dec. 10, 1937.

7. "I'm sick to death": ML, quoted in Schallert, "She's Tired of Being a Wife," 26.

8. "I'm determined": L. B. Mayer, quoted in Crowther, *Hollywood Rajah,* 83.

9. "The sanctity": Production Code, reprinted in Mast, *Movies in Our Midst,* 332–33.

10. a laundry list: Breen to Jason Joy, April 2, 1936, PCA files for *To Mary— with Love,* AMPAS; paying Myrna $3,000 a week: May 25, 1936, George Wesson letter, Fox Collection, UCLA.

11. "hash-over": *Variety,* Sept. 2, 1936; "It begins": quoted in *Hollywood Reporter,* Nov. 6, 1936.

12. "That woman": ML, quoted in Chierichetti, "Myrna Loy Today," 10; "Please put": Breen to Mayer, Nov. 12, 1936, PCA files for *Wife vs. Secretary,* AMPAS.

13. "Myrna Loy performs": *Hollywood Reporter,* Feb. 14, 1936.

14. "You wouldn't": Hall, "That Other Me," 4.

15. "Naturally": quoted in *Philadelphia Bulletin,* "I Want a Wife like Myrna Loy," July 13, 1947.

16. "Present treatment": Breen to Mayer, July 1, 1936, PCA files for *Libeled Lady,* AMPAS.

17. "reflects unfavorably": Breen to Mayer, Aug. 31, 1936, PCA files for *Libeled Lady,* AMPAS.

18. "When I": Weingarten, quoted in "Hollywood in the Thirties," 2; Harlow . . . did want to join: Stenn to the author, Sept. 28, 2008; Thalberg had agreed: Ford, *John Ford,* 148.

19. "the balancing": *Time,* Oct. 19, 1936.

20. "In those days": Weingarten, quoted in "Hollywood in the Thirties," 7.

21. "reek with": *Variety,* Nov. 4, 1936; Schallert: *LA Times,* Oct. 8, 1936; Canby: *New York Times,* Feb. 1, 1981; Hepburn: quoted in Weales, *Canned Goods as Caviar,* 224.

22. "this huge": Greene, *The Graham Greene Film Reader,* 139.

23. total of 250 tailors: Gutner, *Gowns by Adrian,* 58.

24. rights to the story: *Variety,* Feb. 27, 1935; Burke's biographer: Hayter-Menzies, *Mrs. Ziegfeld,* 160.

25. she later said: Rainer, quoted in Brenner, "The Last Goddess," 397.

26. "Miss Loy": *New York Times,* April 9, 1936; Cecilia Ager: *Variety,* April 15, 1936; Harrison Carroll: *LA Herald Express,* April 16, 1936.

27. "No matter": Breen to Thalberg, Dec. 4, 1935, PCA files for *Parnell,* AMPAS. Earlier drafts of the identical letter were first sent to Walter Wanger Productions and to Jason Joy at Fox.

28. "about as fiery": *New York Times,* June 4, 1937.

29. "some twenty": ML, quoted in Hall, "So You Want to Be a Movie Star?" 3.

30. Gable blamed Crawford: Thomas, *Joan Crawford,* 93.

31. "Myrna Loy behaves": *Time,* June 14, 1937; "showing physical contact": Breen to Mayer, Aug. 29, 1936, PCA files for *Parnell,* AMPAS.

32. *Parnell* preview postcards: John Stahl Collection, USC.

33. The *Infidelity* screenplay is part of the University of South Carolina's Warner Bros./Turner Entertainment F. Scott Fitzgerald Screenplay Collection; Fitzgerald had listed: Latham, *Crazy Sundays,* 86.

34. "a deep bow": Fitzgerald to Hunt Stromberg, June 27, 1938, in Fitzgerald, *Correspondence,* 509; "the whole thing": quoted by Charles McGrath, "Fitzgerald as Screenwriter," *New York Times,* April 22, 2004.

35. "Thalberg was dead": Crawford, quoted in Newquist, *Conversations with Joan Crawford,* 181; "The world of art": quoted in Thomas, *Thalberg,* 321; "he'd taken": Loos, *Kiss Hollywood Good-by,* 134.

36. "The public": *Photoplay,* July 1938, 9.

12. TROUBLE

1. had begun dating someone else: Stenn, *Bombshell,* 190–93.

2. Harlow's medical care: Stenn, *Bombshell,* 201; Golden, *Platinum Girl,* 210.

3. "I just don't": ML, quoted in Hall, "So You Want to Be a Movie Star?" 5; salaries: *LA Evening Herald Express,* April 7, 1939.

4. "Hell, they were": quoted in Bull and Lee, *The Faces of Hollywood,* 68.

5. Lombard had been trying: Swindell, *Screwball,* 208.

6. "Daddy": quoted in Stenn, *Bombshell*, 194.

7. "Minnie": Dr. Saxton Pope to ML, undated [June 1937] letter, MLP, Box 32, folder 1.

8. "L. B. Mayer sent": Loos, *Kiss Hollywood Good-By*, 161.

9. "temporary colostomy": "Surgery," *Time*, May 10, 1963; "Bill Powell was": *LA Evening Herald Express*, April 7, 1938.

10. ranked as the fourth: *Variety*, Jan. 5, 1938; "a complete": *Variety*, Oct. 26, 1938.

11. "Christ, he": Joseph Mankiewicz, quoted in Geist, *Pictures Will Talk*, 88.

12. "might have figured": *Motion Picture Herald*, April 23, 1938.

13. "Judicious cutting": *New York Daily Mirror*, April 16, 1938.

14. "An Earthbound Boy": E. B. White, *New Yorker*, May 21, 1938, 164.

15. "Miss Loy": *New York Daily News*, July 23, 1939; "I was the brave": ML, quoted in Hall, "That Other Me," 4.

16. Collins's widow: *Variety*, July 13, 1938.

17. "unnecessary drinking": Breen to Mayer, April 20, 1937, PCA files for *Test Pilot*, AMPAS.

18. "Comes now": quoted in Skolsky, *Hollywood Citizen News*, Dec. 11, 1937; "Spencer Tracy would have": Strickling, quoted by Tornabene, *Long Live the King*, 206.

19. "had all the authority": Crawford, quoted in Newquist, *Conversations with Joan Crawford*, 113.

20. 838 planes: *Hollywood Reporter*, April 15, 1938.

21. Fleming replaced him: Michael Sragow, *Victor Fleming*, 592.

22. "a woman's place": *London Evening Standard*, Oct. 15, 1938; "Studios Turn": *Variety*, June 22, 1938.

23. "Clark was always": ML, quoted in Chierichetti, "Myrna Loy Today," 10; "very beautiful": ML, quoted in Barthel, "Quartet of Queens."

24. as late as 1974: ML, interview by James Day, "Day at Night," Jan. 27, 1974, WNET-TV.

25. References to the Italian invasion: Douglas Churchill, *New York Times*, June 26, 1938.

26. third place: *Variety*, May 10, 1939.

27. "That near-war": Joe Laurie Jr., *Variety*, Oct. 5, 1938.

28. "if the crisis": Joe Laurie Jr., *Variety*, Sept. 28, 1938.

29. "the only 'ism'": Dorothy Parker, quoted in Rosten, *Hollywood*, 133.

30. "The town has become": Ruth Rankin, *Photoplay*, June 1938, 25.

31. "I have very few": ML, quoted in Arthur, "Interview with Myrna Loy," 8.

32. French warships: *LA Examiner*, July 14, 1939.

33. *Confessions of a Nazi Spy*: Schatz, *Boom and Bust*, 267.

34. At a private: Donald Ogden Stewart, *By a Stroke of Luck*, 236.

35. Motion Picture Artists Committee: *LA Evening News*, Dec. 1, 1937; Gianos, *Politics and Politicians in American Film*, 61.

36. Hollywood Anti-Nazi League: May 6, 1955, affidavit in ML's FBI file, Dept. of Justice, FBI archives; backers: Stuart and Thompson, *I Just Keep Hoping*, 46.

37. Myrna's signature: FBI report on ML, Feb. 10, 1965, Dept. of Justice, FBI archives.

38. Herbert Hornblow: *LA Evening Herald Express,* Sept. 15, 1938; die of a stroke: *New York Times,* May 7, 1942.

39. *The Rains Came* premiered: *LA Examiner,* Sept. 15, 1939.

40. story conference: notes to August 26, 1938, conference on *The Rains Came,* 20th Century–Fox Collection, Performing Arts Archives, USC; British consul: notes to May 13, 1938, conference on *The Rains Came,* 20th Century–Fox Collection, Performing Arts Archives, USC.

41. "I want to be wicked": ML, quoted by Ed Sullivan, *New York Daily News,* Aug. 7, 1939.

42. "I'm pretty much": ML, quoted in a 1939 20th Century–Fox press release, film file for *The Rains Came,* Core Collection, AMPAS.

43. Joseph Breen had warned: Breen to Selznick, Dec. 10, 1937, PCA files for *The Rains Came,* AMPAS.

44. "No picture in years": Parsons, *LA Examiner,* Sept. 15, 1939; "Fox reported": 20th Century–Fox press release, film file for *The Rains Came,* Core Collection, AMPAS.

45. interstudio agreement: Loan-out agreement for ML, Spencer Tracy, and Robert Taylor, Dec. 12, 1937, Fox Collection, UCLA; "She should be": notes on August 26, 1938, conference on *The Rains Came,* 20th Century–Fox Collection, Performing Arts Archives, USC.

46. "Miss Loy has": James Francis Crow, *Hollywood Citizen News,* Sept. 7, 1939.

47. he'd be the wind: Barthel, "Quartet of Queens."

48. "only sporadically": *New York Herald Tribune,* Sept. 9, 1939; brooding atmosphere: *Daily Variety,* Sept. 7, 1939; "one of her finest": *Hollywood Reporter,* Sept. 7, 1939.

13. THINGS FALL APART

1. sojourn in Big Sky country: *New York Journal American,* Feb. 28, 29, 1940.

2. purchase part of the . . . ranch: Probate court document, Dec. 10, 1942, Estate of David F. Williams.

3. "I'm not the perfect": ML in *San Francisco Examiner,* Dec. 3, 1939.

4. "still another actress": *Photoplay,* Feb. 1941, 52.

5. elite circles: Leonora Hornblow obituary, *Guardian,* Nov. 16, 2005.

6. "*I* was the love": Leonora Hornblow to the author, June 10, 2005.

7. brief fling with Kay Francis: Kear and Rossman, *Kay Francis,* 113; "caused her great unhappiness": *San Francisco Chronicle,* June 2, 1942.

8. "can't read": Hopkins, quoted in Marx, *Mayer and Thalberg,* 174.

9. Arthur took everything: Quit-claim, Jan. 2, 1941, Arthur Hornblow papers, courtesy Michael Hornblow. The collection has been donated to the Margaret Herrick Library, AMPAS.

10. postnuptial agreement: Feb. 5, 1937, Hornblow papers, AMPAS; handed her a bill: agreements dated Jan. 2, 1941, and May 14, 1942, Hornblow papers, AMPAS.

11. "too tired to know": ML, quoted in Hall, "So You Want to Be a Movie Star?" 6.

12. "The men who work": Carole Lombard, quoted in Crawford and Ardmore, *A Portrait of Joan,* 90; "Her friends knew": Owens, "Why the Perfect Wife's Marriage Failed," 52.

13. he saw her: Grant, "She's My Dream Wife," 51.

14. "would prefer": Hedda Hopper, *San Francisco Examiner,* May 6, 1940.

15. "I saw a lot": Irene Selznick to Leonora Hornblow, quoted in Aronson, "Legendary Lives," 54.

16. "Myrna Loy Admits": *LA Times,* Nov. 16, 1940; "We have tried": Arthur Hornblow Jr. in unsourced clip, Nov. 16, 1940, ML clippings file, NYPL.

17. "Myrna Loy has won": Parsons, *San Francisco Examiner,* Jan. 4, 1941.

18. "The marriages of": Owens, "Why the Perfect Wife's Marriage Failed," 52.

19. "When they were not": *San Francisco Examiner,* Sept. 28, 1941; "She says no more": *San Francisco Examiner,* June 26, 1941.

20. "Mr. Poo": Diana Lewis in undated *Photoplay* article on Powell's third marriage, William Powell clippings file, NYPL.

21. "When lovely Myrna": Fred Dickenson, "When the Perfect Wife Rebels," *Albuquerque Journal,* April 4, 1941.

22. Stanley Cavell: Cavell, *Pursuits of Happiness.*

23. "Heretofore I've always": ML, quoted in *New York Post,* Aug. 10, 1940.

24. "one of the best": *Hollywood Reporter,* Aug. 6, 1940; "the steady progression": *New York Times,* June 6, 1941; MGM's top ten: *Variety,* Sept. 3, 1941.

25. "The Last Time I Saw Paris": *Time,* Dec. 23, 1940.

26. At a benefit: *LA Times,* July 14, 1940; sold cigarettes: undated 1940 or 1941 photo in Constance McCormick scrapbooks, vol. 1, Constance McCormick Collection, USC.

27. There was talk of camouflaging; "Yachts and pleasure craft": *Variety,* Dec. 10, 1941.

28. "The Charleses": *New York Times,* Nov. 21, 1941.

29. "but you don't": Mayer to Douglas, quoted in Arthur, *The Political Career of an Actor,* 56–57.

30. slurs against Douglas: Arthur, *The Political Career of an Actor,* 84; "parlor pink": *LA Times* editorial, May 31, 1940.

31. "all born abroad": Senator Nye, quoted in *New York Times,* Sept. 10, 1941; "You may correctly": Harry Warner testimony, quoted in Sperber and Lax, *Bogart,* 174.

32. money for Greek War Relief: report on broadcast in *Moberly Monitor Index and Democrat,* Feb. 7, 1941.

33. Navy Relief Show: *New York Herald Tribune,* March 7, 1942; She persuaded: *Variety,* Jan. 21, 1942; Bundles for Bluejackets canteen: clipping, Dec. 31, 1941, in Constance McCormick scrapbooks, vol. 2, Constance McCormick Collection, USC.

34. Dolly Tree . . . topcoat: *LA Times,* Feb. 21, 1940.

35. "We had our first": Russell and Chase, *Life Is a Banquet,* 109.

36. private funeral: *LA Times,* Jan. 22, 1942.

37. reward for Gable's capture: Tornabene, *Long Live the King,* 311.

38. Mayer pulled strings: Eyman, *Lion of Hollywood,* 304; FDR's 1942 birth-

day celebration: press release from Hollywood Victory Committee, Feb. 27, 1942, Hollywood Victory Committee file, Special Collections, AMPAS.

39. *Motion Picture Herald* list: Dec. 18, 1940; *Variety*'s reckoning: Sept. 3, 1941; Lamour: *Variety*, Dec. 31, 1941; *Motion Picture Herald*, Dec. 26, 1942.

40. Gladys Rowley: *San Francisco Examiner*, April 20, 1942; "a gray tweed": *San Francisco Examiner*, June 2, 1942.

14. REBOUND

1. "Myrna Loy Bride": *New York Times*, June 7, 1942.

2. John Jr.: obituary, *Variety*, May 18, 1968; obituary, *New York Times*, May 13, 1968; see also Somer, *Ticonderoga*.

3. "I am one of those": ML, undated *Screenland* article, "Why Hollywood Turned Down Myrna Loy," MLP, Box 29, folder 1.

4. "Mrs. Hertz": Unsourced clip dated June 15, 1942, ML clippings file, NYPL.

5. "technical suspension": *New York Times*, May 21, 1944.

6. Betty Black considered: transcript of interview fragment by Kotsilibas-Davis, MLP, Box 30, folder 21, 2189.

7. "The Perfect Wife and": *San Francisco News-Call* photo caption, Sept. 29, 1942, San Francisco History Room, San Francisco Public Library.

8. business affairs: Martin Gang, attorney, to Mary Wall [secretary to Myron Selznick], July 7, 1942; Della Williams to Mary Wall, June 26, 1942; Myron Selznick & Co. to Martin Gang, June 24, 1942, MLP, Box 7, folder 6.

9. *A Guy Named Joe*: *San Francisco Examiner*, Oct. 1, 1942; Irene Dunne: *Hollywood Reporter*, Oct. 30, 1942.

10. Army Emergency Relief show: *New York Times*, Oct. 1, 1942.

11. "the President's favorite": Grace Tully, *F. D. R., My Boss*, 85; FDR viewed: *Variety*, Feb. 12, 1935, and April 24, 1934.

12. "That old gal": ML, quoted by Betty Black, transcript of interview fragment by Kotsilibas-Davis, MLP, Box 30, folder 19, 2187.

13. "First Lady Takes Role": *New York Times*, June 24, 1943.

14. "Recently": ML, quoted in *LA Times*, June 10, 1945; "Once you have seen": ML, quoted in Ben Maddox, undated *Screenland* article on *The Best Years of Our Lives*, Core Collection film file on *The Best Years of Our Lives*, AMPAS.

15. "Those incredible": ML, quoted in *LA Times*, July 15, 1945; "The blind soldiers": ML, quoted in *New York Post*, March 1, 1980.

16. Hearst newsreel: "Hollywood Stars Entertain Wounded Soldiers," [Jan.?] 1945, UCLA Film and Television Archive.

17. "I received": ML, quoted in *San Francisco Examiner*, May 21, 1946.

18. Ruth Mack Brunswick: Roazen, *The Historiography of Psychoanalysis*, 269.

19. taking nothing: Betty Black, transcript of interview fragment by Kotsilibas-Davis, MLP, Box 30, folder 19, 2186.

20. salary: memo from Harry Sokolov, Oct. 30, 1944, Myron Selznick Collection, Harry Ransome Humanities Research Center, Austin, Texas.

21. "Myrna Loy has never": Parsons, *San Francisco Examiner*, April 16, 1944; ML, quoted in ibid.

22. "He was constantly": obituary of Myron Selznick, *LA Times,* March 24, 1944.

23. "her favorite shade": 1944 MGM press release for *The Thin Man Goes Home,* British Film Institute.

24. "a sort of one-finger Thalberg": Fitzgerald, quoted in Latham, *Crazy Sundays,* 159.

25. taken on to please his brother: Scott, *In Capra's Shadow,* 156; "dreadfully dull": quoted in ibid., 157.

26. tippling . . . would be banished: *Hollywood Reporter,* April 5, 1944; "In real life": Sikov, *Screwball,* 209.

27. "production as a whole": *Variety,* Nov. 22, 1944.

28. Mexico to divorce: *LA Times,* Aug. 2, 1944.

29. "I heard the unmistakable": Leonora Schinasi Morris to Arthur Hornblow Jr., undated [1944], Hornblow Collection, Special Collections, AMPAS.

30. "Myrna said five": Leonora Schinasi Morris to Arthur Hornblow Jr., Dec. 17, 1944, Hornblow Collection, Special Collections, AMPAS; "a wonderful": ibid., undated [1944].

31. "she was dewy-eyed": Young, quoted in Leonora Schinasi Morris to Arthur Hornblow Jr., undated [1945], Hornblow Collection, Special Collections, AMPAS.

32. "Myrna Loy shared": *Washington Post,* Sept. 17, 1944; " 'Is you is' ": "Town Talk," *Washington Post,* Feb. 13, 1945.

15. POSTWAR

1. "was more than the amicable": Scheuer, *LA Times,* June 10, 1945; "broken away one by one": ibid.

2. "I've got to trip": ML, quoted in Scheuer, *LA Times,* June 10, 1945.

3. agreement with RKO: *Variety,* July 4, 1945.

4. *Best Years* came into being: Berg, *Goldwyn,* 393.

5. "we would spend": Wyler, "No Magic Wand," 11.

6. "The name of no other": contract dated Jan. 4, 1946, Goldwyn Collection, folder 4859, AMPAS.

7. "looks young": Robert Sherwood, *The Best Years of Our Lives,* Final Shooting Script, May 22, 1946, scene 68, p. 33, Goldwyn Collection, AMPAS.

8. "You loved each other": ibid., scene 240, p. 173.

9. "I can't believe": quoted in Chierichetti, "Myrna Loy Today," 15; seeing them meet: Kevin Thomas to the author, Dec. 16, 2007.

10. attaching a headset: Herman, *A Talent for Trouble,* 287.

11. "and he came down": Margaret Tallichet Wyler, quoted in Davis, *The Glamour Factory,* 245.

12. "Willy Wyler and Toland": Teresa Wright, quoted in Windolf, "From Best Years to Our Years," 21; "Thanks to depth of field": Bazin, "William Wyler," in *Bazin at Work,* 8.

13. "not only": *New York Times,* Nov. 22, 1946; "a horse-drawn": Farber, "Nervous from the Service," *New Republic,* Dec. 2, 1946.

14. "force, beauty" and "he now seems": Agee, *The Nation,* Dec. 14, 1946.

15. 1958 lawsuit: *New York Times,* July 1, 1958; Herman, *A Talent for Trouble,* 293.

16. "This time": *San Francisco Examiner,* Jan. 4, 1946.

17. According to Betty Black: Betty Black, transcript of interview fragment by Kotsilibas-Davis, MLP Box 30, folder 21, 2189.

18. "a delightful lady": Melinda Markey Van Dyke to the author, Sept. 29, 2007.

19. He once chastised her: Jack Larson to the author, July 3, 2006.

20. "The symbol": ML, talk delivered to California Women's Council, "Women United for the United Nations," March 23, 1948, MLP, Box 8, folder 2.

21. Woll's attack: reprinted in *Hollywood Reporter,* Sept. 30, 1946.

22. Joan Crawford hated: Newquist, *Conversations with Joan Crawford,* 151; Esther Williams found him: Williams and Diehl, *The Million Dollar Mermaid,* 155.

23. "I happen to know": Parsons, *San Francisco Examiner,* Oct. 2, 1946.

24. "I am not": ML, in *Hollywood Reporter,* Oct. 2, 1946.

25. Martin Gang filed: *LA Times,* Oct. 4, 1946; "that she has not": Woll, quoted in *LA Times,* Oct. 22, 1946.

26. "it suddenly became": Bacall, *By Myself,* 177.

27. contributed $1,000: list of contributors to the Committee for the First Amendment, William Wyler Collection, folder 596, AMPAS; "one of the most": FBI report on ML, Feb. 10, 1965, Dept. of Justice, FBI archives.

28. Schary . . . testified: quoted in *LA Times,* Oct. 30, 1947; "Whenever a serious": Douglas and Arthur, *See You at the Movies,* 161.

29. *Hollywood Fights Back:* ABC radio broadcasts, Oct. 26 and Nov. 2, 1947, tape recordings heard at the Paley Center for Media, New York.

30. secret list: *Variety,* Oct. 29, 1947; "a Communist device": *Variety,* Oct. 22, 1947.

31. "It is unfortunate": William Wyler to ML, Sept. 20, 1947, MLP, Box 32, folder 1.

32. "Film Industry Rules": *Variety,* Nov. 26, 1947.

33. "I dare them": ML to Wyler, Sept. 24, 1947, MLP, Box 32, folder 1.

16. BREAKING AWAY

1. "traitorous": quoted in Francisco, *Gentleman,* 217.

2. For *The Bachelor and the Bobby-Soxer:* RKO production files, UCLA.

3. split directing duties: Schary, *Heyday,* 140.

4. Grant threatened: Black, *Child Star,* 402.

5. "the calmness": " 'Oh shucks' ": Grant, "She's My Dream Wife," 64, 51.

6. "For the most part": *New York Herald Tribune,* July 25, 1947.

7. Shot in just: RKO production files, UCLA; duplicate outdoor sets: Hodgins, "Mr. Blandings Goes to Hollywood," n.p.

8. Norman Panama and Melvin Frank guessed: Hodgins, "Mr. Blandings Goes to Hollywood," n.p.; RKO . . . in red ink: Richard B. Jewell, "RKO Film Grosses, 1929–1951," n.p.

9. *Variety* complained: March 31, 1948.

10. "a bull's eye": James Agee, *The Nation*, April 24, 1948.

11. *Blandings* advertising tie-ins: Jurca, "Hollywood, the Dream House Factory," 29.

12. "I love her": Grant, "She's My Dream Wife," 74.

13. "they're too much alike": Kael, "The Man from Dream City," *New Yorker*, July 14, 1975, n.p.

14. "a big star": Lewis Milestone, AFI Oral History, Milestone Collection, folder 172, 209, AMPAS.

15. Salaries for *The Red Pony:* Ibid.

16. Linzer said: transcript of interview fragment by Kotsilibas-Davis, MLP, Box 30, folder 20, 957.

17. "many of the tensions": ML, quoted in *San Francisco Examiner*, May 13, 1948.

18. "simple and gracious": Henrey, *A Journey to Vienna*, 18.

19. "It did my heart": Mike Mansfield, quoted in *LA Times*, Dec. 2, 1949.

20. took a pay cut: *Cheaper by the Dozen* contract, Oct. 3, 1949, in 20th Century–Fox Collection, UCLA.

21. "How are the poplars?": Gene Markey to ML, undated [1949], MLP, Box 7, folder 5.

22. "We were away": Markey, quoted in *London Daily Mirror*, Jan. 10, 1950; "Myrna Loy Admits": *San Francisco Examiner*, Jan. 9, 1950.

23. "I shan't": Markey to ML, undated [1950], MLP, Box 7, folder 5.

24. "another storm": Markey to Martin Gang and Robert Kopp, Feb. 13, 1950, private collection.

25. "It's too painful": ML, quoted in *LA Times*, Aug. 17, 1950.

26. "There are a few": Markey to ML, undated [1950], MLP, Box 7, folder 5.

17. MRS. HOWLAND SARGEANT

1. "I want you": Eleanor Roosevelt to ML, quoted in Arthur, "Interview with Myrna Loy," 11; "I don't know enough": ML, *Extra*, June 1950, 3.

2. "a smart little" and "There's a new": *Long Beach Press Telegram*, March 25, 1951.

3. Myrna's close women friends: transcripts of interview fragments by Kotsilibas-Davis, MLP, Box 330, folder 19, 2191, 2020, 2139.

4. "a mismanaged": *New York Times*, May 5, 1952.

5. "Myrna Loy, known as": *Washington Post*, Oct. 7, 1952.

6. "It strikes me": Acheson, quoted in *New York Herald Tribune*, March 7, 1952.

7. pay cut: ML contract for *Belles on Their Toes*, July 18, 1951, 20th Century–Fox Collection, UCLA.

8. "a marshmallow mélange": *Time*, May 5, 1952.

9. "professionally and personally": ML to Passport Office, May 6, 1955, letter and affidavit, FBI file on ML, Dept. of Justice, FBI archives.

10. "a fine actress": Olivia de Havilland to the author, Sept. 21, 2006.

11. "He would shake": Jack Larson to the author, July 3, 2006.

12. United Artists agreed: financial agreement between Dore Schary Produc-

tions and United Artists, Aug. 15, 1958, Dore Schary Collection, Box 128, folder 51, Wisconsin Center for Film and Theater Research, Madison.

13. "Daddy loves": Jill Robinson, quoted in Peary and McGilligan, "Dore Schary," 24.

14. "Where's the corruption?": Clift, quoted in Bosworth, *Montgomery Clift,* 333; "With due respect": *New York Times,* March 5, 1959.

15. "There were sparks": quoted in Bosworth, *Montgomery Clift,* 338; Leone Rosson diaries, Joyce Marie Faust Collection. Dates for subsequent diary quotations will be included in the text.

16. "wonderful to Monty": Larson to the author, July 3, 2006.

17. "Dear Howland": notebook draft of ML letter to Sargeant, private collection.

18. Howland represented: Linzer, transcript of interview fragment by Kotsilibas-Davis, MLP, Box 30, folder 20, 967.

19. "The 54 year old": *LA Examiner,* June 1, 1960.

18. NEW YORK ENDING

1. "Hollywood seems to have": ML, quoted in *San Francisco Examiner,* Jan. 31, 1965; "There are *no*": ML, quoted in Braun, "Myrna Loy on Comedy," 9.

2. "One problem": ML, quoted in *LA Examiner,* Jan. 2, 1960; "People don't dress": ML, quoted in *LA Times* obituary, Dec. 15, 1993.

3. "I don't know why": "Star Admits Her 59 Years," *San Francisco Examiner,* Sept. 14, 1964; Joan Crawford confessed: Newquist, *Conversations with Joan Crawford,* 164.

4. "Work is important": ML, quoted by Dorothy Manners, *LA Examiner,* July 10, 1960; "I wish I'd had": ML, quoted by Margaret McManus in *San Francisco Chronicle,* Pink Section, April 2, 1967.

5. "Myrna was": Wynn Handman to the author, Oct. 11, 2006.

6. "You have a big voice": Handman, quoted in *New York Morning Telegraph,* Nov. 13, 1970.

7. "In films": ML, quoted in *New York World Telegram Sun,* Jan. 16, 1965.

8. a new house record: *New York Times,* Sept. 25, 1961.

9. "ML is a deft": *Variety,* Sept. 16, 1961; "her voice": Frank Prial on *There Must Be a Pony, Newark Evening News,* Aug. 29, 1962; "perfectly lucid": *LA Times,* Oct. 5, 1974.

10. "I never really": ML, quoted in *New York World Telegram and Sun,* Jan. 16, 1965.

11. a distinguished-looking gentleman: Richard Benjamin to the author, Sept. 12, 2009.

12. "got a little in the way": ML, quoted by Paine Knickerbocker, *San Francisco Chronicle,* Feb. 12, 1965.

13. "Christina wouldn't": ML, quoted in Chandler, *Not the Girl Next Door,* 265.

14. "Sorry to hear": ML to George Cukor, Dec. 1978, Cukor Collection, AMPAS; refusal to talk: Christina Crawford, *Mommie Dearest,* 285.

15. Sarah Siddons Award: *Chicago Tribune,* Jan. 22, 1966.

16. Christmas holiday: Deborah Hornblow to the author, Oct. 15, 2005.

17. told the TV interviewer: quoted on James Day, *Day at Night,* Jan. 27, 1974.

18. "completely intoxicated": Laurel Taylor recollections, email to the author, July 3, 2008.

19. "I'll go to bed": ML, quoted in *Women's Wear Daily,* July 30, 1981; Pope Brock: in *People,* April 4, 1988, 47.

20. "Now it is not": Barnes, *New York Times,* April 26, 1973.

21. "I looked like": Lainie Kazan to the author, Jan. 3, 2007.

22. Myrna told the crowd: Ron Bowers, email to the author, Sept. 6, 2006; "warm and cool": Springer and Hamilton, *They Had Faces Then,* 168.

23. Founder's Reception: Program, Nov. 21, 1963, American Place Theatre, MLP, Box 18, folder 3.

24. "Mr. Fonda and Miss Loy": John O'Connor, *New York Times,* Dec. 30, 1981.

25. "Dear, dear Cary": ML to Cary Grant, undated [1982], Grant Collection, AMPAS.

26. "That trip gave me": James Kotsilibas-Davis, quoted in *New York Post,* Nov. 5, 1987.

27. "There were many days": Kotsilibas-Davis and ML, quoted in *Philadelphia Inquirer,* Nov. 29, 1987.

28. American Place Theatre benefit gala: *New York Times,* Nov. 7, 1987.

29. "the reason she never": Robert Osborne, in *Hollywood Reporter,* Dec. 17, 1993.

30. tribute to be held at Carnegie Hall: *LA Times,* Jan. 17, 1985; *New York Post,* Jan. 16, 1985; *New York Times,* Dec. 15, 1993; event Program, Academy Awards Collection, AMPAS.

31. "You've made me": ML, at 63rd Annual Academy Awards, March 25, 1991.

32. "lovely and mysterious": Ronald Reagan, Dec. 4, 1988, Kennedy Center Honors, www.reagan.utexas.edu/archives/speeches/1988.

33. After a party: Miles Kreuger to the author, Aug. 19, 2006.

34. "Myrna Loy, Model of Urbanity": *New York Times,* Dec. 15, 1993.

35. "one of the least vain": Roddy McDowall, eulogy, Dec. 18, 1993, Frank E. Campbell Funeral Chapel, MLP, Box 25.

36. "rueful acceptance": Robert Lantz tribute, undated [1993], MHS clipping.

37. "If you want to know": ML, quoted in *Life,* Dec. 1984.

Bibliography

Alonso, Harriet Hyman. *Robert E. Sherwood: The Playwright in Peace and War.* Amherst: University of Massachusetts Press, 2007.

Als, Hilton. "The Cameraman" [Gregg Toland]. *New Yorker,* June 19, 2006.

American Film Institute Catalog of Feature Films, 1893–1971. http://afi.com/.

Anderegg, Michael A. *William Wyler.* Boston: Twayne, 1979.

Anonymous. "D. T. Williams." Undated typescript SC 2081. Myrna Loy Papers, Montana Historical Society Research Center, Helena.

———. "Surgery: How Not to Die of Cancer." *Time,* May 10, 1963.

———. "A Young Lady of Uncommon Good Sense." *Entertainment,* June 19, 1933.

Ardmore, Jane. "Myrna Loy Brings Excitement, and Finds Exciting New Talent in Hollywood." Undated (c. 1978) typescript. Jane Ardmore Papers. Margaret Herrick Library, Academy of Motion Picture Arts and Sciences.

Armstrong, Richard. "*The Best Years of Our Lives:* Planes of Innocence and Experience." *Filmint* 5, no. 6 (2007): 83–91.

Aronson, Steven M. L. "Legendary Lives: Memory and Desire." *Town and Country,* July 1993.

Arthur, Thomas Hahn. "Interview with Myrna Loy" [Transcript]. Call no. 75–034. Melvyn Douglas Project, Indiana University Center for the Study of History and Memory, Bloomington, 1975.

———. *The Political Career of an Actor: Melvyn Douglas and the New Deal.* Ann Arbor: University Microfilms, 1981.

Astor, Mary. *A Life on Film.* New York: Delacorte Press, 1971.

Atkinson, Brooks. *Broadway.* New York: Limelight, 1985.

Bacall, Lauren. *By Myself and Then Some.* New York: HarperCollins, 2006.

Bachardy, Don. *Stars in My Eyes.* Madison: University of Wisconsin Press, 2000.

Balio, Tino, ed. *The American Film Industry.* Rev. ed. Madison: University of Wisconsin Press, 1985.

————. *Grand Design: Hollywood as a Modern Business Enterprise, 1930–1939.* New York: Charles Scribner's Sons, 1993.

Barthel, Joan. "Quartet of Queens." *Life,* Feb. 19, 1971.

Basinger, Jeanine. *The Star Machine.* New York: Knopf, 2007.

Bazin, André. *Bazin at Work: Major Essays and Reviews from the Forties and Fifties.* Edited by Bert Cardullo. Translated by Alain Piette. New York: Routledge, 1997.

Bennett, Joan, and Lois Kibbee. *The Bennett Playbill.* New York: Holt, Rinehart, and Winston, 1970.

Berg, A. Scott. *Goldwyn: A Biography.* New York: Knopf, 1989.

Bergman, Andrew. *We're in the Money: Depression America and Its Films.* New York: New York University Press, 1971.

Bernstein, Matthew. *Walter Wanger: Hollywood Independent.* Berkeley: University of California Press, 1994.

Black, Shirley Temple. *Child Star: An Autobiography.* New York: McGraw-Hill, 1988.

Bosworth, Patricia. *Montgomery Clift: A Biography.* New York: Harcourt, Brace, Jovanovich, 1978.

Bowers, Ron. "Frances Goodrich and Albert Hackett." *Films in Review* 28, no. 8 (1977): 463–66, 490.

————. "Legendary Ladies of the Movies." *Films in Review* 24, no. 6 (1973): 321–29.

Braun, Eric. "Myrna Loy on Comedy." *Films and Filming,* no. 14 (March 1968): 9–11.

Brenner, Marie. "The Last Goddess" [Luise Rainer]. *Vanity Fair,* April 1998.

Brock, Pope. "Myrna Loy: So Perfect in Her Way." *People,* April 4, 1988.

Bromfield, Louis. *The Rains Came.* New York: Grosset and Dunlap, 1937.

Brownlow, Kevin, and David Gill. *Hollywood: The Pioneers.* Thames Video, 1980. VHS.

Bryant, Roger. *William Powell: The Life and Films.* Jefferson, NC: McFarland, 2006.

Buehrer, Beverley Bare. *Cary Grant: A Bio-Bibliography.* Westport, CT: Greenwood, 1990.

Bull, Clarence Sinclair, with Raymond Lee. *The Faces of Hollywood.* South Brunswick, NJ: A. S. Barnes, 1968.

Calvino, Italo. *The Road to San Giovanni.* Translated by Tim Parks. New York: Pantheon, 1993.

Cameron, Evan William, ed. *Sound and the Cinema: The Coming of Sound.* Pleasantville, NY: Redgrave, 1980.

Cannom, Robert. *Van Dyke and the Mythical City of Hollywood.* Culver City: Murray and Gee, 1948.

Capra, Frank. *The Name above the Title: An Autobiography.* New York: Da Capo Press, 1997.

————. "Reminiscences." In Cameron, *Sound and the Cinema,* 77–84.

Carr, Larry. *More Fabulous Faces: The Evolution and Metamorphosis of Dolores Del Rio, Myrna Loy, Carole Lombard, Bette Davis, and Katharine Hepburn.* Garden City, NY: Doubleday, 1979.

Cauthorn, Benjamin Ross. "Trip to Montana by Wagon Train" [1865]. Manuscript, Special Collections, Harold B. Lee Library, Brigham Young University. American Memory website: http://memory.loc.gov.

Cavell, Stanley. *Pursuits of Happiness: The Hollywood Comedy of Remarriage*. Cambridge, MA: Harvard University Press, 1981.

Ceplair, Larry, and Steven Englund. *The Inquisition in Hollywood: Politics in the Film Community, 1930–1960*. Urbana: University of Illinois Press, 2003.

Chandler, Charlotte. *Not the Girl Next Door: Joan Crawford, a Personal Biography*. New York: Simon and Schuster, 2008.

Chandler, David. "Willy Makes the Stars Tremble." *Collier's*, Feb. 4, 1950.

Cheatham, Maude. "The Perfect Wife Has a Past." *Screen Book*, Feb. 1938.

Chierichetti, David. *Mitchell Leisen: Hollywood Director*. Los Angeles: Photoventures Press, 1995.

———. "Myrna Loy Today." *Film Fan Monthly*, March 1973.

Colman, Richard. "The Siren from Montana." *Photoplay*, Sept. 1929.

Conrad, Barnaby, III. *Ghost Hunting in Montana: A Search for Roots in the Old West*. Guilford, CT. Lyons Press, 1994.

Cook, Blanche Wiesen. *Eleanor Roosevelt*. Vol. 1, *1884–1933*. New York: Penguin, 1993.

Coward, Noel. *Diaries*. Edited by Graham Payn and Sheridan Morley. Boston: Little, Brown, 1982.

Crafton, Donald. *The Talkies: American Cinema's Transition to Sound, 1926–1931*. Berkeley: University of California Press, 1999.

Crawford, Christina. *Mommie Dearest*. New York: William Morrow, 1978.

Crawford, Joan, with Jane Kesner Ardmore. *A Portrait of Joan; the Autobiography of Joan Crawford*. Garden City, NY: Doubleday, 1962.

Crowther, Bosley. *Hollywood Rajah: The Life and Times of Louis B. Mayer*. New York: Holt, Rinehart, and Winston, 1960.

Curtis, James R. *W. C. Fields: A Biography*. New York: Knopf, 2003.

Custen, George F. *Twentieth Century's Fox: Darryl F. Zanuck and the Culture of Hollywood*. New York: Basic Books, 1997.

Davis, Ronald L. *The Glamour Factory: Inside Hollywood's Big Studio System*. Dallas: Southern Methodist University Press, 1993.

Denby, David. "The Aristocrat Next Door." *Premiere*, Nov. 1993.

Di Battista, Maria. *Fast-Talking Dames*. New Haven, CT: Yale University Press, 2001.

Doherty, Thomas. *Pre-code Hollywood: Sex, Immorality, and Insurrection in American Cinema, 1930–1934*. New York: Columbia University Press, 1999.

———. *Projections of War: Hollywood, American Culture, and World War Two*. New York: Columbia University Press, 1993.

Douglas, Melvyn, and Tom Arthur. *See You at the Movies: The Autobiography of Melvyn Douglas*. Lanham, MD: University Press of America, 1986.

Drees, Rich. "*The Thin Man*: Dashiell Hammett in Hollywood." *Films in Review* 46, no. 7/8 (1995): 46–53.

Dunne, Philip. *Take Two: A Life in Movies and Politics*. New York: McGraw-Hill, 1980.

Eames, John Douglas. *The MGM Story*. New York: Crown, 1975.

Edwards, Anne. *Katharine Hepburn: A Remarkable Woman.* New York: St. Martin's, 2000.

Eyman, Scott. *Lion of Hollywood: The Life and Legend of Louis B. Mayer.* New York: Simon and Schuster, 2005.

———. *The Speed of Sound: Hollywood and the Talkie Revolution, 1926–1930.* New York: Simon and Schuster, 1997.

Fairbanks, Douglas Jr. *The Salad Days.* New York: Doubleday, 1988.

Federal Writers Project of the Works Progress Administration. *Montana: A State Guide Book.* New York: Viking, 1939.

Ferguson, Otis. *The Film Criticism of Otis Ferguson.* Edited by Robert Wilson. Philadelphia: Temple University Press, 1971.

Finler, Joel W. *The Hollywood Story.* London: Wallflower Press, 2003.

Fischer, Lucy. *Designing Women: Cinema, Art Deco, and the Female Form.* New York: Columbia University Press, 2003.

Fisher, James. *Spencer Tracy: A Bio-Bibliography.* Westport, CT: Greenwood, 1994.

Fitzgerald, F. Scott. *Correspondence.* Edited by Matthew J. Bruccoli and Margaret M. Duggan. New York: Random House, 1980.

———. *The Last Tycoon.* 1941. New York: Collier, 1986.

Fontaine, Joan. *No Bed of Roses.* New York: William Morrow, 1978.

Ford, Dan. *Pappy: The Life of John Ford.* New York: Da Capo Press, 1998.

Ford, John. *John Ford: Interviews.* Edited by Gerald Peary, with Jenny Lefcourt. Jackson: University Press of Mississippi, 2001.

Francisco, Charles. *Gentleman: The William Powell Story.* New York: St. Martin's, 1985.

Fury, David. *Maureen O'Sullivan: No Average Jane.* Minneapolis: Artist's Press, 2006.

Gehring, Wes D. *Carole Lombard: The Hoosier Tornado.* Indianapolis: Indiana Historical Society Press, 2003.

Geist, Kenneth L. *Pictures Will Talk: The Life and Films of Joseph L. Mankiewicz.* New York: Da Capo Press, 1983.

Gianos, Phillip. *Politics and Politicians in American Film.* Westport, CT: Greenwood, 1998.

Glancy, H. Mark. "MGM Film Grosses, 1924–1948: The Eddie Mannix Ledger." *Historical Journal of Film, Radio and Television* 12, no. 2 (1992): 127–49.

———. "Warner Bros. Film Grosses, 1921–1951: The William Schaefer Ledger." *Historical Journal of Film, Radio and Television* 15, no. 1 (March 1995): 55–73.

Golden, Eve. *Platinum Girl: The Life and Legends of Jean Harlow.* New York: Abbeville Press, 1991.

Gomery, Douglas. *The Hollywood Studio System: A History.* London: British Film Institute, 2005.

Goodrich, David Lee. *The Real Nick and Nora: Frances Goodrich and Albert Hackett, Writers of Stage and Screen Classics.* Carbondale: Southern Illinois University Press, 2004.

Grant, Cary. "She's My Dream Wife." *Photoplay,* Aug. 1948.

Greene, Graham. *The Graham Greene Film Reader.* Edited by David Parkinson. New York: Applause Theatre Books, 1994.

Gutner, Howard. *Gowns by Adrian: The MGM Years, 1928–1941.* New York: Harry N. Abrams, 2001.

Hackett, Albert. "Reminiscences of Albert Hackett" (1958). Interview transcript, 37 pages. Columbia University Oral History Research Office.

Hall, Gladys. "Should a Girl Forgive?" [1934?] Typescript, Gladys Hall Collection. Margaret Herrick Library, Academy of Motion Picture Arts and Sciences.

———. "So You Want to Be a Movie Star?" 1937. Typescript, Gladys Hall Collection. Margaret Herrick Library, Academy of Motion Picture Arts and Sciences.

———. "That Other Me." [1938?] Typescript, Gladys Hall Collection. Margaret Herrick Library, Academy of Motion Picture Arts and Sciences.

———. "The Truth about the Mysterious Miss Loy." *Modern Screen,* Aug.-Sept. 1935.

Hamann, G. D., ed. *Myrna Loy in the 30s.* Hollywood: Filming Today Press, 1996.

Hamilton, Sara. "Myrna Loy's Honeymoon House." *Movie Mirror,* July 1937.

Hammett, Dashiell. *Selected Letters of Dashiell Hammett, 1921–1960.* Edited by Richard Layman, with Julie M. Rivett. Washington, DC: Counterpoint, 2001.

———. *The Thin Man.* 1934. New York: Vintage Crime / Black Lizard Editions, 1992.

Harrington, Lee. "The Marriage Code of Myrna Loy." *Photoplay,* May 1937.

Harris, Marlys J. *The Zanucks of Hollywood.* New York: Crown, 1972.

Harris, Warren G. *Clark Gable.* New York: Harmony Books, 2002.

Haver, Ronald. *David O. Selznick's Hollywood.* New York: Knopf, 1980.

Hay, Peter. *MGM: When the Lion Roars.* Atlanta: Turner Publishing, 1991.

Hayter-Menzies, Grant. *Mrs. Ziegfeld: The Public and Private Lives of Billie Burke.* Jefferson, NC: McFarland, 2009.

Heller, Karen. "Myrna Loy: Back in the Limelight." *Philadelphia Inquirer,* Nov. 29, 1987.

Hellman, Lillian. "Dashiell Hammett: A Memoir." *New York Review of Books,* Nov. 25, 1965.

Henderson, Jessie. "It Takes 3 to Make a Love Affair." *Hollywood,* June 1938.

Henrey, Mrs. Robert. *A Journey to Vienna.* London: J. M. Dent and Sons, 1950.

Henstell, Bruce. *Sunshine and Wealth: Los Angeles in the Twenties and Thirties.* San Francisco: Chronicle Books, 1984.

Herman, Jan. *A Talent for Trouble: The Life of Hollywood's Most Acclaimed Director, William Wyler.* New York: G. P. Putnam's Sons, 1996.

Higham, Charles. *Hollywood Cameramen: Sources of Light.* Bloomington: Indiana University Press, 1970.

———. *Merchant of Dreams: Louis B. Mayer, M.G.M., and the Secret Hollywood.* New York: Donald I. Fine, 1993.

———. *Warner Brothers.* New York: Scribner, 1975.

Hodgins, Eric. "Mr. Blandings Goes to Hollywood." *Life,* April 12, 1948.

Holden, Anthony. *Behind the Oscars.* New York: Simon and Schuster, 1993.

Holloway, Grace, and Edna Gaab. *Broadwater Bygones: A History of Broadwater County.* Bozeman, MT: Broadwater County Historical Society, 1977.

"Hollywood in the Thirties: Discussion and Questions." Interviews with Thirteen Actors, Actresses, and Directors. Sept. 29–Dec. 1, 1969. Discussion Transcript. Margaret Herrick Library, Academy of Motion Picture Arts and Sciences.

Houston, David. *Jazz Baby.* New York: St. Martin's, 1983.

Howard, Joseph Kinsey. *Montana: High, Wide, and Handsome.* New Haven, CT: Yale University Press, 1959.

International Motion Picture Almanac. New York: Quigley Publications, 1934–1938.

Internet Accuracy Project. www.accuracyproject.org/cbe-Loy,Myrna.html.

Jewell, Richard B. "RKO Film Grosses, 1929–1951: The C. J. Tevlin Ledger." *Historical Journal of Film, Radio and Television* 14, no. 1 (1994): 37–49.

Johnson, Diane. *Dashiell Hammett: A Life.* New York: Random House, 1983.

Johnston, Alva. "Lord Fauntleroy in Hollywood." *New Yorker,* Sept. 28, 1935.

———. "Myrna Loy—from Asia to America in 100 Reels." *Woman's Home Companion,* May 1935.

Jurca, Catherine. "Hollywood, the Dream House Factory." *Cinema Journal* 37, no. 4 (1998): 19–36.

Kael, Pauline. *5001 Nights at the Movies.* New York: Henry Holt, 1991.

———. "The Man from Dream City." *New Yorker,* July 14, 1975.

Kay, Karyn. *Myrna Loy.* New York: Pyramid, 1977.

Kear, Lynn, and John Rossman. *Kay Francis: A Passionate Life and Career.* Jefferson, NC: McFarland, 2006.

Kellow, Brian. *The Bennetts: An Acting Family.* Lexington: University Press of Kentucky, 2004.

Kendall, Elizabeth. *Where She Danced: The Birth of American Art-Dance.* New York: Knopf, 1979.

Kennedy, Matthew. *Joan Blondell: A Life between Takes.* Jackson: University Press of Mississippi, 2007.

Kobler, John. *Damned in Paradise: The Life of John Barrymore.* New York: Atheneum, 1977.

Koppes, Clayton R., and Gregory D. Black. *Hollywood Goes to War: How Politics, Profits, and Propaganda Shaped World War II Movies.* New York: Free Press, 1987.

Koszarski, Richard. *Hollywood Directors, 1914–1940.* New York: Oxford University Press, 1976.

LaGuardia, Robert. *Monty: A Biography of Montgomery Clift.* New York: Arbor House, 1977.

Lambert, Gavin. *Norma Shearer.* New York: Knopf, 1990.

Lane, Virginia. "Myrna Talks about Marriage." *Modern Screen,* Aug. 1936.

La Salle, Mick. *Complicated Women: Sex and Power in Pre-code Hollywood.* New York: St. Martin's, 2000.

Lasky, Betty. *RKO, the Biggest Little Major of Them All.* Englewood Cliffs, NJ: Prentice-Hall, 1984.

Latham, Aaron. *Crazy Sundays.* New York: Viking, 1971.

Leider, Emily W. *Dark Lover: The Life and Death of Rudolph Valentino*. New York: Farrar, Straus and Giroux, 2003.

Lewis and Clark County, First District Court, Helena, Montana. Probate Records. Estate of David Franklin Williams, deceased November 7, 1918.

Loos, Anita. *Kiss Hollywood Good-By*. New York: Ballantine, 1975.

Loy, Myrna. "My Own Life Story." *Picture Show*, Nov. 26, 1938.

———. "Reminiscences of Myrna Loy" (1958). Interview transcript, 57 pages. Columbia University Oral History Research Office.

Loy, Myrna, and James Kotsilibas-Davis. *Myrna Loy: Being and Becoming*. New York: Knopf, 1987.

Loy, Myrna, and William Powell. "Why We Are an Ideal Team." *Film Weekly*, Dec. 21, 1934.

Lyn, Hilary. "Unmasking Myrna Loy." *Modern Screen*, Aug. 1938.

MacQueen, Scott. "Noah's Ark: Making and Restoring an Early Vitaphone Spectacle." *Perfect Vision* 12 (1991): 35–45.

Maddox, Ben. "My Daughter, Myrna Loy, as Told by Della Williams." *Modern Screen*, March 1937.

———. "The Mystery of Myrna Loy." *Movie Show*, April 1948.

Madsen, Axel. *William Wyler, the Authorized Biography*. New York: Crown, 1973.

Malone, Michael P., with Richard Roeder and William Lang. *Montana: A History of Two Centuries*. Rev. ed. Seattle: University of Washington Press, 1991.

Manners, Dorothy. "At Last, the Heart-Stirring Love Story of Myrna Loy." *Photoplay*, Aug. 1936.

———. "I Know Myrna Loy—But Not Very Well." *Photoplay*, Aug. 1935.

Mannix, Eddie. The Eddie Mannix Film Ledger. Howard Strickling Collection. Margaret Herrick Library, Academy of Motion Picture Arts and Sciences.

Marx, Samuel. *Mayer and Thalberg: The Make-Believe Saints*. New York: Random House, 1975.

Mast, Gerald, ed. *Movies in Our Midst: Documents in the Cultural History of Film in America*. Chicago: University of Chicago Press, 1982.

McBride, Joseph. *Frank Capra: The Catastrophe of Success*. New York: St. Martin's, 2000.

———. *Searching for John Ford: A Life*. New York: St. Martin's, 2001.

McCarthy, Todd. *Howard Hawks: The Grey Fox of Hollywood*. New York: Grove Press, 1997.

McClelland, Doug. *Forties Film Talk: Oral Histories of Hollywood*. Jefferson, NC: McFarland, 1992.

McDonald, Elizabeth. "Myrna Knows All the Answers." *Modern Screen*, Nov. 1935.

McDowall, Roddy. *Double Exposure, Take One*. New York: Delacorte Press, 1966.

McGilligan, Pat, ed. *Backstory: Interviews with Screenwriters of Hollywood's Golden Age*. Berkeley: University of California Press, 1986.

———. *George Cukor: A Double Life*. New York: St. Martin's, 1991.

McGrath, Charles. "Fitzgerald as Screenwriter: No Happy Ending." *New York Times*, April 22, 2004.

McTeague, James H. *Before Stanislavsky: American Professional Acting Schools and Acting Theory, 1875–1925*. Metuchen, NJ: Scarecrow, 1993.

"Metro-Goldwyn-Mayer: Portrait of a Vertically Integrated Company." *Fortune*, Dec. 1932. Repr. in Balio, *The American Film Industry*, 311–33.

Meyers, Jeffrey. *Gary Cooper: American Hero*. New York: Morrow, 1998.

Mintz, Steven, and Susan Kellogg. *Domestic Revolutions: A Social History of American Family Life*. New York: Free Press, 1988.

Moak, E. R. "The Girl Hollywood Couldn't Beat." *Hollywood*, July 1937.

———. "Myrna Loy a Victim of Sudden Success." *Silver Screen*, March 1933.

Mohr, Hal. "Reminiscences." In Cameron, *Sound and the Cinema*, 69–76.

Moore, Tom. "Early Day History of Radersburg." Undated manuscript. Boston University, Myrna Loy Papers, Box 32, Folder 32.

Mordden, Ethan. *The Hollywood Studios*. New York: Knopf, 1988.

Morehead, Don, and Ann Morehead. *A Short Season: Story of a Montana Childhood*. Lincoln: University of Nebraska Press, 1998.

"Myrna Loy: A Class by Herself." Episode 694 of the *Biography* television series. Produced by Kevin Burns. A&E Network. Orig. air date July 9, 1998. Copyright 20th Century Fox. Van Ness Films: Los Angeles.

Nelson, Nancy. *Evenings with Cary Grant: Recollections in His Own Words and by Those Who Knew Him Best*. New York: William Morrow, 1991.

New Jersey Center Dance Collective. *Denishawn: The Birth of Modern Dance*. Long Branch, NJ: KULTUR, 1988. VHS.

Newquist, Roy. *Conversations with Joan Crawford*. Secaucus, NJ: Citadel Press, 1980.

Nochimson, Martha. *Screen Couple Chemistry: The Power of 2*. Austin: University of Texas Press, 2002.

Nolan, William F. *Hammett: A Life at the Edge*. New York: Congdon and Weed, 1983.

Nollen, Scott Allen. *Boris Karloff: A Gentleman's Life*. Baltimore: Midnight Marquee Press, 2005.

O'Brien, Scott. *Kay Francis: I Can't Wait to Be Forgotten: Her Life on Film and Stage*. 2nd ed. Albany, GA: BearManor Media, 2007.

Oller, John. *Jean Arthur: The Actress Nobody Knew*. New York: Limelight, 1999.

Owens, Elizabeth. "Why the Perfect Wife's Marriage Failed." *Photoplay*, Feb. 1941.

Paris, Barry. *Louise Brooks*. New York: Anchor Books, 1990.

Parish, James Robert, and Ronald L. Bowers. *The Golden Era: The MGM Stock Company*. New Rochelle, NY: Bonanza, 1972.

Peary, Gerald, and Patrick McGilligan. "Dore Schary." *Take One* 7, no. 8 (1979): 23–28, 45–47.

Pennington, Lucinda, and William K. Baxter. *A Past to Remember: Culver City*. Culver City: City of Culver City, 1976.

Petrik, Paula. "If She Be Content: The Development of Montana Divorce Law, 1865–1907." *Western Historical Quarterly* 18 (1987): 261–92.

———. *No Step Backward: Women and Family on the Rocky Mountain Mining Frontier, 1865–1900*. Helena: Montana Historical Society Press, 1987.

Polk's City Directory for Helena, Montana. Salt Lake City: R. L. Polk, 1910–18.

Quirk, Lawrence J. *The Films of Myrna Loy.* Secaucus, NJ: Citadel Press, 1980.
———. *Joan Crawford: The Essential Biography.* Lexington: University Press of Kentucky, 2002.

Rapf, Maurice. *Back Lot: Growing Up with the Movies.* Lanham, MD: Scarecrow, 1999.

Reed, Rex. "Myrna's Back—and Boyer's Got Her." *New York Times,* April 13, 1969.

Reiter, Joan Swallow. *The Women.* Alexandria, VA: Time-Life Books, 1978.

Roazen, Paul. *The Historiography of Psychoanalysis.* New Brunswick, NJ: Transaction, 2000.

Rosson, Leone. Diaries [unpublished] 1959–1985, incomplete. Private Collection.

Rosten, Leo C. *Hollywood: The Movie Colony, the Movie Makers.* New York: Harcourt, Brace, 1941.

Rubin, Jay. "Jay Rubin Interviews Myrna Loy." *Classic Film Collector,* winter 1976.

Russell, Rosalind, and Chris Chase. *Life Is a Banquet.* New York: Random House, 1977.

Salt, Barry. "Film Style and Technology in the Thirties." *Film Quarterly* 30, no. 1 (1976): 13–31.

Samuels, Lenore. "Loyal to Loy." *Silver Screen,* Sept. 1935.

Sarris, Andrew. *You Ain't Heard Nothin' Yet: The American Talking Film: History and Memory, 1927–1949.* New York: Oxford University Press, 1998.

Schallert, Elza. "She's Tired of Being a Wife." *Modern Screen,* Oct. 1939.

Schary, Dore. *Heyday: An Autobiography.* Boston: Little, Brown, 1979.

Schatz, Thomas. *Boom and Bust: The American Cinema in the 1940s.* Berkeley: University of California Press, 1999.

Schickel, Richard. "Hollywood Remembers: Myrna Loy—So Nice to Come Home To." Warner Home Video: Burbank, 2005. DVD.

Schroeder, John W., and James R. Graff. *Historic Helena, 1864–1964: An Early Day Photographic History.* Helena: Thurber Printing, 1970.

Scott, Ian. *In Capra's Shadow: The Life and Career of Screenwriter Robert Riskin.* Lexington: University Press of Kentucky, 2006.

Selznick, David O. *Memo from David O. Selznick.* Edited by Rudy Behlmer. New York: Viking, 1972.

Selznick, Irene Mayer. *A Private View.* New York: Knopf, 1983.

Sharpe, Howard. "W. S. Van Dyke." *Photoplay,* Dec. 1936.

Shawn, Ted. "Dancing Cures the Nerves." *Physical Culture,* Nov. 1922.

Sherman, Jane. *Denishawn: The Enduring Influence.* Boston: Twayne, 1983.
———. *The Drama of Denishawn Dance.* Middletown, CT: Wesleyan University Press, 1979.

Sherwood, Robert. "The Best Years of Our Lives." Final Shooting Script, May 22, 1946. Goldwyn Collection. Margaret Herrick Library, Academy of Motion Picture Arts and Sciences.

Shindler, Colin. *Hollywood Goes to War.* London: Routledge, 1979.

Sikov, Ed. *Screwball: Hollywood's Madcap Romantic Comedies.* New York: Crown, 1989.

Slide, Anthony. "Hollywood's Fascist Follies." *Film Comment* 27, no. 4 (1991): 62–67.

Somer, Jack A. *Ticonderoga: Tales of an Enchanted Yacht.* New York: Norton, 1997.

Sperber, A. M., and Eric Lax. *Bogart.* New York: Morrow, 1997.

Springer, John, and Jack Hamilton. *They Had Faces Then: Super Stars, Stars, and Starlets of the 1930's.* Secaucus, NJ: Citadel Press, 1974.

Sragow, Michael. *Victor Fleming: An American Movie Master.* New York: Pantheon, 2008.

Starr, Jimmy. *Barefoot on Barbed Wire: An Autobiography of a Forty-Year Hollywood Balancing Act.* Lanham, MD: Scarecrow, 2001.

Starr, Kevin. *Material Dreams: Southern California through the 1920s.* New York: Oxford University Press, 1990.

Steel, Harold. "Myrna Loy." *Mon Ciné,* Feb. 20, 1930.

Stenn, David. *Bombshell: The Life and Death of Jean Harlow.* Raleigh, NC: Lightning Bug Press, 2000.

———. "It Happened One Night at MGM." *Vanity Fair,* April 2003.

Stewart, Donald Ogden. *By a Stroke of Luck.* New York: Paddington Press, 1975.

Stone, Patricia. "Somewhat of a Cinderella, Myrna Loy." *Entertainment,* Oct. 22, 1934.

Stuart, Gloria, with Sylvia Thompson. *I Just Keep Hoping.* Boston: Little, Brown, 1999.

Studlar, Gaylyn. "Out-Salomeing Salome: Dance, the New Woman, and Fan Magazine Orientalism." In *Visions of the East,* edited by Matthew Bernstein and Gaylyn Studlar, 99–129. New York: Routledge, 1997.

Sullivan, Mark. *Over Here, 1914–1918.* Vol. 5, *Our Times, 1900–1925.* New York: Scribner, 1933.

Swindell, Larry. *Screwball: The Life of Carole Lombard.* New York: Morrow, 1975.

"This Is Your Life [Myrna Loy]." Television script, writer uncredited. May 16, 1956. Ralph Edwards Productions. Boston University, Myrna Loy Papers, Box 18, Folder 3.

Thomas, Bob. *Joan Crawford: A Biography.* New York: Simon and Schuster, 1978.

———. *Thalberg: Life and Legend.* Garden City, NY: Doubleday, 1969.

Thomson, David. *A New Biographical Dictionary of Film.* New York: Knopf, 2004.

———. *The Whole Equation: A History of Hollywood.* New York: Knopf, 2005.

Tornabene, Lyn. *Long Live the King: A Biography of Clark Gable.* New York: G. P. Putnam's Sons, 1976.

Tranberg, Charles. *The Thin Man: Murder over Cocktails.* Albany, GA: BearManor Media, 2009.

Troyan, Michael. *A Rose for Mrs. Miniver: The Life of Greer Garson.* Lexington: University Press of Kentucky, 1999.

Tully, Grace G. *F. D. R., My Boss.* New York: Charles Scribner's Sons, 1949.

Turk, Edward Baron. *Hollywood Diva: A Biography of Jeanette MacDonald.* Berkeley: University of California Press, 1998.

Van Dyke, W. S. *W. S. Van Dyke's Journal: White Shadows in the South Seas, 1927–1928: And Other Van Dyke on Van Dyke.* Edited by Rudy Behlmer. Lanham, MD: Scarecrow, 1996.

Van Neste, Dan. "Leslie Howard: Unmasking the Pimpernel." *Films of the Golden Age,* winter 1999.

Vieira, Mark. *Hollywood Dreams Made Real: Irving Thalberg and the Rise of M-G-M.* New York: Abrams, 2008.

———. *Irving Thalberg: Boy Wonder to Producer Prince.* Berkeley: University of California Press, 2009.

Vineberg, Steve. *High Comedy in American Movies: Class and Humor from the 1920s to the Present.* Lanham, MD: Rowman and Littlefield, 2005.

Walker, Alexander. *The Shattered Silents: How the Talkies Came to Stay.* New York: William Morrow, 1979.

———. *Stardom.* New York: Stein and Day, 1970.

Walker, Joseph B., and Juanita Walker. *The Light on Her Face.* Los Angeles: ASC Press, 1984.

Ware, Susan. *Holding Their Own: American Women in the 1930s.* Boston: Twayne, 1982.

Warner, Jack L., with Dean Jennings. *My First Hundred Years in Hollywood.* New York: Random House, 1965.

Watters, James. *Return Engagement: Faces to Remember—Then and Now.* New York: Clarkson Potter, 1984.

Weales, Gerald. *Canned Goods as Caviar: American Film Comedy of the 1930s.* Chicago: University of Chicago Press, 1985.

Williams, Della. *Montana Reminiscences of Della Johnson Williams, Interviewed by Cora Poole.* Audiocassette OH63. Helena: Montana Historical Society Research Center, ca. 1960.

———. "Myrna Loy's Family Album." *Modern Screen,* Feb. 1938.

Williams, Esther, with Digby Diehl. *The Million Dollar Mermaid.* New York: Simon and Schuster, 1999.

Willson, Dixie. "The Revealing True Story of Myrna Loy." *Photoplay,* Part 1: May 1938; Part 2: June 1938; Part 3: July 1938.

Windolf, Jim. "From Best Years to Our Years." *New York Observer,* March 24, 1997.

Winokur, Mark. *American Laughter: Immigrants, Ethnicity, and 1930s Hollywood Film.* New York: St. Martin's, 1996.

Wyler, William. "No Magic Wand." *Screen Writer* 2, no. 9 (1947): 1–14.

Young, Alma. "Interview by Robert Gitt and Anthony Slide." 1977. Manuscript. Private Collection of Gitt and Slide.

York, Cal. "Doug's Office Boy Makes Good." *Photoplay,* Jan. 1929.

Zeitlin, Ida. "Behind the Mystery of Myrna Loy." *Screen Book,* March 1936.

———. "Happy Ever After." *Motion Picture,* Nov. 1936.

———. "Myrna's Maid Tells on Miss Loy, as Told by Theresa Penn." *Modern Screen,* Oct. 1938.

Acknowledgments

Writing a biography is a collaborative enterprise. It's a pleasure to thank the following for their help:

INTERVIEWEES

Diana Anderson, April 2, 2008

Rudy Behlmer, January 29, 2008, and via email

Richard Benjamin, September 12, 2009

Alice "Boaty" Boatwright, October 12, 2006

David Chierichetti, February 16, 2007, and March 17, 2008

Bruce Dancis, June 26, 2008

Olivia de Havilland, by letter, September 21, 2006

Rhonda Fleming, September 17, 2007

Jim Frasher, October 17, 2007

Barbara Handman, October 11, 2006

Wynn Handman, October 11, 2006

Deborah Hornblow, October 13, 2005, and via email

Doris Hornblow, May 13, 2005

Dr. John Terry Hornblow, April 20, 21, 2005

Leonora Hornblow, June 10, 2005

Michael Hornblow, June 10, 2005

Marsha Hunt, March 18, 2006

Lainie Kazan, January 3, 2007

Richard Lamparski, multiple conversations

Robert Lantz, August 3, 2006, and March 18, 2007

Jack Larson, July 3, 2006

Bob Lasanka, December 20, 2007

A. C. Lyles, June 17, 2008

Arnie Malina, September 27, 2005

Leonard Maltin, December 5, 2007

Marvin Paige, several conversations

Rex Reed, March 11, 2009

Lisa Ryan, October 25, 2008

June Springer, November 26, 2007

Laurel Taylor, August 24, 2008, and via email

Kevin Thomas, December 16, 2007

Joan Van Ark, September 10, 2009

Jeffrey Vance, July 30, 2007

Melinda Markey Van Dyke, September 29, 2007

LIBRARIANS AND ARCHIVISTS

Noelle Carter at Warner Bros. Archives, University of Southern California.

Ned Comstock at the University of Southern California Cinematic Arts Library for his extraordinary generosity and thoughtfulness.

Julie Graham and Lauren Buisson at the UCLA Performing Arts Library, Special Collections.

Barbara Hall, Kristine Krueger, Faye Thompson, Stacey Behlmer, and Linda Mehr at the Margaret Herrick Library, Academy of Motion Picture Arts and Sciences.

J. C. Johnson at the Howard Gotlieb Archival Research Center, Boston University.

Lisa Kallow, Clerk of the District Court, Lewis and Clark County, Montana.

Jane Klain and Richard Holbrook at the Paley Center for Media, New York.

Rebecca Kohl at the Montana Historical Society.

Harry Miller at the Wisconsin Center for Film and Theatre Research.

Charles Silver and Ron Magliozzi at the Museum of Modern Art Film Study Center, New York.

Josie L. Walters-Johnson, Rosemary Hanes, and Madeline Matz at the Library of Congress Motion Picture Division. Walter Zvonchenko at the Library of Congress Performing Arts Division.

Valerie Yaros, Screen Actors Guild historian.

In addition I would like to thank Kevin Brownlow, for opening his files, reviewing several chapters, and answering endless queries; Bob Gitt and Tony Slide for comments and corrections on my chapter on the transition to sound; Cat Nielson for genealogical research; Karie Bible for her work on the filmography and her research assistance; Cari Beauchamp, Matt Shelby Black, Ron Bowers, Jim Curtis, Dick DeNeut, Scott Eyman, Joyce Marie Faust, Carmen Bley Gilley, Eve Golden, Samuel Goldwyn Jr., Donna Hill, Ann Kahn, Brian Kellow, Matthew Kennedy, John Kern, Terence Kingsley-Smith, Mick LaSalle, Betty Lasky, Tim Lithgow, Christina McKillip, Lisa Mitchell, Scott O'Brien, Jim Parish, Maxine Savitz, Judy Wyler Sheldon, Charlene Spalding, David Stenn, Roy T. Thorsen, Mark Vieira, Shelly Wanger, Ernest Young, and Gwenda Young; my agent, Jin Auh, and Jacqueline Ko, her assistant, at the Wylie Agency; my excellent editor at UC Press, Mary Francis, ably assisted by Eric Schmidt, Suzanne Knott, and ace copy editor Joe Abbott; and my first reader, Bill Leider, for his bottomless support and for watching movies with me. Of course he fell for Myrna Loy.

Index

TEXT
10/13 Sabon

DISPLAY
Sabon (Open Type)

COMPOSITOR
Integrated Composition Systems

INDEXER
Barbara Roos

PRINTER AND BINDER
Thomson-Shore, Inc.